THE
LEGAL
UNIVERSE

Observations on the Foundations of American Law

Vine Deloria Jr. and David E. Wilkins

FULCRUM

GOLDEN, COLORADO

Library of Congress Cataloging-in-Publication Data

Deloria, Vine.
The legal universe : observations on the foundations of American law / Vine Deloria, JR., David E. Wilkins.
  p. cm.
Includes bibliographical references and index.
ISBN 978-1-55591-361-8 (pbk.)
1. Minorities--Legal status, laws, etc.--United States. I. Wilkins, David E. (David Eugene), 1954- II. Title.
KF4755.D455 2011
342.7308'73--dc22
          2011009373

Printed in the United States on recycled paper
0 9 8 7 6 5 4 3 2 1

Design by Jack Lenzo

Fulcrum Publishing
4690 Table Mountain Dr., Ste. 100
Golden, CO 80403
800-992-2908 • 303-277-1623
www.fulcrumbooks.com

To Vine and Barbara Deloria,
outstanding mentors and the dearest of friends

CONTENTS

FOREWORD

WE ARE TAUGHT TO SEEK KNOWLEDGE THROUGH BOOKS, and each generation of students reexperiences the wisdom of the past, reading the works of philosophers such as Plato, Aristotle, Locke, and Hobbes, as well as those of the framers of American political thought, including Jefferson, Adams, and Franklin. But what would happen if we read those works through the "pedagogy of liberation" that bell hooks posited in *Talking Back*? What would we see and what would the impact be? In the words of hooks, we would experience "an oppositional world view—different from that of our exploiters and oppressors, a world view that would enable us to see ourselves not through the lens of racism or racist stereotypes...but one that would enable us to... see ourselves first and foremost as striving for wholeness, for unity of heart, mind, body, and spirit."

The Legal Universe exemplifies the spirit of a pedagogy of liberation. The cojoined voices of the late legendary scholar Vine Deloria Jr. and his protégé David Wilkins probe the foundations of American legal thought, hewing the sacred icons of American Western legal thought—including the social contract, the US Constitution, and the institution of property—to examine the effect of various legal texts and opinions upon the lived experience of many groups in the United States. This work interrogates the status of corporations, which embody the spirit of American entrepreneurship, as well as the changing legal and political status of African Americans, Asian Americans, Native Americans, Mexican Americans, women, and children in their respective "efforts to have their self-determination and humanity respected."

These respective journeys are a testament to the value of *difference* in the quest for equality, dignity, freedom, and humanity. If, as the preamble to the Constitution says, it is true that "all men are created equal, that they are endowed by their Creator with certain inalienable Rights," including "Life, Liberty and the Pursuit of Happiness," then who counts as worthy of the Creator's bounty, and what "rights" express from that status? The "mystery of the law" is defined relationally, in this work, through the experience of each group with Western legal thought and American legal institutions. But, it is the different group journeys through injustice that reveal the majesty of the law, meaning "the manner in which we want the law to work."

Deloria and Wilkins claim that "the social contract, in removing humans from the state of nature, severs them from the rest of nature in a fundamental sense; we participate in the world but with no ultimate relationship to physical reality." Within this view, humans have no responsibility to the rest of the natural world. The social contract is a mechanism to elevate "civilized" humans, thereby freeing them from the dark and empty space of nature. Significantly, the catalyst for the forward evolution of mankind is the institution of property, which Locke deemed to be the chief end of the social contract. Individuals surrendered certain forms of individual authority in exchange for the impartially administered law of a central government designed to protect individual property. It was a fair exchange to all—at least all those who were capable of *holding* property, either in themselves or in relationship with others. But what about everyone else?

Deloria and Wilkins skillfully interrogate the political and legal history of disparate groups to reveal the "semiconscious assumptions about the nature of reality that lurk behind...the Constitution and laws of the United States." For example, why does article 1 of the Constitution, governing apportionment, refer to "free persons" as "whole," while counting only "three-fifths of all other persons"? Why does it exclude "Indians not taxed" from being counted at all? Are Indians even considered to be legal "persons"? And if some human beings within American society lack equal personhood and consequently can be denied basic rights, then how can the US Supreme Court in 2010 declare in *Citizens United v. Federal Election Commission* that corporations are legally entitled to exercise the political free speech rights of individuals, as though they *are* human beings?

If legal personhood raises a perplexing set of quandaries, then consider access to justice. Deloria and Wilkins recount, for example, the failed effort of Dred Scott in the years preceding the Civil War to sue for freedom from his legal status as the property of a white slaveholder; the failed effort of Homer Plessy in the years following the Civil War to prove that, as a person of one-eighth African American blood and seven-eighths Caucasian blood, he had the requisite identity to sit in the first-class railroad coach; and the failed effort of the Cherokee Nation to assert, through the Supreme Court, its political identity as a foreign nation against the state of Georgia, whose nineteenth-century laws were systematically obliterating the federally guaranteed treaty rights of the Cherokee people. They further explore the denial of treaty rights to citizens of Mexico in the years following the Treaty of Guadalupe Hidalgo, which annexed Mexican lands and citizens into the United States, and the denial of treaty rights to Chinese immigrants, who were first guaranteed and then summarily dispossessed of their "inalienable rights" when freely entering the United States.

And lest we think that injustice is a feature of our collective and unenlightened past, Deloria and Wilkins lead us directly into the most contentious issues of the modern world, including the rights of the many nonhuman citizens of the natural world. Have we entered an era where animals can have rights? If ships have rights (and a gender), why can't animals have rights? After all, they are sentient beings and part of the divine Creation. Or is it the case that animals *do* have rights, but lack access to justice? Corporations and ships are human creations and have the access to justice enjoyed by their creators. Animals are divinely created and have no access to justice within the human institutions that serve the interests of individuals in society. These issues are not merely abstract esoteric ramblings. They are vitally important in a natural world that is being thrown into disarray in the era of climate change. Polar bears are drowning as the Arctic melts, and yet the multinational corporations that drive energy development have no legal duty to protect the natural world by modifying their technologies.

In their effort to recast the definition of property that lies at the heart of the social contract, Deloria and Wilkins leave us with a final intriguing thought:

> Since the creation of property depends upon individual minds looking at nature in new and unsuspected ways, the proper and primary role of the social contract should be education, creating the conditions under which the maximum number of minds and personalities can be developed most completely.

This is the pedagogy of liberation that marks the turning of an era of consciousness in which we acknowledge our humanity and our relationship to the natural world, knowing that our very survival as a species depends upon the health of our planet and its ability to sustain all the component parts of a divine creation more complex and mysterious than we can ever imagine.

—Rebecca Tsosie
Sandra Day O'Connor College of Law
Arizona State University

PREFACE

IN 1992–1993, I HAD THE GOOD FORTUNE to receive a postdoctoral fellowship from the Ford Foundation and the even better fortune of having Vine Deloria Jr., who I had already known for more than a decade, agree to serve as my academic host while he was still teaching at the University of Colorado at Boulder. I was there to revise my dissertation into a book. And while I made significant progress on that enterprise, I also had the opportunity to sit in on several courses that Vine taught that year, one of which was a seminar that he led at the law school titled The Legal Universe.

Having been his student at the University of Arizona between 1980 and 1982, where I earned a master's in political science with a concentration in federal Indian policy, I well remembered how intellectually challenging and stimulating Vine's classes always were. This course was no exception. But where most of those early courses had focused on indigenous politics, federal Indian law, and treaties, this course was far more comprehensive and richly comparative, and it dealt with a much broader range of topics that at least symbolically embraced the legal universe.

It was a stunningly diverse and intellectually riveting course, and it required each of us students to be open to the possibility that the law and the legal universe as we had known those terms were far more convoluted and deceptive concepts than many of us had been led to believe they were from our previous law and political science courses. As we read books, essays, and copious numbers of court opinions from various philosophers, law professors, and judges and justices, we came to realize how manipulable the language of law was and how it could be used to either diminish or enrich the lives of various groups—corporations, racial and ethnic groups, women, and so forth—depending on the ideological framework of the jurists, the economic stakes involved, and the pigmentation of the various parties, to name but a few of the variables that may affect how judicial rulings are made.

Several years later, and after Vine and I had published our first book together, *Tribes, Treaties, and Constitutional Tribulations*, he and I met for a dinner in Tucson, Arizona, and he handed me a detailed chapter outline for what would become this book. He told me that he had already drafted a number of the chapters, particularly those in the first half of the book, but that several additional chapters needed to be written. He wondered whether I was interested in joining with him as a collaborator yet again. I was thrilled with this second opportunity to write a book with Vine, and he and I launched our writing strategy.

Unfortunately, as sometimes happens in the writing process, each of our efforts to work on this book were stymied as we were required to redirect our time and energies toward other projects. We would occasionally remind one another that this was a project that warranted our attention, but other duties stalled our return to it. I was eventually able to write several chapters, and we had just turned our attention back to the book when Vine's health began to deteriorate.

About a year after he passed away, in November of 2005, I contacted his wife, Barbara, and talked to her about the book project. She graciously and enthusiastically encouraged me to proceed. This I have done, though it has been a terribly slow process, in large part because it has been an emotionally and intellectually arduous path without Vine's companionship and broad knowledge. Vine was the most brilliant person I had ever known, and his ability to critique and explain complicated concepts in multiple fields was unparalleled. During the writing of our first book, whenever I had questions or needed clarification on anything, he was a phone call or e-mail away, and we could discuss the issue until it was clear to me. Not having the opportunity to discuss, debate, or simply share my views with him during the final editing and writing phases of this project has made this a most difficult task, since Vine's intellectual skills were unrivaled and my interpretation of specific cases, laws, or theorists' perspectives are not comparable to the understanding that Vine might have had. Nevertheless, I have vigorously sought to maintain the high intellectual standards that Vine always operated from and hope that his spirit and his family, especially Barbara, will be pleased with the final product.

Writing about the legal universe is a daunting assignment. And even though we never intended to address every constituent part of the extremely diverse and ever-expanding legal world, we believe that our underlying theoretical framework and our thorough analysis of a broad swath of primary and secondary literature will help readers gain a deeper and more realistic understanding of how and why the legal universe, or important elements of it, unfolded as it did for the various entities we describe in the United States.

Thanks to Sam Scinta for his unstinting and enthusiastic support of this project, and to Carolyn Sobczak for her insightful and clarifying editorial skills.

I am grateful, as always, for the love and support afforded me by my wife, Evelyn (Lini) Donald Wilkins—and our beautiful children: Sion, Niltooli, and Nazhone.

—David E. Wilkins
University of Minnesota (2011)

INTRODUCTION

WHENEVER RACIAL, ETHNIC, AND OTHER MINORITIES in the United States have raised voices of protest against the conditions under which they have been forced to live, they have been admonished to work within the system rather than seek its abolition. Purveyors of this good counsel point to the many institutional checks and balances that have been devised to protect the rights of the minority: the division of sovereignty between the national government and the states, the tripartite arrangement of the federal government itself, which inhibits any one of the three branches from dominating the affairs of government, and the provisions for frequent popular elections and limited terms of office—all of which are further modified by the American propensity to seek a social consensus by offering disputing parties a reasonable compromise on any major issue. These provisions, minorities have been told, are sufficient to prevent the miscarriage of justice in almost every instance. These institutional and procedural devices, however, are designed as much to protect a lethargic majority against activist minorities as they are to afford minorities a shield against the oppression of the majority. Moreover, the minority that *is* protected is a political minority—a fictional entity consisting of people who temporarily share a political opinion on a specific issue. No individual is a permanent member of a political minority except by his own choosing; and even this minority is not always protected in instances of national hysteria.

We should not confuse a political minority with other nonpolitical minorities in society. Nonpolitical minorities are permanent minorities that have always been outside the social contract and the protection of the Constitution: racial and ethnic groups, the isolated cultural enclaves that diverge radically from the majority culture, small religious communities (Amish and Rastafarians, for example), obese individuals, children, the elderly, gays and lesbians, criminals, the natural world, and the largest group of all, women. For the members of many of these groups, individuals have no choice concerning membership—especially those in racial, ethnic, age, or gender groups. Their physical characteristics alone permanently classify them as part of the group.

Individuals in religious and cultural groups, on the other hand, derive most of their values and certainly their personal identities from distinctive beliefs and practices. Surrendering this unique understanding of life is akin to spiritual and psychological obliteration, because no power on earth, particularly a secular government, is considered equal in importance to the central core of beliefs that distinguishes these people from the rest of society.

Gays and lesbians, obese persons, the natural world, and criminals also encounter special problems and experience discriminatory treatment, and each of these groups is also plagued by particular perceptual difficulties that make their situation problematic. Homosexuals, for example, are frequently told that they have a choice in their sexual preferences or that their behavior is either immoral or unnatural. Obese individuals are also often told that they, too, have a choice in being grossly overweight and therefore do not deserve equal opportunity. And criminals, even after being released from incarceration, continue to be treated in a manner that makes it difficult, if not impossible, to get reacclimated to society.

Nonpolitical minorities have no significant constitutional protection, nor have they ever. Insofar as they enjoy constitutional rights and protections, their status is the result of an intense and continuing struggle for respect and equal treatment in the courts and legislatures of the land. Their task has been to force open the definitions that describe the American social contract and extend its applicability beyond the narrow scope originally envisioned by the constitutional fathers. Thus, Chief Justice Roger Taney might well have been describing all of the nonpolitical minorities when, in discussing the status of African Americans in *Dred Scott v. Sandford* (1857),[1] he noted:

> [T]hey are not included, and were not intended to be included, under the word "citizens" in the Constitution, and can therefore claim none of the rights and privileges which that instrument provides for and secures to citizens of the United States. On the contrary, they were at that time considered as a subordinate and inferior class of beings, who had been subjugated by the dominant race, and, whether emancipated or not, yet remained subject to their authority, and had no rights or privileges but such as those who held the power and the Government might choose to grant them.[2]

In the postwar decades, speakers for nonpolitical minorities have typically cited racism, sexism, ageism, speciesism, and ethnocentrism as the primary barriers preventing them from enjoying full rights as citizens in American society. These accusations have much to recommend them, and these are serious social problems; they do not, however, fully explain the continuing failure of the nonpolitical minorities—notwithstanding the 2008 election of the first African American to the presidency, Barack Obama, or his appointments of Sonia Sotomayor in 2009, the first Latina Supreme Court justice, or Elena Kagan in 2010, a female Jewish Supreme Court nominee—to achieve a greater measure of legal equality within the American political system.

We suggest that a hidden conceptual barrier exists that inhibits not only the permanent minorities but members of the majority as well. That barrier is the inadequate development of the philosophical framework that provided the foundation for the American social contract. In the form in which the men who framed the Constitution received it, the philosophy of social contract was oriented wholly toward a certain restricted class of individuals and could neither include any divergent groups nor provide any significant guidance or protection for the mass of people. Its primary virtue was to encourage a clever, established elite to benefit at the expense of others and perpetuate itself.

Identifying the flaw in US philosophical roots requires that we move beyond the intellectual and emotional climate in which the Constitution was conceived and adopted. The meanings of concepts and words change with use, and even the Supreme Court has admitted that the original perspective of the American social contract has been altered by the passage of time. In *Dred Scott,* Chief Justice Taney recited the familiar refrain of the Declaration of Independence: "We hold these truths to be self-evident: that all men are created equal; that they are endowed by their Creator with certain inalienable rights,"[3] and so forth, and then suggested that the words "would seem to embrace the whole human family, and if they were used in a similar instrument *at this day* would be so understood."[4] But he also remarked that if these words had originally possessed this meaning at the time of the American Revolution, then the conduct of the men who framed the Declaration of Independence "would have been utterly and flagrantly inconsistent with the principles they asserted; and instead of the sympathy of mankind, to which they so confidently appealed, they would have deserved and received universal rebuke and reprobation."[5]

With its narrowly restricted view of the human family, the intellectual world of the American Revolution would not have countenanced the acceptance of African Americans (or women, indigenous peoples, and other racially distinct groups) as equal and participating members of a social contract society. Self-evident truths are generally limited to the era in history in which they are accepted with minimal critical examination. So the fact that nonpolitical minorities are not included in the concept of *man* as defined by the nation's organic documents is not really debatable. But we are not concerned with the changing opinions of the sociopolitical world as any generations experience it, rather with the internal logical consistency of the philosophical system that is thought to justify the social contract form of government, the manner in which the words relate to each other.

In the two centuries prior to the American Revolution, the European intellectual world was undergoing profound change. The universal Catholic Church that had defined both secular and sacred truth and knowledge for medieval Europe was being superseded by smaller, secular institutions that seemed to be more in tune with contemporary views about the world. Of the two traditional sources of acceptable truth, revelation and reason, the latter, as demonstrated by observation, experiment, and the use of mathematical languages to describe physical reality, was clearly emerging as the most sensible way of describing the world. Reason substantially undermined the political doctrine of the divine right of kings because it required that government and other social institutions be grounded in a principle, internal to themselves, that contained the same potential for objectivity and neutrality that secular scientific thinkers were achieving in the natural sciences. That someone might inherit political power because of the accident of birth seemed increasingly absurd and irrational.

Of the European philosophers who had a measure of influence on American political beliefs, John Locke, Baron de Montesquieu, and Thomas Hobbes were most prominent. They all sought to understand the phenomenon of government by postulating probable primordial conditions that would require human beings to gather together for mutual aid and benefit. Human nature was thought to be a constant factor because of its divine creation; therefore, discovering the principle of human social organization meant for these men the possibility of grounding political institutions in a concept of justice that was reasonable and self-evident and could be accepted by individuals exercising free will. A government based upon a reasonable, original choice was believed to be compatible with what they understood about the natural world, God, and human nature. The existence of a fundamental rational principle thus gave a respectable status to social contract theory and made it acceptable within the civilized world. No wonder that the Founding Fathers, when confronted with the need to justify first their revolution against an established and divinely constituted authority and then the organization of their new government, appealed to social contract philosophy with its idea of natural law free from ancient prejudice and practices, a law self-evident in its simplicity.

Postulating the conditions under which individuals were free to conceive and establish a social institution, to which they cede the power to regulate their individual behavior, required adopting a specific view of the critical components of human nature, which then determined how the political principles would function. Hobbes and Montesquieu took somewhat emotional views of human nature—the motivation of forming the social contract was not clearly intellectual or rational. Hobbes saw aggression and fear as fundamental attributes of our original condition, while Montesquieu postulated a primeval sense of inferiority.[6]

John Locke saw human nature as excessively and almost exclusively rational. The individual's actions were wholly predictable once the possibilities within a situation were known, since Locke's original men, relying solely on reason, would always objectively choose their own apparent best interests in defiance of any other considerations, hardly an accurate human response to life. All three philosophers agreed that protecting person and property was the primary purpose of government.

Of the three men, John Locke, because he was English and his writings were easily accessible, probably had the most influence on the direction of American revolutionary thinking. More important, Locke's model for the primary state of nature was the New World; America was often cited in his writings when he was discussing the original conditions of the social contract. In his second essay on civil government, for example, he wrote that "in the beginning, all the world was America, and more so than that is now."[7] It was natural, therefore, that Americans would pay close attention to Locke's ideas.

Accepting the historical reality of the primordial wilderness paradise of Eden, Locke admitted the existence of a theological argument for justifying government based upon the Adamic heritage of individual sovereignty but dismissed it, not because it was unacceptable, but because the lineage could never be traced accurately. Presumably, if one took biblical views literally, everyone would jointly share Adam and Eve's sovereignty as First Man and First Woman; therefore, a social contract would not only be possible but unavoidable because theoretically everyone was equally Adam and Eve's descendants. This Adamic kin relationship would be the most comprehensive social contract conceivable and would require the most rigorous sense of democracy and equality. But Locke studiously avoided this solution and turned instead to other ideas then preying on English minds—personality and property.

Civil government for Locke was not found in nature but was a necessary invention because it was a "remedy for the inconveniences of the state of Nature,"[8] the inconvenience being primarily the state of absolute freedom, which gave no divine guidance for one's choices. "To understand political power aright, and derive it from its original," he argued, "we must consider what estate all men are naturally in, and that is, a state of perfect freedom to order their actions, and dispose of their possessions and persons as they think fit, within the bounds of the law of Nature, without asking leave or depending upon the will of any other man."[9]

The freedom of individual sovereignty thus meant an absolute power of control over person and property. The social contract occurred when the individual surrendered part of this absolute right to control and protect their person and property to the group and received in return its protection. The primary characteristic of human freedom, for Locke and also for the constitutional fathers, was not the need to survive, or even the need to relate to others, but merely a concern of maintaining control over person and property with the right to dispose of property according to one's own will or whims. Since the annoying little revenue taxes were the emotional burrs under the saddle of the American Revolution, there was no reason to have inquired further about the philosophical principles underlying the social contract. In making the arbitrary use of property a fundamental cause of the Revolution and the protection of property a major goal of the Constitution, the constitutional fathers uncritically accepted Locke's explanation of the relationship of person and property. Locke conceived of these concepts as always being together, making the social contract dependent upon their interaction and inseparability, and directing people's attentions thereafter to the most tangible aspect of the problem, which was physical property. Thus, he stated:

Though the earth and all inferior creatures be common to all men, yet every man has a "property" in his own "person." This nobody has any right to but himself. The "labour" of his body and the "work" of his hands, we may say, are properly his. Whatsoever then, he removes out of the state that Nature hath provided and left it in, he hath mixed his labour with it, and joined to it something that is his own, and thereby makes it his property. It being by him removed from the common state Nature placed it in, it hath by his labour something annexed to it that excludes the common right of other men. For this "labour" being the unquestionable property of the labourer, no man but he can have a right to what that is once joined to, at least where there is enough and as good left in common for others.[10]

Property has two different meanings or functions here: one is the personal freedom or sovereignty that naturally accrues to the individual because of his or her individuality; the other is the material object that humans create by mixing their labor with the raw materials of nature to produce something of value within a social context.

The property that people have in themselves can only operate responsibly within the social contract if property and person are understood simply as the two essential perspectives of the primordial sociopolitical world that bear the same intrinsic relationship to each other as do matter and energy in modern physical science. Without property, a person has no standing; without a person, property has no meaning. If property and person are understood as inseparable functions of each other, when one appears the other must also be present to close the logical universe in which the two ideas make sense. Social contract theory therefore does not depend upon a single definitive concept that has principles of action that illuminate and inform people of the purpose and functions of their political institutions. It never decides whether person or property is the dominant consideration for any human social organization. American constitutional law reflects this confusion. And since Americans still generally enjoy immense material blessings compared to much of the rest of the world, it is assumed that the social contract has the proper philosophical configurations, and few people probe further into the underlying philosophical thicket.

The problems of nonpolitical minorities take on added significance when they are placed within the philosophical framework of the social contract. Although racism, sexism, and speciesism are dominant attitudes that continue to oppress and diminish or exclude the rights of minorities, they cannot be manifested directly in law and are not nearly as inclusive and effective as is the lack of property, which frequently leaves the individual person nearly defenseless and quite vulnerable. Indeed, the original American situation is considerably more serious. At the time of the adoption of the Constitution, two minorities, women and African Americans, were regarded as someone else's property. Members of both groups had to overcome this idea before they could begin to speak of rights of equality of treatment. In the subsequent course of American history, the members of one set of minority groups—Native nations—were largely stripped of their property through treaties and statutes, and the other minorities who attempted to gain standing within the social contract were generally prohibited from acquiring property or deprived of their claim to property by federal and state action.

Indigenous peoples were the original proprietors of the continent, the quintessential practitioners of the original social contract. Through a legal fiction called the doctrine of discovery, the Supreme Court adopted the bizarre argument that European explorers, sailing along the coasts of North America, gained a superior title to the lands they saw, leaving a mere right of temporary occupancy for the indigenous owners.[11] Since Native nations were not believed to hold absolute legal title to their lands, the national government claimed the power to administer their property. Thereafter, the government became concerned about indigenous peoples' welfare only insofar as it needed to take or exploit the remainder of their lands. Although perceived collectively as a minority group, Native peoples in reality became a function of the property that the government held on their behalf.

Mexican Americans, we shall see, particularly in California, were deprived of their property through the operation of a court of claims that was more interested in confirming title for the invading Euro-American claimants than in upholding their existing property rights, which had been respected for generations.[12] Asian Americans, the data will show, were denied the right to own land for many decades under state alien land laws.[13] And when the federal government began its persecution of the Mormons, a radically divergent religious group, the most effective measure taken was that which confiscated church property.[14]

With the property side of the social contract equation denied them, racial, ethnic, and other minority groups have had little choice but to seek to develop some legal recognition and therefore constitutional protections for their personhood. They quickly discovered, however, that seemingly innocuous yet descriptive terms such as *citizen* and *person* could be made to function against their interests by any judge or justice willing to engage in legalistic sophistry. Once removed from the philosophical context of the social contract, where it is reasonably specific, the word *person* has radically different content depending on the context in which it is used. *Person* appears in article 1 of the Constitution, where it enabled the Founding Fathers to include African American slaves for purposes of state representation by euphemistically referring to them as "three-fifths of all other Persons,"[15] and in section 9, where the slave trade is described as "the Migration or Importation of such Persons as any of the States now existing shall think proper to admit."[16] It is also used in the Fourteenth Amendment to place the civil rights of African Americans within constitutional protection, rights that had previously been clarified by a federal statute that was rigorously ignored. And *person* is used in the Twenty-second Amendment, which prohibits more than two elected terms of office for the president. But the Fifteenth and Nineteenth Amendments, which give African Americans and women the vote, respectively, use the word *citizen* to designate the groups intended to be the beneficiaries of these changes in the Constitution.

The use of *citizen* is the result of long struggles by women and African Americans to pin down the judicial use of words. In *Dred Scott,* Chief Justice Taney declared that

> "people of the United States" and "citizens" are synonymous terms, and mean the same thing. They both describe the political body who, according to our republican institutions, form the sovereignty, and who hold the power and conduct the Government through their representatives. They are what we familiarly call the "sovereign people," and *every citizen is one of this people, and a constituent member of this sovereignty.*[17]

Presumably women were included in this broad definition of the sovereign people. Yet, later in the opinion, Taney amended this broad definition by remarking that

> a person may be a citizen, that is, a member of the community who form the sovereignty, although he exercises no share of the political

power, and is incapacitated from holding particular offices. Women and minors, who form a part of the political family, cannot vote; and when a property qualification is required to vote or hold a particular office, those who have not the necessary qualification cannot vote or hold the office, yet they are citizens.[18]

Those disqualified from exercising the voting franchise were defined as women, children, and males lacking property because of who they were. In *Minor v. Happersett* (1874),[19] in an almost tongue-in-cheek opinion, Chief Justice Morrison Waite admitted that "sex has never been one of the elements of citizenship in the United States. In this respect men have never had an advantage over women. The same laws precisely apply to both."[20] But, the Court concluded, "the Constitution of the United States does not confer the right of suffrage upon any one, and...the constitutions and laws of the several States which commit that important trust to men alone are not necessarily void."[21] Suffrage, the basic right to participate in the social contract, is not a right deriving from that contract. In this case, the allocation of sovereign powers between the states and the federal government, which was supposed to protect the minority, became a device for turning one away.

In varying degrees, the ensuing chapters will show that the other minorities did not do as well as women and African Americans or that they became victims of even stranger sophistry. In *United States ex rel. Standing Bear v. Crook* (1879),[22] American Indians were declared persons but only insofar as they could file a writ of habeas corpus. In *Elk v. Wilkins* (1884),[23] although Elk, a Winnebago Indian, had fulfilled all the legal requirements for voting in Nebraska, including serving in the state militia and paying taxes, he was found not to be a citizen with suffrage. *Elk*, in fact, is now being cited in a backhanded manner by some conservative Republicans to abuse the rights of the children born to undocumented immigrants. Some federal lawmakers, like Lindsey Graham of South Carolina, are seriously proposing to revisit the Fourteenth Amendment in an attempt to deny birthright citizenship to those children.

When a minority could not be easily classified, it was sometimes forced into a definition that had been created for another group in order to deny its members their legal rights. Thus, in *People v. Hall* (1854)[24] and *Gong Lum v. Rice* (1927),[25] Chinese individuals were classified as "black" in order to keep them from giving testimony against whites and attending school with them. In *Ozawa v. United States* (1922),[26] a Japanese immigrant was denied naturalization because, while his skin was white, he was determined not to be an Aryan or a Caucasian. In *United States v. Thind* (1923),[27] a high-caste Hindu Aryan suffered the same rejection because, while he was certainly an Aryan, his skin was not white.

When the cases dealing with nonpolitical minorities are compared, a common theme emerges. A minority may find its progress blocked because it is compared with another minority not recognized as having civil rights or legal status. The fact that women could be citizens without political rights, for example, made it easy for the Supreme Court to deny Dred Scott his freedom by observing that American society already had citizens with no legal standing who could exercise no rights. The exclusion of African Americans from schools became an excuse to prohibit other races from enjoying a public education. Try as they might, minority group members have not been able to secure a clear and consistent definition of *person* or *citizen* from the courts. The result is that two different definitions of *person* emerge.

The most easily understood definition of *person* and the meaning that generates the most respect from the courts is that favored by business interests. Beginning with Daniel Webster's eloquence and John Marshall's confusion in *Trustees of Dartmouth College v. Woodward* (1819),[28] corporations became persons in law. Once granted eternal life existing in contemplation of law, the corporation made steady progress until it was able, through the well-compensated and therefore greatly suspect memory of Roscoe Conkling, to argue that the Senate, in considering the Fourteenth Amendment, had corporations, not freed African American slaves, in mind. In *Santa Clara County v. Southern Pacific Railroad Co.* (1886),[29] the Supreme Court made the corporate person the dominant actor in the American social contract with almost unlimited rights and protections. In the succeeding decades, one of the few limitations imposed on corporate behavior involved the restriction of the corporate powers of Berea College, when it showed the all-too-human and liberal tendency to reach out and offer blacks an integrated education.[30]

In fact, as evidence of the almost humanlike character of corporations, in 2010 the Supreme Court in *Citizens United v. Federal Election Commission*[31] held that the government could not, under the First Amendment, suppress the free speech rights of a corporation. As Justice Anthony Kennedy put it, "[T]o exclude or impede corporate speech is to muzzle the principal agents of the modern free economy. We should celebrate rather than condemn the addition of this speech to the public debate."[32]

On March 2, 2011, the Supreme Court handed down a somewhat contradictory decision involving corporations, *Federal Communications Commission v. AT&T Inc.* In this case, the justices unanimously (Justice Elena Kagan did not participate in the ruling because she had worked on the case as the solicitor general) held that corporations have no personal privacy rights for purposes of the Freedom of Information Act. The opinion, however, never mentioned the *Citizens United* decision, which had said that corporations do have First Amendment rights to spend money in candidate elections. Adam Liptak, writing for *The New York Times*, suggests that the difference in the two cases hinged on the fact that *Citizens United* involved a constitutional question, while *Federal Communications* only considered the meaning of a federal statute. Interestingly, Chief Justice Roberts concluded the ruling by noting, "We trust that AT&T will not take it personally."

The other definition of *person* is that nebulous status thrust upon minorities when an individual may well be a citizen of both state and national governments, but he or she is still not that *particular* person that the Founding Fathers or subsequent Congresses had in mind when they wrote the Constitution or passed statutes fulfilling its purposes. The only effective solution, minorities have discovered, has been a constitutional amendment in which the social contract is forced open and a new meaning attached to its words. Thus, the United States adopted the Thirteenth, Fourteenth, Fifteenth, and Nineteenth Amendments, which provide African Americans and women a measure of equality in society.

Minorities that have been unable to secure amendments to clarify their rights have remained on the periphery of the social contract both in their persons and in their property, achieving a measure of status only when the public perspective has unintentionally included them. It is important to note, however, that women and African Americans were the only groups originally regarded as property, so the amendments that assist them are basically expanding the narrow view of the world held by the constitutional fathers. But the logic of the social contract still does not allow a natural progression outward to embrace excluded groups. Women have continued to seek another constitutional amendment to protect and stabilize the progress they have made in the past century. Again they have been told that existing constitutional law is sufficiently broad to take care of all foreseeable circumstances.

And some scholars[33] have called for an amendment to acknowledge the distinctive cultures, governments, and sovereignty of Native nations, a constitutional process that has occurred, though with mixed results, in Canada, Argentina, Nicaragua, Brazil, Mexico, and Guatemala.[34]

The Pages Ahead

This book's contents are grouped into three fairly discernible, but not categorized, parts. The first four chapters establish the theoretical framework and philosophical paradigm for the balance of the study. We analyze the oft-ignored emotional dimension of the law and discuss the inherent limitations of law and the social contract, especially insofar as how these have already affected the status of nonpolitical minorities. A fair amount of attention is devoted to detailing the pertinent writings of John Locke, Thomas Hobbes, and Baron de Montesquieu and the manner in which property, personhood, and citizenship have been defined and manipulated in a way that frequently violates minority groups, but elevates and venerates the status of corporations.

In the middle chapters we focus on African Americans, Native nations, and women, the most established of the nonpolitical minorities and therefore the ones with the longest track record showing how state and federal policy makers have often gone to great lengths to deny or suppress the humanity of these groups' members in order to prevent them from securing a firm foothold in the social contract.

There are both striking similarities and profound differences between the members of these three groups, with property, gender, and cultural differences playing key roles. Women, of course, while occupying a unique property status, are also distinctive in the sense that they are *not* a numerical minority. Native nations, on the other hand, as the original proprietors of North America, are also distinctive in that they have longed to retain a measure of political, legal, and cultural autonomy and have been much less enamored with being assimilated than other groups.

African Americans arrived as the property of others, and this powerful practical and legal reality dominated their status in American society for a very long time.

The next four chapters focus on the status of Mexican Americans, Asian Americans, children, and the natural world—both the environment and animal life. The chapter on nature, we believe, is particularly timely, given the instances of recent ecological devastation: Hurricane Katrina in Louisiana in 2005, and BP's Deepwater Horizon drilling rig explosion in the Gulf of Mexico in 2010, which killed nearly a dozen workers and unleashed more than five million barrels of oil, decimating wildlife and despoiling the Gulf waters and much of the coastline—the largest oil calamity in US history.

There were, of course, other chapters that might easily have been included—religious minorities, the disabled, gays and lesbians, Appalachian whites, the obese, and others. But Vine's passing, the existence of numerous other scholarly studies that focus on these groups, and the book's already hefty girth dictated that we cap the study at its current scope and length.

We believe that our intimate portrayal of the respective journeys that each of these diverse groups has traveled in their efforts to have their self-determination and humanity respected provides critical knowledge that will enlighten and uplift all those committed to equality, justice, and respect. The considerable efforts that have been waged both historically and today by the institutions of finance and governance that influence and control the American state to deny, disparage, but also to occasionally suppport the members of these groups are cause for both deep concern but also some measure of optimism as well. The United States, as a distinctive polity, like every other state and nation in the world, is subject to ecological forces of nature, as well as to human-led forces of nature that spotaneously surge forward, demanding freedom and dignity. This study is a contribution to that effort, and we hope that it will prove useful to all those engaged in such pursuits.

CHAPTER 1
The Majesty of Law

ONE OF THE MOST PERSISTENT DEBATES IN AMERICAN SOCIETY revolves around the question of the size of government. We consider it too big if it interferes in our personal affairs and too small when it fails to provide us with benefits and services we believe we are entitled to. But we do not really mean the size of government at all; we mean the role of government, its function and purpose. The various amendments to the US Constitution give eloquent testimony to the fact that we have both wrestled with this question and been confused by it most of our national life. Moreover, the birth of the Tea Party movement, the global and national economic recession, and the Obama administration's eye-popping efforts to address the massive financial problems—the $787 billion stimulus package, substantial banking intervention, attempts to shore up the American automotive market by, for example, forcing Chrysler into bankruptcy, and the president's long-term goal to reduce the degree to which the United States is a consumer-driven economy—are the most recent iterations of that age-old question: what should be the role of the government, particularly in dire economic situations?

Nothing seems quite as clear as the general philosophical propositions that undergird our political institutions. The preamble to the Constitution declares, "We hold these truths to be self-evident, that all men are created equal, that they are endowed by their Creator with certain inalienable Rights, that among these are Life, Liberty and the Pursuit of Happiness." These self-evident truths, like many commonsense propositions, are difficult to understand and almost impossible to realize. Their majesty resides in their inspirational value, not in their application. When we attempt to realize them in our daily lives, through the establishment of governments and the promulgation of laws, we soon discover that a simple idea such as equality takes on disturbing proportions and implications when it must be applied to our immediate social situation.

All human societies strive, as part of their maturation process, to turn their philosophical beliefs into a reality. Nevertheless, the United States has frequently fallen short of its goals and has both experienced and created the most dreadful incidents of injustice. We can often understand why these things happen, but we generally lack the skill and knowledge to establish the procedures whereby we can avoid such problems in the future. Only after prolonged agony and experiment, it seems, are we sometimes able to construct the proper mechanisms for at least coping with, if never entirely solving, the problems that bedevil our national soul. The following story is a historical illustration of the agony and profound difficulty that the members of one group we will be examining, African Americans, experienced in their struggles to have their humanity recognized and respected by the US legal system.

On the dark, sultry night of September 30, 1919, a small group of impoverished black sharecroppers gathered in a little church in the backcountry of Arkansas. They shared a common lot of poverty, systematically enforced ignorance, and racial discrimination. The Progressive Farmers and Household Union of America, which had called the meeting, had offered to help them organize and hire a lawyer to represent them in their continuing struggle against the white landowners who were oppressing them. Thus, one by one, they straggled into the rural church that evening with cautious optimism for the future and hoping that their meeting would not attract the attention of the whites who controlled the county. But their hopes were in vain. Word of the gathering had reached the sheriff, and he quickly dispatched Deputy Sheriff Pratt with two other men to keep track of what the sharecroppers were doing. Along the way, other whites, looking for an evening's entertainment, decided to accompany the law officers to the church.

The meeting never took place. From the shadows surrounding the church came hoots, catcalls, and curses. As each sharecropper walked toward the church, they were identified by name and immediately threatened. When they showed no fear and no sign of dispersing, the hidden whites became annoyed and fired a gun in the air, warning that they meant business. When there was no response from those assembled inside the church, they fired shots closer to the building. Soon general shooting broke out, and in the confusion one of the white men who had accompanied the deputy sheriff was killed. The black sharecroppers scattered into the countryside, some hiding, others trying to reach their homes.

As word of the white man's death spread through the county, the incident was completely distorted by local whites. The sharecroppers were blamed for starting the violence, and white citizens were told that a general black insurrection was taking place. During the next day and night, gangs of armed whites roamed the hills, beating and killing many African Americans. In all, between 200 and 250 blacks were killed, and five whites died. Arkansas governor Charles Brough, when informed that Phillips County was suffering a major black "uprising," appointed the Committee of Seven—prominent white citizens who he charged with bringing law and order to the area.

The committee did little to soothe tempers; they told a growing crowd of frightened, angry whites at the Phillips county seat of Helena that the Progressive Farmers and Household Union of America was a dangerous revolutionary organization dedicated to starting a race war between blacks and whites. How the committee reached this conclusion was unclear, but it served to keep the whites in a frenzy. When someone killed a second white man the following day, every black who could be taken alive was brought to the county jail for interrogation, although the circumstances of this second killing suggested that the man might have been slain by a fellow white to settle an old score. Nevertheless, 122 blacks were indicted by the grand jury on charges growing out of the riot, and 73 were charged with murder.[1] Not a single white person was indicted.

When news that the killers had been identified reached the mob assembled in front of the jail, cries of "Lynch!" filled the air. On the following day, October 2, federal troops were sent to the county to prevent any further violence. The crowd, in an increasingly agitated mood, continued to surround the jail and dispersed only when the Committee of Seven appeared and promised that if the crowd let the law take its course, the accused blacks would be properly executed by the state. Satisfied, the crowd gradually dispersed.

Having weathered the immediate crisis, the committee and local law officers began gathering evidence for the trials. Blacks who had not been accused of crimes were whipped and tortured for information about the killings until finally several men agreed to testify that they had witnessed the accused blacks, standing in a group, kill a white man with a high-powered rifle.

The lawyer who had agreed to assist the sharecroppers prior to their meeting, O. S. Bratton, fared almost as badly as his intended black clients. He barely escaped being killed by the mob the morning after the church attack. On October 2, when the Committee of Seven was promising that law would prevail, he was arrested and held in jail on a murder charge.

He remained there for the rest of the month. On October 31, he was indicted for battery but later that day was secretly taken from jail by the county judge who would later try the case. Hustled into a closed automobile,

Bratton was driven four miles to West Helena, where he was put on the train just ahead of the mob that had heard of his release and was looking for him. After his forced departure, the court appointed a defense lawyer more ideologically in tune with the racist sentiments of the community.

One of the trials lasted a mere forty-five minutes. It featured a simple declaration that a white man had been killed and the rehearsed stories of the two black witnesses. No defense witnesses were called. There was no cross-examination of prosecution witnesses, no conflicting evidence presented, no closing defense argument—in short, no defense. It took five minutes for the jury to return its verdict for all the defendants: guilty of murder in the first degree. The convicted blacks received the promised death sentence and were sent to the state penitentiary at Varner to await execution. The other trials followed similar patterns. In all, twelve men were sentenced to death. Additionally, another sixty-seven individuals were sent to prison on various other charges.

By the spring of 1920, the case had gained national attention and thousands of letters expressing sympathy and demanding clemency or suggesting a commutation of the death sentences began arriving at the governor's office. Local citizens began to fret over the delay caused by the appeal and demanded the immediate execution of the sharecroppers. Five original members of the Committee of Seven wrote the governor that "all of our citizens are of the opinion that the law should take its course." In October 1920, a meeting of nearly four hundred members of the Richard L. Kitchens Post of the American Legion in a resolution addressed to the governor reminded him that "a solemn promise was given by the leading citizens of the community, that if these guilty parties were not lynched, and let the law take its course, *that justice would be done and the majesty of the law upheld.*"[2] They urged the governor to proceed with the executions.

The governor, of course, could not act to carry out the sentence in the face of orders to stay the executions issued first by the higher state courts and then by the federal courts. In 1923, the sharecroppers' case finally arrived at the US Supreme Court, in *Moore v. Dempsey*, where the high court reviewed the Arkansas federal district court's denial of the writ of habeas corpus filed by the condemned blacks.[3] Justice Oliver Wendell Holmes, writing for the majority, cited numerous instances of prejudicial acts that had precluded a fair trial for the accused, and the Court reversed the decision and sent the case back for further hearings. But the Court's decision was not unanimous.

Torture to elicit damning testimony, systematic exclusion of blacks and impartial whites from the jury, and the denial of the right to a counsel of their own choice were not believed to be sufficient evidence of a lack of due process by Justices James McReynolds and George Sutherland, who argued that the solemn adjudications of state courts ought not be overturned on the basis of mere ex parte affidavits from the convicts.

This incident is known as the Elaine Race Riot or the Phillips County Race Riot in Arkansas and is typical of the treatment of African Americans in the South in the early decades of the twentieth century. The arrest, indictment, prosecution, trial, verdict, and sentencing certainly followed the form of legal process, but all the evidence indicated that justice had been badly abused at each step in the procedure. Eventually, after a struggle that lasted for a decade and a half, the blacks were freed. *Moore v. Dempsey* is usually cited as a landmark case in the movement incorporating Fifth and Fourteenth Amendment protections for state citizens. But more interesting, for our purposes, is the idea of law held by whites in this case.

It has been said that we get our understanding of the law from observing the actions of people around us rather than from our reading of statutes and ordinances. Yet there must be some correlation between what we know the law to be and the situations in which we demand its application. There is a startling disparity between the form and substance of law in this case that cannot be avoided. How could the American Legion Post, for instance, nearly a year after the trial, have petitioned the governor for immediate executions when it was apparent to nearly everyone in the country that the convicted blacks had been denied any semblance of justice? And in their petition, how could they insist that "the majesty of law" would be enhanced if the men were summarily executed before their appeals had been decided? In view of the mass of evidence presented before the Supreme Court concerning the abuses of the legal system, how could two justices describe the proceedings in the state courts as "solemn," thereby lending judicial dignity to a process that could only be described as loathsome?

We can answer these questions only by supposing that the promise made by the Committee of Seven to the mob assembled outside the Phillips County jail represented a higher vision of justice and served a greater social purpose than did the orderly operation of an impartial judicial system. We must suppose that the mockery of a trial and demand for immediate execution of these poor African American cotton farmers was more resonant with the philosophy of the Declaration of Independence and the Constitution than any other way of handling the case. And this supposition is impossible to contemplate. No system of law can accommodate itself to satisfy the emotional demands of a mob, and after tempers had cooled, people should have understood that fact and relented. But they did not. The committee's promise, long after the racist fever of the moment had subsided, was regarded as a legally binding resolution of the incident by the people and elected officials of Arkansas. Where is the correlation between justice and law in this instance?

In the Elaine riot and its subsequent legal activities we have an instance in which law is seen as an instrument to enforce a view of the world that is wholly subliminal, emerging only in dire circumstances to become an embarrassment to everyone. The critical words *majesty* and *solemn* seem to indicate a strong belief that law must be reliable and relentless in its operation, almost in defiance of the justice that it promises to administer. Once the formal process has been acted out, we seem to say, the substance of justice has been realized and no other considerations need be made. *Moore v. Dempsey*, regardless of the constitutional issues it presents, gives us an opportunity to critically examine how much our domestic law is the product of emotions and to what degree it represents the lofty philosophical propositions of the nation's organic documents.

Law and human emotions have always had an intimate and perplexing relationship. Traditionally we have been told that so-called primitive societies allow themselves the luxury of engaging in swift, brutal retaliation and that the hallmark of civilized life is our avoidance of bloodlust retributive justice. But this image of scowling and bloodthirsty savages seeking to exact eye-for-an-eye vengeance is, in fact, a fundamental misconception about aboriginal life, which, more often than not, focused on peacemaking and restorative justice when disharmony arose in the community.[4] More often it has been the allegedly "civilized" peoples who have formed the frenzied mobs that have carried out vicious campaigns against those accused of various offenses.

Nazi Germany is not the only example of a people and law gone astray. We need only remember vigilante groups that terrorized cities in the western United States, the sordid record of southern lynchings of African Americans, and the brutal attacks on workers at Ludlow and Haymarket to realize that mob violence is more often a product of mass society than it is a characteristic of indigenous peoples. More recently under the George

W. Bush administration's two terms, we have witnessed a series of actions and policies—military tribunals at Guantanamo Bay, Cuba, and the use of "enhanced interrogation techniques," also known as torture—all executed under the color of law that has cast a pall over the democratic soul of the nation, both internally and in the eyes of the world.

Efforts to understand the emotional dimensions of law have usually focused on formulations of legal concepts rather than analyzing our response to law and what exceptions we place on it. Thurman Arnold, a prominent Washington attorney and a former assistant attorney general of the United States, suggested that law was the "great reservoir of emotionally important symbols" undergirding the status quo "by creating a realm somewhere within the mystical haze beyond the courts, where all our dreams of justice in an unjust world come true."[5] This nebulous realm, above daily experiences, beyond our sense perceptions, and immune from logical analysis, projects a transcendent feeling for justice, which we feel but have great difficulty expressing.

Theodore F. T. Plucknett, in his study *A Concise History of the Common Law*, saw emotion in considerably broader terms.[6] "[T]he ideas which most powerfully influence conduct in every department of life," according to Plucknett, "are not the ideas of a systematic philosophy deliberately held, but rather the vague notions and unconscious prejudices, habits of mind, and so forth, of which we are for the most part unaware." More important than the clear but inconsistent doctrines and beliefs of which we are certain, Plucknett believed, was the "half-conscious formation of ideas which is bound to go on in the mind of every active practitioner."[7] It may not be the substance of law that we are able to explain objectively in our conduct, but rather the hidden wellspring of emotions and the habits of mind that catch us unaware in a crisis that are the factors that actually determine our behavior.

Benjamin Nathan Cardozo, in his classic treatise *The Nature of Judicial Process*,[8] attempted to identify these half-conscious ideas and concluded that precedents are ultimate sources of law. As such, the history behind precedents "are the basic juridical conceptions which are the postulates of judicial reasoning, and farther back are the habits of life, the institutions of society, in which those conceptions had their origin, and which, by a process of interaction, they have modified in turn."[9] Cardozo's view suggests a polarity in which judicial conceptions of law are at one end and represent intellectual clarity, and the habits and values of our lives are at the other end, representing everything emotional and subjective. The ebb and flow between emotions and intellect produces a living law that grows as it derives new ideas from human experience and expresses them in principles that in turn modify and direct human behavior.

In the essay "The Paradoxes of Legal Science," Cardozo suggested an intimate connection, if not an identity, between law and philosophy at the deepest level of individual and social perception. "We fancy ourselves to be dealing with some ultra-modern controversy, the product of the class of interests in industrial society," he wrote, but after examination "the problem is laid bare, and at its core are the ancient mysteries crying out for under-standing—rest and motion, the one and the many, the self and the not-self, freedom and necessity, reality and appearance, the absolute and the relative. We have the claims of stability to be harmonized with those of progress. We are to reconcile liberty with equality, and both of them with order."[10] The resolution of the most difficult legal problems are eventually exercises in posing, understanding, and reconciling philosophical alternatives and applying them in the practical realm of human life.

It is in the correlation of philosophy and daily reality that law becomes mysterious and complicated. Legal doctrines are built upon an abstract indi-vidual who inerrantly follow the dictates of the law and avoids all penalties and prohibitions. Legal scholars, it seems, spend a considerable amount of time describing this ideal individual and it is from an understanding of this idealized individual's behavior that Americans derive their legal doctrines in most areas of jurisprudence. Thurman Arnold, commenting on the irony of law and economics, said that "law and economic theories maintain their consistency by relation to themselves, not to actual men, but to an abstract man, who represents men as they ought to be." "The theories," he argues, "are tested not by comparison with reality but by checking them up with the abstract man behind them."[11]

This abstract person pervades all legal thinking. This individual is par-ticularly important in the law of torts, and Cardozo explains how this per-son is useful to legal thinking. "The standard of care as measured by the conduct of a reasonable man is at times the expression of a minimum of duty rather than a maximum. If the individual has special skill or opportu-nities for knowledge, he may be required to do whatever a reasonable man would do if equally favored by nature and occasion."[12] Although abstract, the ideal person is not a static personality. The individual takes on and discards knowledge and reasonable deliberations as the occasion warrants. This person is believed to act prudently and with foreknowledge of the results of their actions and they range throughout the field of law setting a good example to the rest of us who stumble along with only a minimal amount of information and deliberation in comparison. Not only is American legal philosophy constructed on the basis of this abstract individual, their religious beliefs and behavior, their ethical codes and social customs, and their social sciences all feel this idealized individual's influence. Perhaps only in athletics do we ever encounter the exploits and achievements of real people and that is because Americans are so insistent about keeping records and maintaining athletic statistics. But theologically, they spend funds according to wise investment procedures, never exceeding their budgets unless they find the occasion for reasonably certain speculative investments. Psychologically, Americans judge their mental activities and emotional state by comparison with statistical people who provide them with a norm for their behavior.

Cardozo, Plucknett, and Arnold all suggest that law is somewhere between the nebulous prejudices of unconsciousness and the clearly defined activities of the abstract person of law as they are compared to that individual by judges and justices. The abstract individual does provide Americans with a majesty of law but only because this idealized individual's behavior enables Americans to construct logically consistent doctrines that purport to give them certain answers to the nagging question of how to judge human behavior. It was the certainty of execution and death that the Arkansas mob expected, that made them believe in the majesty of law. But the majesty of law, as represented by the Supreme Court, where passions were minimal, turned aside their demands and made them conform to the standards under which the abstract person would have felt constitutionally protected.

Because there is this interaction between law and prejudice, the model of law suggested by these three legal scholars can be exceedingly useful in examining the treatment of racial, ethnic, gender, age, and other minorities within the American constitutional framework. Traditionally, Americans have acted as if minority groups were a subspecies of the majority, lacking only a few attributes that distinguish the majority from any preceding generation of humans in world history. Americans frequently use the terms *disadvantaged* and *plight* to explain the status of minorities and imply that if there were some way for minorities to overcome the handicaps they inherently possess, justice of a more profound nature might be theirs for the taking.

Although these attitudes continue to exist at the level of policy making, in general the rights of minorities have been significantly expanded during the post–World War II years, and this expansion has, in many respects, continued into the twenty-first century. It is doubtful that anything remotely approaching the Elaine riot could happen today without an instantaneous outcry of rage by the public. Indeed, the linkage of the nation through television, the Internet, cell phones, and dramatically improved transportation and communication facilities has made us one nation, whether we wish to recognize it or not.

Prior to Barack Obama's election, many people believed that the United States had reached a plateau in race relations and that only an additional effort by minorities would improve existing conditions. The election of an African American (who happens to be half white) to the presidency, however, helped, at least temporarily, to ameliorate race relations on certain levels. But Obama's reluctance to directly address black/white racial issues—except for his awkward treatment of the affair involving Harvard's Henry Louis Gates and the Cambridge police officer, and the hasty firing and subsequent reinstatement of Shirley Sharrod, an African American employee at the US Department of Agriculture, for alleged discriminatory treatment of a white farmer, instigated by a conservative white blogger and accepted without verification by news organizations, the NAACP, and the USDA—shows that tensions remain.

And the immigration issue, especially as it affects those undocumented immigrants from Mexico who settled in Arizona, which passed a draconian law in 2010 that sought to criminalize virtually all brown-skinned Latinos and Latinas, continues to be a major issue that has not been adequately addressed by local, state, or national lawmakers. Not suprisingly, most Latinos heartily oppose Arizona's measure, but a majority of white Americans support it.

Thus, we have no way of accurately predicting how minorities will fare in the future. The task of creating the American Dream for every citizen is far from finished, but the future of minorities seems to be one of defending the present status rather than projecting new paths by which progress can be made.

One of the major objections raised in recent years by many American minority groups is the propensity of the Euro-American majority to judge minorities by criteria applicable primarily to itself. This accusation is no doubt true, but it is predictable because both majority and minority tend to judge the world according to their own experiences and expectations. We cannot predict the future of minorities because we are unable to find a means by which we can distinguish a future homogenous social condition from the projections made by the majority. That is to say, we cannot presently find a vision of society in which the amalgamation of majority and minorities finds a new expression that transcends the heritage of each. In many ways, perhaps, we are in a situation similar to that described by Cardozo. The habits of life and institutions of society continually exert so much influence on the development of law that the system has become closed and merely recycles old problems, occasionally giving us some new insights on old questions, but little in the way of hope for the future.

The model for understanding the experiences of the various minorities in constitutional history suggests that we move from prejudice to clarified expressions of law and with the enforcement of law an additional movement in the hazy realm where prejudice, which may or may not be more violent and narrow than what preceded it, continues to persist despite the construction of new law. In order to establish the foundation or starting point for our examination, it is necessary that we discover the basis upon which the Euro-American majority established its conception of the social contract and promulgated the image of the abstract person from which minorities of various persuasions—racial, ethnic, gender, age—were initially excluded and into which these same minorities have only recently intruded and achieved a modest, though still vulnerable, status.

Exploring the legal history of American law involves more than a recitation of the wrongs experienced by American minorities. Rather, we need to know what the original conception of law and society was and be able to trace the entrance of minorities into the American social contract through the gradual expansion of the idea of the abstract person to include minorities. In effect, we must construct a universe of legal realities that must have undergirded the original American social contract and explore the correlation of law and emotions that expanded this idea into our present condition.

Christopher Stone, in his famous essay on ecological law, "Should Trees Have Standing? Toward Legal Rights for Natural Objects," pointed out that "the world of the lawyer is peopled with inanimate right-holders: trusts, corporations, joint ventures, municipalities, Subchapter R partnerships, and nation-states, to mention just a few." He also noted that ships not only had a legal existence but also a gender—feminine. In dealing with the problem of *standing*, the technical term for the recognition by law of the right of an entity to participate in the legal process, Stone remarked that "[i]t is not inevitable, nor is it wise, that natural objects should have no rights to seek redress in their own behalf. It is no answer to say that streams and forests cannot have standing because streams and forests cannot speak. Corporations cannot speak either; nor can states, estates, infants, incompetents, municipalities or universities. Lawyers speak for them, as they customarily do for the ordinary citizen with legal problems."[13] Stone also astutely observed that "throughout legal history, each successive extension of rights to some new entity has been, therefore, a bit unthinkable. We are inclined to suppose the rightlessness of its rightless 'things' to be a decree of Nature, not a legal convention acting in support of some status quo. It is thus that we defer considering the choices involved in all their moral, social, and economic dimensions."[14]

The subsequent development of legal concepts and the correlative rights that entities achieve in law are a product of the struggle to overcome the belief that Nature has decreed certain things to be true and the demonstration that the world will not be the worse for allowing entrance into the legal universe of entities previously unwelcome and forbidden. This belief of Nature's decree is certainly an apt description of the view of minority rights held by many Euro-Americans, and especially by white male Americans, at the adoption of the US Constitution. With the exception of a handful of "civilized" or "praying" Indians and freed blacks, minority groups, including women and children, were certainly not felt to have any legal rights within the constitutional framework. Thomas Jefferson may have wanted to free his slaves and demonstrate that all men were created equal. The fact is that he did not do it.

We can suppose, for the sake of discussion, that the legal universe at the time of the adoption of the US Constitution was peopled primarily by male members of the white majority. What obstacles had to be overcome, what steps had to be taken, and what changes had to be made in order for American society to have moved forward into the far more progressive stance in evidence today? Social conditions and attitudes certainly had to change and it would not be difficult to trace out the history of minority struggles to achieve equality, reciting all the incidents that inspired laws and constitutional amendments, and then draw our conclusions quite easily. But such a history would illustrate primarily the change in American society and the changes in law would be seen as technical adjustments to an already-existing social contract. Such a study would be useful but would have little predictive value and would even lack the precision that is necessary to accurately mark the changes in legal concepts that made such progress possible.

We will want to watch the changes in the law itself, not because law is something that stands above ordinary experience or the temper of the times, but because legal doctrines summarize the state of social perceptions at the time they are articulated. They represent the reconciliation between what we emotionally experience and are willing to accept. Laws do not always look forward, but even in looking backward it helps to reorganize that hazy realm of our habits of mind and social institutions and call forth new energies for the potential resolution of problems that we can feel but not always explain.

Let us suppose, then, that the legal universe at the time of the adoption of the Constitution was peopled by this one entity—the white, propertied male who willingly gave his consent to the establishment of the social contract. Let us next trace the progress of several of the major American minority groups as they attempt to make their way into this social contract—or in the case of Native nations, seek to maintain a degree of political, legal, and cultural autonomy—and attempt to discover in this journey what other relevant aspects of law and legal doctrines assisted or inhibited their progress. If we can identify additional elements and presuppositions of the original social contract, it may be possible to gauge how well minorities have overcome the barriers that presently confront them. Finally, we can suggest ways of viewing the status of minorities, which may themselves suggest the path of the future.

Attempting to establish an interpretation of legal history that purports to be able to predict patterns of development and identify problems is a hazardous and, more importantly, highly speculative task. We can be content if we discover new ways of looking at old problems, raise a few conceptual questions that have not previously been considered, and simply lay the groundwork for future discussions of where problems persist. While we could certainly demonstrate the interaction between the historical events and the development of law, let us confine our discussions to legal concepts and doctrines themselves. The final result of any examination of the law should be to raise our conception of the majesty of law, and this task can best be accomplished by restricting our investigation and discussion to the expressions of the courts, particularly the US Supreme Court, where the majesty of the law in the form of "opinions" is most prominently displayed.[15] A clear vision of the majesty of law in itself is a powerful experience and calls us to new responsibilities. Lacking this vision, we are inclined to attribute majesty to the manner in which we want law to work, and this desire is the ultimate debasement of the legal process.

CHAPTER 2
The Social Contract

THE THREE CENTURIES PRECEDING THE AMERICAN REVOLUTION recast foundations of Western institutions. The power of the Christian Church, once the self-proclaimed arbiter of universal conflict and center of earthly authority, had declined after the Protestant Reformation. Individual conscience rather than ecclesiastical tradition now served as a primary source of religious belief, paralleled by the homogeneity of Christendom, giving way to national churches. The great landed nobility, the repositories of individual and national wealth, no longer controlled a majority of national income. International commerce and colonial exploitation brought greatly increased luxuries to a new merchant class; traders and industrialists rather than feudal lords entered the new aristocracy of every nation.

During the Middle Ages, the Pope, Christ's vicar upon earth, possessed the power to sanctify the dynastic changes that periodically occurred among the ruling families of Europe. The doctrine of the divine right of kings became commonly accepted as an explanation of the origin and basis of political institutions. Truth consisted of two complementary sources, revelation and reason, and the image of God as a lawgiver extended far beyond the customs and traditions of social life to embrace the perceptions of the natural world as well. As reason continued to gain in ascendancy and revelatory authority eroded with individual interpretation of the biblical scriptures, rationally minded thinkers began to shift their point of view from the divine right of kings to different principles that could explain the origin and stability of political institutions in terms acceptable to the spirit of the times.

While the Christian interpretation of history still maintained its way, it became apparent that much knowledge of human institutions, geography, and human cultures was to be found outside the opening books of the Old Testament. Therefore, to save the truth of the Old Testament while accounting for the existence of other peoples and societies in newly encountered foreign lands, Western philosophers had to posit an original state of nature and the operation of natural law in human society. In this way, the Old Testament could be preserved and a plentitude of new anthropological information could be assimilated to supplement the Holy Scriptures. Natural law, whether in the realm of physical events or in the spontaneous human activities, dominated knowledge. In the same way that the individual stood before God in a bargaining position, so individuals composing society were thought to have once bargained with political figures to create a contract or compact for the conduct of human affairs.

Three major figures represent the shift that European civilization experienced after 1500: Thomas Hobbes, John Locke, and Baron de Montesquieu. While they disagreed considerably about the origin and principles of political institutions, they did agree upon one principle. All three began assuming a hypothetical state of nature from which they derived natural laws of historical institutional development. Hobbes and Montesquieu observed a more pragmatic view of humans than did Locke, but their realism created a pessimistic philosophy that did not reflect the optimism of the times. Hobbes imagined the life of an individual striving for survival in a state of nature as "solitary, poor, nasty, brutish, and short," and he eventually concluded that might generally makes right. Montesquieu found in his state of nature not the gentle confidence of Locke or the aggressive individual of Hobbes, but a timid and fearful soul. "Such a man would feel nothing in himself at first but impotency and weakness; his fears and apprehensions would be excessive; as appears from instances (were there any necessity of proving it) of savages found in forests, trembling at the motion of a leaf, and flying from every shadow. In this state every man would fancy himself inferior, instead of being sensible of his equality. No danger would be therefore of their attacking one another; peace would be the first law of nature."[1] This analysis might have been correct, but it was not appealing to the adventurous European civilizations expanding over earth and oceans with rather brutal colonial tactics.

Of the three philosophers, there can be little doubt that John Locke was the most influential with respect to the fathers of the American Revolution. They regarded themselves as Englishmen but were treated as second-class subjects, equal in some respects to the very peoples they were displacing on behalf of the mother country. Even more important, Locke was an employee of the Whigs during the reign of Charles II, and his writings were designed to justify the Glorious Revolution of 1688. Much of his original intent in writing *On Civil Government* was to provide the theoretical basis for a settlement in Georgia and another American colony had the revolution failed. His writings emphasized an idealized state of nature, specifically located in America, and references to America scattered throughout his writings indicate that he saw an opportunity to empirically prove his theory. In the second essay on civil government, Locke wrote that "in the beginning, all the World was *America*, and more so than that is now."[2] Such a direct reference could hardly have been overlooked by the American political theorists searching for an articulation of natural law upon which they could justify their rebellion against the king of England.

Locke's political philosophy began politely by recognizing the theological beliefs still potent in European minds. He argued that the biblical Adam had lacked total authority over his children, either by the laws of nature on through a positive act of God, concluding that "it is impossible that the Rulers now on Earth, should make any benefit, or derive any the least shadow of Authority from that, which is held to be the Fountain of all Power, *Adam's Private Dominion and Paternal Jurisdiction*."[3] In acknowledging conventional religious truth but placing it in opposition to historical development, Locke set the stage to separate church and state while maintaining the subjective intimacy of theology and political science, a strange combination that has continued as an unarticulated feature of law throughout American history. By eliminating revelation from consideration, Locke elevated reason to a position of primacy in the origin of human institutions. Within his subsequent state of nature is lodged the assumption that institutions have meaning insofar as their constituents have a rational basis for participation. Many commentators often neglect this aspect of Locke's political philosophy, but it should be kept firmly in mind in discussing the social contract because for Locke, both religious and political ideas shared an aura of rationality even though only the political concepts managed to achieve objective expression in constitutions and laws. The religious ideas continued to lurk in the background, like James Fenimore Cooper's Indians, appearing to be reasonable, and therefore escaping serious analysis, but destined for extinction nonetheless—mere museum pieces. [4]

"To understand Political Power right, and derive it from its Original," Locke argued, "we must consider what State all Men are naturally in, and that is, a *State of perfect Freedom* to order their Actions, and dispose of their Possessions, and Persons as they think fit, within the bounds of the Law of Nature, without asking leave, or depending upon the Will of any other Man."[5] This picture hardly refers to a historical condition. It describes an archetype of chaos in which freedom is conceived primarily as the ability to act arbitrarily within a limited sphere. Appearing simultaneously are both the state of nature and the law of nature, leading some commentators to suggest that Locke's "original men" had already responded to both aspects when they are first encountered. They have conceived of and appropriated property; they have appended the boundaries of natural law that give validity to their acts. This state of nature is not a serious defect, however, for it corresponds to the manner in which many people conceive the origins of society; and thus if it is not logically correct, it has surrendered such clarity for the more constructive purpose of communicating a framework within which human experience is readily recognized.

The law of nature in Locke's first description of the world has two components: reason and common equity, "which is that measure God has set to the actions of Men, for their mutual security,"[6] and it is the possibility that individuals will overstep this measure of their individuality, ordained by the deity, that provides the motivating force for the establishment of civil society. Civil government, in fact, emerges as the "proper Remedy for the Inconveniences of the State of Nature,"[7] although it is not certain whether Locke saw, as did Hobbes, that individuals were inevitably condemned to intrude upon others. Hobbes seemed to attribute a savage and perhaps evil motivation to individuals; Locke, more in tune with the conception of the complexity of natural laws in the realm of physical science, seemed to assume that even with sincerity and reasonable conduct, conflict of some kind was unavoidable. At any rate, civil government emerged almost immediately from the state of nature because of the uniqueness of individuals and their close proximity to one another. Geography may be said to provide a significant but unarticulated factor in Locke's ideas, and it is important to note this aspect now because geography will emerge again as an important aspect of political thought.

Locke hinted at this dimension of political organization when he cited contemporary conditions as indicative of the state of nature. He asked rhetorically, "*Where are,* or ever were, there any *Men in such a State of Nature?*" and concluded that "since all *Princes* and Rulers of *Independent* Governments all through the World, are in a State of Nature, 'tis plain the World never was, nor ever will be, without Numbers of Men in that State."[8] International relations might have been a better point of departure for Locke since the great cultural differences among nations, comparable in many respects to the quirks of individual personalities, might have led him to examine that nebulous realm of beliefs and ill-formed ideas that play so potent a role in human perceptions of social institutions. Nevertheless, he began with individuals and expanded his analysis outward to embrace the world of his time. His methodology is crucial to understanding the Anglo-Saxon American political tradition, where in legal theory it has been the practice to study the behavior of individuals and then project that activity to a more generalized social scheme, that is, "What if everyone did it?" Such a projection is not often accurate or useful. The what-if scenario assumes that legal principles, functional with respect to the individual, can be projected indefinitely to describe group, crowd, and mass behavior. This projection would only hold if the members of a crowd, or mob, held a common belief about the world, and thus assumes that culture plays no significant part in human institutions.

Not every compact, according to Locke, resolves the inconveniences of the state of nature, "but only this one of agreeing together mutually to enter into one Community, and make one Body Politic; other Promises and Compacts, Men may make one with another, and yet still be in the State of Nature."[9] Locke failed to clarify exactly what these other compacts might be that would preserve the state of nature yet be fully deliberate as agreements between individuals. Hanna Pitkin, in an incisive essay, "Obligation and Consent," wrote that "strictly speaking, of course, Locke's contract sets up *society* and government is established by society as a trust."[10] If we consider Locke's identification of the rules of the nations as existing in a state of nature, Pitkin's interpretation cannot possibly hold because these societies are already in existence and simply require an agreement in objective form to regulate their activities to escape the state of nature. Society thus exists prior to the establishment of a social contract and the instrument that removes society from the state of nature is an objective agreement articulating principles by which individuals, and for that matter nations, agree. The distinctions between society and government are crucial since the law of nature would appear to be more closely followed in societies than by governments because of the failure of societies to transcend the state of nature. Societies would thus be more compatible with other aspects of nature, particularly natural law as it relates to physical entities, than would governments operating according to generally acceptable propositions and principles.

The social contract, in removing humans from the state of nature, severs them from the rest of nature in a fundamental sense; we participate in the world but with no ultimate relationship to physical reality. Gradually we come to project our own beliefs about the world back upon it and transform it into an artificial entity that has existence only with respect to our political institutions. This alienation, although a theoretical separation initially, explains why Anglo-Saxon and American legal theory took the radical step of viewing land, water, air, and even outer space as legal entities capable of subdivision and ownership. We will return to this problem in our last substantive chapter, when we view the treatment of the natural world in American case law. It is sufficient to note that the contradictory status that is accorded the natural world is inherent in Locke's effort to ground political institutions in the transcendence of natural law and the state of nature.

Several other approaches to the state of nature were used by Locke to show the universality of his philosophy. "Men living together according to reason, without a common Superior on Earth, with Authority to judge between them," he suggested, "is *properly the State of Nature*." And he emphasized this point by remarking that the "*want of a common Judge with Authority, puts all Men in a State of Nature.*"[11] The two definitions appear to be synonymous, but they contain a radical difference in viewpoint. If natural law can be intuitively or rationally discovered, it should produce a state of affairs in which a judge would be unnecessary. Judgment, in fact, would never enter into the situation since universal reason would produce identical conclusions for anyone exercising this faculty based on commonly shared experiences. The lack of a common judge with authority can characterize the state of nature only in those instances where emotional factors would tend to create chaos in rational processes and lead to divergent conclusions from the same conglomerate of factual data. Thus, while we observe Locke's effort to develop a thoroughly consistent philosophy of self-evident principles, we note that he continually leans on nonlogical factors to justify his rational system. Failure to confront the metaphysics lurking in the half-conscious background produces a philosophy that has validity only during lucid and unemotional moments, and these are rare occasions in human experience.

The same wandering between rational principles and half-intuited facts of human personality characterized Locke's efforts to define his central political concept—property. Locke's theoretical individuals survey nature from a lofty and, one might say, abstract position beyond space and time, and then move into the natural world to appropriate its benefits. The process by which this movement into the physical world occurs deserves citation at length because it forms the subsequent theoretical basis upon which Americans justify their occupation of a continent. Locke argued:

Though the Earth, and all inferior Creatures be common to all Men, yet every Man has a *property* in his own *person*. This no Body has any Right to but himself. The *Labour* of his Body and the *Work* of his Hands, we may say, are properly his. Whatsoever then he removes out of the State that Nature hath provided, and left it in, he hath mixed his *Labour* with, and joyned to it something that is his own, and thereby makes it his *Property*. It being by him removed from the common state Nature placed it in, hath by this *labour* something annexed to it, that excludes the common right of other Men. For this *Labour* being the unquestionable Property of the Labourer, no Man but he can have a right to what that is once joyned to, at least where there is enough, and as good left in common for others.[12]

This argument is the central theme of Locke's political philosophy. All other ideas are corollary to this major argument, and it is this belief that calls forth torrents of emotions from Americans whenever political ideas are discussed.

The crux of this argument is that every individual is entitled to all the fruits of his or her labor, and that society and government, no matter how defined or conceived, always exists to protect this fundamental interest. It is possible to dwell on this proposition to the exclusion of any other Lockean idea because it has such vast implications. Here one discovers echoes of Adam and Eve's expulsion from the Garden of Eden, and the traditional Western belief that one acquires status and benefits in society by working. The conception of the human being that we find hidden here has little to do with human personality. Individuals are deemed worthy to the degree that their physical activities qualify the person for consideration. We see this belief inherent in the current social welfare programs administered by the federal and state governments, and the strange but fanatical obsession with eligibility requirements in those same welfare programs.

Insofar as nature is inexhaustible, work should not be a requirement for political rights or social status since there is an adequate amount of material wealth in nature beckoning the individual to share in a general prosperity. But Locke, like other philosophers and theorists before and since, assert that nature is limited and thus they have jumped ahead to set "natural" boundaries to the process of appropriation from nature. Individual ownership seems to depend upon the rather unique stamp that individual labor impresses upon nature. Property, it would seem, has very little to do with material things but a great deal to do with the manner in which those things are used. Property thus describes a particular type of relationship that the human species has with the natural world.

We can now see why failing to distinguish between compacts that preserve a state of nature and those that take our species out of the state of nature proved so confusing to Locke. Obviously, those societies still living in a state of nature and appropriating from nature with a minimum interference of natural processes are living in the most sophisticated harmony with the rest of the universe. The task of any society would appear to be that of regaining the intimate relationship that the state of nature provides. The measure of civilization would then be a mature acknowledgment of our species' contribution to nature and instead of creating massive disruptions of nature, the preservation of the natural state would be understood as the highest value. Locke most likely could not take this path of reasoning because of the very complicated institutions that were already in existence in Europe that cried out for philosophical clarification and justification. But he may have been more than Andrew Sinclair characterizes him: "a propagandist for that lust after property which was the basis of the European's self-justification for dispossessing the Indian."[13] At least part of the problem may have been that very ancient Western Manichaean belief that humans and nature stand in alienation to one another. This may well have been lurking in Locke's unconscious and existed so comfortably as a truth that it required no examination.

Before we leave this discussion of the role of nature in the creation of property, it is important to note that Locke, like many later Europeans and Americans, assumed that nature was boundless. While he limits human appropriation from nature, he provides no reasonable criterion for determining that limit. His failure to discuss limits fit perfectly, until late in the twentieth century, with contemporary Euro-American optimism that nature was inexhaustible. While this belief is now being challenged by increasing numbers of scientists, environmentalists, and others, it still continues to fester, despite the growing realization by many—largely because of accumulated scientific and anecdotal data on global climate change—that nature's resources are not, in fact, limitless.

The process of appropriation that Locke described simply is a more difficult idea than most Western theorists have realized. Appropriation involves more than willingness to work, a unique idea for using natural resources or features, or a commonly acceptable use of natural objects. The product must be understood as a wholly artificial construction having no ultimate value and being little more than an adaptation or adjustment that our species makes with respect to its environment. It was not so understood by Western people, and is seen this way by few Americans today. The appropriation and uses to which nature was put by Western peoples became determinative of reality, and the process of appropriation, observed in the daily lives of people, became a belief in progress. It has manifested itself in our day as the continual striving for novelty. In several centuries we have moved from a simple appropriation and recasting of nature to a demand for newness and a disrespect for old things. In many ways we can be said to be appropriating even the artificial constructs of former generations and replacing them with modern projects that are becoming increasingly abstract and inhuman. Appropriation, although originally conceived as simply an adjustment of our species to nature, is in its final phase a consumer of history and human values and the absolutization of activity as the meaning of human existence. John Locke leads directly to Al Gore's documentary, *An Inconvenient Truth*.

Appropriation, in Locke's scheme of things, was limited by the amount of natural resources that a person could constructively use. "As much as any one can make use of to any advantage of life before it spoils," he suggested, "so much he may by his labour fix a Property in. Whatever is beyond this, is more than his share, and belongs to others."[14] Had this theory been restricted solely to the gathering of berries and crops, hunting, or fishing, it would have been adequate. But in more sophisticated societies, where commerce was already in operation, it was possible to represent perishable goods by money, bonds, and counting. Appropriation is a plausible doctrine for natural societies, and a perfectly dreadful one for large abstract governments.

Following the appropriation of nature into property, the organization of government for Locke became imperative, the next logical step in the creation of human institutions. "The great and *chief end* therefore, of Mens [*sic*] uniting into Commonwealths, and putting themselves under Government," he concluded, "*is the Preservation of their Property*. To which in the state of Nature there are many things wanting."[15] The state of nature, according to Locke, lacked three things government supplied: (1) an established, settled, known law, received and allowed by common consent to the standard of right and wrong; (2) a known and indifferent judge with authority to determine all differences according to this established law; and (3) a source of power to support and execute the decisions of the judge. These characteristics are both the minimum and maximum functions of government. They assume a rather benign attitude.

Every partner in the social contract, according to Locke, had property to protect and decided to surrender some individual authority in exchange for the security of impartially administered laws. Government receives power through individuals ceding their natural right of retaliation and self-defense. More important, the individual surrenders his or her judgment about *when* to act. Governments are established by rational individuals seeking security through commonly accepted rules and regulations instead of personal judgment.

This system of government, while avoiding difficult questions of moral responsibility, provided a framework within which property owners could remain unmolested. Coming at a time in history when the acquisition of immense wealth seemed within the grasp of every European, when the English colonists were busy subduing a large continent in a state of nature, Locke's social theory proved immensely popular. Locke failed to understand that the recently acquired wealth of Europe was largely created by the different values that Europeans placed in certain products of the natural world, and this difference was being wrought by new ways of using things. Charles Reich, in his classic analysis of the idea of property, argued that "wealth or value is created by culture and by society; it is culture that makes a diamond valuable and a pebble worthless. Property, on the other hand, is the creation of law. A man who has property has certain legal rights with respect to an item of wealth; property represents a relationship between wealth and its 'owner.'"[16] Europeans seemed poor and desperate to many non-Europeans when they first appeared, and stories abound about the minerals that "drive the white man crazy," which illustrate the cultural basis of value and, ultimately, property itself.

Locke suggested that human labor was the primary constituent that made both value and property important. "'Tis *Labour* then which *puts the greatest part of Value upon Land*, without which it would scarcely be worth any thing: 'tis to that we owe the greatest part of all its useful Products: for all that the Straw, Bran, Bread, of that Acre of Wheat, is more worth than the Product of an Acre of as good Land, which lies wast, is all the Effect of Labour."[17] But Europeans were not performing physical labor to produce either wealth or value. Both commercial and industrial activities were moving toward an increasing abstractness wherein new and complicated uses of physical goods were creating a new type of property. To use examples of agricultural activity at the very period of history when Europeans were frantically moving out of that stage of existence to an urban, industrial, and highly sophisticated form of living meant that Locke's conception of property would always be conceived in the popular mind as the possession of physical assets and their transformation by physical work. If Western civilization has been overly materialistic, it is because the most incisive theorists insisted on using images that were more comprehensive and pictorial than accurate reflections of the way people were behaving.

Once we transcend the physical images of agriculture that Locke insisted on using, we discover a hidden dimension of property that has merit yet today. In an aside, Locke attempted to clarify his conception of property and remarked, "By *Property* I must be understood here, as in other places, to mean that Property which Men have in their Persons as well as Goods."[18] The idea of a property right in one's person may seem strange, but it is the proper conception for Locke in trying to explain human adjustment to nature and the resulting institutions.

Property in one's person transcends the ability to perform physical labor and denotes Locke's ability to conceive of nature as more than the physical world. This notion becomes more familiar when we remember that Greek philosophy conceived the reality of the universe to be that of ideas as well as or more than the phenomenal world. Property is thus a creation of genius, not labor, which is simply the tangible expression of genius. When genius is seen as a product of and a responsibility of culture, then the real basis of Locke's political philosophy finally emerges. The education of individuals in society becomes the real basis of property, not the boundless plenitude of nature. A series of individuals can all view natural resources and, depending upon the unique viewpoint of individuals, may produce a variety of products, each of which is property, but some of which, like treated adobe bricks, may be infinitely more valuable than the majority of the others, such as the famous adobe submarines of the Mexican Navy.

The requirements of education are usually seen in Locke's philosophy as a means of ensuring responsible, rational individuals who calmly and carefully agree to the social contract and who ensure that the laws of this contract are commonly accepted. To understand the need for education as a property-producing device rather than as a means of producing good citizens is a radical break with traditional interpretations of the social contract that enables us to pierce farther into the hazy realm of the unconscious where justice dwells. For if nature is conceived as boundless because it is primarily intellectual and creative, then we have a basis for maintaining the social contract once we understand that government is responsible for generating conditions at property creation. Education then becomes the major task of government. If Locke had intuited this aspect of his time, Europeans and Americans might have become lovers of wisdom instead of pursuers of wealth.

Political philosophy has largely missed this aspect of Locke's thought and, indeed, Locke himself seemed to misunderstand it. More often the commentaries on Locke's work have devoted a great deal of energy analyzing the various implications of either property or consent. Charles Reich, for example, took the idea of property and demonstrated the extremely valuable role that it plays in protecting the individual from the intrusions of government on human personality. "Property draws a circle around the activities of each private individual or organization," Reich wrote.[19] He went on to note that "within that circle, the owner has a greater degree of freedom than without. Outside, he must justify or explain his actions, and show his authority. Within, he is master, and the state must explain and justify any interference."[20] Obviously, Reich followed Locke's misconception that property is primarily a physical entity and Reich's task was to resolve the problem of clarifying public and private use of physical things. Thus he argued that "it is as if property shifted the burden of proof; outside, the individual has the burden; inside, the burden is on the government to demonstrate that something the owner wishes to do should not be done." For Reich, the function of property in a legal sense is "to draw a boundary between public and private power."[21] This boundary line prevents the American majority from completely overriding the various societal minorities, but the assumption of conflicts that must be resolved by law or otherwise will be resolved by force. American history would indicate the validity of Reich's analysis, but events have tended to produce these situations of majority-minority conflict because property was originally conceived in materialistic fashion, limiting horizons to immediate possession of physical things.

John Rawls, in his most famous work, *A Theory of Justice*, and in several later works, took the social contract dimension of Locke's thesis and produced an immense analysis of it under the characterization of "justice as fairness."[22] "In justice as fairness," Rawls wrote, "the original position of equality corresponds to the state of nature in the traditional theory of the social contract."[23] Justice as fairness advanced the proposition that rational individuals would construct the best possible political institution by general agreement if they understood all the conditions and positions in that society prior to the time they entered it, but knowing that they might be assigned any particular status within that system. Thus the inclination of individuals would be to ensure adequate protections and procedures for the deprived as well as the privileged since they would have no assurance that they would be among the favored. Therefore, everyone would take care to create adequate and tolerable conditions for everyone else as insurance against misfortune and ill fate.

Rawls's system could equally find its parentage in Hobbes, for his concern was not with justice in a transcendent sense but with full recognition of the perverse activities of human beings in a social context. "Private society is not held together by a public conviction that its basic arrangements are just and good in themselves," Rawls realistically argued, "but by the calculations of everyone or of sufficiently many to maintain the scheme, that any practicable changes would reduce the stock of means whereby they pursue their personal ends."[24] This polite manner of describing individual greed made Rawls's social contract a formidable accomplishment because he anticipated uncontrolled self-interest and attempted to control it by prior agreement. "If justice as fairness is more convincing than the older presentations of the contract doctrine," Rawls stated, "I believe it is because the original position...unites in one conception a reasonably clear problem of choice with conditions that are widely recognized as fitting to impose on the adoption of moral principles."[25]

Anticipating moral dilemmas is a much more sophisticated analysis of the political institutions than we encounter in Locke's conception of government, but like his explanation we discover that judgments are ceded to the central institution and, perhaps, to a much greater degree than Locke himself would find comfortable. Missing in both systems is the role of rationality following the agreement on the principles of the social contract. Both Rawls and Locke seem to project rational individuals who exercise their faculties until they have consented to be governed by an objective set of rules and regulations. After this pledge of allegiance, reason seems to play the role of conscience rather than a creative innovator to enable government to meet change. We might well have remained with Montesquieu and his fearful and inferior individuals as to posit the existence of creatures whose only rational act is to assent to principles that will thenceforth follow with dogged determination in exchange for security.

In a practical, realistic, and historical sense, as Dan Lacy pointed out, "the equality of all men, proclaimed by Locke and the Americans alike, really meant the equality of all active members of the political community—of those who were assumed to be parties to the social contract and who had a requisite stake in the polity formed by the contract."[26] Jack Rakove concurred on the important issue of representation in early American political life when he stated, "if one maxim reflected Americans' ideas of representation as much as the 'solecism' of *imperium in imperio* governed their notions of sovereignty, it was the belief that a representative assembly 'should be in miniature an exact portrait of the people at large. It should think, feel, reason and act like them.'"[27]

Here we again enter the realm of hazy existence beyond the objective institutions and expressions of the law. Once the government is instituted by common consent, nonrational factors take control and determine who are thereafter participants and beneficiaries of the government. Hanna Pitkin argued "that the historical accuracy in the contract doctrine is basically irrelevant—that the contract is a logical construct. The only 'consent' that is relevant is the hypothetical consent imputed to hypothetical, timeless, abstract, rational men."[28] In a theoretical sense, this is true. Absent a continuing role for creative intellectual activity membership in the social contract is an inherited right, and exclusion from active membership becomes an irremovable status to which individuals are bound against their will.

Pitkin concluded from this hypothetical consent "that your obligation to obey depends not on any special relationship (consent) between you and your government, but on the nature of that government itself. If it is a good, just government doing what a government should, then you must obey it; if it is a tyrannical, unjust government trying to do what no government should, then you have no such obligation."[29]

This goes to the heart of political theory and is reflected in the dissenting opinion of Justice Hugo Black in the freedom of speech cases of the 1950s, when he argued against suppression of unorthodox political beliefs under the rationale that they were un-American. In his James Madison lecture on the Bill of Rights, Black summarized his understanding of the right of free speech:

The Framers knew, better perhaps than we do today, the risks they were taking. They knew that free speech might be the friends of change and revolution. But they also knew that it is always the deadliest enemy of tyranny. With this knowledge they still believed that the ultimate happiness and security of a nation lies in its ability to explore, to change, to grow and ceaselessly to adapt itself to new knowledge born of inquiry free from any kind of governmental control over the mind and spirit of man. Loyalty comes from love of good government, not fear of a bad one.[30]

Free speech is simply the objective manifestation of the freedom to think, and the criterion of a good government must be one that exists to provide ever-increasing opportunities to think. The Supreme Court's two opposing 2007 decisions—the first, popularly called the "Bong Hits 4 Jesus" case, allowing school officials to censor and punish student speech that could be interpreted as celebrating the use of illegal drugs[31]; the second holding that the restriction on corporate and union-sponsored television advertising contained in the 2002 McCain-Feingold campaign finance law threatened to curb core political speech[32]—are contemporary examples of how the now staunchly conservative Court has shown a far greater willingness to support corporate and business interests over those of individual rights and liberties.

Raymond Polin concluded that "property is the external manifestation, the necessary outward expression, of a liberty which has become effective and of a right which is capable of being exercised on things." Equating liberty and property means, according to Polin, "that there can be no right, no justice, without property. For Locke, that is an ontological truth."[33] But although property and liberty can be equated in some respects, and certainly in historical terms we can see this aspect more starkly than any other, yet it also assumes that government must accept responsibility for and help justify arbitrary human actions. Liberty in this sense has a tendency toward moral irresponsibility while otherwise conforming to the law. D. D. Raphael distinguishes two forms of liberty that, taken together, form a transitional phase that we can observe in the development of American law. He identifies rights to be *allowed* something and rights to be *given* something, and concludes that these rights can be characterized as negative and positive aspects of liberty.[34] Again, this explanation leads to a restrictive sense of the social contract that produces government and thus ultimately limits property to tangible, physical things. This interpretation, we would argue, is an aborted version of Locke's because the unarticulated idea of property—potential genius—is one of the major misunderstandings in social contract theory.

We now see the basic outlines of Locke's civil government developed from the premise of a state of nature together with his insistence on property as the major factor in government. These fundamental ideas had an important role in the minds of the framers of the American State Papers in that they helped to justify the belief that a new form of government could be created by their deliberate actions.

The importance of exploring such tangential subjects as the distinction between society and government is that these implications of Locke's philosophy that were not fully explored by Locke himself were not explored by succeeding generations of political thinkers either, and they emerged in later decades as problems, some of which have yet to be resolved. Suggesting that Locke might have followed his reasoning a bit further to identify education as the creator of property allows us to project a framework within which we can examine the subsequent case law dealing with those groups not assumed to share in the American social contract, and in this way we can test the validity of our conjectures as well as provide an additional dimension in which to understand what developments were necessary to expand the legal universe to include these groups.

Whether Locke had direct textual influence over the creation of the American Constitution pales beside the recognition that within the general context of his thoughts we can discover the principles that still contain for our time adequate means of bringing justice to society. We are now in a position to move directly to an examination of the principles articulated by the Founding Fathers of the United States with the analytical tools to uncover the semiconscious assumptions about the nature of reality that lurk behind, as they do *The Deerslayer*, the Constitution and laws of the United States.

CHAPTER 3
Certain Inalienable Rights

IN THE BEGINNING PARAGRAPHS OF *THE SPIRIT OF LAWS*, Baron de Montesquieu asserted that laws "should be relative to the climate, whether hot or cold, of each country, to the quality of its soil, to its situation and bigness, to the manner of living with the natives, whether husbandmen, huntsmen, or shepherds; they should have a relation to the degree of liberty which the constitution will bear; to the religion of the inhabitants, to their inclinations, riches, number, commerce, manners, and customs."[1] Not surprisingly, the US Constitution reflects these concerns. In tracing the legal universe predating the Constitution, our first step is to sketch out aspects of colonial life that influenced individual and group rights.

The colonies lacked a tradition of political participation. Most were originally founded as business ventures by politicians in England who had secured land grants and charters from the king. The organization of political institutions was distinctly a secondary matter for these entrepreneurs and it evolved as local settlers attempted to deal with problems primarily local in scope. Other colonies began as religious sanctuaries for dissident groups that had been driven from European countries because their religious divergence was viewed as politically disruptive by the political and religious establishment. Maryland, Delaware, and Pennsylvania, all of which enjoyed the personal patronage of English political figures, were considered the property of these figures for decades. Any widespread political activity by these settlers had to conform to the wishes of the proprietary family.

Feudalism provided the European nations with a social and political structure that made radical change unlikely, and some efforts were made in the different colonies to reproduce a type of feudalism here. John Locke's "Fundamental Constitution for the Carolinas" featured landgraves and caciques, but the attempt to institute these titles failed miserably. Maryland had a brief experience with manors whose lords had quasi-feudal powers over their estates, but the constant movement into the backcountry made stability impossible, and this effort also failed. The closest that any colony came to feudal rights that carried a respected and inherited status was the development of patronages in New York by the Dutch. Some important families gained control over vast estates along the Hudson River that incorporated both Dutch traditions and a special legal position in colonial law.

But during and after the Revolution, most of these large estates were broken up and confiscated, leaving the families with a recognized social standing as old settlers and little more.

In the South, the colonies attempted to use traditional legal devices to maintain large landholdings. Primogeniture, the right of succession belonging to the firstborn, and entailing, the bequeathing of property so that it remains within a family, were common practices in most of the southern colonies. Economic factors were as important as the social and political aspects of maintaining large estates. However, since the principal crops—tobacco and, later, cotton—involved the cultivation of large tracts of land and the use of a great deal of human labor, smaller tracts were simply not economically feasible. With the development of new lands to the west and the constant movement of people to the mountain ranges to the north, there was little opportunity to use these legal concepts to develop an inherited aristocracy in the old European sense.

Universal manhood suffrage in the modern sense did not exist in the colonies. People considered themselves subjects, not citizens. The customary property requirement in most colonies was ownership of fifty acres of land, or land or property that had an annual rental income of two pounds (one pound was equal to the value of one pound of silver—not an inconsiderable amount at the time). In some colonies, particularly those that had been founded by religious groups, church membership was an additional requirement for political participation, at least with respect to matters above the simple local peacekeeping level. The property requirement was not as onerous as it would seem. A person intent upon entering the political arena in any serious way had simply to move to unsettled lands and stake out a homestead. With this open frontier always beckoning to people of low social and economic status, most colonies were practical democracies even though they had not yet articulated the theory that would explain their behavior.

The most important aspect of revolutionary America was population increase. Between 1750 and 1775, the population more than doubled. Many of the Scottish and Irish immigrants had little affinity for the English. Even if there had been traditions of self-government in the colonies, such an influx would have strained them. As it was, most American settlements faced social and political problems in an immediate practical manner. Most colonies had in fact recently exercised more self-government than any of the nations in the world; they had simply failed to reflect on the implications of their activities. This reflection would be provided by Thomas Paine, Samuel and John Adams, James Wilson, John Hancock, James Otis, Thomas Jefferson, Jonathan Mayhew, Patrick Henry, and James Monroe in the series of crises leading to a formal revolutionary break with England.

The decade following the French and Indian War saw continual conflict between the colonies and the mother country. England had emerged victorious over France but was nearly bankrupted by the conflict. Policy makers urged the king to make colonial administration self-supporting in order to avoid a continual drain on the British treasury. Therein lay the problem. For centuries, both England and France had made extensive claims to lands in North America, and their rivalry over the title to lands precluded any necessity to actually govern these areas. With England's victory in North America and the eclipse of French threats, the English discovered that they now had to govern their claimed lands. No precedents existed for the administration of such a vast geographical area. Given this unpopular task, England probably could not have avoided the American Revolution. The Sugar Act, the Stamp Act, the Boston Tea Party event, and other English efforts to bring the colonies under economic control only irritated the colonists. Violence began in 1765 after royal officers were commissioned to enforce the Stamp Act. On August 14, 1765, Andrew Oliver, a royal stamp distributor in Boston, was hanged in effigy, his office destroyed, and his home wrecked. Soon, other royal collectors were similarly harassed and driven to seek refuge in the royal military posts. Thereafter it was simply a matter of logical unfolding of traditional political responses between people and government. Colonist incidents would spark a harsh governmental response, which in turn would trigger more disobedience and provide evidence that even more severe measures should be taken to bring the colonists and conditions under control. Dan Lacy suggests that "most of the imperial issues involved in the later Revolution were actually decided in 1765 and 1766."[2] The Revolution, then, was an unfortunate afterthought when considered from a theoretical viewpoint.

England had little chance of preserving its political sovereignty over the colonies. Collectively, the colonies had three million people at the time of the Revolution; England had nearly seven million people. Outside of the seaports and large cities where British soldiers and officials supervised commercial activities, there were few other places in North America not controlled by the colonists. Even the complement of troops available to quell disturbances was minimal. The Americans supplied themselves from the bountiful produce of the immediate vicinity, but the English, for the most part, had to transport their supplies across a three-thousand-mile-wide ocean. It is inconceivable, therefore, that the English could have ever subdued and ruled the colonies, even with a century of warfare.

If the colonists had won nearly every issue that would later be decided permanently in the Revolution, and if there was no conceivable chance that England could have defeated the colonists, what motivated the two nations to engage in a destructive war over impractical and largely fabricated issues? Laying aside the punitive political motivations that helped to escalate military activities, we can probe the minds of the Americans of that time to discover how they understood their situation. Lacy noted that

> at the culmination of more than a decade of debate over the rights of the colonists, especially their rights as Englishmen under the British Constitution, the Declaration [of Independence] summarized the whole underlying philosophy of the state, deriving from Locke and the liberal thinkers who followed him, in one classic statement—a statement that does not assert the rights of Americans or Englishmen at a particular time under a particular charter or constitution, but rights that were claimed for all men, everywhere, always, under their natural birthright as equal sons of God.[3]

This universal philosophy expressed in the Declaration of Independence, which seeks to transcend all particular considerations of political rights, was probably as much a surprise to most Americans as it was to the nations of the world. "In practice, however eloquent the appeals to natural law, the specific rights that were asserted were rights of Englishmen, developed under English law, and were defended as such."[4] When we carefully analyze the parts of the Declaration of Independence in these contradictory terms, we discover that such a schizophrenic view does exist there. The abstract principles of equality form the opening and concluding parts of the document and the major body of the Declaration includes a long list of grievances against the king of England that could only be validly conceived as wrongs if the colonists enjoyed the same rights as Englishmen living in England.

We can understand the American Revolution, then, as a necessary experience wherein the Euro-American people of the New World were forced to come to grips with the reality of their situation. They were not Englishmen but Americans, and yet no one understood what an American was. At the time, Americans were understood as sharing every cultural characteristic that represented the British Isles, yet the colonists were fundamentally and undeniably different, and this basic fact of life had to find some expression in a common experience of birth. Americans were born in the years of the Revolution, when they were forced to surrender, one by one, those ties of emotional loyalty that many of them still unconsciously held for the mother country. There are, of course, other interpretations of the meaning of the American Revolution, and a number of these interpretations suggest that economic interests were of critical importance in initiating and sustaining the struggle for independence. When we view the events leading up to the Revolution, the documents that justified it, and the creation of the Constitution several years later, as these developments and documents naturally lead to the developments in American legal history, this interpretation will become more comprehensible and important. The American Revolution was primarily an emotional experience of a people attempting to create and enact cultural identity. That identity inevitably had to take shape in political terms.

If John Locke and the liberal thinkers of the time had an influence over the fathers of the Revolution, who encouraged them to appeal to natural law as the justification for their rebellion, the mood of the times had not changed radically when, after ten years of national existence under the Articles of Confederation, the states adopted the present US Constitution. Dean Alfange, writing of the adoption of the Constitution, described it as a revolution since it reflected the Americans' instinct for self-preservation but was also of significant economic importance. Alfange maintained that unlike earlier developments, the revolution to transform the confederated states into a unified polity had been initiated by men with substantial property interests.[5]

There certainly were economic interests that created a need for a strong central government that could untangle the snares and confusion in commercial matters that had grown up under the Articles of Confederation. But to describe the adoption of the Constitution solely as an economic revolution is to miss "the mood of the times that existed in the cultural milieu which Americans and Englishmen still shared." Lacy observed that "in the mid-eighteenth century the government of Britain, both national and local, single-mindedly represented not the traditions of England or its military glory, its feudal past, or its religious passion, but its property."[6] And the trend of political thought in England, as well as the practical political changes, involved the elevation of property rights as fully as did the adoption of the Constitution in the United States, indicating that while an ocean might have separated the two nations, in terms of those nebulous half-conceived beliefs about the world, they shared a common view of society. If the changes were initiated by the propertied class, they represented intuitive responses to the times, not a deliberate or systematic effort to install a particular philosophy that people fully understood.

Two additional factors played a greater role in the composition of the Constitution and its adoption: the incorporation of the contemporary conception of natural law in the scientific sense, and the fear of central authority. Several scholars have argued that the scientific ideas of the time had a major influence on the manner in which the authors of the Constitution conceived its operating principles would work. F. S. C. Northrop suggests that "it is in the theoretically constructed constitutional law entered into by a contract modeled on the universal laws of Newton's natural science and grounded in man's equality before such laws that Jefferson, Adams, Franklin and their fellow authors of the Declaration of Independence and the Constitution of the United States found the spiritual source of the equality and freedom of their countrymen under law."[7] And Don Price, discussing the relationship between government and science, endorsed this interpretation, suggesting that "it may have been only by crude analogy, but some of the Founding Fathers were certainly conscious of the correspondence between their proposed system of constitutional checks and balances and Sir Isaac Newton's system of mechanics, in which the universe was held together and kept in order by a balance of counteracting forces set in motion by a Prime Mover, but working endlessly thereafter by a sequence of cause and effect."[8] This conception still has immense emotional and intellectual support today, and few people recognize the ideological roots as primarily eighteenth-century scientific beliefs.

The mechanical checks and balances were felt necessary because of the experience that Americans had had with the arbitrary exercise of political power under the king of England. Alexis de Tocqueville, in his classic study, *Democracy in America*, in describing the generation of men who were responsible for both the Declaration of Independence and the Constitution, noted:

They had all grown up at a time of social crisis, when the spirit of liberty had been in constant conflict with a strong and dominating authority. When the struggle was over, and when, as is usual, the passions aroused in the crowd were still directed against dangers which had long ceased to exist, these men called a halt; they looked at their country more calmly and with greater penetration; they were aware that a final revolution had been accomplished and that henceforth the perils of threatening the people could only spring from abuses of liberty. What they thought, they had the courage to say; because they felt in the bottom of their hearts a sincere and ardent love for the same liberty, they dared to speak about restraining it, because they were sure they did not want to destroy it.[9]

So the task was one of preserving the hard-won liberty while remaining aware that any framework of government provided opportunity for oppression on occasion. In *The Federalist Papers*, we find Alexander Hamilton frankly acknowledging this uncertainty:

But what is government itself, but the greatest of all reflections on human nature? If men were angels, no government would be necessary. If angels were to govern men, neither external nor internal controls on government would be necessary. In framing a government which is to be administered by men over men, the great difficulty lies in this: you must first enable the government to control the governed; and in the next place oblige it to control itself. A dependence on the people is, no doubt, the primary control on the government; but experience has taught mankind the necessity of auxiliary precautions.[10]

The new Constitution was as much an imposition of a certain form of behavior as it was an articulation of principles of freedom. The auxiliary precautions mentioned by Hamilton established limits beyond which the government could not proceed. Justice Hugo Black, a dissenting voice against congressional and judicial effort to suppress freedom of speech, in his James Madison lecture on the Bill of Rights, remained faithful to the vision of the constitutional fathers, commenting: "To my way of thinking, at least, the history and language of the Constitution and the Bill of Rights which I have discussed with you, make it plain that one of the primary purposes of the Constitution with its amendments was to withdraw from the Government all power to act in certain areas—whatever the scope of those areas may be."[11]

One of the most significant features of the auxiliary precautions, and certainly one of the most radical political innovations in human history, was the division of sovereign powers between the states and the federal government affected by the Constitution. In effect, two entirely independent political entities were created, state governements and the national government, each of which derived its powers from the people on differing occasions and by independent means, and each of which had specific sets of relationships with respect to the other, with both occupying the same geographical areas. Only when one reflects upon this arrangement does the genius become apparent, for when the larger political entity is forbidden to intrude on certain areas through the device of making clear for which subjects it shall have responsibility, then the major impetus of growth and development is properly vested in the intangible processes of human sensitivities.

"The proposed Constitution," Madison explained further,

> therefore, even when tested by the rules laid down by its antagonists, is, in strictness, neither a national nor a federal Constitution, but a composition of both. In its foundation it is federal, not national; in the sources from which the ordinary powers of government are drawn, it is partly federal and partly national; in the operation of these powers, it is national, not federal; in the extent of them, again, it is federal, not national; and finally, in the authoritative mode of introducing amendments, it is neither wholly federal nor wholly national.[12]

Using the machine as an analogy, the Constitution's authors and advocates explained the new government in external and internal terms. Federal powers, which were carefully defined, were designed to be exercised "principally on external objects [such] as war, peace, negotiation, and foreign commerce" while the powers reserved to the states were understood as internal and covered "all the objects which, in the ordinary course of affairs, concern the lives, liberties, and properties of the people, and the internal order, improvement, and prosperity of the State."[13]

The Constitution's founders assumed that states would gain ascendancy over the federal government because they dealt with the ordinary course of affairs. "The proof of this proposition," Hamilton continued, "turns upon the degree of influence which the State governments, if they administer their affairs with uprightness and prudence, will generally possess over the people." This, he went on, was "a circumstance which at the same time teaches us that there is an inherent and intrinsic weakness in all federal constitutions; and that too much pains cannot be taken in their organization to give them all the force which is compatible with the principles of liberty."[14] The real power that the Constitution gave to the federal government, not only protecting it but eventually making it supreme, was union. James Brown Scott, reviewing Madison's notes on the constitutional convention, commented:

> Since the Constitution was adopted in its entirety by the people of each of the several States, it was not only the supreme law, but it could only be amended, and the relations between the Union and the States changed, by the legislatures or conventions of three-fourths of the States, in accordance with the Fifth Article. There is here, therefore, no room for withdrawal, for the people of a State could only change its relations to the Union by the vote of three-fourths of the States. It is difficult to see how the people of a State could withdraw from their own Constitution, which they themselves and in conjunction with the other States had made their supreme law. Secession could only be revolution.[15]

Thus, geographical division of sovereignty was ultimately a fraud in the sense that the seeds for a truly national federal government were inherent in the constitutional scheme and only needed the passage of time to come to fruition. Because the national dimension to American life was inherent and not explicit, it was unnoticed by most Americans as a legal problem but remained an emotional belief throughout most of the succeeding centuries. We can trace one aspect of this national growth by examining the manner in which federal influence and activity has increased.

National power, Alfange observed, "expanded through the development by the courts of implied federal powers—i.e., powers that could be derived by reasonable implication from such explicit grants as the taxing power, the power to regulate interstate commerce, and the power to coin money."[16] Once reasonable implication became an accepted canon of interpretation, there really was no limit whatsoever to the powers of the federal government apart from withdrawal, which, as we have noted, was impossible.

Explicit description of the scope of federal activity thus formed the outlines of a universe of concepts within which American law developed. Americans *assumed* they were a nation, but *understood* they had one federal and several state governments, which operated with checks and balances. Indeed, John Jay joyously wrote in *The Federalist Papers*:

> With equal pleasure I have as often taken notice that Providence has been pleased to give this one connected country to one united people—a people descended from the same ancestors, speaking the same language, professing the same religion, attached to the same principles of government, very similar in their manners and customs, and who, by their joint counsels, arms, and efforts, fighting side by side throughout a long and bloody war, have nobly established general liberty and independence.[17]

And Tocqueville, writing several decades later, commented that "the government of the Union rests almost entirely on legal fictions. The Union is an ideal nation which exists, so to say, only in men's minds and whose extent and limits can only be discerned by the understanding."[18] Because this understanding existed in no one's mind, the objective legal expression of national citizenship became the last important political principle to emerge in American constitutional law. William Swindler wrote that the Supreme Court "has avoided developing to their full potential dimensions either the concept of national citizenship or the privileges and immunities which attach to this status, partly because the terms are too general and partly because, conversely, the due-process and equal-protection clauses have offered more viable alternatives."[19] It should be noted in this respect that the two major groups receiving belated national citizenship—African Americans and women—achieved this status through constitutional amendment, not through the orderly processes of logical implication from constitutional premises.

Assuming that the states would be responsible for the "ordinary course of affairs" had important consequences. "Almost the entire domain of the common law is comprehended with the residual powers of the states," Alfange noted. "They include the whole field of criminal jurisprudence, torts, domestic relations, corporations, and, in general, the laws dealing with contractual obligations and the disposition of property."[20] With only their English heritage to draw from, the states began a piecemeal adoption and adaptation of the common law. These Anglo-Saxon concepts provided the substance of American law, insofar as they affected the individual until well into the twentieth century, when national citizenship began to influence the definition and solution of local problems. Thus, in the first part of the twentieth century we still find labor-management problems phrased in the old conceptual framework of the right to contract, even though industrialization had made such laws obsolete if not ludicrous.

Price argued that any constitutional system that sought to protect freedom by dividing power had to be based on a separation between the governing institutions that wielded political power and those that were engaged in what he called "the search for truth."[21] He was obviously referring to the modern intimacy between knowledge and the political institutions that undergirds the military-industrial-academic complex. But his contention is worth noting because it transcends immediate situations and accurately describes an important distinction that must always be considered in political processes. Truth, and indeed common sense, were inherited complexes of ideas for most Americans in the exuberant manner in which John Jay described them. Lacking institutions dedicating themselves to truth, Americans accepted then current beliefs about the world and vested American society with a substantial view of the world derived from Locke and the English empiricists rather than initiating a process in which truth could be continually brought into a role of influence in political affairs.

Thus Tocqueville observed that "the Anglo-Americans regard universal reason as the source of moral authority, just as the universality of the citizens is the source of political power, and they consider that one must refer to the understanding of everybody in order to discover what is permitted or forbidden, true or false."[22] The American political system, while very sophisticated as a self-operating machine, was built upon a very tenuous premise in the last analysis. "In nations where the dogma of the sovereignty of the people prevails," Tocqueville commented, "each individual forms an equal part of that sovereignty and shares equally the government of the state." But more important for our understanding, Tocqueville concluded, "each individual is assumed to be as educated, virtuous, and powerful as any of his fellows."[23] Therein lay the seeds for continual unrest in American society.

Americans mistakenly believed that equality before the law in the sense of an imperial treatment also meant cultural and intellectual homogeneity. Madison objected to this belief, noting that "theoretic politicians, who have patronized this species of government, have erroneously supposed that by reducing mankind to a perfect equality in their political rights, they would at the same time be perfectly equalized and assimilated in their possessions, their opinions, and their passions."[24] Even Montesquieu, whose thinking was familiar to the essayists of *The Federalist Papers*, had observed:

> The principle of democracy is corrupted, not only when the spirit of equality is extinct, but likewise when they fall into a spirit of extreme equality, and when each citizen would wants to be upon a level with those he has chosen to command him. Then the people, incapable of bearing the very power they have intrusted, want to do every thing of themselves, to debate for the senate, to execute for the magistrate, and to strip for the judges.[25]

So there had to be a means of avoiding the excesses of extreme equality while preserving its semblance. Northrop, discussing the philosophical principles underlying the American political understanding, argued that "according to the spirit of the people of the United States it is not the relation of men to one another in society but their relation to nature and to nature's universal laws before which all men are equal that is the criterion of the just, the good and the divine."[26]

The constitutional founders had enabled both individuals and society to escape the inevitable leveling process equal political rights might produce. They found their answer in the concept of private property. As Charles Reich argued, the Bill of Rights depended on the existence of private property. He went on to note that political rights presupposed that individuals and private groups have the will and the ability to act independently. And since individuals are generally motivated by self-interest, their personal well-being must first be independent. "Civil liberties," Reich concluded, "must have a basis in property, or bills of rights will not preserve them."[27] Property seemed the perfect solution for the protection of the individual because it was conceived in the physical sense of owning land and therefore incorporated the best provisions of feudalism with the economic opportunity then available to many Americans. Price explained that the primary reason why private property was once considered the most effective safeguard against centralized political power was that it was so unique. He gave the examples of presidents Washington and Jefferson, noting that even while they served they also looked forward to turning over authority and retiring to their farms once their service to the nation was complete. "Property in the land," said Price, "called for the exercise of individual virtues, not power over others; it committed its owners to a sense of public responsibility, but also to the defense of personal rights against impersonal power."[28] Former president George W. Bush evoked similar sentiments when he discussed his relationship to his property in Texas. When property began to take more abstract forms, however, personal responsibility declined and impersonal power began its ascendancy.

The final product, then, of the American constitutional system, was to assume that a society existed within which a government could be formed and the fear of centralizing power led to the specific definition of a federal system of government where a national social reality should have existed. Property became the dominant consideration of the political institutions, and the individual became a function of the relationships of property. The seeds of a national society were inherent in the constitutional framework because once a new territory had joined the union, it was thereafter bound by the beliefs and aspirations of the majority of the people to the Union. The Constitution mapped out the boundaries where government could exercise authority, and the task of Americans was to fill that outline with substantial content. The content, of course, would be an expression of America, its history, its lands, its cultures, its religions, it peoples, and all of the other characteristics that Montesquieu believed created the laws of nations.

There was, perhaps, no other way that such a process of national growth and self-awareness could be initiated, nurtured, and kept within the bounds of reason. Americans could hardly thrust off their English heritage and adopt a culture radically distinct from their memories and understandings of the Old World. But their failure to pursue the implications of social contract theory meant that a great many problems in resolving the question of social existence lay ahead. Because the American State Papers, the Declaration of Independence, the Articles of Confederation, and the Constitution, with its amending Bill of Rights, defined an objective legal universe that the federal government made tangible, certain aspects of human existence were vested with immutable status that was not easily changed.

African Americans, women, and aboriginal peoples were doctrinally excluded from participation in American society. The world was presumed to represent rational, white, propertied men, and therefore women did not even receive consideration. African Americans were viewed as a quasi property, and only a war of secession resolved that question. Indigenous peoples were not presumed to actually own property but merely to occupy it, thereafter making them subject to "parental" control by the federal government.

In 1765, when the agitation against England began and John Adams was working for the creation of a common school system, he declared that "the preservation of the means of knowledge among the lowest ranks is of more importance to the public than all the property of all the rich men in the country."[29] When Adams intuitively saw behind the Lockean philosophy to recognize that education was the prime creator of property and political rights, or whether he simply wished to create an intelligent, reasonable society, he located the element in a democratic structure without which it cannot function. Democracy depends ultimately upon the political participation of intelligent, rational citizens exercising their keenest insights into the nature of life. Property depends upon the most inclusive minds discovering in the natural world material uses not previously recognized. Beneath the developments of American legal theory, the innovation and educational opportunities have always been potent, if unarticulated, political forces and influences.

CHAPTER 4
"Existing in Contemplation of Law": Corporations and the Law

IN THE UNITED STATES, THE MOST PROMINENT AND INFLUENTIAL INHABITANT of the legal universe for the past two centuries has been the corporation, with its variant forms of partnership, joint ventures, and so forth. Its origin is clouded with controversy as historians still debate which medieval organization provided the ideological pattern for the modern corporation. Did corporations begin as a monastic effort to avoid paying taxes to the king, or did they arise when towns and cities wrested self-government and independence from the king? In English history, the period before the American Revolution saw a struggle between corporations and the Crown over Parliament's and the King's power to grant or confiscate private charters. In the early 1700s, the South Sea Company, a speculative group engaged in foreign trade, had generated enormous inflation in England. The South Sea bubble finally burst, however, leaving a sour taste in the mouths of investors that resulted in restrictive legislation in the House of Commons against corporate ventures.

A characteristic of these early corporations was their independence from politics. "They might depend on it, as many American corporations did by relying on tariff protection," Don Price wrote, "and they might try with some success to control it, but they were not incorporated into its administrative system, they did not receive support from taxation, and the main directions of their new enterprises were controlled by their owners and managers."[1] So isolated were corporations from the political institutions in the American colonies that there were not more than a few dozen corporations in America at the time of the Revolution. The state legislatures were not eager to authorize the creation of any more, and corporate existence during the period when the great state debates were being conducted was hardly considered any cause for alarm. Where states did allow corporations to form, the charters were severely restricted.

Adam Smith, in his classic study, *The Wealth of Nations*, did not predict any significant future for corporations. Assuming that avarice would overcome the human desire for economic security, Smith reasoned that the modern industrial corporations as we know them today could not arise because individuals would not work as efficiently and as loyally for a corporation as they would for themselves. But Smith, like many other thinkers, did not anticipate the tremendous changes that the Industrial Revolution would spawn. Commercial enterprises eventually needed more capital than could be raised by individuals, and the corporate form, wherein a group of individuals contributed shares of money to form a large capital base, became the only feasible way to finance large-scale manufacturing and foreign trade. Unable to foresee the massive expansion of commerce, legal and political thinkers drew analogies between corporations and human beings.

The legal recognition of the corporation required a combination of jurisprudence and economics in ways hardly understood by Western fore-casters: the corporation was an economic creature that was therefore subject to the laws of economic change; yet its political existence was defined by the world of real human beings, with whom it competed for economic survival. Human beings were subject to the whims of personal belief; corporations were subject to changes in natural economic law. In the half-conscious minds of the corporate shareholders, however, these two influences combined, the glue being the emotion of the risk involved in a commercial enterprise. Capitalist corporate economic behavior thereby seemed an overpowering instance of national civilized human behavior.

Alfred North Whitehead wrote in *Adventure of Ideas* that "the development of economics was, in truth, affected by the moralizing tendency of the class mainly concerned. Their ideal of commercial activity as the main occupation of perfected civilization led to the consideration of economic laws which *should* hold, and to the neglect of economic procedures which in fact did *hold*."[2] Thurman Arnold was more critical of the combination of law and economics. "Clothe any situation with the atmosphere of law and it becomes our duty to formulate logical rules and systems," he wrote. "On the other land, clothe the same situation with a business or commercial atmosphere, and it becomes our duty to let it alone—to avoid artificial or man-made restrictions, to shun panaceas, to keep constantly in mind that every time man has attempted to control his destiny in an orderly manner he has failed."[3] He added: "Law has set up moral ideas for business and dressed huge corporations in the clothes of small individuals. Economics has excused the law from doing anything more than dramatizing these ideals, by the invention of greater and more fundamental principles even than those of the law."[4]

The background, then, that the corporation brings to the legal universe is one of unconceived potential in the innocent guise of activities laying just beyond the reach of individual property holders who wish merely to expand their holdings one more small step. Investments produce income, which in turn are reinvested in additional production. Suddenly there is no conceivable horizon beyond which the corporation cannot travel. People crave more and better implements, additional exotic foods, a more comfortable life, so why limit commercial activities? Indeed, the emotional commitment is to strengthen business organization so humans can enjoy more and more products. Corporate law, like the corporation, simply grew. But it grew with astonishing speed and apparently benevolent results that overshadowed the fundamental changes that corporations inevitably caused in the American political and legal systems.

The first major case in American law involving corporations involved their definition. Prior to the American Revolution, King George III had given a charter of incorporation to a group of people headed in America by Eleazar Wheelock and in England by the Earl of Dartmouth. They sought to establish a school in the wilds of New Hampshire to educate Indian children. The board of trustees was empowered to solicit funds for support and to appoint their own successors. The state of New Hampshire, in 1817, feeling that education was a responsibility of the state, and certainly harboring a continuing mistrust for an institution deriving its powers from the king of England, began to agitate for the incorporation of the school in the state's educational system. In 1816, the legislature passed a law incorporating a new body called the Trustees of Dartmouth College. The trustees of the existing college were directed to surrender their books and offices to the new corporation.

The Supreme Court of New Hampshire upheld the acts of the state legislature. The college appealed to the US Supreme Court on a writ of error. Daniel Webster, acting as attorney for the plaintiffs, argued that while the state of New Hampshire had certainly stepped into the shoes of the king insofar as the exercise of sovereign power was concerned, not even the king could have altered the charter of a corporation without its consent. By the same token, New Hampshire was restricted from changing the corporate powers of the college. The attorney for the state argued that the change brought about by the American Revolution dissolved any legal rights the original trustees possessed. The attorney general of New Hampshire also argued that the Revolution had destroyed the legal estate the trustees possessed and shifted that right to the holders of the equitable state—the beneficiaries of the educational institution—represented by the state of New Hampshire.

The Supreme Court could have denied the state's contention that the American Revolution destroyed prior corporate rights. Or it could have restricted their discussion to the prohibition against violation of contracts contained in the Constitution. Instead, Chief Justice John Marshall and Justice Joseph Story described at length the peculiar status of corporations. Marshall wrote, in words repeatedly quoted by corporate attorneys seeking expanded powers for their clients:

> A corporation is an artificial being, invisible, intangible, and existing only in contemplation of law. Being the mere creature of law, it possesses only those properties which the charter of its creation confers upon it, either expressly, or as incidental to its very existence...Among the most important are immortality, and, if the expression may be allowed, individuality; properties, by which a perpetual succession of many persons are considered as the same, and may act as a single individual...It is chiefly for the purpose of clothing bodies of men, in succession, with these qualities and capacities, that corporations were invented, and are in use. *By these means, a perpetual succession of individuals are capable of acting for the promotion of the particular object, like one immortal being.*[5]

This definition introduced into the natural rights of humans a new being, a being capable of surviving the twists and turns of fortune that inevitably afflict the human species. The corporation now stood in the shoes of the church, which prior to this time had been the only nonpolitical organization having eternal existence. Marshall, however, denied any political nature to the corporation, arguing that its "immortality no more confers on it political power, or a political character, than immortality would confer such power or character on a natural person."[6] With this remarkably upbeat analogy, Marshall blithely anticipated no problems with corporate structure other than the efforts of government to regulate its activities.

Justice Story agreed with Marshall's personifying corporate existence and even expanded the analogy beyond Marshall's conception. Agreeing that a corporation was a collection of individuals united together for a common purpose, Story characterized such a group as "an artificial person, existing in contemplation of law, and endowed with certain powers and franchises which, though they must be exercised through the medium of its natural members, are yet considered as subsisting in the corporation itself, as distinctly as if it were a real personage."[7] The shift from "artificial being" to "artificial person" was not considered significant at the time since the terms then were virtually interchangeable. Yet the undeveloped definition that allowed corporations every human attribute except morality and mortality posed conceptual problems and invited further theoretical exploration.

The original trustees of Dartmouth College prevailed, and the New Hampshire statute was found to violate the right to contract in the disposition of property. "As a result of Marshall's interpretation of the contract clause," historian Benjamin Wright commented, "the Court gave an amount of protection to corporations which had not been anticipated, save possibly by Hamilton."[8] The contract clause did protect the status of corporations as fictional legal entities existing, as Story described them, "in contemplation of law." But whether the law would only contemplate was another matter. In the next decade, two problems in the nature of corporations surfaced: (1) what residual rights did the stockholders transmit to the corporations? and (2) what residence did an artificial being, a legal fiction, actually have?

In *Bank of Augusta v. Earle* (1839), a question arose concerning whether a Georgia bank could lawfully exercise its corporate powers within the neighboring state of Alabama.[9] Daniel Webster appeared once again in a critical role as attorney for the corporate interests. He argued for the application of the privileges and immunities of citizenship phrase of the Constitution to protect corporate interests. Since corporations were composed of individuals doing business together, Webster reasoned that limiting the geographic scope of their activity would be impressing a secondary citizenship upon them. In effect, he sought to accomplish the transfer of individual personal rights to a corporate entity as if the corporation were an informal partnership. Webster's intuition about the future was correct; his perception of how the new idea should be phrased was premature and ill conceived.

The Supreme Court, at least temporarily having refused to vest corporations with personal rights to liberty, did not provide any guidance regarding which attributes normally attach to human beings or, in this case, to artificial beings who dwelt in the realm of legal contemplation. The first effective step in this direction involved the legal residency of the corporation. Until 1844, the courts had generally regarded corporate residence as wherever most of the stockholders lived, because most of the corporations were local groups having little intercourse outside their immediate locale. The definition made practical sense, yet it had tremendous implications for legal procedure. Federal courts rarely entertained corporate cases because of the difficulty in accurately identifying the place of citizenship. The cases were thought best limited to state courts. Then in 1844, a unanimous Supreme Court in *Louisville Railroad Co. v. Letson* clarified the residency issue by declaring that corporations would henceforth be considered citizens of the state in which they were incorporated.[10] They were creatures of the state legislatures, not national beings. With this clarification it became possible to determine precisely where the corporation lived. The sole remaining question involved whether a definition of *commerce* could bring interstate corporate activity within the range of the federal constitution. Legal and popular conceptions of commerce still considered all trade a local affair, so not until much later in the century would this question be resolved.

In the meantime, Supreme Court decisions seemed to be moving toward further limitations of corporate activity. Although states were extending corporate franchises to canal and railroad companies, manufacturing, industrial and mining concerns, and to service agencies and certain public utilities, the implications of Marshall's perpetual economic individual remained unclear until after the Civil War. At first, the cases decided by the Supreme Court following the war seemed to severely restrict corporate activity. An 1869 case, *Paul v. Commonwealth of Virginia*, raised the question of corporate citizenship in a different manner than Daniel Webster had originally phrased it, and the novel terminology required further clarification. [11]

The case involved an 1866 Virginia statute prohibiting a foreign corporation, one not chartered in Virginia, from conducting business in that state without previously obtaining a license. A subsequent Virginia statute supplemented the first one by prohibiting any Virginian from acting as an agent for out-of-state insurance companies unless they had obtained a state license. Samuel Paul, the defendant, represented several insurance companies chartered in New York. Although Paul promised to comply with the Virginia statutes, he failed to do so. He was indicted and subsequently convicted of violating the law. On appeal, Paul's attorneys argued that the New York insurance companies, under the privileges and immunities clause of the Constitution, were exempt from the Virginia statute.

Justice Stephen Johnson Field, writing for a unanimous court, rejected Paul's argument and declared that "the term 'citizens' as there [the Constitution] used applies only to natural persons, members of the body politic, owing allegiance to the State, not to artificial persons created by the

Legislature, and possessing only the attributes which the Legislature has prescribed."[12] The distinction between natural and artificial persons preserved for human beings all the protections that had been secured by the Constitution and announced as basic principles of natural law by the Declaration of Independence without drastically injuring the corporate entity. Field noted the proliferation of corporations and remarked:

> There is scarcely a business pursued requiring the expenditure of large capital, or the union of large numbers, that is not carried on by corporations. It is not too much to say that the wealth and business of the country are to a great extent controlled by them. And if, when composed of citizens of one State, their corporate powers and franchises could be exercised in other States, without restriction, it is easy to see that, with the advantages thus possessed, the most important business of those States would soon pass into their hands. The principal business of every State would, in fact be controlled by corporations created by other States.[13]

Field believed that this distasteful result had never been intended by the Constitution's founders when they protected individual privileges and immunities. With regard to the argument that the commerce clause did not cover corporate activity, Field pointed out that the world had been dominated by large British corporations such as the East India and Hudson's Bay companies when the Constitution was adopted, and that the federal commerce clause almost certainly was intended to cover their activities.

The one flaw in Field's conception of corporate status was in his definition of commerce. Like other thinkers of his era, he conceived of commerce as being primarily the business of transporting goods from one place to another, and he saw most business activities related to the law of contracts and not to the sequence of manufacture, transportation, and sale. Thus he concluded with the belief that since insurance dealt with contractual obligations, corporate law had to remain a function of state rather than federal law. "Issuing a policy of insurance is not a transaction of commerce," he argued. Continuing, he declared that

> the policies are simple contracts of indemnity against loss by fire, entered into between the corporations and the assured, for a consideration paid

by the latter. These contracts are not articles of commerce in any proper meaning of the word. They are not subjects of trade and barter offered in the market as something having an existence and value independent of the parties to them. They are not commodities to be or forwarded from one State to another, and then put up for sale. They are like other personal contracts between parties which are completed by their signature and the transfer of the consideration. Such contracts are not inter-state transactions, though parties may be domiciled in different States. The policies do not take effect—are not executed contracts—until delivered by the agent in Virginia. They are, then, local transactions, and are governed by the local law.[14]

The Virginia statute was held constitutional, at least partially, because insurance policies were considered proper subjects of local, not federal, law. While corporations made little headway in this case, and Field's sharp distinction between natural and artificial persons created a powerful barrier against corporations successfully claiming the inalienable rights, privileges, and immunities of natural citizens, the case actually lowered every other barrier. Defining commerce with such severe and narrow guidelines meant that should a corporate entity achieve parity with a natural person, it would be difficult to bring it under federal control. Almost every avenue for their activity remained open, unsupervised, and unrestricted by any political entity equal to the largest corporations.

The Thirteenth, Fourteenth, and Fifteenth Amendments had been adopted in 1865, 1868, and 1870, respectively, as a means of protecting the newly freed slaves from arbitrary and discriminatory acts of the states in which they lived. Like any new adjustment of the basic constitutional framework, they required specific application before they could be fully understood. In the *Slaughter-House Cases* of 1873, the first effort to extend the meaning of these amendments occurred.[15] The decision seemed to close the door on further development of corporate law, but proved to be the foreclosing of an era of states' right and the opening of a new era of national development of unparalleled economic expansion that favored the corporate entity.

Louisiana's legislature passed an act in 1869 that granted an exclusive twenty-five-year right to the Crescent City Live-Stock Land and Slaughter-House Company to maintain landings for cattle, yards for holding cattle, and slaughterhouses for butchering cattle. This state monopoly covered a

1,154-square-mile area embracing three parishes, including the city of New Orleans. This statute effectively eliminated all competition in the meat-processing trade in the New Orleans region. Independent butchers and meat markets could continue in business only if they used the Crescent City facilities. Independent butchers sued Crescent City and maintained that they had been placed in a position of involuntary servitude, as defined by the Thirteenth Amendment.

Justice Samuel F. Miller, speaking for the majority, restricted the meaning of *involuntary servitude* to its racial connotations. "Undoubtedly while negro slavery alone was in the mind of Congress which proposed the thirteenth article," Miller wrote, "it forbids any other kind of slavery, now or hereafter."[16] And he suggested that if "Mexican peonage" or "Chinese coolie labor" were the subject of the suit, it would fall under the protection provided by the amendment. Miller said that the Louisiana statute was a valid exercise of the state legislature, a police regulation that protected the health and comfort of the people. He made a careful distinction between citizenship of the United States and the citizenship that individual states might define, and having drawn this distinction, Miller promptly placed almost every right that could be exercised by an individual under the category of state citizenship, reserving only rights that would naturally occur in conjunction with foreign affairs in the classification of national citizenship. Miller feared the eventual control of all state functions by Congress and wrote with regard to the argument that the Fourteenth Amendment provided individuals with federal protection against confiscation of their property by the states, that

> such a construction followed by the reversal of the judgment of the Supreme Court of Louisiana in these cases, would constitute this court a perpetual censor upon all legislation of the States, on the civil rights of their own citizens, with authority to nullify such as it did not approve as consistent with those rights, as they existed at the time of the adoption of this amendment…when the effect is to fetter and degrade the State governments by subjecting them to the control of Congress, in the exercise of powers heretofore universally conceded to them of the most ordinary and fundamental character; when in fact it radically changes the whole theory of the relations of the State and Federal governments to each other and of both these governments to the people.[17]

The Supreme Court thus virtually repealed the civil rights amendments by profoundly limiting their application. Justice Field, in dissent, denied any distinction between state and national citizenship. In phrases surprisingly modern, Field argued that involuntary servitude included arbitrary prohibitions against different types of economic activity. Part of the rights of a free man, Field concluded, was the right to pursue an avocation without restraint. "A prohibition to him to pursue certain callings, open to others of the same age, condition, and sex, or to reside in places where others are permitted to live, would so far deprive him of the rights of a freeman, and would place him, as respects others, in a condition of servitude."[18] Justice Joseph P. Bradley, also writing in dissent, was even more eloquent in his protest against Miller's interpretation of the amendments. "The amendment was an attempt to give voice to the strong National yearning for that time and that condition of things, in which American citizenship should be a sure guaranty of safety, and in which every citizen of the United States might stand erect on every portion of this soil in the full enjoyment of every right and privilege belonging to a free man, without fear of violence or molestation."[19] This vision, magnificent as it is, has yet to be realized, and we will discuss the *Slaughter-House Cases* again in conjunction with the effort of the African American community to achieve a more stable place in the legal universe.

The *Slaughter-House Cases* did not directly affect the status of the corporation, serving only to confirm the Louisiana statute as a valid exercise of the state's police power. But they indirectly erected a formidable barrier against federal intervention in state regulation of business. Corporations remained creatures of state government, with no apparent national or federal implications. Commerce was a local matter. The legal fiction that corporations were creatures of the state legislatures left them virtually immune from federal control, a belief that applied even to the transcontinental railroads.

At the end of the Civil War, the transcontinental systems had started moving into the heartland of America. As they transformed agriculture from a local to a national business, conflict arose between the farmers and the railroads over who controlled the access to market. Freight rates seemed to fluctuate according to the whims of the railroads, and farmers saw their potential profits taken from them by the bewildering variety of prices imposed by the corporations. In 1867, the National Grange of the Order of Patrons of Husbandry, popularly known as the Grangers, began to combat the unfair practices of the railroads. By 1874, the National Grange had twenty thousand local branches and a membership of approximately 1.5 million. Although the Grangers publicly disavowed any formal political activity, they were powerful enough to force the major political parties to initiate reform of railroad practices in several of the midwestern states. These state laws set an upper limit on charges by railroads, warehouses, and grain elevators, and they established commissions to regulate business practices.

The corporations quietly complained, insisting that their businesses were exempt from state regulation and that states had deprived them of property without due process of law. A series of Granger cases challenging the state's regulations eventually arrived at the Supreme Court. Most of the cases involving railroads characterized railroad companies as quasi-public entities, and it was under this guise that the Supreme Court upheld state regulation of railway rates and freight charges. Chief Justice Morrison Waite, speaking for a majority of the Court, declared in *Chicago, Burlington and Quincy Railroad Company v. Iowa* that

> railroad companies are carriers for hire. They are incorporated as such, and given extraordinary powers, in order that they may the better serve the public in that capacity. They are, therefore, engaged in a public employment affecting the public interest, and, under the decision in *Munn v. Illinois*, just announced, subject to legislative control as to their rates of fare and fright, unless protected by their charters.[20]

Benjamin Wright, discussing this and other railroad cases, noted that "from the statement in the first paragraph of the railroad cases, it seems apparent that the Court simply assumed that a corporate person was entitled to protection under the Fourteenth Amendment."[21] If such an assumption was made by the Court, it was not readily apparent. Two years later, the *Sinking Fund Cases* presented the question of whether a railroad with a federal charter could be directed by congressional legislation to establish a sinking fund—these are assets and their earnings that are earmarked for the retirement of bonds or other long-term obligations. Chief Justice Waite, delivering the opinion of the court, declared that the United States "equally with the states...are prohibited from depriving *persons or corporations* of property without due process of law."[22] A distinction, then, still remained between corporations and persons.

The Court confronted this distinction between corporations and persons directly in 1882 in *San Mateo County v. Southern Pacific Railroad Company*.[23] Appearing for the railroad was former senator Roscoe Conkling, one of the framers of the Fourteenth Amendment. Conkling argued that the provisions of the first article of the amendment were intended to protect corporate property as well as civil rights. William F. Swindler, writing about this case, described Conkling's presentation to the Court by noting that "by inference rather than direct allegation, Conkling repeatedly pointed out to the Court that the Amendment had been intended to distinguish between 'citizens'—Negroes and others—whose 'privileges and immunities' were to be protected, and 'persons' who could be 'legal persons' (i.e., corporations) as well as real persons."[24] Although the Court did not immediately approve this interpretation of the amendment, it wholeheartedly accepted Conkling's theory four years later in the important case *Santa Clara County v. Southern Pacific Railroad Co.*, when it ruled that corporations enjoyed the same rights under the Fourteenth Amendment as did natural persons.[25]

James W. Ely Jr. has shown in a detailed study of railroad law that "there is little evidence to support the contested thesis that courts devised legal rules in the nineteenth century to subsidize economic growth [for railroads] at the expense of the weaker segments of society," and that "it is impossible to sustain the contention, initially advanced by Populists and Progressives but echoed too casually by modern historians, that the Supreme Court invariably sided with rail enterprise in the nineteenth and early twentieth centuries."[26] Nevertheless, it is true that once corporations had been conceived as persons within the scope of constitutional protections, no judge or justice dared challenge this doctrine until young Hugo Black, newly arrived on the Supreme Court, vigorously attacked it in a dissenting opinion in the 1938 case *Connecticut General Life Insurance Co. v. Johnson*.[27] In his opinion, Black argued that "the history of the [Fourteenth] amendment proves that the people were told that its purpose was to protect weak and helpless human beings and were not told that it was intended to remove corporations in any fashion from the control of state governments."[28] The documentary evidence overwhelmingly supports Black's interpretation of the amendment. When the secret journals of the Joint Committee on Reconstruction were reprinted in 1914 by Professor Benjamin Kendrick, they gave little comfort to Conkling's strained interpretation of the distinction between *citizen* and *person*.

Yet American society willingly accepted that corporate ownership represented the next stage of civilized growth. Dean Alfange, describing the mood of society in those decades, wrote:

> A popularized, and hence inevitably distorted, brand of Darwinism transferred such scientific concepts as natural selection, survival of the fittest, evolution and progress to the eminently unscientific domain of social and international relations. As a result, predatory capitalism and imperialism were invested in the eyes of many who were not even remotely touched by their material benefits with the sanctity of natural laws and cosmic processes.[29]

Unrestricted corporate development assumed the posture of natural law even though the corporation itself was an artificial device for accumulating property and power. In fact, Charles Reich argued, "property became power over others; the farm landowner, the city landlord, and the working man's boss were able to oppress their tenants or employees."[30] And Reich suggested that "the defense of private property was almost entirely a defense of its abuses—an attempt to defend not individual property but arbitrary private power over other human beings."[31]

Commenting on the shift in legal perception created by the identification of the corporation as a person, Thurman Arnold remarked that "liberty of individuals to live unmolested by the power of overlords has become confused with the liberty of great industrial overlords to hold in their uncontrolled discretion the livelihood of individuals."[32] Legal understanding of the principles of American government shifted to accommodate this practical reality. "The Declaration of Independence is now the symbol of great business organizations, that holding companies are entitled to life, liberty and the pursuit of power."[33] The private area, which had been sacrosanct as a sphere of life from which government should be banned or severely limited, became the arena in which private corporate governments ruled. "When the corporations began to stop competing, to merge, agree, and make mutual plans," Reich noted, "they became private governments."[34] Arnold suggested further that the "great organizations became the actual government of the people in their practical affairs. The governments at Washington and at the state capitols became the spiritual government whose chief function was that of a repository of ideals and ceremonies."[35]

Arnold, Reich, and Whitehead all compared this transition of economic life from single local business to international commerce as the reinstitution of feudalism. "There is a marked similarity between the partnership of the feudal states and the church during the Middle Ages and the relationship of great corporations and our National Government at Washington. The medieval church, like our modern constitutional government, was the repository of the ideals of the people, and was unconcerned with the distribution of goods to them," Arnold argued.[36] Whitehead went even further in his analysis:

> The modern evolution of big business involves a closer analogy of feudalism, than does feudalism to slavery. In fact, the modern social system with its variety of indispensable, interlocked avocations necessitates such organization. The only questions at issue are the freedom of individuals to circulate among the grades, and satisfactory legal conceptions of the variety of relations of the grades with each other. Individualists and socialists are merely debating over the details of neo-feudalism which modern industry requires. *The self-sufficing independent man, with his peculiar property which concerns no one else, is a concept without any validity for modern civilization.*[37]

In large measure, then, corporations replaced human beings in the political/judicial framework. Human beings become components of the business organization. The subtleties of Lockean natural law were transformed into Darwinian economic jungles in which artificial entities demanded the respect due human beings. "Toward the end of the [nineteenth] century the vast increase in regulatory statutes coming before the Court raised a question quite as fundamental as that produced by the slavery struggle," Wright explained. He went on to note that the problem involved determining "whether the Constitution of 1787 could be interpreted to serve as an instrument of government for an industrial population."[38] Corporate interests, of course, pretended that their interpretation of legal rights, particularly due process, was the true intent of the constitutional founders. But it appeared, Wright argued, "that the economic and social individualism of the seventies and eighties was created by that generation rather than inherited from the founders."[39]

By the end of the nineteenth century, in spite of sporadic efforts of state and federal governments to regulate corporate interests, the law had developed almost insurmountable barriers to protect the giant economic organizations. Three basic doctrines stood out as the foundations of corporate rights as the century closed: (1) freedom of contract, (2) commerce as transportation, and (3) Fourteenth Amendment due process requirements. Other subsidiary concepts clustered about corporate interests; but these three ideas, taken together, made the corporate legal position nearly impregnable. It took the Great Depression of the 1920s and 1930s to shake judicial belief in the application of these ideas in favor of the corporate entity; and the Obama administration's initial efforts ("Obamanomics") to combat the national and global recession that began in 2008 has reinserted the federal government as a dominant player in the private market economy, to the chagrin of conservatives who still adhere to the idea that the power of markets is the key to innovation and prosperity.

The sanctity of contract that provided Marshall with his framework for rescuing corporate existence in *Dartmouth College* protected the corporations for most of the nineteenth century. Viewed as the creatures of state legislatures with charters considered more as contracts than as licenses, corporations escaped regulation by the federal government and were not subject to restrictive legislation in states until the populist movements of the 1800s forced state legislatures to introduce reforms. In many cases the larger corporations controlled the state legislatures. With the recognition of the corporation as a person, the sanctity of contract shifted perceptibly to provide protection against efforts of labor to organize against them. The relationship between an individual worker and the corporation was characterized by the courts as a negotiation of two individuals contracting for service and employment. Collective bargaining was therefore a violation of the sacred right of individuals to contract and was therefore illegal.

Corporations began their legal existence as a venture of individuals combining their physical assets to engage in activities beyond the economic scope of any one of them. Since state legislatures were believed to be the creators of corporations, and since the early charters severely restricted the economic activities of corporations, people came to believe that commerce was the physical transportation of finished goods and agricultural products from their place of production to markets rather than the whole scope of commercial activities. This definition of commerce as basically transportation was tenaciously held by judges far beyond the time when it was a reasonable description of corporate activity. By restricting the idea of commerce to transportation, by arguing that the Constitution provided only that the federal government regulate commerce among the states, and by phrasing much commercial activity in contractual terms that separate the administrative aspects of business from its physical activities, courts were able to leave a large realm in which corporations were virtually exempt from legislation.

The capstone of this legal edifice was the identification of corporations as persons within the constitutional framework. The Fourteenth Amendment prohibited the states from depriving any person of property without due process of law. Due process originally meant the application of the principles of the common law to produce a fair trial. With the recognition of corporations as persons, and with state legislatures trying feebly to regulate these business giants by setting rates and conditions of work, due process came to involve the question of legislative intent. Asking whether the basis for state action was reasonable in the light of conditions became a due process question. Courts thereby became the primary source of standards by which a fair return on corporate investments was determined. In *Wabash, St. Louis & Pacific Railway Co. v. Illinois* (1886), the Supreme Court held that states had no power to regulate railroad rates for interstate shipments.[40] *Wabash* did not completely deny states of all interstate power, but the case did create a regulatory void by making rate regulation of interstate shipments a federal power. Congress responded to this decision by creating the Interstate Commerce Commission in 1887.

Three years later, in *Chicago, Milwaukee & St. Paul Railroad Co. v. State of Minnesota* judicial power was reified further.[41] In this case, Minnesota had established a commission to set rates for railroads, which, after finding that the rate on milk charged by the Chicago, Milwaukee and St. Paul Railroad was excessive, ordered a reduction. But the Supreme Court, looking at the same evidence considered by the state commission, decided that new rates were so low as to be confiscatory and declared the Minnesota statute unconstitutional. Dissenting, Justice Joseph Bradley, joined by Justices Lucius Lamar and Horace Gray, disagreed with the view expressed by the majority "that the judiciary, and not the legislature, is the final arbiter in the regulation of fares and freights of railroads and the charges of other public accommodations."[42] While corporations might be creatures of the legislature, their perpetual existence and activities thereafter were subject to the discretion of the judicial branch.

There were, of course, continual efforts after 1880 to curb corporate excesses. The popular image of Theodore Roosevelt, the muckrakers, and the

Populist movement as opponents of trusts and national monopolies come to mind when we discuss this period. Their efforts, however, seldom loosened the grip of the ever-enlarging corporations over the American economy. Of more importance was the Great Depression, when the invisible hand of natural economic law failed to preserve a system with corporations running amuck. The collapse of the free enterprise system meant a retrenchment of belief in uncontrolled greed as the single most important factor in economic life. Americans demanded and received several bold new interventions by the federal government in the nation's economic activities.

More recently were the gross corporate excesses and ever-increasing disparity between the wealthiest class, the dwindling middle class, and the ever-expanding lower-income classes in the 1990s and early 2000s. This led to the crippling economic recession in the United States and abroad beginning in 2008 and compelled the newly elected President Obama and Congress to take several dramatic steps aimed at averting a long-term recession. This included a nearly $800 billion stimulus package, major infusion of money into the banking industry and other financial institutions, and significant loans and curt demands for a radical restructuring of two of the three major automobile companies—General Motors Corporation and Chrysler Corporation. Such efforts, while not necessarily moving the United States toward a social democratic state, are nevertheless telling and indicate an important modification in the relationship between government and corporate America.[43]

Our immediate concern centers on the intellectual and emotional perceptions of the legal and popular minds of the corporation as a person protected by the Constitution, so we need not review the legislation presented during the New Deal era or even the post-Bush era in an effort to control corporate activity. But in remembering the Great Depression, Wright said that "viewed in terms of governmental power, the most notable change from the doctrine of 1935–1936 is the great increase in the scope of Congressional authority under the commerce clause. The distinction between commerce and production is perhaps not entirely gone, but the conception of commerce as transportation has departed."[44] It is too early to tell what, if any, long-term effects the Obama administration's efforts will have on corporate America. But at present, it appears that the modifications being made, in a theoretical sense, mark a movement—as they did during the Great Depression—from exclusion to inclusion of economic activities subject to government regulation.

Returning to the Great Depression, before the government's control could be consolidated, World War II and the succeeding decades of the cold war again altered the relationship between corporations and government. The United States developed sophisticated new weapons systems for the seemingly perpetual conflict with Communism, and private corporations were encouraged to conduct research and development for the military through a most uncapitalistic system of cost-plus profit contracts. So large and complicated were some of these weapons, and so restricted in their possible peaceful uses, that no profitable corporation could be expected to develop the necessary tools of production and products. Price argued that the uncertainty of the research and development process compelled business and government to work out a mutual arrangement that would benefit both entities.[45] He then described the new relationship between business and government as "more like the administrative relationship between an industrial corporation and its subsidiary than the traditional relationship of buyer and seller in a free market."[46] This relationship expanded in the twenty-first century in the US war on terrorism, with the federal government engaging in detailed economic relationships with myriad private corporate contractors— security, construction, financial, and so forth—who were and are involved in the front lines of the conflicts in Iraq, Afghanistan, and other lands as well. And as noted above, the national and global economic recession only intensified this dynamic, with the federal government embedding itself in the inner sanctums of a multitude of corporate offices and acquiring substantial share control over several corporations.

It is difficult, therefore, to adequately describe the new legal status of corporations in the broad and philosophical terms appropriate to jurisprudence. Gone is the old idea of independent economic existence. In its place we discover a quasi-public, quasi-private organization dependent to a large degree upon government subsidization. Price remarked that "you can no longer tell, by identifying an institution as a private corporation in legal form, whether it competes in the market economy, or is simply a new type of government agency, or is somewhere along a highly varied spectrum in between."[47] Once creatures of the state, corporations now inhabit a nebulous realm of governmental policy and depend upon politics, lobbying, and administrative favor for their existence. Price went on to suggest that a great amount of private enterprise was now intimately suffused in the interstices of government contracts. In other words, "what the grant-in-aid programs did to the arguments for states' rights, the new contractual systems are doing to those for pure private enterprises."[48] The American economic system has changed irretrievably, and is changing still, taking with it the original articulation of human rights and federalism.

The modern corporation, despite the problems encountered during the recession that began in 2008, continues to occupy a dominating position in the legal universe today, a position that has been considerably strengthened by the Supreme Court, led by Chief Justice John Roberts. A *New York Times* article in 2010 declared this august body to be "The Most Conservative Court in Decades."[49] For example, in 2006–2007 the Court handed down two major decisions—*Leegin Creative Leather Products Inc. v. PSKS Inc.* and *Philip Morris USA, Inc. v. Williams*—indicating its pro-business slant. In *Leegin*, an antitrust ruling, the Court opted to overrule a 1911 decision in which it was always illegal for a manufacturer and retailer to agree on minimum resale prices. Instead, the 5–4 majority, led by Justice Anthony Kennedy, held that the legality of price maintenance would now be judged not by a bright-line per se rule, but by a "circumstance-specific 'rule of reason'" for its impact on competition.[50]

In *Philip Morris*, another 5–4 decision, the Court relied on the due process clause in an unusual way and acted to curb punitive damages by overturning a $79.5 million award against the tobacco giant. The Court said that the jury that granted the award to the widow of a smoker may have improperly calculated the figure to punish the cigarette maker for harm to other smokers as well, despite the fact that the corporation had for decades misrepresented the devastating harm its chief product causes to smokers and those directly exposed to secondhand smoke. One commentator, Adam Cohen, assessing the Supreme Court's 2006–2007 term, noted that "we are not in a new *Lochner* era, but traces of one are emerging." Cohen continued: "This court is already the most pro-business one in years, and one or two more conservative appointments could take it to a new level."[51]

More recently, on January 21, 2010, and in another bitterly contested 5–4 decision, the five conservative justices, led by Justice Kennedy, ruled in *Citizens United v. Federal Election Commission*[52] that the federal government could not ban political spending by corporations in candidate elections. The Court overturned two earlier precedents—*Austin v. Michigan Chamber of Commerce* (1990)[53] and *McConnell v. Federal Election Commission* (2003)[54]—involving the First Amendment rights of corporations and held that the government lacked the power to regulate the political free speech rights of corporations who now have the right to directly spend unlimited sums of money on political campaigns.

President Obama called *Citizens United* "a major victory for big oil, Wall Street banks, health insurance companies and the other powerful interests that marshal their power every day in Washington to drown out the voices of everyday Americans."[55] Justice John Paul Stevens, who wrote a ninety-page dissent, argued that the majority erred in treating corporate speech the same as that of human beings, though even Stevens conceded that corporations were broadly covered by the First Amendment. *The New York Times* pithily editorialized that this decision had "thrust politics back to the robber-baron era of the 19th century" since corporations will now be able to use their vast resources to overpower and heavily influence elections and will be able to intimidate government officials to do what they want.[56]

In public utilities, computers, energy production, insurance, banks, entertainment, and others, corporations have virtually dictatorial control over large sectors of American life. The legal fictions that continue to justify their power become galling to many Americans. The corporation may be a person in law but is not a person in fact. Economists may eulogize the free marketplace, but Microsoft and other major corporations consistently seek to stifle competition. Corporations may simply be a benign conglomerate of American investors, but management, through proxy votes, has long since severed any real decision making from the hands of individual stockholders. Some corporations have such excess profits that their management groups can purchase and retire all outstanding stock, thus making control of the corporation just short of hereditary.

Some adjustment must be made within the legal universe to bring the corporate person under social control, including attempts at congressional legislation to curb corporate abuse. But since our task is to explore the interrelationships of inhabitants of the legal universe, our suggested solution must be consonant with concepts and doctrines that originally served to provide a theoretical structure for that universe. "Multiple ownership of corporations helped to separate personality from property, and property from power," Reich argued.[57] Perhaps by linking together these now isolated elements we may discover a means to equity in the legal universe, an equity between individual and the corporate person.

Louis Kelso and Patricia Hetter, in their classic book *Two-Factor Theory: The Economics of Reality*, discussed how modern corporations distribute income differently and thereby prevent further concentration of wealth. They suggest that economic thinking is two centuries out of date in analyzing the factors of production. "The idea that inanimate things produce wealth in the same sense that animate things do, and thus can be productive surrogates for personal toil in the economic world," they suggest, has apparently never occurred to Western economists. "Nor could it, as long as economic speculation was dominated, as it has been throughout the history of political economy, by pre-industrial mores and modes of thought that interpret all industrial reality in terms of only one of the two factors of production: man's labor." They conclude, and this proposition forms their basic assumption, that "one-factor economic thought is incapable of explaining a physical world in which major productive instruments are nonhuman."[58]

Thus, Kelso and Hetter advocate a thorough-going capitalism and label it *universal capitalism*, the ownership of instruments of production by the mass of people. "The theory of universal capitalism introduces symmetry and logic into an industrial economy where the bulk of wealth is produced, not by human labor as under pre-industrial conditions, but by capital instruments."[59] The old linkages between people, property, and the power that comes from controlling property are reestablished with universal ownership of the means of production, not in a socialist or communist sense, but as great masses of people owning stocks in private corporations. In terms of our analysis thus far, such a widespread ownership would introduce democracy into the private economic governments called corporations. "The political objective of universal capitalism is maximum individual autonomy, the separation of political power wielded by the holders of public office from economic power held by citizens, and the broad diffusion of privately owned economic power."[60] A universal private ownership of corporate stocks would provide individuals with sufficient economic strength to exert political independence and reduce the activities of corporations in political affairs.

Kelso and Hetter suggest that "corporate strategy has consisted entirely of ideas on how to maximize output, minimize cost, and maximize profit. But since output has no rational ultimate purpose except to satisfy the consumer needs of individuals," they argue, "the traditional goals of the corporation are insufficient and incomplete."[61] Corporations should be as concerned with the generation of individual purchasing power as with profits so that socioeconomic planning can be placed on a rational basis and not be subjected to fluctuations of affluence and sparsity that presently plague many in American society. The most important aspect of developing consumer affluence, they argue, is to see that the consumers become stockholders and have access to dividends that will form an important part of their annual income.

With widespread private ownership of corporate stock, the corporations would pay little or no income tax after they distributed all or nearly all profits directly to stockholders, retaining a minute percentage of earnings as surplus. This adjustment in the tax structure would accomplish fundamental, long-lasting changes. It would place the major burden of federal taxation on individual income, still maintained in graduated scale, but would radically increase the incomes of stockholders so that no drastic reduction in federal income would result. It would restore the original theoretical framework of the corporate venture as one in which individuals invest their surplus wealth and receive a percentage of the return now absent the great percentage of income that it retained and becomes the property of the corporation itself as reserves. Finally this change would provide a mechanism for distributing the income produced by machines, not by human labor, thus enabling all of society to enjoy the benefits of the Industrial Revolution and post-industrial revolution.

The Kelso-Hetter plan is one of a number of possible legal adjustments that can limit corporate domination of society. It would restore a sense of continuity with American political tradition, once again linking human beings and legal fictions in a more humane relationship. Something must be done within the realm of law to allow humans once again to control institutions and organizations. The usefulness of the corporate person in modern law, in view of the present merging of corporate and government interests, needs reevaluation.

As a result of the global economic recession that began in 2008, other commentators have been proposing a series of equally radical solutions that they believe would help restore a measure of balance in the economy and the nation. As Leo Hindery Jr. and Donald Riegle Jr. put it: "The right way to earn our way back to long-term prosperity is through stimulus efforts that will help develop, broadly deploy, fairly compensate and, especially, fully employ our human capital, which will always be our greatest source of national wealth."[62]

Their proposal would require congressional action that included, at a minimum, enactment of the Employee Free Choice Act, which allows workers to freely join unions; a national pension plan that would resurrect retirement savings; a long-term plan of public investment to upgrade and reconstruct the nation's infrastructure; an effort to reinstitute the tax-policy link between productivity growth and wage gains; and authorization and full funding of programs similar to the depression era's Civilian Conservation Corps that would provide employment for some of the more than six million high school and college graduates.[63]

President Obama, in an economic speech in 2009, hinted at the redirection that needs to take place when he said, "We must lay a new foundation for growth and prosperity—a foundation that will move us from an era of borrow and spend to one where we save and invest, where we consume less at home and send more exports abroad."[64]

But in the end, we still face the less-clearly defined factors present in corporate legal existence. The words of Tocqueville continue to haunt: "I believe that the recurrence of these industrial crises is an endemic disease among all democratic nations in our day. It can be made less dangerous, but not cured, for it is not due to accident but to the essential temperament of these people."[65]

CHAPTER 5
"Three-fifths of All Other Persons": African Americans and the Law

TWO RACIAL MINORITIES ARE SPECIFICALLY MENTIONED in the Constitution and *The Federalist Papers*—African Americans and American Indians. The various Native nations and African Americans presented the new country with immense difficulties, and neither group was recognized as a participant in the original social contract. Throughout American history these two distinctive communities have provided polar, if malleable, extremes in American social and religious thought, at times the object of waves of sympathy, at other times the subject of intense discrimination and oppression.

Alexis de Tocqueville said it best when he wrote: "The Indians die as they have lived, in isolation; but the fate of the Negroes is in a sense linked with that of the Europeans. The two races are bound one to the other without mingling; it is equally difficult for them to separate completely or to unite."[1] This important distinction summarizes historic reaction of the majority of Euro-Americans. We shall take up the status of indigenous peoples after we first examine the intimate connection between African Americans and Euro-Americans in American legal and political history.

The roots of the African American–Euro-American relationship began prior to the discovery of America. Peter Kolchin, a historian, observed that "in order to understand the unfree origins of the United States, it is useful to put American developments in a broader world context, for until the nineteenth century unfree status of one type or another—slavery, serfdom, peonage—was the lot of much of humankind."[2]

While many other societies practiced slavery and other forms of unfree status, European and Euro-American slavery rested upon a deeper and more fundamental presupposition than had most previous slavery systems. Ancient slaves were generally captives of war, conquered peoples, or merchandise of slave traders who existed at the boundaries of the civilized world. Anyone could be a slave; by the same token, any slave could earn his or her freedom. While slavery was a status, it was a legal status that could be changed. "The ancients bound the slave's body but left his spirit free and allowed him to educate himself," Tocqueville wrote in *Democracy in America*. "In this they were acting consistently; at that time there was a natural way out of slavery; from one day to the next the slave could become free and equal to his master."[3] Slavery fluctuated with an individual's fortunes and was seldom if ever considered a manifestation of the natural order.

European and Euro-American slavery was a different matter. "From the moment when the Europeans took their slaves from a race different than their own, which many of them considered inferior to the other human races, and assimilation with whom they all regarded with horror," Tocqueville suggested, "they assumed that slavery would be eternal, for there is no intermediate state that can be durable between the excessive inequality created by slavery and the complete equality which is the natural result of independence."[4] Western slavery, in fact, was a direct product of European expansion and was most emphatically a system of labor. And as Kolchin noted, it was started to meet the serious labor shortage that developed wherever white landholders sought to develop important crops, like sugar, coffee, tobacco, rice, and especially cotton, in parts of the country where population was relatively scarce.[5]

Slavery, as Africans and African Americans experienced it under the Europeans and Euro-Americans, only superficially dealt with legality and remotely connected with personal fortunes, luck, or fate. Africans, indeed all the darker-skinned peoples, were believed so inferior that some whites would argue that slavery was benevolent because it placed these peoples in close proximity with white civilization. While the origin of this belief must certainly lie within the realm of Christian teachings during the formative decades of slavery in the West,[6] evolutionary social theory that began to supplant specifically religious interpretations of racial origins did nothing to correct the erroneous teachings. Indeed, evolutionary thinking viewed all darker-skinned peoples as culturally and technologically inferior to the fairer-skinned Europeans and Euro-Americans and provided powerful pseudoscientific support for nineteenth-century European colonialism.

As James Oakes showed, "racism—the proposition that blacks are by nature, and not by law, a distinct and inferior race of people—emerged in the late eighteenth century almost as a counterweight to the doctrine of human equality. Drawing on a host of European prejudices against blackness, heathenism, cultural difference in general,...racism distinguished itself by unifying those prejudices under the framework of a pseudo-scientific geneticism specific to the Enlightenment."[7]

European and American slavery was qualitatively distinct from ancient slavery in another way, in that it affected great masses of people, not merely unfortunate tribes, villages, or individuals. Although precise figures are impossible, an estimated ten to eleven million living slaves crossed the Atlantic between the sixteenth and nineteenth centuries.[8] Many more died in wars and in transit, so the total population affected is actually much higher.

The slave trade, slave mass production, became the object of European commercial efficiency. Andrew Sinclair remarked that "no civilization had ever subjected the ancient institution so stringently to the laws of commerce. The mechanisms of Europe, from the account-book to the design of the between-decks of the slave-ship, from the auction in Charleston to the drunken haggling with the kings of Bonny, was designed to degrade man's view of man."[9] And, perhaps in the final horror of commercial abstraction, in defining slaves as the property of their masters this accelerated the reduction of their labor force to that of a mere commodity, not dissimilar to other items, cotton and tobacco, being bought and sold on the open market. Such a level of commodification explains why the South could "simultaneously embrace the practice of human slavery and the principle of human equality. For it is the nature of commodity exchanges that it appears to be equitable."[10] The objectivity, then, of western slavery, provides the final criteria by which it must be judged. Out of centuries of insensitivity and degradation, African Americans have had to claim their rights in the legal universe.

Climate and land played an important role both in making slavery feasible in the United States and in eliminating it. The lands of the southern states were fertile and capable of producing cash crops such as tobacco and cotton. The moderate temperature and longer growing season meant that no large supply of provisions was needed to support settlements. But because these cash crops required large parcels of land and many field hands, slavery became the most feasible mode of planting existence. New England, on the other hand, had rocky, sometimes quite barren soil, incapable of producing much more than the foods needed to support a single family. With a shorter growing season and much harsher winters, New Englanders could not afford extra mouths during most of the year and additional workers would not have added much to New England's agricultural capability. Thus the southern soil tended to produce plantations and aristocrats, the New England hills independent small farmers and tradesmen. Equality was seemingly more natural to New Englanders, foreign to southerners, and, eventually, when abolitionists convinced the Yankees of the evils of slavery, the movement for human equality originated in and was strongly supported by New England people.

Religions also played an important role in American slavery. The South generally had established the Church of England or the Episcopal Church, whose basic theology claimed its validity from the apostolic succession and emphasizes ceremonies and hierarchy, both vital elements of southern aristocratic life. In addition, southern evangelical Protestants were increasingly present. They tended to stress the importance of "individual piety and not social regeneration."[11] The Calvinists, along with Presbyterians, Congregationalists, and to a lesser extent Quakers, "were more inclined to equate slavery and sin."[12]

While slavery was practiced everywhere, it was not destined to last long in New England. Shortly after the Revolution, as states began to adopt formal constitutions, slavery was eliminated either by judicial interpretation, as it was in Massachusetts in 1780, or by specific provision, as in the Vermont Constitution, adopted in 1777. The aim of northern opposition, ending slavery, was not always so quickly achieved. In fact, most northern states passed post-nati ("those born after") abolition laws, which stated that "slaves born prior to enactment of the legislation would remain in slavery while those born thereafter would be freed when they reached adulthood."[13] Thus, when the Constitutional Convention convened, slavery was one of its most divisive problems, with half the states having already abolished the institution and the other half zealous in preserving and expanding its scope.

The Federalist Papers reflected the difficulties experienced in the drafting and ratification of the Constitution. Although they did not reveal the popular image of African Americans and slavery, the debates at the convention and the individual essays written by Alexander Hamilton, James Madison, and John Jay did express the general conceptions held by most American statesmen. Sections 2 and 9 of article 1 in the Constitution were compromises over slavery. In neither case were slaves or blacks expressly mentioned:

> *Section 2.* Representatives and direct Taxes shall be apportioned among the several States which may be included within this Union, according to their respective Numbers, which shall be determined by adding to the whole Numbers of free Persons, including those bound to Service for a Term of Years, and excluding Indians not taxed, *three-fifths of all other Persons.* (emphasis added)

> *Section 9. The Migration or Importation of such persons as any of the States now existing think proper to admit,* shall not be prohibited by the

Congress prior to the Year one thousand eight hundred and eight, but a Tax or duty may be imposed on such Importation, not exceeding ten dollars for each Person. (emphasis added)

The fifty-fourth essay in *The Federalist Papers* sought to phrase southern attitudes toward both slavery and African Americans in rather specific northern terms. Hamilton constructed a synthetic status that he supposed African Americans to occupy midway between property and persons, denying that slaves could be regarded as exclusively one or the other. With respect to the status of African Americans as property, he argued:

> In being compelled to labor, not for himself, but for a master; in being vendible by one master to another master; and in being subject at all times to be restrained in his liberty and chastised in his body, by the capricious will of another—the slave may appear to be degraded from the human rank, and classed with those irrational animals which fall under the legal denomination of property.[14]

Involuntary servitude did not class slaves with purportedly irrational animals since, according to Hamilton, the primary characteristic of slaves was a restraint of liberty that did not necessarily imply an inadequate set of human facilities. Thus by defining why southerners regarded African Americans as property, Hamilton studiously avoided the critical question of their obvious humanity.

The same criticism could be applied to Hamilton's contention that slaves had personal worth: "In being protected, on the one hand, in his life and in his limbs, against the violence of all others, even the master of his labor, and his liberty; and in being punishable himself for all violence committed against others—the slave is no less evidently regarded by the law as a member of the society, not as part of the irrational creation; as a moral person, not as a mere article of property."[15] Again we see a shifting of concepts beyond any connection with the true situation.

Slaves, Hamilton argued, were "protected" even against their masters because they were persons; yet, insofar as they remained property, they were subject to chastisement, even death, by their master. The confusion is somewhat alleviated when Hamilton explained the constitutional compromise revealing that he was perhaps personally opposed and wished to reduce it to a legal impediment: "The federal Constitution, therefore, decides with great propriety on the case of our slaves, when it views them in the mixed character of persons and of property. This is in fact their true character. It is the character bestowed on them by the laws under which they live."[16]

The original constitutional conception of slavery and, by extension, of African Americans was a conception that legally defined a mixed character. Hamilton continued by noting that it was "only under the pretext that the laws have transformed the Negroes into subjects of property that a place is disputed them in the computation of numbers"; and, he added, "it is admitted that if the laws were to restore the rights which have been taken away, the Negroes could no longer be refused an equal share of representation with the other inhabitants."[17]

This argument concedes that, except for law enacted by the Euro-American majority, African Americans would be admitted to full citizenship. The compromise, then, which this "mixed character" of slaves required, is partial representation through computing the number of representatives each state will send to Congress. Hamilton concluded: "Let the case of the slaves be considered, as it is in truth, a peculiar one. Let the compromising expedient of the Constitution be mutually adopted which regards them as inhabitants, but as debased by servitude below the equal level of free inhabitants; which regards the *slave* as divested of two fifths of the *man*."[18]

The other slavery section of the Constitution involved the foreign slave trade. Congress was prohibited from interfering with the importation of slaves for twenty years, after which further importation was banned. Madison, author of the forty-second Federalist essay, expressed his wish that the slave trade had been immediately prohibited: "It were doubtless to be wished that the power of prohibiting the importation of slaves had not been postponed until the year 1808, or rather that it had been suffered to have immediate operation."[19] Madison hoped that slavery itself would be discouraged by the new federal government so that, through the enlightened leadership of those states that had already prohibited slavery, it would eventually vanish in the United States.[20]

Clearly the northern statesmen were unhappy in this waffling. Their attitude forecast a continuing struggle over slavery. The mixed character of slaves, partially property, partially persons, proved to be a useful legal formula only for determining the number of southern representatives. Popular social belief was submerged beneath legal fictions so that the prejudicial attitudes of Euro-Americans toward African American slaves remained hidden in those murky realms of emotion. Most indicative of the continuing American attitude toward African Americans was Tocqueville's pithy observation on race relations in the United States, made some four decades after the adoption of the Constitution: "To debauch a Negro girl hardly injures an American's reputation; to marry her dishonors him."[21]

Other nations, however, recognized the evils of slavery and began to agitate for its abolition. England was the reluctant and begrudging leader in this movement, and eventually rid itself of the institution in a two-step process. "Two parliaments determined the new policies," Alfred North Whitehead explained. "They were composed of aristocratic land-owners and evangelical bankers and merchants, one parliament Tory and the other Whig."[22] In 1808, the same year that importation of slaves was forbidden in America, England banned the slave trade in its dominions. A quarter of a century later, in 1833, Parliament finally authorized the purchase and freeing of all slaves in territories controlled by the British Empire. The purchase of slaves cost the government nearly twenty million pounds and at a time when it was suffering severe financial distress. Yet the British reformers were determined to rid their nation of this evil system.

Could Americans have followed Great Britain's lead and manumitted slaves through government purchase? Slavery in the British dominions was a class phenomenon; in America, among other things, it was a regional political institution. The southern states had suspected the federal government from the beginning, and nullification of federal powers by state laws had always been a popular political theory. Any movement to eliminate slavery brought threats of secession. For seventy years, the nation witnessed the cautious game of balancing slave and free representation in Congress, it absorbed bitter disputes over slavery in the territories, and it heard growing demands for abolition from radical northerners. Fugitive slave laws were subverted by underground railroads that smuggled slaves north to freedom.

Tocqueville predicted that only a violent confrontation between north and south could resolve this question. "The Negro race will never again leave the American continent, to which the passions and vices of Europe brought it; it will not disappear from the New World except by ceasing to exist." And he warned that "the inhabitants of the United States may postpone the misfortunes they dread, but they cannot now remove their cause."[23] Tocqueville was not merely discussing the legal protection given to slavery, but the deeply rooted prejudices as well. "Thus," he observed, "it is that in the United States the prejudice rejecting the Negroes seems to increase in proportion to their emancipation, and inequality cuts deep into mores as it is effaced from the laws."[24]

The nation survived several crises revolving about slavery. The Missouri Compromise of 1820, by banning slavery in the territories but admitting Maine and Missouri as matching states to keep voting strength in the Senate equally paired, enabled one generation to postpone the question. The Compromise of 1850 again attempted to postpone the question for a later generation to solve, but within the decade a case arrived at the Supreme Court that summarized the history and politics of race and servitude. The Court, in deciding the case, reviewed previous efforts to resolve the question yet dodged the vital issue. Slavery was upheld, a victory truly Pyrrhic because no incident fanned abolitionist fires as did the 1857 *Dred Scott v. Sandford* decision.[25]

Dred Scott was an African American slave and house servant owned by an army surgeon, Dr. Emerson. In 1834, Emerson and Scott moved from Missouri, a slave state, to the army barracks at Rock Island, Illinois, a free state. They lived there two years, after which the army transferred Emerson to Fort Snelling, Upper Louisiana Territory, located in present-day Minnesota. Emerson purchased Harriet, the slave of another officer, at Fort Snelling. She and Scott were married in 1836, and in 1838 both went with Emerson to Jefferson Barracks, in Missouri.

In 1854, while still living in Missouri, Scott sued Sandford, now regarded as his owner, for assault against himself, his wife, and his children. Sandford denied that Scott was a citizen under the laws of Missouri and asked that the suit be dismissed. The Circuit Court of St. Louis County ruled in favor of Scott, the Supreme Court of Missouri reversed, and the case arrived at the US Supreme Court on Scott's exceptions to the jury instructions. The case was argued twice, once in 1855 and again the next year. Each justice wrote an opinion on the case, six deciding that the Missouri Compromise was unconstitutional. Two justices wrote lengthy dissents to protest Chief Justice Roger Taney's introduction of race into the case.[26]

In a technical sense, the Court answered two questions: (1) did Dred Scott escape slavery by having lived in either Illinois, a free state, or the Upper Louisiana Territory, free under the Missouri Compromise? and (2) did this new freedom prevent the reinstitution of Scott's slave status on his return to Missouri? The arguments, however, divided into three general categories that transcended these technical questions and raised broader concerns of historical understanding, perceptions of race, and challenges to American federalism. Many of the theories discussed by the majority and the dissent in *Dred Scott* became paradigms for phrasing legal theories to resolve the social and moral dilemmas of racism in America.

Chief Justice Taney wrote a sweeping opinion; the concurring justices added shorter comments on specific issues they considered important. Taney articulated racial attitudes and antagonisms that were widespread at the time. He maintained that African Americans could never become citizens of the United States because they were originally excluded from that nebulous body he described as the "sovereign people." Taney twice reiterated the point that the only issue before the Court was whether African Americans, characterized as a class of persons, could by any means achieve full citizenship. Writing about colonial attitudes toward African Americans, the chief justice declared that

> [African Americans] had for more than a century before been regarded as beings of an inferior order and altogether unfit to associate with the white race, either in social or political relations; and so far inferior, that they had no rights which the white man was bound to respect; and that the Negro might justly and lawfully be reduced to slavery for his benefit. He was bought and sold, and treated as an ordinary article of merchandise and traffic, whenever a profit could be made by it. *This opinion was at that time fixed and universal in the civilized portion of the white race. It was regarded as an axiom of morals as well as in politics.*[27]

Regarding the Declaration of Independence and the Constitution, Taney said:

> They show that a perpetual and impassable barrier was intended to be erected between the white race and the one which they had reduced to slavery, and governed as subjects with absolute and despotic power, and which they then looked upon as so far below them in the scale of created beings, that intermarriages between white persons and Negroes or mulattoes were regarded as unnatural and immoral, and punished as crimes, not only in the parties, but in the person who joined them in

marriage. And no distinction in this respect was made between the free negro or mulatto and the slave, but *this stigma, of the deepest degradation, was fixed upon the whole race.*[28]

While each of the justices wrote separate opinions, only two, Justices John McLean and Benjamin R. Curtis, dissented. They used a combination of analogy and expansion of the word *color* to show that the Constitution did not vest political rights in only the white race while denying them to nonwhites. McLean pointed out that "several of the States have admitted persons of color to the right of suffrage, and in this view have recognized them as citizens; and this has been done in the slave as well as the free States. On the question of citizenship, it must be admitted that we have not been very fastidious. Under the late Treaty with Mexico, we have made citizens of all grades, combinations, and colors. The same was done in the admission of Louisiana and Florida."[29]

Curtis denied that the Constitution was made exclusively by and for the white race, citing evidence that five of the thirteen original states allowed African American citizens to exercise the voting franchise at the time of the Constitution's adoption. Curtis argued that the posterity for which the Constitution was adopted included African Americans as well as Euro-Americans. And he adopted the *Federalist Papers* interpretation of the status of slavery, describing it as a local municipal ordinance. "This is not only plain in itself, and agreed to by all writers on the subject," Curtis argued, "but is inferable from the Constitution, and has been explicitly declared by this court. The Constitution refers to slaves as 'persons held to service in one State, under the laws thereof.' Nothing," Curtis concluded, "can more clearly describe a status created by municipal law."[30]

The Supreme Court majority was unable and unwilling to admit that times and conditions had changed, that slavery was now on the verge of being morally unacceptable to Americans. Taney, a strict constitutional constructionist, denied that any change of public opinion could alter the legal status of African Americans because the Constitution could only be interpreted as the Founding Fathers understood it.

Taney's description of race relations touched on all the nebulous ideas that had been used to justify African American slavery, an eloquent exploration of the emotional factors that had served to keep America half slave, half free for nine decades. If any of the constitutional provisions were unjust,

Taney said, "there is a mode prescribed in the instrument itself by which it may be amended; but while it remains unaltered, it must be construed now as it was understood at the time of its adoption."[31]

The nature of citizenship seemed to be pivotal in *Dred Scott*, but the twists and turns that Taney gave it made any final definition hazardous at best. In one respect he seemed to advocate dual citizenship when he distinguished between state and national citizenship. This meant that the jurisdictional question—whether or not federal courts could deal with this question—could be avoided. Arguing for two levels of citizenship, Taney wrote that

> we must not confound the rights of citizenship which a State may confer within its own limits, and the rights of citizenship as a member of the Union. It does not by any means follow, because he has all the rights and privileges of a citizen of a State, that he must be a citizen of the United States. He may have all the rights and privileges of the citizen of a State, and yet not be entitled to the rights and privileges of a citizen in any other State.[32]

On the surface, Taney devised an insurmountable barrier between state and federal citizenship. But on closer examination, it is clear that he was advocating a society in which slavery dominated everything, whether at the state or federal level. With respect to the constitutionality of the Missouri Compromise, Taney argued:

> It is the opinion of the court that the Act of Congress which prohibited a citizen from holding and owning property of this kind in the territory of the United States north of the line therein mentioned, is not warranted by the Constitution, and is therefore void; and that neither Dred Scott himself, nor any of his family, were made free by being carried into this territory; *even if they had been carried there by the owner, with the intention of becoming a permanent resident.*[33]

This doctrine went far beyond the simple articulation of states' rights or the preservation of slavery. Under this doctrine, slave owners could move en masse from slave states to any area of the nation, bringing their slaves with them, and they would be protected in the possession of their human property. Thus, Taney obliterated any constitutional prohibition against slavery that a state or territory possessed. Instead of being an avid states' rights activist, however, Taney used the concept of property to extend the southern slave economy beyond the boundaries of that region to any state.

Taney hewed to a rigid definition of the federal government as a union of sovereign states that conceived of new territories as standing almost at arm's length from the federal government until it was sufficiently settled and organized to apply for statehood in the union. And he denied Congress the power to legislate for the territories when he declared that "there is certainly no power given by the Constitution to the Federal Government to establish or maintain Colonies bordering on the United States or at a distance, to be ruled and governed at its own pleasure; nor to enlarge its territorial limits in any way, except by the admission of new States."[34]

Taney concluded that no laws were needed from Congress respecting territories except the willingness to accept newly formed states into the Union. Then, he suggested, no laws would be needed since the Constitution already defined the rights of states and their citizens. "But no power is given to acquire a Territory to be held and governed permanently in that character," he declared.[35] *Dred Scott* was a desperate attempt by the Supreme Court to resolve social conflict through manipulation of the law. But the Court's political solution was to impose the southern view of slavery on the rest of the nation, an action that only served to infuriate abolitionists.

American slavery was a peculiar creature, half economic, half social prejudice, intertwined with history and political theory. Its solution would have required a spontaneous recognition by a majority of Americans that human beings, whatever their origins, deserved respect. Such a view was impossible in the nineteenth century. Interpretations of the Declaration of Independence and the Constitution remained mired in parochial emotions. A few perceptive outside observers saw the nature of the American dilemma, but even the visionaries in the United States could not understand it. Tocqueville, in one of his typically incisive commentaries on American life, observed that "when they have abolished slavery, the moderns still have to eradicate three much more intangible and tenacious prejudices: the prejudice of the master, the prejudice of race and the prejudice of the white."[36]

If we regard Tocqueville's observation as an accurate prognostication, events following the *Dred Scott* ruling make a great deal of sense. In 1862, only five years after the case, on the eve of the inauguration of Abraham Lincoln as president of the United States, South Carolina announced its secession from the Union. Other southern states followed in turn, Lincoln resisted, and the Civil War followed. Americans faced the task of preserving or dividing the Union by force. In January 1863, as part of the war strategy, President Lincoln issued the Emancipation Proclamation, which freed slaves in states or parts of states in rebellion. During the Civil War, nearly twenty thousand of the newly freed slaves served in the Union forces, and in this sense the Emancipation Proclamation provided a respectable entrance of some African Americans into American society, while serving an important military purpose as well.

But the situation in the southern states would prove extremely difficult. As the Union armies gained control over the rebellious states, and as the social, political, and economic institutions of the South broke down, the problem of caring for thousands of homeless ex-slaves became critical. With actual combat still raging, emancipated slaves often followed the Union armies, seeking both protection and direction. In March 1865, Congress passed a bill establishing a new program within the War Department, the Bureau of Refugees, Freedmen, and Abandoned Lands, with responsibility for bringing order to the southern states. This bureau became, over the next decade, the Freedmen's Bureau and it was charged with the herculean task of rehabilitating ex-slaves and defending their newly established rights.[37]

Lincoln's persistence in treating the southern states as if they had never seceded, and then Andrew Johnson's mild treatment of the rebellious states, meant that the most powerful political figures in the South maintained a grip on the region's political institutions. In 1865, most of the southern states immediately passed black codes designed to keep African Americans in servitude.[38] These codes preserved the antebellum slave codes through a slight rephrasing of terms. In effect, the South proposed to keep African Americans in slavery, but a slavery enforced and required by individual land-owners. On the pretense of resolving the problem of vagrancy, for instance, the codes profoundly restricted the movements, behaviors, and rights of freed slaves. Any relationship between employers and workers was described as "contractual," with harsh penalties ensuring that the "contracts" were kept by the workers. African Americans were restricted to prewar domestic or agricultural work, and the phraseology of the codes left no doubt that African Americans, while technically free, were still considered inferior and were destined to fill only servile functions in the new South.

Northern abolitionists felt, with good reason, that they had won the war and that the black codes were a flagrant attempt to reverse the war's outcome. A federal civil rights bill passed in 1865 nullified the codes, but it was considered insufficient. The Emancipation Proclamation meant that the returning southern states would have more representatives in the Congress because the three-fifths clause no longer limited their population. Thus, future congresses might repeal the Civil Rights Act if southern congressmen could find common cause with northern Democrats. The radicals in Congress, therefore, thought it best that civil rights be the subject of specific constitutional amendments, placing them, presumably, forever beyond the reach of future congressional coalitions.

In 1865, the Thirteenth Amendment was adopted, prohibiting slavery or involuntary servitude in the United States. In 1868, the Fourteenth Amendment was adopted, prohibiting states from abridging the privileges and immunities of any American citizen. It also eliminated the three-fifths count of blacks, prohibited former Confederate officials from serving in political office, and validated the war debt.

The newly formed southern state governments then introduced, under their states' rights to determine voting qualifications, grandfather clauses, which restricted the voting franchise to citizens whose grandfathers were eligible to vote, thereby virtually eliminating the suffrage of African Americans. In 1870, to prohibit this type of disenfranchisement, the Fifteenth Amendment was ratified, which prohibited any abridgment of voting rights on the grounds of race or previous condition of servitude. In these three crucial amendments the prejudice of the master, expressed in immediate rewriting of state laws, was finally curbed by federal constitutional provisions.

The original barrier raised against African Americans had been a legal formula by which they had been defined partially as property. This formula created a status for them in the Constitution from which they could not escape by their own efforts, except on rare occasions. Elimination of this legally inferior status by constitutional amendment meant that the racial problem shifted from controversy over objective legal concepts to the indefinite realm where half-formed concepts structure the manner in which people think of law. African Americans, then, entered the legal universe as a result of the Civil War and through the succeeding amendments which placed them, at least in a legal sense, on a level of equality with Euro-Americans. Law had to confront race directly, and there were few available concepts. Because the reaction of the South in constructing black codes had been immediately countered by Congress's passage of the Civil Rights Act, civil rights and racial difficulties became synonymous in American minds. Benjamin Wright pointed out that "before 1865 there was but a single case in which an act was held invalid because it violated a civil right."[39] After 1865, civil rights cases would occupy an increasing amount of attention from the courts and congresses.

Much of the controversy revolved about the Fourteenth Amendment's imprecise description of the "privileges and immunities" of American citizens. Raoul Berger, in *Government by Judiciary*, his study of the amendment's history, described the intent of the framers: "The purpose of the framers was to protect blacks from discrimination with respect to specified 'fundamental rights,' enumerated in the Civil Rights Act and epitomized in the §1 'privileges and immunities' clause. To achieve that purpose they made the black *both* a citizen 'of the United States and of the State in which he resides.'" He went on to say that the framers had not intended state citizenship to reduce the rights they had fought so hard to establish, but to stabilize them. "The notion," said Berger, "that by conferring dual citizenship the framers were separating said rights of a citizen of the United States from those of a State citizen not only is without historical warrant but actually does violence to their intention."[40]

Americans had believed that the geographical distribution of sovereignty would protect them from an overzealous and dominating central government. Seventy-five years of political existence had demonstrated that the division of sovereignty created immense difficulty in defining precisely which areas were reserved to the states, which were delegated to the federal government, and which were retained by the people. Although believing themselves to be a people ruled by law, Americans had great difficulty distinguishing the law from their beliefs; indeed, many believed that law was a formal and systematic method of enforcing their beliefs on society. One belief concerned a difference between state and federal citizenship. This belief had been bolstered by the *Dred Scott* case, with few people seeing in the conflict over secession the creation of a new national citizenship transcending this distinction. Thus, the unresolved debate and conflict over the nature of American citizenship was more important than race in a theoretical sense. It would take another century before a majority of people confronted this problem.

The first phase of African American liberation—escape from legal restrictions enforcing an inferior social status and entering into a legal universe where they confronted attitudes and institutions based primarily on emotional prejudice—is typical of the experiences of every minority group in American history. In the next phase of the African American struggle, overcoming these undefined fears and attitudes, the problem shifted dramatically. From the original definition of race as a way to limit freedom, the situation shifted until racial discrimination was enforced through devices that pretended that no racial differences existed in the law. With their large demographic base, their historical concentration in the South, and their slave history, African Americans would be on the cutting edge of any American movement against racial prejudice. Other groups that suffered less from racial discrimination profited by having an easily identified larger group, like African Americans, bear the brunt of prejudice.

The century and a half following the Civil War can be interpreted as an effort by virtually all minority groups in the United States to face the reality of living in a nation that is a nonhomogenous society and an effort to understand and improve upon their particular place within the state and society. The Thirteenth, Fourteenth, and Fifteenth Amendments truly mark the theoretical foundations of this new era. Unfortunately, the civil rights amendments almost immediately became the province of the majority, only much later being effectively applied to protect the various minority groups.

The Civil War settled the question of secession, but failed to establish the nature of federal citizenship. While states could not unilaterally depart from the Union, they preserved most of their power to regulate and control the granting or withholding of citizenship. Federalism remained primarily a posture of unity toward foreign influences despite the attempt to define more specifically the nature of federal citizenship.

Berger argued that the civil rights amendments, in particular the Fourteenth Amendment, were not intended to give African Americans equal social and political rights with Euro-Americans. Amassing a considerable wealth of historical material, Berger sought to demonstrate that the racial antagonisms were so great that even the most radical reformers could not have openly advocated integrated schools, the free exercise of voting rights, and the open use of public accommodations. W. E. B. DuBois had earlier expressed similar sentiments when he noted in *Black Reconstruction in America, 1860–1880*, that "both the Fourteenth and Fifteenth Amendments were thus made innocuous so far as the Negro was concerned, and the Fourteenth Amendment in particular became the chief refuge and bulwark of corporations. It was thus that finance and the power of wealth accomplished through the Supreme Court what it had not been able to do successfully through Congress."[41]

Although the Supreme Court virtually interpreted the Fourteenth Amendment out of existence in the post–Civil War period, it could not have done so unless groundwork had already been laid for distinguishing between state and federal citizenship. This problem, unresolved since the beginning of the republic, took form early in the *Slaughter-House Cases*.[42] The decision in these cases made the later actions nullifying federal efforts to protect the rights of African American citizens inevitable and illustrated the fact that while people conceived of the Union as an indissoluble political arrangement, they had not begun to conceive the difficulties inherent in the geographical divisions of sovereignty and citizenship.

Critical in the *Slaughter-House Cases* was the question of the state's relationship to its citizens. Attorneys for the dissenting butchers and meat-packers equated the restrictions placed upon them as involuntary servitude. Equality before the law girded this approach, and the dissenting justices picked up the argument readily. Justice Stephen J. Field, in his dissent, reasoned that the freedom to pursue a vocation was essential to citizenship and could not be restricted. Indeed, he wrote:

> A prohibition…to pursue certain callings, open to others of the same age, condition, and sex, or to reside in places where others are permitted to live, would so far deprive [one] of the rights of a freeman, and would place him, as respects others, in a condition of servitude. A person allowed to pursue only one trade or calling, and only in one locality of the country, would not be, in the strict sense of the term, in a condition of slavery, but probably none would deny that he would be in a condition of servitude.[43]

Justice Joseph P. Bradley's dissent also addressed fundamental issues as he described the underlying problems that the Thirteenth Amendment sought to confront. But his analysis so departed from the theoretical framework in which the cases were set that it was not convincing, although it perhaps contained more historical and social truth than the opinions of any of the other justices. Bradley frankly wrote that the mischief to be remedied was not merely slavery and its incidents and consequences; but that spirit of insubordination and disloyalty to the National government which had troubled the country for so many years in some of the States, and that intolerance of free speech and free discussion which often rendered life and property insecure, and led to much unequal legislation. The amendment was an attempt to give voice to the strong National yearning for that time and that condition of things, in which American citizenship should be a sure guaranty of safety, and in which every citizen of the United States might stand erect on every portion of its soil, in the full enjoyment of every right and privilege belonging to a freeman, without fear of violence or molestation.[44]

Heady words, incorporating a lofty vision of national citizenship and, coming only four years after the ratification of the Fourteenth Amendment, certainly an indication that Americans intuited a better social condition for all Americans.

Justice Samuel F. Miller, however, writing for the majority, chose to limit the practical application of the Thirteenth Amendment to the question of African American slavery and extended this interpretation only so far as to indicate that Mexican peonage or Chinese coolie labor might also be included under its provisions. In the larger context of the relationship of a state to the rights and privileges of national citizenship, Miller created an artificial distinction that thereafter dominated judicial considerations of the civil rights amendments. "Not only may a man be a citizen of the United States without being a citizen of a State," Miller argued, "but an important element is necessary to convert the former into the latter. He must reside within the State to make him a citizen of it, but it is only necessary that he should be born or naturalized in the United States to be a citizen of the Union."[45]

Here Miller cleverly, or perhaps foolishly, confused two types of citizenship, describing national citizenship in terms of qualifications and restricting state membership to that of the eligibility to participate in the political processes of the state. His conclusion, "that there is a citizenship of the United States, and a citizenship of a State, which are distinct from each other, and which depend upon different characteristics or circumstances in the individual,"[46] can be easily distinguished simply by confirming residency in a state, at which point the two citizenships again merge and should be considered identical.

Yet the two types of political status did not merge in the minds of the justices of the Supreme Court nor in the understandings of the legal profession. Once this distinction was articulated by the highest court in the land, the whole question of citizenship took an approach in which characteristics of constitutional freedoms were allocated either to the states or the national government depending upon the sophistry that could be mustered by the respective counsels on each side of a legal question. In analytical terms, the development of law thereafter restricted the communication of meaning to stark and easily distinguished alternatives. One such case, involving the right of peaceful assembly, *United States v. Cruikshank*, demonstrated the extent to which this division of powers could be twisted to reach preconceived ends.[47]

In 1873, a mob of whites in Louisiana, after harassing and then killing nearly one hundred African American freedmen, were indicted and convicted of multiple counts of hindering and conspiring to hinder the African Americans in the free exercise of their constitutional right to bear arms, assemble, and enjoy the equal protection of the law and due process.[48] The Supreme Court, however, circuitously analyzed the fact situation in order to void the convictions. Describing the right of peaceful assembly as a right found "wherever civilization exists," the Court suggested that this natural right had been allocated to the states even before the adoption of the Constitution. Having completely disposed of this as a federal right, the Court then readmitted it under severely restricted conditions. Chief Justice Morrison R. Waite, writing for the majority, said: "The right of the people peaceably to assemble for the purpose of petitioning Congress for a redress of grievances, or for any thing else connected with the powers or the duties of the national government, is an attribute of national citizenship, and, as such, under the protection of, and guaranteed by, the United States.[49]

National citizenship, then, existed insofar as people exercising constitutional rights did so with the specific intent of establishing a relationship with the federal government, period. Such a severe narrowing of the rights of citizens practically eliminated any concept of the universal rights articulated in the Declaration of Independence and the Bill of Rights. The enforcement of constitutional rights depended upon the pleadings by lawyers.

The *Cruikshank* Court made this interpretation a matter of record, pointing out that "there is no allegation that this was done because of race or color of the persons conspired against. When stripped of its verbiage, the case as presented amounts to nothing more than that the defendants conspired to prevent certain citizens of the United States, being within the State of Louisiana, from enjoying the equal protection of the laws of the State and of the United States."[50] Seemingly, this violation of rights would be sufficient to secure a conviction. Yet the Court then dismissed the indictments as too vague since they did not specifically list the federal rights that had been violated. As if to deepen their judicial injury, Chief Justice Waite, for the Court, said, "We may suspect that race was the cause of the hostility; but it is not so averred. This is material to a description of the substance of the offence, and cannot be supplied by implication. Every thing essential must be charged positively, and not inferentially. The defect here is not in form, but in substance."[51]

But if we consider that the race of a person must be pleaded in order for them to enjoy full citizenship rights, then there can be no full enjoyment but only a limited and restrictive participation in society based upon protections that are given to an allegedly inferior race. Thus to plead race is the denial of equality and pleading race is a matter of form that enables one to avoid dealing with substance.

The conception of the federal government, used by Chief Justice Waite, fully corresponded to David Kairys's description in *With Liberty and Justice for Some*, in which the philosophical and practical content of the Supreme Court's rulings involving racial, ethnic, and gender minorities are made empty by the clever use of definitions and the apparent ease by which important words or phrases are deprived of meaning and content.[52] Thus, Waite wrote that the federal government was, "for certain purposes, a government of the people." And, he contended, "its powers are limited in number, but not in degree. Within the scope of its powers, as enumerated and defined, it is supreme and above the States; but beyond, it has no existence. It was erected for special purposes, and endowed with all the powers necessary for its own preservation and the accomplishment of the ends the people had in view. It can neither grant nor secure to its citizens any right or privilege not expressly granted or by implication placed under its jurisdiction."[53] If, therefore, any right is treated as the Court handled the right to free assembly, defining it as a natural right preceding the Constitution but returned specifically in a federal purpose is clearly shown, then the attributes of national citizenship are reduced to the clever manipulation of words. In effect, this case characterizes the approach used by the Supreme Court following the

Civil War to negate the meager gains made by African Americans as a result of that war.

Louisiana proved to be the testing ground of the citizenship problem in post–Civil War decades. Most of the important cases that defined state and federal citizenship were generated in this state. In 1869 the Louisiana legislature, then still under the control of the carpetbaggers, who depended upon African American voters, passed an act designed to enforce the thirteenth article of the state constitution that guaranteed that "all persons shall enjoy equal rights and privileges upon any conveyance of a public character."[54] It was not long before this act was tested in the courts. Mrs. De Cuir, an African American woman, booked passage on the steamboat *Governor Allen*, which made a regular run from New Orleans, Louisiana, to Vicksburg, Mississippi. Her destination was the landing at Hermitage, a plantation upriver but still within the state of Louisiana. She was refused accommodations with the white passengers and brought action under the 1869 statute against the captain of the vessel. The state supreme court ruled in her favor and the case was appealed to the US Supreme Court.

Chief Justice Waite, writing for the majority, restricted the discussion in *Hall v. De Cuir* severely: "For the purposes of this case," he wrote, "we must treat the act of Louisiana of February 23, 1869, as requiring those engaged in inter-state commerce to give all persons traveling in that State, upon the public conveyances employed in such business, equal rights and privileges in all parts of the conveyance, without distinction or discrimination on account of race or color."[55] Waite then proceeded to construct hypothetical conditions that, he maintained, would cause such confusion and disruption as to make the state statute a burden on inter-state commerce. "No carrier of passengers can conduct his business with satisfaction to himself," Waite suggested, "or comfort for those employing him, if on one side of a State line his passengers, both white and colored, must be permitted to occupy the same cabin, and on the other be kept separate. Uniformity in the regulations by which he is to be governed from one end to the other of his route is a necessity in his business, and to secure it Congress, which is untrammeled by State lines, has been invested with that exclusive legislative power of determining what such regulations shall be."[56]

Waite then concluded that the commerce power, allocated by the Constitution to the federal government, excluded the states from attempting to regulate public conveyances within their borders. In reaching this conclusion, the chief justice intruded upon state sovereignty in a rather backhanded manner, writing that "while recognizing to the fullest extent the principle which sustains a statute, unless its unconstitutionality is clearly established, we think this statute, to the extent that it requires those engaged in the transportation of passengers among the States to carry colored passengers in Louisiana in the same cabin with whites, is unconstitutional and void. *If the public requires such legislation, it must come from Congress and not from the States*."[57] Congress had, as a matter of fact, already passed two civil rights acts—in 1866 and 1875—that should have been regarded by the Court as a statement of federal policy on the matter of racial discrimination. In fact, the 1875 act was the last piece of federal civil rights legislation until 1957.[58] But both the Fourteenth Amendment and the Civil Rights Act of 1875 were cleverly shunted aside by concurring Justice Nathan Clifford in an opinion that appears suspiciously designed to answer any criticism of the Court's concentration on the interstate commerce clause:

> Vague reference is made to the Civil Rights Act and to the preceding amendment to the Constitution, as if that act or the said amendment may supersede the operation and legal effect of the coasting license as applied to the case before the court; but it is clear that neither of those provisions, nor both combined, were intended to accomplish any such purpose. Enough appears in the language employed in those provisions to show that their principal object was to confer citizenship, and the rights which belong to citizens as such, upon the colored people, and in that manner to abrogate the rule previously adopted by this court in the *Dred Scott* case.[59]

Clifford finished his opinion by pretending that the Civil Rights Act of 1875 conflicted with but did not supersede the act of Congress for "the enrollment and licensing of ships and vessels for the coasting trade."[60]

In *De Cuir*, the Court utilized a familiar device, sometimes characterized as "the parade of the imaginary horribles," in which it judges a policy by its conceivable ultimate conclusion if pressed to its limits, and held a state statute prohibiting discrimination on public carriers to be an undue burden on interstate commerce.[61] In 1875, Congress acted in the Civil Rights Act to prevent discrimination against African Americans on public conveyances, in hotels and inns in the course of travel, and in theaters and other forms of public amusement. Sufficiently impressive penalties were provided for persons convicted of denying or inciting another to deny equal rights to African Americans in these particular areas. But a majority of white Americans were not yet ready to deal with full or even partial citizenship opportunities for the former slaves. A considerable amount of litigation resulted from the Civil Rights Act of 1875, and by October 1882 the Supreme Court was ready to hear a number of cases contesting different provisions of the act. Kansas, California, Missouri, New York, and Tennessee had been notorious in the way their white citizens and institutions of governance discriminated against African Americans, and of the cases taken, two dealt with hotel accommodations, two with access to theaters and places of public amusement, and one with discriminatory practices of interstate railroads.[62]

The Court had already closed the interstate commerce door on itself, and a holding of constitutionality based on the federal powers to regulate commerce would have pushed both the Court and American society further than either wished to move. In the *Civil Rights Cases* (1883), Justice Joseph Bradley, writing for a majority of the Court, gave a very limited interpretation of the Fourteenth Amendment. "Positive rights and privileges are undoubtedly secured by the Fourteenth Amendment," Bradley wrote, "but they are secured by way of prohibition against state laws and state proceedings affecting those rights and privileges, and by power given to congress to legislate for the purpose of carrying such prohibition into effect; and such legislation must necessarily be predicated upon such supposed state laws or state proceedings, and be directed to the correction of their operation and effect."[63] In other words, the Fourteenth Amendment was not to be understood as protecting rights that people might wish to exercise but was to be held in reserve in case any state made specifically discriminatory laws identifying African Americans as the particular object of discrimination.

"It is absurd to affirm that, because the rights of life, liberty and property (which include all civil rights that men have) are by the amendment sought to be protected against invasion on the part of the state without due process of law, congress may, therefore, provide due process of law for their vindication in every case,"[64] Bradley argued, explaining that simply because the amendment prohibited discrimination did not mean that Congress could establish positive laws to ensure equal protection. He then characterized the actions of the defendants as simply "private wrongs," which could be rectified by private lawsuits, not acts that required federal intervention or protection.

Bradley assumed that hotels, theaters, and railroads, although licensed by the state and, if in corporate forms such as railroads most certainly were, a creature of the state, really had little relationship with state governments. He rejected the argument that treatment as second-class citizens was a form of servitude, restricting the interpretation of this phrase to the actual state of slavery with which Americans were all too familiar.

Justice Bradley's nullification of the Civil Rights Act of 1875 became the battle cry of a generation of segregationists who would thereafter vehemently argue that although African Americans were the same as other citizens, they preferred to remain different:

> When a man has emerged from slavery, and by the aid of beneficent legislation, has shaken off the inseparable concomitants of that state, there must be some stage in the progress of his elevation when he takes the rank of a mere citizen, and ceases to be the special favorite of the laws, and when his rights as a citizen, or a man, are to be protected in the ordinary modes by which other men's rights are protected.[65]

And Bradley strangely reasoned that prior to the abolition of slavery, thousands of African Americans had lived in the North and did not feel deprived when they were forbidden equal rights in public conveyances and accommodations. He conveniently ignored the constant fear under which these freed individuals had lived and refused to acknowledge that they could easily have been kidnaped, transported south, and reduced to a state of slavery without any legal redress. Bradley's characterization of the progress of African Americans as now demanding that they be treated as other citizens and not remain as the "special favorites" of the law was an approach to racial questions wherein the courts pretend that very little or no discrimination actually exists and interprets the legal protections given to minority groups as "special" privileges that handicap them from achieving full citizenship. This theory, revived by the conservative majority on the Roberts court, is a favorite device for exploiting indigenous nations and other racial, ethnic, and gender groups as well.[66]

Justice John Marshall Harlan filed a vigorous dissent. "The Thirteenth Amendment, my brethren concede, did something more than to prohibit slavery as an *institution*, resting upon distinctions of race, and upheld by positive law," Harlan insisted. "They admit that it established and decreed universal *civil freedom* throughout the United States. But did the freedom thus established involve nothing more than exemption from actual slavery? Was nothing more intended than to forbid one man from owning another as property?"[67] Harlan had reached the crux of the matter. The majority of the Court in this case, and in the *De Cuir* case, were content to interpret the civil rights amendments simply as prohibitions against an institution that was already dead, leaving the question of state and federal citizenship, as well as state and federal powers, untouched and unresolved.

Harlan systematically attacked Bradley's definition of inns, places of public amusement, and railroads as essentially private enterprises immune to state laws. He pointed out that railroads, for example, were "created primarily for public purposes, and subject to be controlled for the public benefit."[68] And, he continued, "authorities are sufficient to show a keeper of an inn is in the exercise of *quasi* public employment." As for public amusement parks, Harlan contended that "within the meaning of the act of 1875, [they] are established and maintained under direct license of the law. The authority to establish and maintain them comes from the public. The colored race is a part of that public…[L]icense from the public to establish a place of public amusement, imports, in law, equality of right, at such places, among all the members of that public."[69]

Harlan's reasoning was direct and irrefutable: "Citizenship in this country necessarily imports equality of civil rights among citizens of every race in the same state. It is fundamental in American citizenship that, in respect of such rights, there shall be no discrimination by the state, or its officers, or by individuals, or corporations exercising public functions or authority, against any citizen because of his race or previous condition of servitude."[70] Finally, raising the ultimate question of justice that must always transcend any statement of law, Harlan wrote:

> I venture, with all respect for the opinion of others, to insist that the national legislature may, without transcending the limits of the Constitution, do for human liberty and the fundamental rights of American citizenship, what it did, with the sanction of this court, for the protection of slavery and the rights of the masters of fugitive slaves. If fugitive slave laws, providing modes and prescribing penalties whereby the master could seize and recover his fugitive slave, were legitimate exertions of an implied power to protect and enforce a right recognized by the

Constitution, why shall the hands of Congress be tied, so that—under an express power, by appropriate legislation, to enforce a constitutional provision granting citizenship—it may not, by means of direct legislation, bring the whole power of this nation to bear upon States and their officers, and upon such individuals and corporations exercising public functions as assume to abridge, impair, or deny rights confessedly secured by the supreme law of the land?[71]

There was, of course, no good answer to this question, except that the process to transition African Americans to full citizenship had not been made emotionally or intellectually by a majority of the Supreme Court.

The *Civil Rights Cases*, perhaps the harshest blow struck against African Americans by the Supreme Court since Lincoln's Emancipation Proclamation, marked the end of federal efforts to ensure equal protection of the laws. State citizenship became synonymous with segregation in fact and later in law. African Americans in the northern states made some important gains against segregation in the 1880s, with thirteen states passing laws prohibiting discrimination in restaurants, hotels, and public transportation. But the southern states, realizing that there would be no federal supervision of the treatment of African Americans, and interpreting the decision in these cases as the go-ahead for state legislation separating the races, in the late 1880s and early 1890s passed numerous statutes that forbade equal treatment of blacks, justifying these laws as the exercise of state police powers.

The only additional twist that was given to these new laws was the provision, in most cases, for criminal sanctions for the violation of segregationist ordinances and statutes. Again, Louisiana became the center of attention when in a prearranged situation with railroad officials, Homer Plessy, labeled as an octoroon (a person of one-eighth African American blood) and hardly identifiable physically as an African American, was evicted from the first-class car and later was convicted of having violated an 1890 Louisiana statute, the Separate Cars Act, that required racial segregation on railroads in the state.[72]

When the case reached the Supreme Court in 1896, Justice Henry B. Brown wrote the majority opinion, against which Justice Harlan was the sole dissenter. Brown cited many cases decided prior to the civil rights amendments and relied heavily upon the dicta of previous cases in which the Court argued that slavery and the badge of inferiority that discrimination created were not identical and that while slavery had been abolished, the allocation of African Americans to an inferior legal and social status had not been intended by the amendments.

Brown used baffling logic: "A statute which implies merely a legal distinction between the white and colored races—a distinction which is founded in the color of the two races and which must always exist so long as white men are distinguished from the other race by color—has no tendency to destroy the legal equality of the two races, or re-establish a state of involuntary servitude."[73] Here, Brown mistook social prejudice for an aspect of ultimate reality, bringing forward the elements of emotion that lay hidden within the recesses of the legal universe and justifying segregation as having its origin in natural law, which the Supreme Court was impotent to change or criticize. "The object of the amendment was undoubtedly to enforce the absolute equality of the two races before the law," Brown wrote, "but in the nature of things it could not have been intended to abolish distinctions based upon color, or to enforce social, as distinguished from political equality, or a commingling of the two races upon terms unsatisfactory to either."[74]

Again, Brown placed certain behaviors outside the scope of law. Plessy, however, was not asking for enforced social equality but nullification of enforced social inequality. "Laws permitting, and even requiring, their separation in places where they are liable to be brought into contact do not necessarily imply the inferiority of either race to the other, and have been generally, if not universally, recognized as within the competency of the state legislatures in the exercise of their police power."[75] It is difficult, even now, to reconcile the provision for criminal penalties with the Supreme Court's characterization of segregation laws as "permissive" in separating the races. Yet once this train of logic was adopted and a pretense of law became a description of the Court's interpretation of facts, the reasoning moved inevitably to its conclusion.

Plessy's attorneys, led by Albion Tourgée, a prominent figure in the fight for African American rights, had hit precisely the underlying point of the case when they suggested that the effect of the federal courts' interpretation of the Fourteenth Amendment was to vest an absolute right of property in white skin. Brown handled this contention very badly. He did admit that "the power to assign to a particular coach obviously implies the power to determine to which race the passenger belongs, as well as the power to determine who, under the laws of the particular State, is to be deemed a white, and who a colored person."[76] But Brown refused to relent on the question whether the Constitution allowed racial characteristics to become property. "Conceding this to be so," Brown wrote, "for the purposes of this case, we are unable to see how this statute deprives him of, or in any way affects his right to, such property."[77] So, Brown noted, if the plaintiff was a white man, he had a cause of action for being classified as black; if he were black, he had no right to complain of being discriminated against since he was not entitled to the reputation or privileges of being white.

Brown's concluding remarks set the tone for racial discrimination against African Americans at every level of society for the next three-quarters of a century. "We consider the underlying fallacy of the plaintiff's argument to consist in the assumption that the enforced separation of the two races stamps the colored race with a badge of inferiority," he concluded. "If this be so, it is not by reason of anything found in the act, but solely because the colored race chooses to put that construction upon it."[78] Finally, Brown maintained that "legislation is powerless to eradicate racial instincts or to abolish distinctions based upon physical differences, and the attempt to do so can only result in accentuating the difficulties of the present situation. If the civil and political rights of both races be equal, one cannot be inferior to the other civilly or politically. If one race be inferior to the other socially, the Constitution of the United States cannot put them upon the same plane."[79] The problem, however, was not that Plessy expected the Constitution to cure social defects; he only wished to eliminate the institutionalization of social prejudice by legal doctrines.

Justice Harlan, a Kentuckian and former slaveholder, whose dissent has in our times become famous and is often cited as a basic interpretation of the Constitution, vigorously opposed the majority opinion. "The Thirteenth Amendment does not permit the withholding or deprivation of any right necessarily inhering in freedom," Harlan declared. "It not only struck down the institution of slavery as previously existing in the United States, but it prevents the imposition of any burdens or disabilities that constitute badges of slavery or servitude. It decreed universal civil freedom in this country."[80]

Therein lay the difference in judicial philosophies. The majority, most of whom were railroad attorneys before coming to the Court, said that citizenship alone was involved and that any other attributes that might be attached to that citizenship by the states were beyond the reach of the federal government or even constitutional amendments. Harlan, on the other hand, recognized that freedom and citizenship, stripped of their practical attributes, were simply hollow terms. He characterized segregation laws as a burden, a critical concept because it was only when justices, judges, juries, and attorneys recognized segregation as a burden on all aspects of life that the courts began to attack the practice.

Harlan located the premises of the majority: "It was said in argument that the statute of Louisiana does not discriminate against either race, but prescribes a rule applicable alike to white and colored citizens. But this argument does not meet the difficulty," Harlan suggested. "Every one knows that the statute in question had its origin in the purpose, not so much to exclude white persons from railroad cars occupied by blacks, as to exclude colored people from coaches occupied by or assigned to white persons." And, with a rather jaundiced eye toward his fellow justices, he wrote, "no one would be so wanting in candor as to assert the contrary."[81]

Thus, while Harlan stripped the case to its naked racial prejudice, the time was not yet ripe, the logic not yet sufficiently developed, and the philosophical view of American society not yet mature enough to gain a victory for his accurate and eloquent exposure of the real issues. Americans could not see why constitutional protections should be assured that might lead to social behavior few people cared to contemplate. We clearly have the intrusion of nebulous emotional beliefs and of developed concepts into the supposed precision and logic of law.

None of the civil rights plaintiffs ever contended that social equality could be achieved by legislation. Their intent was to ensure that racial discrimination did not result from formal political action by any level of government. Yet from the Civil War onward, fanatic Euro-American concern over the social status of African Americans dominated legal thinking. White supremacy was written into law. Only a gradual change of consciousness about the nature of race and ethnicity could purge the law of bias.

Harlan summarized his view of the Constitution so powerfully and concisely that today he is quoted by contemporary segregationists, neoconservatives, and Tea Partiers who have helped lead the fight that has nearly dismantled affirmative action programs nationwide.[82] With some bit of grandeur, Harlan wrote that "in view of the constitution, in the eye of the law, there is in this country no superior, dominant, ruling class of citizens. There is no caste here. Our Constitution is color-blind, and neither knows nor tolerates classes among citizens. In respect of civil rights, all citizens are equal before the law."[83] Harlan had once again elevated the Constitution to its proper status as a principled document, expressing ideas of human relationships unbound by time and place. His stirring dissent, however, would not gain a majority of judicial support until nearly six decades had elapsed.

Plessy v. Ferguson (1896) devastated African American civil rights in virtually every sphere: transportation, education, voting, employment, and others. Segregation was not part of the Constitution. "Separate but equal" in practical terms meant "isolated and unequal." The shift in viewpoint accomplished in the thirteen years between the *Civil Rights Cases* and *Plessy* was more than tactical; it encompassed the whole universe of legal concepts. The problem, then, became to demonstrate that segregation harmed whites as well as African Americans, that equality meant more than provision of separate facilities.

The National Association for the Advancement of Colored People (NAACP) Legal Defense and Educational Fund began in the mid-1930s to construct a litigation strategy that would produce "the proper sequence of thought" that eventually led to the conclusion that segregation was unconstitutional. The only conceivable avenue that could be chosen was to challenge on a long-term basis the factual characteristics of equality. Thus began the great program, concentrating initially on graduate education, that demonstrated that education was more than a set of buildings and simple teaching, but was most intimately involved in the free intercourse of ideas that could occur only with the free social relationships of individuals, regardless of color. While contemporary commentators sometimes criticize the court as acting like a "super legislature,"[84] the movement of the Supreme Court along the lines set down by the NAACP cases confirms that there should be little doubt that the program provided a new intellectual context for the reexamination of legal segregation.

Of the civil rights cases since 1896, *Morgan v. Virginia* (1946) stands out because it provided the context of recent civil rights acts, acts almost identical to those passed after the Civil War. In *Plessy*, Harlan's conception of segregation laws imposing a burden on citizenship comparable to slavery was transposed into a new question: does legal segregation impose an undue burden on interstate commerce? Harlan had prophetically warned in the *Civil Rights Cases* and especially in *Plessy* that the Court's rulings would "stimulate aggressions, more or less brutal and irritating, upon the admitted rights of colored citizens,...[and would] encourage the belief that it is possible, by means of State enactments, to defeat the beneficent purposes which the people of the United States had in view when they adopted the recent amendments of the Constitution."[85] State overzealousness in the construction of "separate but equal" policies and laws would, indeed, govern for several decades.

Morgan was an NAACP case argued by future Supreme Court justice Thurgood Marshall and a colleague, William Hastie. The state had passed a statute requiring all buses, both intrastate and interstate, to separate white and black passengers to prevent occupation of contiguous seats by persons of different races. This requirement was unusual because the bus driver had to literally shift and reseat the passengers every time the racial proportions of passengers changed. Such activity made for a very uncomfortable and confusing bus trip. In this case, Irene Morgan, an African American woman traveling from Hayes Store, Virginia, to Baltimore, Maryland, was ordered by the Greyhound bus driver to surrender her seat during a stop in Virginia to make room for a newly arrived white passenger. Morgan refused to move and the driver contacted a local sheriff. The lower court upheld Virginia's contention that this was a valid exercise of police power to regulate highways and carriers in order to maintain peace.[86] The case was then appealed to the Supreme Court.

Justice Stanley Reed wrote for the majority, with Justices Hugo Black and Felix Frankfurter concurring in separate opinions. Justice Harold H. Burton dissented. Reed had difficulty because the *De Cuir* case had struck down a similar state statute under the opposite conditions, but he resolved this problem by creating an abstract principle "that may be taken as a postulate for testing whether particular state legislation in the absence of action by Congress is beyond state power." The abstract principle, according to Reed, "is that the state legislation is invalid if it unduly burdens that commerce in matters where uniformity is *necessary—necessary in the constitutional sense of useful in accomplishing a permitted purpose.*"[87] Reed then compared the Virginia statute with public conveyance statutes in other states: eighteen prohibited segregation on public carriers, ten (all southern states) required it, with Alabama having a provision requiring it unless a ticket purchased in a state that prohibited racial segregation was held by a passenger traveling through Alabama.

Reed declared: "As there is no federal act dealing with the separation of races in interstate transportation, we must decide the validity of this

Virginia statute on the challenge that it interferes with commerce, as a matter of balance between the exercise of the local police power and the need for national uniformity in the regulations for interstate travel." "It seems clear to us," noted Reed, "that seating arrangements for the different races in interstate motor travel require a single, uniform rule to promote and protect national travel."[88] The Virginia statute was found unconstitutional.

Justice Burton, in dissent, raised a question of vital importance. Demonstrating that the problem was diversity of state laws that might affect interstate commerce, Burton argued, "if the mere diversity between the Virginia statute and comparable statutes of other states is so serious as to render the Virginia statute invalid, it probably means that the comparable statutes of those other states, being diverse from it and from each other, are equally invalid."[89] Burton then pointed out that the ten southern states requiring segregation were contiguous and the eighteen states prohibiting it were outside the South, therefore by implication contiguous, and he warned that the Court's findings would probably eventually require elimination of intrastate segregation on buses also. Burton closed his dissent by asserting that "it is a fundamental concept of our Constitution that where conditions are diverse the solution of problems arising out of them may well come through the application of diversified treatment matching the diversified needs as determined by our local governments. Uniformity of treatment is appropriate where a substantial uniformity of conditions exists."[90]

Clearly we see here a shift in perspective from the preservation of state's rights to the recognition of the United States as a unified nation. Commerce bound it together and had erased traditional distinctions that supported geographical divisions of sovereignty. Segregation, based in part upon the prejudices of a rural and largely isolated people, was giving way to the unity of American society. Commerce, already an expanded concept not restricted to the transportation of goods across state lines, now included the objects transported. The legal universe experienced a logic of synthesis replacing the traditional isolation of concepts. *Morgan* moved the nation further toward an acceptable concept of national citizenship.

Destruction of the "separate but equal" doctrine, however, needed a more substantial subject matter than transportation. Education supplied a context in which racial discrimination could be fully challenged because education dealt with the ultimate concept of the individual, and this aspect of the American political system had not been given an objective viewing since the formation of the republic. Lockean theory relied upon the individual; American citizenship was grounded in individualism. But the characteristics of this individual had never been adequately articulated in law; they had been assumed to exist and for nearly two centuries had been conceived only in majority terms and characteristics. Since the Declaration of Independence had posited that all men are equal, and the social contract included all men, and later all women, the law had to discover just how inclusive this belief could become. Americans needed finally to transcend their English roots and admit their actual diversity.

Eventually, four cases dealing with segregated schools in Kansas, South Carolina, Virginia, and Delaware made their way to the US Supreme Court, carefully nurtured and monitored by the NAACP Legal Defense and Educational Fund. The Kansas case, *Brown v. Board of Education of Topeka* (1954), was most critical because it involved a state statute in which segregation was permitted but not required and, most important, all the educational facilities, transportation, curricula, and educational qualifications of teachers were substantially the same.[91] The only question to be resolved was whether segregation itself was constitutional under the equal protection clause. The companion cases in the three other states involved unequal facilities in dual school systems and thus could conceivably be shunted aside with directions from the Court to equalize facilities. Argument on the cases was heard in 1952 and again in 1953, after the parties were asked to comment specifically on the historical background of the Fourteenth Amendment. On May 17, 1954, a unanimous Court released its first decision. *Brown I* unanimously held on the merits that racial segregation of public schools was unconstitutional. The Court then held four days of reargument to consider what the remedy would be. In *Brown II*,[92] the remedy arrived at by the Court a year later was that because the issue of ending segregation varied, the lower federal courts were better positioned to assure compliance. The Court ordered them to act with "all deliberate speed."[93]

In *Brown I*, Chief Justice Earl Warren, who had only recently, in 1953, assumed his position with the sudden passing of then chief justice Fred Vinson, writing for the Court, carefully sidestepped the actual historical record, and he provided a narrow interpretation of the equal protection clause of the Fourteenth Amendment. As one commentator noted, "Warren self-consciously avoided questioning the entire structure of Jim Crow in all of its applications."[94]

According to Warren, the historical circumstances surrounding the adoption and implementation of the Fourteenth Amendment in 1868 were inconclusive: "In the South," noted the chief justice, "the movement toward free common schools, supported by general taxation, had not yet taken hold. Education of white children was largely in the hands of private groups."[95] Warren added that "even in the North, the conditions of public education did not approximate those existing today. The curriculum was usually rudimentary; ungraded schools were common in rural areas; the school term was but three months a year in many states; and compulsory attendance was virtually unknown."[96] He noted that compulsory school attendance laws were not generally adopted by the states until long after the ratification of the Fourteenth Amendment; not until 1918 were such laws in force nationally.

Warren's description of contemporary education and its role in American political life was significant. "Today," the chief justice explained, "education is perhaps the most important function of state and local governments. Compulsory school attendance laws and the great expenditures for education both demonstrate our recognition of the importance of education to our democratic society." And Warren pointed out that education

> is required in the performance of our most basic public responsibilities, even service in the armed forces. It is the very foundation of good citizenship. Today it is a principal instrument in awakening the child to cultural values, in preparing him for later professional training, and in helping him to adjust normally to his environment. In these days, it is doubtful that any child may reasonably be expected to succeed in life if he is denied the opportunity of an education. Such an opportunity, where the state has undertaken to provide it, is a right which must be made available to all on equal terms.[97]

The characterization of education as the most important function of government represented an important change in perspective by the Supreme Court. No longer are we concerned with the allocation of sovereignty into geographical subdivisions and the relationships between the various levels of government. More important was the function of government itself and in this sense the jargon-free and unanimous Warren opinion went to what we have argued was the heart of the Lockean philosophy: education undergirds politics. As Baron de Montesquieu had written, "it is in a republican government that the whole power of education is required."[98] Alexis de Tocqueville put it this way:

> The first duty imposed on those who now direct society is to educate democracy; to put, if possible, new life into its beliefs; to purify its mores; to control its actions; gradually to substitute understanding of statecraft for present inexperience and knowledge of its true interests for blind instincts; to adapt government to the needs of time and place; and to modify it as men and circumstances require.[99]

Rather than stepping outside the mainstream of legal thought, the Warren opinion tamely synthesized political theory and the practical concerns of American society into a weak contemporary restatement of the meaning of national citizenship as expressed through education. *Brown I* transcended racial segregation to reach the nature of equal protection of the laws as the great principle beyond specific prejudices or beliefs.

In *Brown II*, the Court, fearing probable violence to any proposed remedy requiring busing, ignored the urging from the NAACP that desegregation proceed immediately or at least with clearly articulated timetables and instead adopted a view more in line with what the states were proposing—that desegregation proceed, if at all, at a much slower, more deliberate pace.[100] The cases were remanded to the district courts, who were ambiguously ordered to "take such proceedings and enter such orders and decrees consistent with this opinion as are necessary and proper to admit to public schools on a racially non-discriminatory basis with all deliberate speed the parties to these cases."[101]

The staggering developments following the *Brown* decisions have become embedded in the nation's social and political consciousness, for both good and ill. On the positive side, if segregation was wrong in educational institutions, it was now seen to be wrong in all other forms of public life in which the political institutions provided services and programs for all citizens. The Constitution, at least from *Brown II* until the early 1970s, had come full circle, once again color blind, but in a radically different sense than in the days of the American Revolution. Congress passed civil rights acts in 1957, 1960, 1964, 1965, 1968, and 1972, each time expressing the gradual awakening of American society to racial prejudice and the efforts of an aroused majority to prohibit institutional racism. Although these acts differed but little from the civil rights acts of a century before, the legal philosophy behind them differed in one respect—they were justified on the basis of the interstate commerce clause. African Americans thus achieved equal protection of the law in the most ironic development imaginable in political theory. Having entered the constitutional framework as quasi-property, they finally achieved full citizenship as attributes of the interstate commerce clause because discrimination against them was defined as a burden on the economic enterprise of American society.

The *Brown* rulings were also an extremely positive catalyst in that by having relied heavily on social science research on educational psychology, they showed that segregation caused a sense of inferiority among African American students that adversely affected their ability to learn. The logic of this argument dealing with the relationship between self-esteem and education would play a significant role in the discourse used by African American civil rights leaders.[102] And as John Skrentny observed: "After *Brown*, education scholars began to focus on the health of the black psyche outside of the Jim Crow south, such as in poor sections of Harlem. New interest developed in the 'cultural deprivation' of poor (usually black) children."[103] *Brown* also served as inspiration to jurists and lawyers, who paid more attention to the equal protection and due process clauses of the Fourteenth Amendment.

Another direct remedial outgrowth in the wake of the paradigm-shifting *Brown* rulings was the birth, expansion, and slow strangulation of affirmative action policies that began in the 1960s in both education and employment. These policies were an effort to address discriminatory problems by providing tangible opportunities for minority group members who historically had been denied or had profoundly limited job or educational choices.

The legal foundation of affirmative action policies traces to the Fourteenth Amendment's equal protection clause and President Franklin D. Roosevelt's Executive Order 8802, issued in 1941, stating that "there shall be no discrimination in the employment of workers in defense industries or Government because of race, creed, or national origin."[104] That order greatly increased the number of African Americans who were employed in war-related activities and also expanded the notion that government had to take a more active role in confronting institutional racism.[105]

In the 1960s, various federal agencies, in the enforcement of Title VII of the Civil Rights Act of 1964 and Executive Orders 10925 and 11246, emphatically declared that employers doing business with the federal government were prohibited from discriminating in employment because of race, class, religion, sex, or national origin and that those same employers had to act affirmatively to hire and promote qualified minorities and women.[106]

The Supreme Court, beginning in 1971, would play a powerful role that legitimated a more race-conscious approach to civil rights.[107] But in the 1978 decision *Regents of the University of California v. Bakke*,[108] when confronted with a medical school affirmative action plan that set aside 16 of the 100 places in its entering class for minority members, the Court, in a 5–4 ruling, constructed a compromise opinion that said, on the one hand, that the university's plan of action constituted an illegal quota that denied Bakke's (a white male) right not to be discriminated against because of race, but that, on the other hand, race-conscious policies, when adopted as a remedy for explicit discrimination, were still permissible, under the Constitution and the Civil Rights Act of 1964. Interestingly, the medical school's dean, who was actively involved in the suit, "intervened each year in the admissions process on behalf of the children of friends and acquaintances."[109]

After 1980, the Reagan administration engaged in a concerted assault on affirmative action programs, arguing that what it called preferential treatment for minority group members who were not themselves direct victims of discrimination constituted reverse discrimination against whites and thus was a violation of the nondiscrimination requirements of Title VII. In fact, the Equal Employment Opportunity Commission (EEOC) during the Reagan and Bush I years severely curtailed the number of class action lawsuits it filed on behalf of minority members. Instead, it focused on suits brought by individuals, which are far less effective in addressing entrenched institutional racism.[110]

Beginning with appointments made by Reagan and continuing through George W. Bush's two terms, the Supreme Court became increasingly conservative and much less willing to use race as a factor, jeopardizing some of the legal and political gains African Americans and other minorities had made via the courts. As Justice Sandra Day O'Connor wrote in 1993 in *Shaw v. Reno*,[111] a case involving majority-black electoral districts, "racial classifications with respect to voting carry particular dangers. Racial gerrymandering, even for remedial purposes may balkanize us into competing racial factions; it threatens to carry us further from the goal of a political system in which race no longer matters...It is for these reasons that race-based districting by our state legislatures demands close judicial scrutiny."[112]

A decade later, the Supreme Court handed down two major rulings on affirmative action, both involving the University of Michigan: *Gratz v. Bollinger* (2003)[113] and *Grutter v. Bollinger* (2003).[114] In *Gratz*, the Court, 6–3, invalidated the university's undergraduate affirmative action plan because it assigned numerical values to minority applicants. But in *Grutter*, the Court, by a 5–4 split, upheld the law school's plan because it focused on each individual applicant while seeking to achieve a diverse student body and end racial stereotypes. O'Connor, in the latter case, felt emboldened and went so far as to offer a specific time frame on how much longer she believed race might be used in educational admissions policies: "Twenty-five years from now," she said, "the use of racial preferences will no longer be necessary to further the interest approved today."[115]

Melanye T. Price and Gloria T. Hampton point out in a 2010 essay that while African American political and economic leaders, the black middle class, and their white allies were able to prevent the wholesale termination of affirmative action programs, the situation of working-class, poor, and incarcerated blacks, as exemplified in the devastating aftermath and lasting impact of Hurricane Katrina in New Orleans, continues to pose profound problems and does not receive nearly as much attention as the struggle of middle- and upper-class blacks.[116]

Indigenous nations, Mexican Americans, Asian Americans, women, children, and other minority groups tracked the progress of the civil rights movement, contributing their own forms of protest as the African American phase of protest slowly ebbed. While large pockets of prejudice continue to exist throughout American society, the legal universe at least has been purged of the half-articulated racist belief in the alleged inherent inferiority of African Americans. Barack Obama's election as the nation's first African American president was a telling example of how far the nation has gone toward exorcizing some of its racial demons.

CHAPTER 6
"Aliens," "Independent Peoples," or "Domestic Dependent Nations": Indigenous Nations and the Law

THE EUROPEANS' VIEW OF THE WORLD was profoundly transformed by their encounters with the peoples, lands, and resources of the Western Hemisphere. The limited geographical and historical horizons that had formed the European understanding of law and culture were expanded by contact with other peoples, and Europeans responded by trying to incorporate their experiences into a worldview that already made sense to the intellectuals, theologians, and political philosophers of the Old World. Europeans and Euro-Americans were then searching for a new ideological foundation to justify the political changes taking place in their institutional life. The major effort revolved around a system of natural law that seemed reasonable in view of the radical adjustments then occurring.

The indigenous peoples of the so-called New World, operating without literate cultures and rigidly codified laws, seemed to the Europeans to be peoples still living in a primordial state. The tendency was to describe Native peoples as examples of natural beings in an effort to demonstrate that even in early human development, certain principles of law were valid. Thus John Locke, arguing for the efficacy of natural law, referred to the Indians as persons who did not recognize the authority of others: "Those who have the supreme power of making laws in England, France, or Holland are, to an Indian, but like the rest of the world—men without authority."[1] And Baron de Montesquieu, arguing on behalf of a natural law that governed nations as well as individuals, wrote: "All countries have a law of nations, not excepting the Iroquois themselves, though they devour their prisoners: for they send and receive ambassadors, and understand the rights of war and peace. The mischief is that their law of nations is not founded on true principles."[2]

The real mischief, however, was how and why Europeans could not conceive of peoples governing themselves without formal European-styled institutions and written laws. Instead, they projected their own institutions upon the indigenous peoples' methods of resolving social and political disputes and, seeing that the processes and beliefs were not identical, convinced themselves that Native nations lived in a state of savagery and barbarism.[3] And unfortunately for the indigenous nations, Europeans understood civilization as maximizing social control over individuals rather than considering members of society so enamored with their institutions that they required a minimum of state supervision.

John Locke made Native methods of subsistence a property right within his social contract theory, contending that "the fruit, or venison, which nourishes the wild Indian, who knows no enclosure, and is still a tenant in common, must be his, and so his—i.e., a part of him, that another can no longer have any right to it before it can do him any good for the support of his life."[4] Nevertheless, Europeans were reluctant to grant that aboriginal peoples had any rights that commanded respect. The European states, all closely linked with the Christian religion, broadly respected a general theoretical agreement among themselves under which they claimed the non-Christian, that is, indigenous, lands that their explorers, missionaries, pirates, and military adventurers had allegedly discovered or "acquired ownership of land simply by exchanging other commodities and by doing physical labor on the land."[5] The land title, claimed via the doctrine of discovery, was sometimes presumed to have extinguished Native ownership, sometimes to have simply reduced said ownership, and sometimes not to have affected Native ownership at all. Most accurately, the doctrine was understood by European competitors to forbid any other nation, apart from those in a state of war, from exercising any claim in conflict with the original "discoverer" of Native-inhabited lands. It was not understood as having terminated indigenous ownership of their own territory, which had long been recognized in various treaties, laws, and proclamations.[6]

The practical application of the legal fiction of discovery theory, in this final meaning, did not work well in practice, however, and the wars for domination of northeastern North America required Europeans to form strong military and political alliances with the larger indigenous nations since no European nation could afford to transport and supply large armies for its imperialistic purposes. Thus, quite early in the settlement of the eastern seaboard, certain Native nations were recognized as the political equals of the European nations in formal treaty arrangements. The Haudenosaunee (Iroquois) formed an alliance with the English that lasted until after the War of 1812[7]; the Huron allied themselves with France during that nation's brief claim to lands in the Canadian and Mississippi valley regions[8]; and in the South there was continual intrigue between the English, Spanish, and French for the loyalties of the Cherokee, Creek, Choctaw, and Natchez. Leading figures in these Indian nations at times received military appointments from the competing nations and were paid salaries to ensure their loyalty.[9]

The formal alliances between governments were not nearly as important as the conflicts between indigenous communities and European immigrants on the frontier before the American Revolution. Here, enduring attitudes and distinct behavioral patterns formed. The conflicts usually involved direct and profound incursions of European settlements on the lifeways of the Native nations. "As soon as a European settlement forms in the neighborhood of territory occupied by the Indians," Alexis de Tocqueville observed, "the wild game takes fright. Thousands of savages wandering in the forest without fixed dwelling did not disturb it; but as soon as the continuous noise of European labor is heard in the vicinity, it begins to flee and retreat toward the west, where some instinct teaches it that it will still find limitless wilderness."[10] This disruption caused by Europeans was neither welcomed by the Native peoples, nor completely understood by them, since Natives were primarily sedentary peoples who had difficulty comprehending the stunning and devastating environmental impact that Europeans and Euro-Americans had on the natural world.

One of the pithiest assessments of indigenous peoples' attitude toward life compared to that of European immigrants was provided by Tocqueville. Although writing well after the Atlantic coastal areas had been settled by Europeans, he accurately, if ethnocentrically, described the nature of the cultural conflict:

> Gentle and hospitable in peace, in war merciless even beyond the known limits of human ferocity, the Indian would face starvation to succor the stranger who knocked in the evening on the door of his hut, but he would tear his prisoner's quivering limbs to pieces with his own hands. No famed republic of antiquity could record firmer courage, prouder spirit, or more obstinate love of freedom than lies concealed in the forests of the New World. The Europeans made but little impression when they landed on the shore of North America; they were neither feared nor envied. What hold could they have on such men? The Indian knew how to live without wants, to suffer without complaint, and to die singing.[11]

Statements such as these served to reinforce the already prevalent European attitude of indigenous peoples as "noble savages."[12] But any attitude of disdain on the part of Native peoples was nearly a fatal flaw, for it adversely affected their judgment regarding the grave threat that European migration and Euro-American settlement posed for their existence.

Some Native nations, however, were, as early as 1803, realizing how the population and property dynamics were changing in ways that did not bode well for them. President Thomas Jefferson picked up on this, evidenced when, in 1803, in a confidential message to Congress on the need to send an exploratory party to the West to scout out the area, he stated that

> the Indian tribes residing within the limits of the United States, have, for a considerable time, been growing more and more uneasy at the constant diminution of the territory they occupy, although effected by their own voluntary sales; and the policy has long been gaining strength with them, of refusing absolutely all further sale, on any conditions; insomuch that, at this time, it hazards their friendship, and excites dangerous jealousies and perturbations in their minds to make any overture for the purchase of the smallest portions of their land.[13]

Thus, while the United States during and after the Revolutionary War had explicitly recognized the political sovereignty and proprietary rights of Native nations via treaties, congressional statutes, presidential policies, and constitutional clauses, the War of 1812 and two subsequent indigenous/US conflicts—the Battle of the Thames, in 1813, and Andrew Jackson's decisive defeat of the Creek at Horseshoe Bend, in 1814—gave the United States "military supremacy over the Indian tribes from the Great Lakes to the Gulf of Mexico and from the Atlantic to the Mississippi."[14]

With the diminution of the military capability of the eastern Native nations, the federal government, and particularly the Congress, opted to reconsider its relationship to the Natives. Previously, Congress had been charged with making the necessary appropriations to carry out the federal government's treaty commitments and to enact laws, such as the Trade and Intercourse Acts, to oversee commercial relations with Native nations. But in 1819, Congress adopted a law aimed at "civilizing" Native people.[15] It was titled "An Act making provisions for the civilization of the Indian tribes adjoining the frontier settlements," and with its passage the federal government officially decided to seek the cultural transformation rather than the physical obliteration of indigenous peoples.

"There were only two roads to safety open to the North American Indians," Tocqueville would later observe, "war or civilization; in other words, they had either to destroy the Europeans or become their equals."[16] At the very earliest stage of European colonization, the indigenous nations could have easily destroyed the tiny European settlements, but they chose to offer the food and assistance necessary for European survival. Very soon it became too late to dislodge the foreigners; too many Europeans had arrived in North America to be evicted by any Indian tribe. And, like the Europeans, the Native nations were unwilling to permanently align themselves in a massive transnational organization to face their common destiny, although some regional intertribal alliances were forged that enjoyed a measure of temporary success—for example, the All Indian Pueblo Council and Tecumseh's military alliance, among others.[17]

In suggesting that Native peoples emulate the Europeans, Tocqueville was urging a course of action later adopted by the Japanese to forestall European conquest of their islands. But Indian nations were not living on islands, and thus expansion into vacant areas automatically impinged upon their independence. In addition, according to Tocqueville, "the Indians' misfortune has been to come into contact with the most civilized nation in the world, and...the greediest, at a time when they are themselves half barbarians, and to find masters in their instructors, having enlightenment and oppression brought to them together."[18]

The American Revolution proved critical to the future of indigenous nations. The Americans, seeking to secure the frontier against the combination of British regulars and their Native allies, signed several treaties with various Indian tribes that seemed favorably inclined toward their cause.[19] These treaties were approved by the Continental Congress and established the precedent of dealing with Native nations on a formal contractual basis, complete with sonorous documents that promised services in return for military assistance and the cession of lands. The British insisted that the Americans treat the Indian tribes as political entities fully capable of exercising European-style powers of self-government. Even at the Treaty of Paris, which closed the war, England sought a provision that would have established an Indian buffer state between the newly independent colonies and their possessions in Canada. Not until the Treaty of Ghent, in 1815, did the British reluctantly surrender this strategy for containing the Americans.

Native peoples also figured prominently in several of the points of controversy aired in *The Federalist Papers*. Arguing for a strong federal government, John Jay wrote that "not a single Indian war has yet been produced by aggressions of the present federal government, feeble as it is; but there are several instances of Indian hostilities having been provoked by the improper conduct of individual States, who, either unable or unwilling to restrain or punish offences, have given occasion to the slaughter of many innocent inhabitants."[20] Americans would always characterize their losses as "slaughtered innocents" as a means of justifying the continual intrusion by white settlers onto Native lands. Beneath this self-serving rhetoric, however, lay an unresolved problem, one that has yet to be settled definitively. The geographical division of sovereignty between the states and federal government meant, in practical terms, exploitation of the Native nations by state governments until such time as the federal government felt impelled to intervene. James Madison tried to explain how conflicting claims of sovereignty would operate with respect to commerce but utterly failed to anticipate how complicated the matter would become. Madison observed:

> The regulation of commerce with the Indian tribes is very properly unfettered from two limitations in the Articles of Confederation, which render the provision obscure and contradictory. The power is there restrained to Indians, not members of any of the States, and is not to violate or infringe the legislative right of any State within its own limits. *What description of Indians are to be deemed members of a State, is not yet settled, and has been a question of frequent perplexity and contention in the federal councils.*[21]

Not only had the Constitutional Convention failed to resolve this question, but, according to Madison, they had a difficult time properly phrasing the nature of the dispute: "And how the trade with Indians, though not members of a State, yet residing within its legislative jurisdiction can be regulated by an external authority, without so far intruding on the internal rights of legislation, is absolutely incomprehensible."[22]

The resolution of this problem was, of course, already partially solved in the precedent of ratifying treaties with the Indian nations that foreclosed any state action dealing with Indians. Alexander Hamilton outlined the status of treaties that the United States entered into with other polities, and this definition seemed clear and satisfactory, at least with respect to eliminating the diversity of jurisdiction that would occur if each state were allowed its option in upholding the treaty: "The treaties of the United States, to have any force at all, must be considered as part of the law of the land. Their true import, as far as respects individuals, must, like all other laws, be ascertained by judicial determinations. To produce uniformity in these determinations, they ought to be submitted, in the last resort, to one SUPREME TRIBUNAL."[23]

But Hamilton was worried, and with good cause, about the distinctions that might be made between the interpretation of treaties and the laws of the states conflicting with them. "So great a proportion of the cases in which foreigners are parties involve national questions," Hamilton wrote, "that it is by far most safe and most expedient to refer all those in which they are concerned to the national tribunals."[24]

A question never satisfactorily answered concerned the application of state laws to Native nations who were in a treaty relationship with the United States. Presumably, if Indian treaties were of similar legal stature as foreign treaties, the Native nations were entitled to the same respect. John Jay, too, recognized that the states suspected the constitutional provision that made treaties the supreme law of the land. "They [the states] insisted," Jay wrote,

> and profess to believe, that treaties, like acts of assembly, should be repealable at pleasure. This idea seems to be new and peculiar to this country, but new errors, as well as new truths, often appear. These gentlemen would do well to reflect that a treaty is only another name for a bargain, and that it would be impossible to find a nation who would make any bargain with us, which should be binding on them *absolutely*, but on us only so long and so far as we may think proper to be bound by it.[25]

This attitude toward treaties was never put to rest in favor of a lofty stance upholding national commitments that, when applied to Indian treaties, proved disastrous.

"Though a wide ocean separates the United States from Europe," Hamilton wrote, "yet there are various considerations that warn us against an excess of confidence or security." He outlined the claims of England and Spain that encircled the United States on all sides, and although the Native peoples were not yet perceived at the same threat level to the Americans, Hamilton accurately predicted that conflict was inevitable. "The savage tribes on our Western frontier ought to be regarded as our natural enemies, their natural allies, because they have most to fear from us, and most to hope from them."[26]

The new federal Constitution, adopted in 1789, contained four clauses that directly implicated the indigenous/United States relationship: (1) Article 1, section 1, clause 3, mentions "Indians not taxed" in connection with the method of figuring representation and direct taxes (this phrase was later repeated in section 2 of the Fourteenth Amendment, which changed the formula to reflect African American citizenship); (2) Article 1, section 8, clause 3 gave Congress the power "to regulate Commerce with foreign Nations, and among the several States, and with the Indian tribes"; (3) Article 4, section 3, clause 2, declares that "the Congress shall have Power to dispose of and make all needful Rules and Regulations respecting the Territory or other Property belonging to the United States"; and (4) Article 6, section 2, states that "all Treaties made, or which shall be made, under the Authority of the United States, shall be the Supreme Law of the land; and the judges in every State shall be bound thereby."

These clauses affirmed that the national government—and Congress in particular—had exclusive authority to deal with indigenous nations in regard to issues of representation, trade and intercourse, diplomacy, and land issues. While each would prove significant, the commerce clause was the only source of explicit power claimed by the federal government. In theory, this clause should not have extended to Congress any greater authority over Native nations than it exercises over states. In both historical and contemporary practice, however, such has not been the case. As indigenous dominion waned during the course of the nineteenth and early twentieth centuries, the federal government used the commerce clause (and other self-generated powers) to justify many new assertions of national authority over Native peoples.

Along with the commerce clause, the property clause and the claims of the United States to North American lands would also prove pivotal. Although it rarely plays a major role in congressional decisions or federal court rulings when indigenous issues are being addressed, an analysis of critical Supreme Court opinions suggests that the property clause, "and/ or the fact of American claims to legal title to lands in North America under the doctrine of discovery, plays an important part in determining the posture and actions of the United States toward Indians."[27] The critically important case of *Johnson v. McIntosh*, handed down in 1823, gave the Court its first opportunity to define the federal government's claims to land historically owned by Native nations.[28]

In *McIntosh*, the Court institutionalized a revised doctrine of discovery and engaged in a convoluted discussion of the doctrine of conquest. The results were oppressive to the sovereignty and proprietary rights of indigenous nations. According to Chief Justice John Marshall, not only had the discoverer gained the exclusive right to appropriate Native lands, but the tribes' sovereign rights were diminished and their right to sell land to whomever they wished was fatally compromised. Marshall acknowledged that both the discovery and conquest doctrines were self-serving, yet relied on them nonetheless. "However extravagant the pretension of converting the discovery of an inhabited country into conquest may appear," he asserted, "if the principle has been asserted in the first instance, and afterwards, sustained; if a country has been acquired and held under it; if the property of the great mass of the community originates in it, it becomes the law of the land, and cannot be questioned."[29]

The Court transformed these extravagant theories into legal terms for largely political and economic reasons: increasing indigenous resistance to land loss, uncertainty over what Spain's, France's, and Russia's long-term intentions were on the continent, and its own desire to formulate a uniform American law of real property. Marshall himself had a keen interest in seeing this case through to the conclusions that were reached. Lindsay Robertson's book *Conquest by Law* reveals that Marshall's primary rationale for redefining the discovery doctrine was not so much to forever disregard the land rights of Native peoples, but to shore up institutional and state support for the high court and, more importantly, to clear the way for Virginia's Revolutionary War veterans to secure land grants they had been promised in western Kentucky.[30]

Still, although it denied that indigenous nations could alienate their lands to whomever they wished, the Court conceded that Natives retained a right of perpetual occupancy that the United States had to recognize. It also determined that the federal government had to secure Indian consent before it could extinguish Indian occupancy title. In these respects, the Court displayed a desire to adhere to, at least in theory, just and humane standards that recognized the prior existence and a measure of their property rights title, even as it embraced the racist and ethnocentric view of the technological and proprietary superiority of western nations.

No further conflict of as great a magnitude occurred until the late 1820s, when the state of Georgia, impatient with the pace at which the United States was extinguishing the Cherokee Nation's title to lands within Georgia's demarcated borders, took things into its own hands and precipitated what became a national political crisis.[31]

The Cherokee had a long series of treaties with England and the United States that guaranteed the right of self-government and political independence to their nation, beginning with a treaty in 1719 specifically outlining the borders of Cherokee lands. In 1802, as part of the series of compromises that states made with the federal government to fund Revolutionary War debts through selling western lands, Georgia ceded to the United States a large amount of land it claimed that lay within its original borders. Georgia expected the United States in return would extinguish the Indian title to lands lying within the state's new borders. As political pressure increased, George Washington, John Adams, and James Monroe refused to force the Cherokee to cede their aboriginal and treaty-recognized lands, Washington going so far as to threaten to call out military troops to protect the Cherokee. Georgia fluctuated between wanting the Cherokee lands and demanding that the federal government enforce the tribal boundary provisions. On the nineteenth of November, 1814, the following resolution was adopted by the Georgia legislature:

> Whereas, many of the citizens of this state, without regard to existing treaties between the friendly Indians and the United States, and contrary to the interest and good policy of this state, have gone, and are frequently going over, and settling and cultivating the lands allotted to the friendly Indians for their hunting ground, by which means the state is not only deprived of their services in the army, but considerable feuds are engendered between us and our friendly neighbouring Indians:
>
> Resolved, therefore by the Senate and House of Representatives of the state of Georgia in general assembly met, that his excellency, the governor, be, and is hereby requested to take the necessary means to have all intruders removed off the Indian lands, and that proper steps be taken to prevent future aggressions.[32]

The Georgians, it seemed, in 1814 wanted a peaceful relationship with the Cherokee through the enforcement of the treaty provisions. But as the Cherokee Nation continued their cultural, political, and legal evolution—incorporating elements of western law into their own, developing a written language, crafting a formal constitution modeled loosely after the federal constitution, and in 1827 formally announcing their political independence—these developments, combined with the discovery of that most precious of metals, gold, on Cherokee lands, compelled Georgia's lawmakers to act.

Beginning in 1828, the state's legislature passed a series of acts annexing Cherokee lands to certain counties, extending state civil and criminal laws over the Cherokee, annulling Cherokee laws, prohibiting the Cherokee from appearing as witnesses in state courts, and providing for surveying Cherokee lands. The Cherokee Nation's leadership appealed directly to the US Supreme Court, their diplomatic partners, for an injunction restraining the state. As they drew up their complaint, Georgia convicted and executed a Cherokee named George Tassels under the new laws.[33] Georgia refused to file an answer to the Cherokee's complaint and refused to appear in court, emphatically declaring that it would not be bound by an adverse decision. It was generally known that President Andrew Jackson supported the removal of eastern Native peoples to lands west of the Mississippi. The Court's decision, *Cherokee Nation v. Georgia*, handed down in 1831, held on procedural grounds that since the Cherokee were neither a state or a foreign nation within the meaning of the federal constitution, they had no right to file a petition directly to the Supreme Court and their suit was dismissed.[34]

But rather than end the case there, the chief justice, John Marshall, who astutely sought to avoid a direct confrontation with Georgia and President Jackson, went to considerable lengths to spell out the political relationship between Native nations and the federal government.

In outlining the Cherokee case as presented to the Court, Marshall isolated two aspects of the problem that had a material impact on an understanding of the issues. The chief justice outlined the Cherokee record of acculturation, which should have been sufficient to sustain their cause had Tocqueville's analysis of the "two roads" open to Indians been correct:

> They have established a constitution and form of government, the leading features of which they have borrowed from that of the United States; dividing their government into three separate departments,

legislative, executive and judicial. In conformity with this constitution, these departments have all been organized. They have formed a code of laws, civil and criminal, adapted to their situation; have erected Courts to expound and apply those laws, and organized an executive to carry them into effect. They have established schools for the education of their children, and churches in which the Christian religion is taught; they have abandoned the hunter state, and become agriculturists, mechanics, and herdsmen; and, under provocations long continued and hard to be borne, they have observed, with fidelity, all their engagements by treaty with the United States.[35]

This indisputable transformation from a hunting economy to a European inspired lifestyle, however, was not considered sufficient by the majority on the Court to protect the legal rights of the Cherokee. The conflict between Native nations and the United States was not one over cultural similarity or homogeneity, but involved a deeper, far less clear, largely unstated complex of beliefs and emotions.

The original European and Euro-American claim to Cherokee lands rested upon the assertion by Christian monarchs that "pagans" could not hold valid title to land in a world dominated, or intended to be dominated, by those who adhered to or operated under the banner of the Christian religion. No argument was made by the Cherokee that, having adopted the religion of the foreigner, they had entered the family of Christian nations and were entitled to the respect and protection of the larger nations. The Cherokee relied upon federally sanctioned and Senate-ratified treaty guarantees made by the United States, and this placed the issue of federal-state relations directly before the Court. Without realizing it, the Cherokee had inadvertently intruded upon the one area—intergovernmental dynamics—that could not be satisfactorily resolved by the Americans then or in succeeding generations.

Marshall reviewed the tactics of the state of Georgia that had forced the Cherokee to sue in the Supreme Court as the court of original jurisdiction:

While these laws are enforced in a manner the most harassing and vexatious to your complainants, the design seems to have been deliberately formed to carry no one of these cases to final decision in the state Courts; with the view, as the complainants believe and therefore allege, to prevent any one of the Cherokee defendants from carrying those cases to the Supreme Court of the United States, by writ of error for review, under the twenty-fifth section of the act of Congress of the United States, passed in the year 1789, and entitled 'an act to establish the judicial Courts of the United States.'[36]

This practice of arresting and harassing Indians under the color of law but dropping the case, or shifting the charges to unrelated crimes that avoided the federal question, began with the Cherokee but was adopted by nearly all states as a method to nullify federal protections guaranteed to Native individuals. State courts, especially those in the South, became politicized against the continuation of tribal existence, and the geographical allocation of sovereignty meant that indigenous peoples fell between the cracks in the constitutional edifice. Consequently, few landmark cases were produced dealing with the status of Indians.

"The Indian territory is admitted to compose a part of the United States," Marshall began his opinion. "In all our maps, geographical treatises, histories, and laws, it is so considered. In all our intercourse with foreign nations, in our commercial regulations, in any attempt at intercourse between Indians and foreign nations, they are considered as within the jurisdictional limits of the United States, subject to many of those restraints which are imposed on our own citizens."[37] While this evidence was generally accurate, it more directly reflected the attitude of the United States toward any foreign efforts to retain or regain a foothold on the North American continent, not a reasoned position adopted by mutual consent as a result of the various treaty negotiations between the United States and Native nations. Marshall at this time cleverly avoided describing the actual political relationship that had been developed by the mutual agreement of the Cherokee Nation and the United States.

One of Marshall's principal tasks was to eliminate any conception of the Cherokee as a foreign nation because foreign nations are authorized under the Constitution to appeal directly to the Supreme Court. To accomplish this, he constructed a set of terms that have plagued legal scholars and Native peoples ever since. Native nations, declared Marshall, "may, more correctly, perhaps, be denominated domestic dependent nations." "They occupy a territory to which we assert a title independent of their will, which must take effect in point of possession when their right of possession ceases. Meanwhile they are in a state of pupilage. Their relation to the United States resembles that of a ward to his guardian."[38] It is important to note that Marshall did not say that the relationship *was* that of a guardian to a ward—only that it *resembled* that arrangement. Marshall was presuming that there would be a time when one of two things would occur: (1) Native peoples would become so acculturated in the ways of civilized nations that they would become fully capable of exercising political powers and thus joining the family of nations, or (2) the United States would confirm the Cherokee title to lands forfeiting its claim which existed independent of the will of the Cherokee.

Moving to an interpretation of the commerce clause, Marshall wrote that Indian nations were clearly distinguishable both from foreign nations and from the states of the Union. "They are designated by a distinct appellation; and as this appellation can be applied to neither of the others, neither can the appellation distinguishing either of the others be in fair construction applied to them. The objects, to which the power of regulating commerce might be directed, are divided into three distinct classes—foreign nations, the several states, and Indian tribes."[39] Although this interpretation at first glance appears self-explanatory, it is still somewhat vague. The federal government did not, in fact, regulate the commerce of foreign nations or the several states but instead oversaw commerce *with* these other polities. Thus a proper interpretation, if Marshall's thinking was to be consistent, would have been to recognize that the federal government regulated its own citizens in their trade and commercial dealings with Native peoples, not the Indians in their trade with American citizens.

A final pivotal comment in the chief justice's opinion completed the refusal to admit indigenous rights into the constitutional framework. "The bill requires us to control the legislature of Georgia," he suggested, "and to restrain the exertion of its physical force. The propriety of such an interposition by the Court may well be questioned. *It savours too much of the exercise of political power to be within the proper province of the judicial department.*"[40] Here Marshall was clearly wrong. A few decades before, to allow Dartmouth College to maintain its corporate status, the Court, under Marshall, had nullified acts by the New Hampshire legislature. New Hampshire's officers had clearly confiscated the books and property of Dartmouth, perhaps not with Georgia's violent force against the Cherokee, but with no less effect. Later cases would continue the power of the Supreme Court to nullify and control the acts of state legislatures. The characterization of the relief needed by the Cherokee as an "exercise of political powers" was simply not true.

What Marshall nervously anticipated, although he craftily disguised it, was that the heightened tension between the national government and the states, and between the executive branch and the judiciary, would probably have erupted if the Supreme Court had openly supported the Cherokee. There is a radical difference between the exercise of political power and an articulation of the laws that is fraught with political consequences. Marshall deliberately obscured this difference and subsequent generations of judges and justices, caught between upholding federal treaty rights and the unpleasant political consequences in the eastern states, but especially in the western states, where most reservations would later be located, followed Marshall's example. Of all the ethnic groups we examine, Native nations and their frequently complicated issues more often become political questions whenever the federal courts are forced to decide controversial questions. Once so declared, the courts can then choose to not hear the dispute, thereby denying indigenous peoples an opportunity to secure justice in judicial proceedings.[41]

The justices in *Cherokee Nation* were hard-pressed to distinguish the Cherokee from other existing small nations who enjoyed a protectorate status with respect to a larger nation. Arguing against recognition of the Cherokee as a foreign nation, Justice William Johnson worried that "the Catawbas, having indeed a few more acres than the republic of San Marino, but consisting only of eighty or a hundred polls, would then be admitted to the same dignity" as smaller European nations. "They still claim independence, and actually execute their own penal laws, such as they are even to the punishment of death; and have recently done so," Johnson remarked. "We have many ancient treaties with them," he continued, "and no nation has been more distinctly recognized, as far as such recognition can operate to communicate the character of a state."[42] There was no question about an Indian tribe being a state in the generic sense of that word. The question revolved about the exact status of an Indian nation and when it could be expected to assume the full political status worthy of respect by the United States and other nations. "They have in Europe sovereign and demi-sovereign states," Johnson admitted, "and states of doubtful sovereignty. But this state [the Cherokee community], if it be a state, is still a grade below them all: for not to be able to alienate without permission of the remainder-man or lord, places them in a state of feudal dependence."[43]

Therein lay the fallacy. Indigenous nations very well could have alienated their lands to any foreign nation they chose. The problem, which everyone recognized, was that few foreign nations at that point were adventurous enough to undertake dealing with the Native nations, an endeavor that most certainly would have led to war with the United States.[44] Legally, however, there was no international law that placed Indian title in a feudalistic property status with a remainder-man interest vested in the United States. Because the variety of legal concepts available were so sparse, Johnson's analogy was the best the Court could devise. Yet Johnson's characterization of the Cherokee's political status conflicted directly with his analysis of their land title. "Their condition is something like that of the Israelites, when inhabiting the deserts," he argued, explaining that:

> Though without land that they can call theirs in the sense of property, their right of personal self government has never been taken from them; and such a form of government may exist though the land occupied be in fact that of another. The right to expel them may exist in that other, but the alternative of departing and retaining the right of self government may exist in them. And such they certainly do possess; it has never been questioned, nor any attempt made at subjugating them as a people, or restraining their personal liberty except as to their land and trade.[45]

The comparison with the ancient Israelites hinted that should the Cherokee exercise their right to migrate from their ancestral lands, they would achieve a higher political status, presumably, because they could secure better title to new lands and a firmer claim to nationhood by moving apart from the United States.

Justice Johnson treated the political question with more sophistication than had Marshall: "The United States finding themselves involved in conflicting treaties, or at least in two treaties respecting the same property, under which two parties assert conflicting claims; one of the parties, putting itself upon its sovereign right, passes laws which in effect declare the laws and treaties under which the other party claims, null and void."[46] No relief could be given, according to Johnson, if the judicial and executive branches of the United States found that a solution would create incalculable evils for all concerned. This interpretation depended on conceiving the federal-state relationship as distinct rather than intimate. But it established the United States and Georgia, and the treaty with the Cherokee, as equal in importance. Importantly, Johnson's explanation rose above the simple declaration that the question was political and not within the province of the Court.

Justice William Thompson wrote the dissenting opinion, joined by Justice Joseph Story. Thompson moved directly to the definition of what constitutes a nation in traditional usage. "Every nation that governs itself, under what form soever, without any dependence on a foreign power, is a sovereign state," Thompson argued. He sought to confine the discussion of political status to the exercise of internal sovereignty, that is to say, police powers and the consent of the governed. "We ought, therefore, to reckon in the number of sovereigns those states that have bound themselves to another more powerful, although by an unequal alliance. The conditions of these unequal alliances may be infinitely varied," Thompson pointed out, "but whatever they are, provided the inferior ally reserves to itself the sovereignty or the right to govern its own body, it ought to be considered an independent state."[47] Here, Thompson took Johnson's inadequately articulated argument regarding Cherokee land title to its logical conclusion:

> Consequently, a weak state, that, in order to provide for its safety, places itself under the protection of a more powerful one, without stripping itself of the right of government and sovereignty, does not cease on this account to be placed among the sovereigns who acknowledge no other power. Tributary and feudatory states do not thereby cease to be sovereign and independent states, so long as self government, and sovereign and independent authority is left in the administration of the state.[48]

The Cherokee, in the dissenters' view, therefore, were a protected nation, foreign in sufficient aspects that the Supreme Court, had it adopted their argument, should have heard the case.

Thompson concentrated on the majority's requirements for determining the foreign nature of the Cherokee. "The progress made in civilization by the Cherokee Indians cannot surely be considered as in any measure destroying their national or foreign character, so long as they are permitted to maintain a separate and distinct government; it is their political condition that constitutes their *foreign* character."[49] He continued by adding that "in that sense must the term *foreign* be understood as used in the constitution. It can have no relation to local, geographical, or territorial position," thereby refuting Marshall's contention that Cherokee national status was determined by boundaries on US maps. "It cannot mean a country beyond sea. Mexico or Canada is certainly to be considered a foreign country, in reference to the United States. It is the political relation in which one government or country stands to another, which constitutes it foreign to the other."[50]

Whereas the majority avoided the treaty issue, there being little grounds to deny the Cherokee's substantial rights under properly ratified treaties, Thompson cited the treaties as made in good faith and as indicating that the United States considered the Cherokee of sufficient political status, a people capable of securing treaties and bargains for themselves. "The treaties made with this nation purport to secure to it certain rights. These are not gratuitous obligations assumed on the part of the United States. They are obligations founded upon a consideration paid by the Indians by cession of part of their territory."[51] It would be strange to say, he thought, that the Cherokee Nation could make a bargain but was incapable of enforcing it. "What is a treaty as understood in the law of nations?" Thompson inquired: "It is an agreement or contract between two or more nations or sovereigns, entered into by agents appointed for that purpose, and duly sanctioned by the supreme power of the respective parties."[52] "And where," he demanded to know, "is the authority, either in the constitution or in the practice of the government, for making any distinction between treaties made with the Indian nations and any other foreign power?"[53]

There were no answers to Thompson's questions. The majority had deftly sidestepped the major issues, dwelt on the technicality of legal standing, and hoped that they could abort the real controversy until it was too late for the Court to be drawn further into the conflict. Thompson, however, pointed out the obvious: "Other departments of the government, whose right it is to decide what powers shall be recognized as sovereign and independent nations, have treated this nation as such. They have considered it competent, in its political and national capacity, to enter into contracts of the most solemn character; and if these contracts contain matter proper for judicial inquiry, why should we refuse to entertain jurisdiction of the case?"[54] He faced directly the responsibility of the Court to resolve treaty cases, and he concluded that jurisdiction should have been taken in the case.

Still, the Cherokee lost. The Supreme Court hoped that it had seen the last of this controversy, but its decision only agitated both parties. Georgia passed more statutes repressing the Cherokee. The Cherokee gained courageous allies in missionaries Elizur Butler, Samuel Worcester, James Trott,

Samuel Mays, Surry Eaton, Austin Copeland, and Edward D. Losure. These men boldly entered the Cherokee Nation, placed themselves under both Cherokee and federal laws, and defied the oath of allegiance that Georgia required of all white men. Convicted of violating the Georgia law, the missionaries were arrested, tried, and sentenced to four years hard labor in the state penitentiary. They appealed on writ of error to the Supreme Court. The controversy was now a national scandal, virtually compelling the Court to grant the writ. John Marshall now applied himself once more to the question of Indian treaties and to describing the relationship between Native nations and states.

Most scholars and judges, when attempting to describe the political status of Indian tribes, rely heavily upon Marshall's characterization of indigenous in *Cherokee Nation* as domestic dependent nations and emphasize his guardian-ward analogy, though the analogy is often wrongly treated as if it formally established a wardship status for Indian nations. Too often they treat the subsequent *Worcester v. Georgia* (1832) decision as if it existed in a vacuum, unrelated to the Cherokee controversy. But the Court had little choice except to try to clarify the convoluted phrases of *Cherokee Nation* and directly confront the problems created by Georgia's actions. Thus, *Worcester* is Marshall's most impressive and most historically verifiable statement on the political status of indigenous nations, a decision that more accurately depicted the actual political and legal status of the Cherokee Nation and more clearly described the intergovernmental relationship between Native nations and the federal and state governments.

Marshall began by reviewing the history of European-indigenous relations. He saw that the particular relationship enjoyed by each Native nation depended upon which European nation the Native community had been primarily associated with, and he concluded that "the United States succeeded to all the claims of Great Britain, both territorial and political," but remarked that "no attempt, so far as is known, has been made to enlarge them."[55] Marshall reduced the "extravagant and pretentious" claims made by the United States under the very doctrine, discovery, that he himself had utilized in the *McIntosh* ruling in 1823. In the present case, he more honestly described the doctrine's proper scope by examining the colonial charters based upon the doctrine:

> The first of these charters was made before possession was taken of any part of the country. They purport, generally, to convey the soil, from

the Atlantic to the South Sea. This soil was occupied by numerous and warlike nations, equally willing and able to defend their possessions. The extravagant and absurd idea, that the feeble settlements made on the seacoast, or the companies under whom they were made, acquired legitimate power by them to govern the people, or occupy the lands from sea to sea, did not enter the mind of any man.[56]

The charters, Marshall said, "were well understood to convey the title which, according to the common law of European sovereigns respecting America, they might rightfully convey, and no more. This was the exclusive right of purchasing such lands as the natives were willing to sell."[57] Here is a far more realistic interpretation of the doctrine of discovery that reflects mercantile nations attempting to regulate competition, rather than the ludicrous claims of absolute land title that latter jurists, settlers, and state officials attributed to it. If Marshall's interpretation of the discovery doctrine was sound, then his conclusion was logical: "the crown could not be understood to grant what the crown did not affect to claim; nor was it so understood."[58] This dispelled Georgia's claims regarding Cherokee lands under the agreement of 1802, which failed to consider prior treaty obligations, ignored Cherokee sovereignty, and denied aboriginal land title.

With respect to the series of treaties between the Cherokee and the United States, again Marshall brought a historical perspective to bear. "During the war of the Revolution," he reminded his brethren on the Court, "the Cherokees took part with the British. After its termination, the United States, though desirous of peace, did not feel its necessity so strongly as while the war continued. Their political situation being changed, they might very well think it advisable to assume a higher tone, and to impress on the Cherokees the same respect for Congress which was before felt for the King of Great Britain. This may account for the language of the Treaty of Hopewell."[59] He added that the Cherokee had not traveled to New York to sign the treaty; the Americans had opted to journey to Hopewell, the Cherokee homeland. The motivation of the Indians in signing treaties with Great Britain and the United States, according to Marshall, was the promise of protection by both countries from the senseless and treaty-violating provocations by the settlers and state officials.

"Protection," Marshall declared, "does not imply the destruction of the protected."[60] Marshall, then, rejected as a surrender by the Indians of the right of self-government. "The great subject of the article is the Indian trade," he maintained. "The influence it gave, made it desirable that Congress should possess it. The commissioners brought forward the claim, with the profession that their motive was 'the benefit and comfort of the Indians, and the prevention of injuries or oppressions.'"[61] Marshall could no longer suppose that the Cherokee had surrendered self-government by casually admitting a nebulous phrase into one treaty. He had, in fact, jettisoned his original views on the political status of Indians. Rather, he adopted Justice Thompson's dissenting opinion in *Cherokee Nation*, which he had urged his associate to write.

Marshall then outlined, step by step, the political status of Native nations in relation to the federal government as derived from treaties:

> From the commencement of our government, Congress has passed acts to regulate trade and intercourse with the Indians; which treat them as nations, respect their rights, and manifest a firm purpose to afford that protection which treaties stipulate. All these acts, and especially that of 1802, which is still in force, manifestly consider the several Indian nations as distinct political communities, having territorial boundaries, within which their authority is exclusive, and having a right to all the lands within those boundaries, which is not only acknowledged, but guarantied by the United States.[62]

Furthermore, Marshall declared: "The treaties and laws of the United States contemplate the Indian territory as completely separated from that of the States; and provide that all intercourse with them shall be carried on exclusively by the government of the Union."[63] Finally, the chief justice concluded:

> The Indian nations had always been considered as distinct, independent political communities, retaining their original natural rights, as the undisputed possessors of the soil, from time immemorial, with the single exception of that imposed by irresistible power, which excluded them from intercourse with any other European potentate than the first discoverer of the coast of the particular region claimed: and this was a restriction which those European potentates imposed on themselves, as well as on the Indians. The very term 'nation' so generally applied to them, means a people distinct from others.' The Constitution, by declaring treaties already made, as well as those to be made, to be the

supreme law of the land, has adopted and sanctioned the previous treaties with the Indian nations, and consequently admits their rank among
those powers who are capable of making treaties. The words 'treaty'
and 'nation' are words of our own language, selected in our diplomatic
and legislative proceedings by ourselves, having each a definite and well
understood meaning. We have applied them to Indians, as we have
applied them to the other nations of the earth. They are applied to all
in the same sense.[64]

Two comments can be made regarding Marshall's conclusions. First, he
implied that the Europeans had restricted themselves as much as they had
restricted the Indians. The Europeans, through discovery, claimed only the
preemptive right to first purchase of lands, not the extinguishment of Native
proprietary rights or the diminution of the national status of Native nations
and their inherent right of self-government. Second, Marshall understood
that the technical vocabulary used by the Court and US policy makers had
originated in federal law and was not of indigenous origin. Thus *treaty* and
nation have definite meanings fixed by the United States. The Cherokee
insistence that their nation qualified as a nation under a protectorate status
is not an indigenous interpretation but derives from common usage by the
United States. The concepts, therefore, are definite, of American origin, and
legally and morally bind the United States to a specific performance of self-
imposed obligations.

Justice Thompson, his previous dissenting theories having been
adopted by Marshall, did not file a separate concurring opinion. Justice
John McLean, apparently converted to the protectorate theory, added some
important considerations in a concurring opinion. "Every State is more or
less dependent on those which surround it," McLean wrote, "but, unless
this dependence shall extend so far as to merge the political existence of
the protected people into that of their protectors, they may still constitute
a state. They may exercise the powers not relinquished, and bind themselves as a distinct and separate community."[65] McLean followed Marshall,
insisting that historical precedents had obligated the United States, and that
"the inquiry is not, what station shall now be given to the Indian tribes in
our country? but, what relation have they sustained to us, since the com-
mencement of our government?"[66] Implicit in McLean's comments were the
legal recognition of Indian treaties and the separation of Native peoples

as distinct, self-governing political communities. The indigenous nations' relationship to the United States depends entirely on the exercise of constitutional powers by the federal government, yet they are not within the constitutional limitations and protections that define American citizenship.

McLean emphasized two aspects of indigenous status undeveloped by the other justices. First, he distinguished between the treatment of Indians and relations with foreign nations under the commerce clause: "In the regulation of commerce with the Indians, Congress have exercised a more limited power than has been exercised in reference to foreign countries. The law acts upon our own citizens, and not upon the Indians, the same as the law referred to act upon our own citizens in their foreign commercial intercourse."[67] This difference limits the power of Congress to those duties specifically associated with commerce and to the fulfillment of express treaty provisions that require congressional action.

Second, he articulated an interpretive framework, later known as the canons of treaty construction, to support Native interpretations of treaty language because of the evident language barriers indigenous negotiators faced in their parlays with Europeans and Americans. In McLean's words:

> The language used in treaties with the Indians should never be construed to their prejudice. If words be made use of which are susceptible of a more extended meaning than their plain import, as connected with the tenor of the treaty, they should be considered as used only in the latter sense. To contend that the word 'allotted,' in reference to the land guarantied to the Indians in certain treaties, indicates a favor conferred rather than a right acknowledged, would, it would seem to me, do injustice to the understanding of the parties. How the words of the treaty were understood by this unlettered people, rather than their critical meaning, should form the rule of construction.[68]

Subsequent courts misunderstood, in some cases completely ignored, McLean's rule of interpretation, giving to treaties a meaning that made sense to them but that, placed in historical context, distorted the political arrangements negotiated between Native nations and the United States. Nevertheless, nearly every court, in attempting to decide a Native case dealing with treaties, has at one time or another referred to McLean's principle as the rule governing their reading of confusing language.

The Cherokee cases, when combined with *McIntosh*, present an ambiguous set of concepts regarding the legal status of indigenous nations and their individual citizens. As long as Native communities retained identifiable, distinct cultural patterns, the various and somewhat contradictory doctrines enunciated by John Marshall—tribal nations are viewed as both domestic dependent nations and distinct independent political communities—held. But unimaginable changes were rapidly occurring. The manner in which Native peoples responded to the ever-increasing and soon overwhelming settlement patterns of whites made it difficult to continue to envision indigenous nations as separate political communities indefinitely. Only those nations capable of offering effective military resistance against the United States obtained favorable treaty provisions—provisions, nevertheless, that were often broken as soon as a tribal nation surrendered its arms. The constitutional linguistic confusion that described Native peoples in both corporate and individual capacities had not been resolved by these early Supreme Court cases, and American jurisprudence responded to Marshall's decisions with confusion, selectively choosing those aspects and doctrines that suited their own personal and institutional agendas. Many judges and justices, both federal and state, read the guardian-ward analogy literally, seeing in indigenous cultures no objectified values. The courts developed and adhered to the racist and ethnocentric notion that Indian wards, when depicted as being in a state of domestic dependency, needed constant federal supervision in their quest to achieve civilized behavior.

After these decisions, two major strands of interpretation intertwined, and it is important at this point to trace each theory separately before we consider them together in an analysis of the present status of Native nations and tribal citizens. Federal policy in the decades after removal of the majority of eastern Native peoples in the 1830s and 1840s fluctuated dramatically between (1) recognizing the political identity of the Native nations through treaties and (2) disaggregating Native lands in an effort to destroy indigenous culture and identity. In the century-long battle over the political identity of Native nations, non-Indians continued and even expanded their parochial attitudes about culture and refused to acknowledge the validity of nonliterature, customary cultural traditions. At the same time, Native legal rights were determined on the basis of immediate conditions, to the neglect of historical antecedents that had created problems that federal policy was supposedly designed to solve.

A People Distinct from Others

Although the Supreme Court, in the three early Marshall opinions, had used the protected nation idea to describe the status of Indian tribes, the practical application of this concept proved nearly impossible. In Europe, where geographical boundaries, political institutions, laws, and ruling families had been established for centuries despite wars of dynastic succession that devastated the continent for centuries, there was never any question about the status of governments. In the case of small duchies and principalities such as those in Germany and Italy, the protectorate status was understood by Europeans, and violations of protectorates would likely involve the errant nation in conflict. Statesmen jealously guarded their alliances large and small.

North America, on the other hand, presented a wide variety of indigenous political institutions making consistency in federal law and policy difficult to sustain. The Iroquois were so determined to preserve their organic political institutions that the federal government reluctantly abandoned efforts to fundamentally change them. The Five Civilized Tribes—the Cherokee, Creek, Choctaw, Chickasaw, and Seminole—driven to what became the Indian Territory in the 1830s and 1840s, adopted governmental structures consonant with the American system, though retaining enough of their customs and values to make their relationship with the United States distinctive and one that warranted federal respect far longer than was extended to most other Native nations. The Pueblo peoples of New Mexico and Arizona, already possessing charters and land grants for their aboriginal lands and confirmation of their governments from the kings of Spain, were also adept at retaining many of their original institutions of governance in the face of persistent assimilative efforts by the Spanish, Mexicans, and Americans. While some social and structural change was inevitable, the Pueblo possessed such efficient and entrenched governments that it was virtually impossible for foreign powers to govern them externally.

Another important group of Native nations presented further problems for the definition of protectorates. The plains nations—the Lakota, Dakota, Cheyenne, Arapahoe, Comanche, and Kiowa—governed themselves according to traditional customs that involved conflict with anyone threatening their territories. If no one intrusively hunted on their lands, illegally dug for gold in their mountains, or interfered with their migratory travels, the Native peoples of this region remained fairly peaceful. But intrusions and minor incidents could quickly provoke them to war, and in battle they oftentimes proved more than a match for the Europeans and American troops. There was, therefore, no question of "protecting" these nations. Eventually the federal government would have to seek to physically and materially subdue them.

Finally, there were the remnants of older and more powerful tribal nations that had sustained great losses as a result of colonialism—smaller nations who desperately needed and sought the protection of the United States. Sometimes these small tribes occupied large tracts of land, but more often they had already signed treaties with the United States and removed themselves to the eastern fringe of the Great Plains. In eastern Kansas, western Missouri, and along the rivers of Nebraska, these smaller Indian nations, the Ponca, Quapaw, Omahas, Miami, Iowa, and Winnebago, for example, resided and attempted to live new lives as farmers. The larger plains tribes often stole their horses, raided their villages, and attacked their hunting parties. In California, Oregon, and Washington, many small Native communities had been ravaged by diseases, nearly exterminated by miners and settlers, or had already faded into tiny remnants by the time the United States arrived in the 1840s. Some of these small nations could be properly considered domestic dependent nations. Generally, these traumatized nations—for instance, the Umatilla, Klamath, Karok, Washoe, Chehali, and Makah—had preserved fewer customs and institutions and required the assistance and the protection of the United States.

The American pattern of settlement differed from that of the colonial European nations. England and Spain had prohibited settlement except when authorized by the Crown, so that tracts of land settled by these nations came under a charter or land grant confirmed by the king, all property and privilege remaining a gift from the sovereign and under his control. But the United States, starting in the 1840s, responded favorably to citizens' demands for land via agricultural homesteads and awarded nearly 300 million acres of aboriginal territory to homesteaders. This policy and later land policies like the Homestead Act of 1862, which authorized any citizen or purported citizen to get 160-acre tracts of land, and massive grants to war veterans, railroad corporations, and wealthy land speculators enabled the Americans to settle the entire continent in less than a century, whereas the English had stalled at the Appalachian frontier for nearly two centuries.[69]

The possibility of a newly settled territory governing itself almost from its inception, becoming a state, and then entering the Union on equal terms with the original states was a potent political idea that the Constitution extended to the great mass of non-Indian settlers moving onto the frontier. Respectability, riches, and political careers could be quickly made in the West in a way impossible in dreams and in land drives that were seldom conducive to respect for Indian property rights. With the western tribal nations having no discernibly fixed boundaries—at least according to whites—and often as not welcoming the first newcomers who entered their lands, the federal government was hard-pressed to protect the western tribes. The western territories, later states, came to consider Native peoples their most potent enemy, and the elimination of Indian nations was their foremost goal.

Two cases, one decided by the US Supreme Court, the other by the Supreme Court of the Territory of New Mexico, show the polarity of ideas about Indians during the post–Civil War period. In *The Kansas Indians* (1867), the US Supreme Court was asked to decide whether the state of Kansas had the right to tax the Shawnee, Wea, and Miami.[70] These small nations had been removed to the eastern plains of Kansas from the Ohio valley during the 1820s and 1830s. They had received new lands with guarantees of federal protection from other tribes and white settlers. Upon its admission to the Union, Kansas was required to agree in its enabling act that it would never attempt to tax or govern the tribes, since the tribes' treaty relationship was with the federal government. But the Shawnee, Wea, and Miami had become very proficient at farming and had generally incorporated with the local whites to a significant degree and had therefore become, in the eyes of state officials, virtually indistinguishable from their white neighbors. Kansas, in defiance of its enabling act, had then levied taxes on the Indians' lands.

Each of the small tribal nations appealed for relief to the federal courts, where the cases were consolidated under the heading *The Kansas Indians*. The Supreme Court, adhering steadfastly to John Marshall's doctrine of federal supremacy in Indian affairs established in the Cherokee cases thirty years earlier, declared:

> If the tribal organization of the Shawnees is preserved intact, and recognized by the political department of the government as existing, then they are a "people distinct from others," capable of making treaties, separated from the jurisdiction of Kansas, and to be governed exclusively by the government of the Union. If under the control of Congress, from

necessity there can be no divided authority. If they have outlived many things, they have not outlived the protection afforded by the Constitution, treaties, and laws of Congress.[71]

The Court took the position that unless and until Congress acted to divest Indian tribes of their treaty rights, they were entitled to retain their distinct political status as separate nations. "It may be, that they cannot exist much longer as a distinct people in the presence of the civilization of Kansas," the Court said, "'but until they are clothed with the rights and bound to all the duties of citizens,' they enjoy the privilege of total immunity from State taxation."[72]

Although this decision correctly supported Indian treaty rights, and did so emphatically, its language would radically affect the manner in which future Americans understood Indian treaties. The Court said that until Indians became full US citizens, as a practical result of the commitment to allow tribes to govern themselves, they "remained immune from state taxation." Behind this privilege was the unstated assumption that at some future time, Native self-government could involve taxation of Indians by their own governments. This was not explained, thereby leaving the public with the impression that treaties had created a privileged class of tax-exempt citizens. The gratuitous comment by the Court helped the courts and Congress move away from the true basis of federal-Indian relationships and into an effort to bring Indians into full American citizenship. Nevertheless, the federal position was clear in *The Kansas Indians*: Native nations were to be protected, the United States must honor its treaty commitments, and states lacked any constitutional authority over Native peoples on their lands.

The New Mexico controversy was another matter. A man named Jose Juan Lucero had settled at Cochiti Pueblo. The US attorney attempted to remove him under the provisions of an 1851 statute that extended the Indian Trade and Intercourse Act to Utah and New Mexico.[73] The Pueblo, however, had land grants confirmed by both Spain and Mexico, were considered self-governing corporate bodies by both governments, and were not easily classified politically as Indians, for whom the 1851 act had been enacted.

The decision, *United States. v. Lucero* (1869), eloquently demonstrated the wide gap between abstract federal doctrines and the hatred, passion, prejudice, and practical needs of the frontier. "Who and what are the Indians for whom said laws were passed, and upon whom they were intended to operate?" the New Mexico court asked. Judge John S. Watts moved quickly and began the recital of the settlers' version of natural law: "They were wandering savages, given to murder, robbery, and theft, living on the game of the mountains, the forest, and the plains, unaccustomed to the cultivation of the soil and unwilling to follow the pursuits of civilized man."[74] Watts then invoked the standard agricultural justification for indigenous dispossession:

> Providence made this world for the use of the man who had the energy and industry to pull off his coat, and roll up his sleeves, and go to work on the land, cut down the trees, grub up the brush and briers, and stay there on it and work it for the support of himself and family, and a kind and thoughtful Providence did not charge man a single cent for the whole world made for mankind and intended for their benefit. Did the Indians ever purchase the land, or pay anyone a single cent for it? Have they any deed or patent for it, or has it been devised to them by anyone as their exclusive inheritance?[75]

There was not a place in the legal universe of the frontier for Native peoples, even allegedly civilized Indians, as the Pueblo nations would later be termed. The political philosophers of Europe who traced the origin of their own civilized institutions to wandering tribes who appropriated wealth and property from an inexhaustible earth would have found few adherents in frontier New Mexico.

"The idea," said Watts, "that a handful of wild, half-naked, thieving, plundering, murdering savages should be dignified with the sovereign attributes of nations, enter into solemn treaties, and claim a country five hundred miles wide by one thousand miles long as theirs in fee simple, because they hunted buffalo and antelope over it, might be beautiful reading in Cooper's novels or Longfellow's Hiawatha, but is unsuited to the intelligence and justice of this age, or the natural rights of mankind."[76]

Indian legal title to land was a legal fiction for New Mexico, even though sanctified through age and practice and accepted by other courts of law in the US and the Old World. The New Mexico court did not care that Indian title was no more a fiction than the idea of a corporation being a person, or of African Americans being property, or that all citizens had ratified a social contract called the US Constitution. These legal fictions had once been considered necessary for the survival of society, and the real question was when a particular fiction would cease to be necessary. And who would decide? An anomaly of jurisprudence, the *Lucero* opinion accurately reflected the predominant western attitudes toward Indians at the time, attitudes making continuing conflict between the states and the federal government inevitable.

In addition to *The Kansas Indians* and *Lucero*, the five years following the Civil War included the Sand Creek massacre of peaceful Cheyenne and Arapahoe, which enraged the plains tribes. The Far West blazed with confrontations between Native war parties and the US Cavalry. After two years of continuous warfare, which included several disastrous defeats, the US Congress authorized a Peace Commission to negotiate treaties with the major Native nations of the area.[77] From July 1867 to December 1868, the commissioners worked and traveled, placating the most determined tribes, making relatively conservative promises, and generally seeking to calm Native tempers by assuring tribal leaders that they would not suffer depredations by whites invading their hunting grounds.

At Fort Laramie, the commission's members met with the Lakota, Northern Arapahoe, Northern Cheyenne, and the Crow. The Fort Laramie sessions were hostile and suspicious gatherings, with tempers always near the explosion point. These Native nations had been in council with the United States once before, in 1851, and since the rights guaranteed under that treaty had been violated by the United States, they were reluctant to grant further concessions until the federal government pledged to renew its 1851 agreements. General John Sanborn, a commissioner, promised material benefits under the new treaties:

> We shall agree to furnish you supplies in clothing and other useful articles while you continue to roam and hunt. We shall agree to furnish cattle, horses, cows, and implements to work the ground to each of your people as may at any time settle down and build a home and wish to live like the whites. Under this treaty you can roam and hunt while you remain at peace and game lasts; and when the game is gone you will have a home and means of supporting yourselves and your children. But you must understand that if peace is not made all efforts on our part to make it are at an end.[78]

General William S. Harney, who had fought the Lakota enough to merit their grudging respect, emphasized the seriousness of the United States:

I am afraid that you do not understand why we want to make peace. Perhaps you think we are afraid. You cannot be such fools as that, I hope. We do not want to go to war with you because you are a small nation, a handful compared with us, and we want you to live. If we go to war we shall send out to meet you a large army. Suppose you kill the whole army, we have another to send in its place. A great many of you will be killed and you have nobody to take their places.[79]

The Lakota were unimpressed with Harney's argument. They had demolished the Americans on the Bozeman Trail and had only seen whites in small numbers so could not conceive of the population, not to mention the technology, that the United States could draw upon in a prolonged battle. So they refused to cooperate until the government promised to remove its forts from their hunting grounds. The Lakota were in a sense bluffing, but the Americans were also bluffing. War on the plains was an unconstructive way to spend money. During three years of warfare, the army had spent incredible sums, had lost a considerable number of men and supplies, and still remained incapable of providing safe passage for white settlers to the West Coast. The commissioners were thus instructed to achieve peace at any price, regardless of the cost in annuities. If the Lakota had known this, they most likely would have driven an even harder bargain.

These plains treaties, coming at a time of rapid white settlement, underscored the national character of Native nations by setting aside large areas for permanent reservations. The treaties assured the Natives a vigorous federal protection from intruders. Article 2 of the 1868 Sioux treaty, for example, provided that

> the United States now solemnly agrees that no persons except those herein designated and authorized so to do, and except such officers, agents, and employes [sic] of the Government as may be authorized to enter upon Indian reservations in discharge of duties enjoined by law, shall ever be permitted to pass over, settle upon, or reside in the territory described in this article.[80]

The Plains Indians were promised "free and undisturbed use and occupation" of their lands.[81] Any future land cession would be invalid unless approved by three-quarters of the adult males of a tribe. Once again, an independent

Indian nation existing within the borders of a future state was used to resolve the continuing conflict between Native nations and white settlers.

As the powerful indigenous nations of the western plains maintained a significant quantum of political independence, the tribal nations of Indian Territory (the eastern part of present-day Oklahoma) continued to endure an arduous transition to "civilization." At the outbreak of the Civil War, the leaders of the Five Civilized Tribes, understanding that they were bound to the United States by treaty, offered assistance to the Union even though some of there members were slaveholders.[82] Northern politicians rejected their offer out of hand: using Indians in warfare, they declared, would be "uncivilized," an atrocity not to be visited upon their white brothers in the South. Few knew that many individual members of the Five Civilized Tribes had been converted to Christianity and were active members of their own Methodist and Baptist churches, no more cruel in their fighting techniques than whites. The myth of Indian savagery persisted.

Rejected by the United States, the leaders of the Five Tribes (and several other Native nations) signed treaties of alliance with the Confederacy.[83] The war exacerbated tension between various political segments in each of the Five Tribes, and some members of each nation joined the side with which they had sympathy, with the most capable leaders becoming officers in the Confederate army. In 1866, those who had signed treaties with the Confederacy were severely punished for their "disloyalty" to the United States, and were required to sign new peace treaties that stripped them of many important rights and much property. Three provisions in particular reflect the changes now thrust upon those Indians who had most fully embraced aspects of American culture. They added another dimension to struggle over the proper relationship between the United States and Indian tribes.

First, the Indians were required to abolish slavery and involuntary servitude. Article 2 of the Creek Treaty, for example, contains the basic provision inserted in each of these post–Civil War treaties: "The Creeks hereby covenant and agree that henceforth neither slavery nor involuntary servitude otherwise than in the punishment of crimes, whereof the parties shall have been duly convicted in accordance with laws applicable to all members of the said tribe, shall ever exist in said nation."[84]

The former black slaves, often referred to as freedmen, were made citizens of the Indian nations in a most peculiar fashion, however. They were granted the right to live and cultivate the soil within their respective Native nations and had the right to participate in certain elections of representatives to national councils:

> And inasmuch as there are among the Seminoles many persons of African descent and blood, who have no interest or property in the soil, and no recognized civil rights, it is stipulated that hereafter these persons and their descendants, and such other of the same race as shall be permitted by said nation to settle there, shall have and enjoy all the rights of native citizens, and the laws of said nation shall be equally binding upon all persons of whatever race or color, who may be adopted as citizens or members of said tribe.[85]

The treaties were signed less than a year after the Thirteenth Amendment was ratified by the requisite number of states, in 1865. The rights of African Americans in the Indian Territory were thus not determined by constitutional amendment but by treaties with the Five Civilized Tribes, indicating that federal officials still intended to acknowledge and respect the distinct national character of these nations although requiring of them, by treaty, recognition of rights that other Americans subscribed to under the Constitution. The issue of African American freedmen continues to be a contentious topic within several of the Native nations in Oklahoma, most notably the Seminole and the Cherokee Nation. In fact, in 2007, when the Cherokee Nation held a national referendum and opted to disenfranchise approximately 2,800 freedmen, this created a major controversy at the national level that has not yet been resolved, although bills were introduced in Congress designed to punish the Cherokee Nation for their action.

The second important provision in these treaties involved the establishment of a US court to handle legal disputes between citizens of the Five Civilized Tribes and noncitizens. The treaties varied considerably on this point. The Creek Treaty contemplated the organization of Indian Territory into an Indian government prior to the creation of the court[86]; the Treaty with the Choctaw and Chickasaw merely gave consent to a federal court but barred it from interfering with the tribal judiciary[87]; the Cherokee Treaty provided elaborate procedural devices for settling disputes[88]; and the Seminole Treaty casually mentioned that such a court could be created.[89] In one sense, the Five Civilized Tribes had been incorporated into the federal judiciary system, and in another sense they remained outside it.

The third important treaty provision created the multinational General Council of the Indian Territory. This council would meet annually and was authorized to organize a government embracing virtually all the tribes in the territory. In July 1870 Congress appropriated $5,000 to pay the expenses of the Native delegates and the first session of the council met in Okmulgee, the Creek capitol, in late September of that year.[90] It created committees on relations with the United States, international business, judiciary, finance, education and agriculture, enrolled bills, and rules. The Education and Agriculture Committee made an impressive report. The other committees, however, hampered by political infighting, accomplished very little. The council was adjourned until December, when a special constitutional committee was scheduled to report. The December meeting experienced credentials controversies, after which a number of minor and trivial amendments were offered to the proposed international constitution. The delegates then returned to their respective nations, few of whom were eager to join a territorial government.

These general councils continued until 1878. They were revived briefly in the late 1880s in reaction to the Dawes Act, also known as the General Allotment Act of 1887. Support in Congress for an Indian state was mixed, however. In 1870, Senator John Harlan, introduced a measure in the Senate authorizing the Council of Indian Tribes to elect a delegate to Congress.[91] This delegate would have had a status comparable to today's representatives from Puerto Rico, Guam, and the District of Columbia. Exercising little legislative power, this individual would nevertheless have been a physical presence in Washington, reminding Congress of its treaty obligations and advocating for the rights of the Native nations. Furthermore, "a realization of such a result," declared Commissioner of Indian Affairs Ely S. Parker, "would give the Indians much additional weight and importance."[92] But suspicion existed that the reason behind Harlan's desire to organize the Indian Territory was to more easily secure railroad lands. For every positive development, a negative aspect frightened the Native leaders, which resulted in a stalemate.

The proposal to make the Indian Territory a permanent political subdivision of the United States represented the best post–Civil War compromise in the search for a workable settlement of Indian political/legal relationships with the United States. The Constitution of Indian Territory contained most of the provisions of the 1866 treaties and seemed to resolve the question of federal jurisdiction over the nations of the territory. But the Native leaders remained a long way from understanding the Euro-American political tradition. They might subscribe to rules and procedures to conform with the white man's way of legislating, but in their hearts they were still devoted to indigenous ways, even in the face of a severe threat to their existence, which precluded cooperation with those outside their respective nations. Parker, the Seneca Indian who was a Civil War general and later commissioner of Indian affairs under Grant, noted in his report on the Okmulgee meeting that

> the Indians are a peculiar people; that from time immemorial their form of government has been based upon a community of interests, and they have not yet been educated to recognize fully the value of individual and exclusive rights in property. Their public men are zealous in guarding every right their people are accustomed to, and time alone can bring them to a just appreciation of the value of personal or individual rights.[93]

The failure to exploit this opportunity to form an Indian political state would have lasting and largely negative repercussions for the peoples of the Five Civilized Tribes. As preparations began for the council meeting at Okmulgee, a special report was being prepared by the Senate Judiciary Committee on the effect of the Fourteenth Amendment on Indian nations and treaty rights. The report reviewed in great detail the treatment of Indians by the executive branch, the many Supreme Court decisions on the relationship between the Indian tribes and the United States, and concluded that

> it is manifest that Congress has never regarded the Indian tribes as subject to the municipal jurisdiction of the United States. On the contrary, they have uniformly been treated as nations, and in that character held responsible for the crimes and outrages committed by their members, even outside of their territorial limits. And inasmuch as the Constitution treats Indian tribes as belonging to the rank of nations capable of making treaties, it is evident that an act of Congress which should assume to treat the members of a tribe as subject to the municipal jurisdiction of the United States would be unconstitutional and void.[94]

The Indian nations, having little familiarity with the congressional and legislative process and most likely no idea that this report even existed, were unable to exploit the Senate Judiciary Committee's conclusion. On the application of the Fourteenth Amendment to Native nations the committee was even more explicit:

> To maintain that the United States intended, by a change of its funda-mental law, *which was not ratified by these tribes, and to which they were neither requested nor permitted to assent*, to annul treaties then existing between the United States as one party, and the Indian tribes as the other parties respectively, would be to charge upon the United States repudiation of national obligations, repudiation doubly infamous from the fact that the parties whose claims were thus annulled are took weak to enforce their just rights, and were enjoying the voluntarily assumed guardianship and protection of this Government.[95]

The committee thus conceived Native nations as remarkably compa-rable to the states of the Union, yet with a political status not subject to the US Constitution because of their preexistence and separate national status. Treaties bound the federal government to obtain the free consent of tribal nations before it could change their status. The following year, however, a rider was attached to the 1871 Indian Appropriation Act in the House:

> That hereafter no Indian nation or tribe within the territory of the United States shall be acknowledged or recognized as an independent nation, tribe, or power with whom the United States may contract by treaty: *Provided further*, That nothing herein contained shall be con-strued to invalidate or impair the obligation of any treaty heretofore lawfully made and ratified with any such Indian nation or tribe.[96]

Considered in the context of the Judiciary Committee report of the year before, this restriction could only serve to guide congressional commit-tees and the executive branch in their dealings with Native nations. There were no hearings on this provision; few people understood exactly what it intended. Interpretations flourished as Americans tried to make sense out of the new status of Indian nations. In 1883, with *ex Parte Crow Dog*, the situation became more complex.[97]

Crow Dog, a Lakota holy man, had killed the famous chief Spotted Tail in a quarrel and, in the traditions of the nation, he and his family offered restitution to Spotted Tail's relatives, who accepted Crow Dog's gifts. The families considered the incident closed.[98] After newspapers complained that a murderer had escaped execution because of Indian custom, the white public was outraged and demanded that the government try Crow Dog for murder. Crow Dog was arrested, tried, convicted by a federal court, removed from the reservation to Deadwood, Dakota Territory, and sentenced to death. Crow Dog asked for permission to visit his family before his execution. Granted this request, he returned to the reservation, where he was released on his word to return. On the appointed day, Crow Dog calmly walked into the federal courtroom. His dramatic surrender created a greater stir than his killing of Spotted Tail. A team of lawyers filed a writ of habeas corpus on his behalf with the US Supreme Court. The question was simple: government prosecutors contended that later statutes superseded treaties with the Lakota and extended civil and criminal jurisdiction over the tribe; Crow Dog's attorneys argued that section 2146 of the Revised Statutes exempted any subject specifically reserved by the tribe in a treaty from federal claims of jurisdiction. Justice Thomas Stanley Matthews, delivering the opinion for a unanimous Court, described the Lakota as members of "a community separated by race, by tradition, by the instincts of a free though savage life, from the authority and power which seeks to impose upon them the restraints of an external and unknown code," which, he noted, "makes no allowance for their inability to understand it."[99] Matthews stayed within *The Kansas Indians* theory by emphasizing that cultural differences made indigenous peoples unique. Extending federal laws over Native rights to self-government was simply unjust and unacceptable:

> It tries them, not by their peers, nor by the customs of their people, nor the law of their land, but by superiors of a different race, according to the law of a social state of which they have an imperfect conception, and which is opposed to the traditions of their history, to the habits of their lives, to the strongest prejudices of their savage nature.[100]

The writ of habeas corpus was granted, and Crow Dog's conviction was overturned. In a conclusion that stands as an irony today, when capital punishment is not always considered cruel and unusual punishment, Justice Matthews wrote that the case was "one which measures the red man's revenge by the maxim of the white man's morality," not realizing or unable to admit that it was the Lakota who resolved murder by restitution and white men who demanded revenge by capital punishment.

The federal government, which for years had sought to extend the full weight of Western law over Native peoples, used the *Crow Dog* decision as the final impetus to impose federal jurisdiction by attaching a provision to the Indian Appropriation Act of 1885, which read in pertinent part:

> That immediately upon and after the date of the passage of this act all Indians, committing against the person or property of another Indian or other person any of the following crimes, namely, murder, manslaughter, rape, assault with intent to kill, arson, burglary, and larceny within any Territory of the United States, and either within or without an Indian reservation, shall be subject therefor to the laws of such Territory relating to such crimes, and shall be tried therefor in the same courts and in the same manner and shall be subject to the same penalties as are all other persons charged with the commission of said crimes.[101]

This section, popularly referred to as the Major Crimes Act, although it failed to amend or repeal any previous treaty provisions, gave the courts and Congress justification for extending federal laws over Indian reservations.

A definitive test of the constitutionality of this act came the next year in *United States v. Kagama*.[102] Kagama and a friend had murdered another Indian on the Hoopa Valley Reservation, in California. This case presented the Court with the question of who had jurisdiction to hear the case: the federal or state government. There was no recognition whatsoever of tribal sovereignty, which would have precluded either of these parties from exercising jurisdiction. Justice Samuel F. Miller, in a unanimous opinion, traced federal primacy over Indian affairs and produced one of the most confused, inconsistent opinions in the history of the US Supreme Court. Citing the commerce clause, Miller concluded:

> we think it would be a very strained construction of this clause, that a system of criminal laws for Indians living peaceably in their reservations, which left out the entire code of trade and intercourse laws justly enacted under that provision, and established punishments for the common-law crimes of murder, manslaughter, arson, burglary, larceny and the like, without any reference to their relation to any kind of

commerce, was authorized by the grant of power to regulate commerce with the Indian tribes.[103]

But, he suggested, "while we are not able to see, in either of these clauses of the Constitution and its amendments, any delegation of power to enact a code of criminal law for the punishment of the worst class of crimes known to civilized life when committed by Indians, there is a suggestion in the manner in which the Indian tribes are introduced into that clause, which may have a bearing on the subject before us."[104] Miller then returned to the original question posed by Chief Justice John Marshall in *Cherokee Nation*: were the Indian tribes foreign nations? Miller seemed to follow Marshall's ideas as they were developed in *Worcester* through *The Kansas Indians* to *ex Parte Crow Dog*. With respect to Native nations, Miller wrote:

> They were, and always have been, regarded as having a semi-independent position when they preserved their tribal relations; not as States, not as nations, not as possessed of the full attributes of sovereignty, but *as a separate people, with the power of regulating their internal and social relations, and thus far not brought under the laws of the Union or of the State within whose limits they resided.*[105]

This description overlooked the fact-based Senate judiciary report that had acknowledged that Native nations had sufficient attributes of sovereignty to rank among treaty-signing nations. But Congress's 1871 act prohibiting further treaty making with indigenous nations may well have influenced Miller's opinion. The conception of Indian nations as protected nations was clearly present for Miller in a legal sense but only vaguely in a cultural sense. Natives were a separate people for whom no fundamental legal barrier existed to prevent them from becoming integrated into American society. Miller's conclusion, following these ideas, is all the more baffling:

> These Indian tribes *are* the wards of the nation. They are communities *dependent* on the United States. Dependent largely for their daily food. Dependent for their political rights. They owe no allegiance to the States, and receive from them no protection. Because of the local ill feeling, the people of the States where they are found are very often their deadliest enemies. From their very weakness and helplessness, so largely

due to the course of dealing of the Federal Government with them and the treaties in which it has been promised, there arises the duty of protection, and with it the power.[106]

Miller failed to make the careful distinctions that the previously developed dependency theory required. Rather than viewing Indians in a collective sense having to rely upon the moral stance of the United States for protection from other nations and their possible intrusions upon aboriginal rights, and thereby signing treaties with the United States to ensure their protection, Miller unilaterally placed each Indian nation in a wardship status, thus profoundly reducing their political rights. Miller justified this severe diminishment in status by arguing that the present tribal dependency had been produced by the actions of the United States. Finally, he used the present dependent condition of aboriginal nations as a justification for discovering power in the federal government to exercise even more control. Instead of specific treaties articulating the rights of certain tribes and placing definite limits on the power of the United States, Miller and the Court generalized treaties into a national promise of protection, or what he termed guardianship, to all Native nations.

The implications of Miller's redefinition of Indian status did not become clear until 1903, when the court decided *Lone Wolf v. Hitchcock*.[107] This case involved an 1892 agreement that had been made with the Kiowa, Comanche, and Apache nations for the allotment of their reservation. The three nations originally agreed to a set of provisions that Congress subsequently so radically changed that it was no longer the contract the Indians had initially confirmed. With legal representation from the Indian Rights Association, they sued, and in a bill of equity claimed that article 12 of the 1867 treaty provided that

> the confederated tribes of Kiowas, Comanches, and Apaches were vested with an interest in the lands held in common within the reservation, which interest could not be divested by Congress in any other mode than that specified in the said twelfth article, and that as a result of the said stipulation the interest of the Indians in the common lands fell within the protection of the Fifth Amendment to the Constitution of the United States, and such interest—indirectly at least—came under the control of the judicial branch of the Government.[108]

It would have been interesting if the Indians had claimed the protections of the Fourteenth Amendment in the sense that they were excluded from the constitutional protections for the very reason that they were a "people separate from others" who enjoyed a definite legal relationship with the United States that could not be breached by an act of Congress.

In their argument, the tribal nations relied specifically on a treaty provision, not Justice Miller's general promise outlined in *Kagama* based upon deteriorating economic and political conditions caused by the United States. The Court, however, now turned aside the Indians' contentions through another remarkable twist of judicial logic. Justice Edward D. White, writing for the Court, declared:

> The contention ignores the status of the contracting Indians and the relation of dependency they bore and continue to bear toward the government of the United States. To uphold the claim would be to adjudge that the indirect operation of the treaty was to materially limit and qualify the controlling authority of Congress in respect to the care and protection of the Indians, and to deprive Congress, in *a possible emergency, when the necessity might be urgent for a partition and disposal of the tribal lands,* of all power to act if the assent of the Indians could not be obtained.[109]

It is difficult to conceive of an emergency in which Congress would have to partition Native lands. If we place this statement within the protected status theory, then it would appear that if the United States were militarily subjugated in a war and had to surrender part of its lands to another nation, and if that nation demanded as part of its booty a portion of the Kiowa, Comanche, and Apache reservation, the proper conditions would exist so that the United States could violate its treaty guarantees without guilt. Apart from that unlikely scenario, it is difficult to conceive why the specific article of a treaty, ratified by Congress, proclaimed by the president, and, according to the Constitution, the "supreme law of the land," would not buffer Indian nations from arbitrary exercises of federal power. The treaty commissioners, after all, had assured the Indians that article 12 protected them against intrusions and encroachments by the federal government and secured legal protection against confiscation of their lands. Presumably, congressional leaders had read both the article and the treaty before ratifying it, as had the president before he proclaimed it. The linguistic argument that

Congress could act in unusual ways in an emergency would later emerge in civil liberties cases to deny both Natives and other minority groups specific rights. This is, in fact, a favorite technique of judicial conservatives who sometimes use exaggerated and invented appeals to "necessity, emergency, fear, and prejudice to justify denial of fundamental constitutional rights."[110] The logic used here to justify the extension of federal powers over the rights of local self-government would characterize the logical meanderings of the judicial branch elsewhere in its efforts to describe national powers in the industrial and postindustrial ages.

Many passages from *Kagama* are sprinkled through *Lone Wolf* and give every indication that *Lone Wolf* was the fully matured child of *Kagama*, the dicta of the former becoming the doctrines of the latter. "Plenary authority over the tribal relations of the Indians has been exercised by Congress from the beginning," the opinion read, "and the power has always been deemed a political one, not subject to be controlled by the judicial department of the Government."[111] Judicial amnesia was at work here, as Justice White was completely ignoring *ex Parte Crow Dog* and a host of other cases that had held just the opposite. "Until the year 1871 the policy was pursued of dealing with the Indian tribes by means of treaties, and of course, a moral obligation rested upon Congress to act in good faith in performing the stipulations entered into on its behalf."[112] Again, the Court radically revised history and reduced indigenous legal rights to moral imperatives or policy considerations.

In *Kagama* and *Lone Wolf* we find a disturbing replacement of legal rights by moral imperatives, the maturing of these moral imperatives into virtually absolute, if nonconstitutionally derived legal powers, and the production of such a welter of confused thinking that the idea of Indians and Indian tribes, clear in the final Marshall opinion, *Worcester*, was placed beyond the realm of rational analysis. Native peoples, who began their presence in American history with an uncluttered identity in the legal universe, by 1903 had been evicted almost entirely from the realm of law, reduced to little more than nebulous, shadowy figures. *Lone Wolf* concluded with a gratuitous comment that sealed the Natives' judicial fate as profoundly diminished sovereigns with few respected treaty or proprietary rights:

> We must presume that Congress acted in perfect good faith in the dealings with the Indians of which complaint is made, and that the legislative branch of the government exercised its best judgment in the

premises. In any event, as Congress possessed full power in the matter, the judiciary cannot question or inquire into the motives which prompted the enactment of this legislation. If injury was occasioned, which we do not wish to be understood as implying, by the use made by Congress of its power, relief must be sought by an appeal to that body for redress and not to the courts.[113]

Native nations, as we have noted, were excluded from the protections of the Fourteenth Amendment because of their separate political and cultural status, with treaties binding them to the federal government. Neither did they ask nor comment on or assent to the amendment. Standing completely outside the constitutional framework, insofar as that framework has protected minorities, *Lone Wolf* thereupon emphatically precluded any judicial redress for aggrieved Natives, their only hope being political lobbying, a slim hope at best in 1903 since most Indians were not American citizens and tribal nations remained extraconstitutional polities. And being the smallest of the minorities, virtually incapable of exercising any significant political influence on US governing institutions, Natives thereafter were far more subject to private, state, and federal exploitation, protected only sporadically by presidential morality or a climate of public opinion that sometimes favored them. Native nations had been largely deprived of their treaty-making capacity and treaty-guaranteed property rights, and did not possess the constitutional status that other Americans enjoyed.

Lone Wolf represented a major step on a path to complete and nearly absolute conceptual confusion on the rights and status of Native nations. Between the Cherokee decisions and the *Lone Wolf* case, the practice of land allotment had divested Indians of their corporate (national) political rights and substituted a formula in which the white man's moral obligations and the Indians' legal rights were synonymous. Adding to the disarray were acts of Congress aimed at a deteriorating situation in the West, together with the Court's determination to connect contemporary events with historical legal concepts to form a rational body of law. The United States once more had to resort to new legal fictions. For example, after disclaiming treaties in 1871 via congressional fiat, the federal government continued to treat formally with Indian nations until 1914. Since these treaties were not consonant with declared congressional policy, another name disguised the fact that the United States was violating its own laws, and so these documents came to be called agreements when discussed by white lawyers, judges and justices, and scholars. When they were being negotiated with Native leaders, however, they were typically presented and referred to as treaties. It was not until 1914 that most Indians discovered that they had been formally deprived of the right to sign treaties with the United States in 1871.

A generation after *Lone Wolf*, Nathan Margold, then solicitor for the Bureau of Indian Affairs (BIA) in the Department of the Interior during the New Deal era, wrote in the introduction to Felix Cohen's *Handbook of Federal Indian Law* that "if the laws governing Indian affairs are viewed as lawyers generally view existing law, without reference to the varying times in which particular provisions were enacted, the body of law thus viewed is a mystifying collection of inconsistencies and anachronisms."[114] By neglecting or deliberately avoiding careful historical analysis, by projecting their own limited understanding into the past, and by pretending that an implied logic of emergency had always undergirded the indigenous/US relationship, the Supreme Court virtually banished both justice and reason from the field. "Federal Indian law," Margold warned, "is a subject that cannot be understood if the historical dimension of law is ignored."[115] The period from 1890 to the present demonstrates the futility of attempting to make sense of this subject by the manipulation of concepts alone. Even while *Kagama* and *Lone Wolf* were being heard, the same courts, congressmen, and presidents established precedents that cut these decisions to manageable size, thereby creating a more coherent concept of the status of Indian tribes.

A Status Higher Than States

Morris Cohen, in his book *Reason and Law*, asked: who are the civilized people? "The naive answer," he said, is that civilized people are "those whose views are like our own, from which it follows that our ancestors were not, and that other people with different conceptions of the requisites of pity and probity are not, civilized." Cohen maintained that this belief "is supported by the fashionable assumption that there is a cosmic law according to which all people must, regardless of diverse circumstances in their environment, evolve along the same uniform line of which we today represent the highest point."[116] But, Cohen noted, historical evidence shows a wide variety in what has been considered civilized behavior. Law, then, depends as much upon the manner in which those in authority apprehend their subjects as upon any articulation of principles, doctrines, and dogmas.

Nowhere is this more evident than with non-Indian conceptions of indigenous nations in the nineteenth century. The Major Crimes Act purported to extend federal jurisdiction over Indians "within any Territory of the United States, and either within or without an Indian reservation."[117] This broad application of federal law appeared to apply to all tribes within the continental limits of the United States. But this was not the case. The Five Civilized Tribes of Indian Territory were not affected by this statute. The argument was raised, by both federal officials and Native officials, that treaties preserved aboriginal jurisdiction over their internal civil and criminal matters. In fact, the Major Crimes Act was passed with the plains tribes specifically in mind, although it did not mention any western tribes by name. An additional argument for the exclusion of the Five Civilized Tribes from federal jurisdiction at the time was that they were capable of governing themselves. But the plains tribes were equally adept at exercising self-government following their own customs, as the high court had explicitly recognized in the *Crow Dog* case.

The real answer to this bifurcation in policy application was that federal lawmakers recognized in the Five Civilized Tribes enough familiar political and legal institutions to reassure themselves that these Native nations understood and at least partially embraced "civilized" life. The Five Civilized Tribes had their own courts, judges, and jails and had long-established written codes; appeals could be taken from these courts to the western district court of Arkansas and then to the US Supreme Court. One of the leading plains nations, the Lakota, allowed no appeals, had no written codes, courts, or judges; all tribal members knew the tribal traditions and were expected to obey them, creating no need to inform outsiders of the efficacy of their government. Non-Indian observers, however, could see no familiar institutions and, lacking verification of what they considered cosmic reality, concluded that the Lakota had no laws and no means of properly controlling human behavior.

Andrew Sinclair explains the radical shift in attitudes that non-Indians experienced with respect to tribal nations and their method of self-government as one of increasing knowledge and sophistication on the part of the non-Indian, not as growing awareness by Natives of the nature of law and civilized life. Sinclair said that prior to 1926, when Branislaw Malinowski's work *Sex and Repression in Savage Society* was being published, anthropology as a discipline was already beginning to show signs of maturation in terms of questions raised and the methods used to gather data about Native peoples. Sinclair noted that contrary to popular myth, indigenous peoples "were the most-law-abiding peoples on earth."[118] But most justices and government officials, usually lagging far behind social science in perceptions of culture, still believed that without familiar white institutions, Indians lived in a state of anarchy and needed the federal government to protect them—from themselves.

In 1892, an incident occurred in Cherokee country exactly paralleling the *Crow Dog* case. A Cherokee named Robert Talton killed another Cherokee and was arrested, tried, and convicted by a Cherokee court. He sued on a writ of habeas corpus, contending that the grand jury that convicted him, being composed of five persons under a Cherokee code revised during the year of his conviction, was unconstitutional under the US Constitution's Fifth Amendment protections. In 1896, the case reached the Supreme Court. In *Talton v. Mayes*, the Court faced the question of whether the powers of local government exercised by the Cherokee Nation were federal powers created by the US Constitution under the treaty relationship and therefore subject to other provisions in the Constitution and to the laws of Congress.[119]

Justice White, who six years later would write the *Lone Wolf* opinion, announced that "by treaties and statutes of the United States the right of the Cherokee Nation to exist as an autonomous body, subject always to the paramount authority of the United States, has been recognized." This recognition, White maintained, enabled the tribe "to make laws defining offenses and providing for the trial and punishment of those who violate them when the offenses are committed by one member of the tribe against another one of its members within the territory of the nation."[120] Once this right to make laws was conceded by the federal government, White implied, everything covered by the Cherokee laws became a local matter no longer subject to constitutional protections. White affirmed aboriginal political rights of the Indian nation:

> The existence of the right in Congress to regulate the manner in which the local powers of the Cherokee Nation shall be exercised does not render such local powers Federal powers arising from and created by the Constitution of the United States. It follows that as the powers of local self-government existed prior to the Constitution, they are not operated upon by the 5th Amendment, which as we have said, has for its

sole object to control the powers conferred by the Constitution on the national government.[121]

Tribal governments, in White's analysis of constitutional law, were comparable to states in that the Bill of Rights did not apply to them even though they were recognized by and somewhat regulated by federal laws.

The *Talton* decision carved out a whole new area of law in the sense that indigenous governments were recognized as having a definite status with respect to their own members that they were denied with respect to the United States. If treaties had been reduced to an expedient means of dealing with policy questions involving Indians, they nevertheless were critical in affirming powers of self-government, powers existing prior to the Constitution, untouched by its adoption, and still existing in the Indian nation. This question seldom arose in the nineteenth century, and not until the mid-twentieth century did the *Talton* doctrine gain force. The courts never really abandoned the Marshall-invented domestic dependent nation concept. Instead, they simply transformed the question they expected that concept to resolve. This approach, though it postponed the solution of the indigenous/federal dilemma, enabled two theories of Indian nationalism to survive. If Native members lacked any legal protection from abuses by their own governments, they at the same time preserved the potential of politically independent and self-sufficient Indian communities.

Other difficult questions arose for the courts: who was an Indian, and what constituted a tribal nation? The answers to these basic questions were at once simple and profoundly difficult. They involved racial and cultural characteristics as well as legal and political concepts applied to novel situations. The treaties, for example, had recognized certain Native groups as political entities; these entities, following the indigenous method of choosing leadership and establishing separate bands, were not always readily discernible. Historically, and after the establishment of the reservation system, Natives tended to group around charismatic leaders who by exerting tremendous influence on the government, or the nearest Indian agent, could deliver tangible and much-needed benefits to their followers. If an Indian leader's charisma diminished and the person lost respect, people clustered to other leaders who might or might not use the same approach to the government. Then, too, promises to maintain order did not always result in peace since a tribal leader could loosely bind only those they influenced by moral example. If others not in the leader's sphere of influence decided to resist white intrusions and fight for their homelands and retain other rights, that was their decision. A tribal leader lacked the coercive authority to interfere in those personal decisions.

By the 1870s, a number of claims had arisen against certain Indian nations by white citizens who claimed that they had lost relatives and/or property in skirmishes with particular tribes. Tedious and time consuming, these so-called depredations claims followed no fixed procedures for obtaining compensation from the tribes, most of whom, in their treaties, had promised to reimburse any white citizen they had injured in a breach of the peace.[122] When tribal peoples discovered that their treaty annuities were being used to pay depredation claims, they complained. Often, it turns out, they had not even injured the alleged claimant or the claims were later shown to be entirely fraudulent.

In 1891, Congress passed the Indian Depredation Act, which allowed all persons with claims against a tribe to file suit in the court of claims.[123] One task of this court very rapidly became to determine what characteristics constituted an Indian tribe. Also, if the alleged depredations had been caused by a tribe not at war with the United States, no recovery could be obtained since the acts would be properly acts of war between hostile nations, not depredations. So, in determining the validity of these claims, yet another conception of the Indian nations was created—less fictional than other conceptions in the past, but most assuredly contributing to the growing legal confusion about the nature and status of Native nations.

A review of cases filed under the Indian Depredation Act reveals that awards usually were made on an ad hoc basis, the object normally being to settle claims as quickly as possible. Yet, out of this plethora of litigation, two cases attempted to deal with the difficult question of Indian political organization. They are important cases because twentieth-century administrative and congressional decisions required a historical understanding of tribes, bands, and other identifiable groups of Indians. These cases, both involving the Apache of Arizona and New Mexico, were clear enough to serve as precedent. In *Dobbs v. the United States and the Apache Indians* (1898),[124] the court of claims reviewed the development of tribal recognition:

> In dealing with this question the court has held, first, that a nation, tribe, or band will be regarded as an Indian entity where the relations of the

Indians in their organized or tribal capacity has been fixed and recognized by treaty; second, that where there is no treaty by which the Government has recognized a body of Indians, the court will recognize a subdivision of tribes or bands which has been recognized by those officers of the Government whose duty it was to deal with and report the condition of the Indians to the executive branch of the Government; third, that where there has been no recognition by the Government, the court will accept the subdivision into tribes or bands made by the Indians themselves.[125]

But, the court continued, still another category existed: "the court has had to go further and recognize bands which simply in fact existed, irrespective of recognition, either by the Department of the Interior or the Indian tribes from which the membership of the band came."[126]

An Indian band's survival in many instances depended upon their political and military skills in encounters with the United States. This transcended Marshall's characterization of tribes as domestic dependent nations, since it recognized Indian political entities entirely unrelated to the government. Native nations could even emerge as identifiable units as a response to the presence of the United States.

When the Supreme Court, in *Montoya v. United States* (1901),[127] confronted the struggles of the court of claims over political identity, it reasoned:

By a 'tribe' we understand a body of Indians of the same or a similar race, united in a community under one leadership or government, and inhabiting a particular though sometimes ill-defined territory; by a 'band,' a company of Indians not necessarily, though often of the same race or tribe, but united under the same leadership in a common design. While a 'band' does not imply a separate racial origin characteristic of a tribe, of which it is usually an offshoot, it does imply a leadership and a concert of action. How large the company must be to constitute a 'band' within the meaning of the act it is unnecessary to decide. *It may be doubtful whether it requires more than independence of action, continuity of existence, a common leadership and concert of action.*[128]

Although this definition of a band was created to determine legal liability for depredations, it raised the question of indigenous characteristics once again, but failed to resolve the issue.

Although Frederick Jackson Turner announced the end of the frontier and sought to describe its influence in 1890, in Indian affairs the frontier spirit continued until 1914, when the United States stopped making agreements with Native peoples—the last negotiated accord was with the Utes of southern Colorado—and settled into a long period of administrative attempts to manage what it was now calling the "Indian problem." The government's concern in a majority of its agreements with tribal nations had been the acquisition of "surplus" Native lands retained during the formal treaty era. "Surplus lands" was a significant euphemism since the Native nations of Oklahoma, the Dakotas, Montana, the desert Southwest, and other arid and semiarid states needed considerable acreage just for subsistence purposes. But the federal policy was to divide Indian lands into 160-acre (or less) farming plots. Tribes were then pressured into one-sided agreements that allotted their remaining lands into small tracts with the balance of their territory then being sold to the federal government. Simultaneously, the strange idea arose that the last vestige of tribal existence was common property and the Indian nations came to be perceived as quasi-corporations possessing immense resources, which, in the opinion of federal policy makers, should be distributed to tribal members.

New Mexico, Arizona, and Oklahoma were still territories as the twentieth century began. As each reached statehood, fundamental changes were made in their relationship to Indian nations. In Oklahoma, the governments of the Five Civilized Tribes were nearly destroyed through so-called agreements reached under such pressure that traditional Indians often resisted by individual acts of violence.[129] The shift in attitudes toward the Five Civilized Tribes, the tribal favorites of liberal elements in national Indian policy making for several generations, came as a result of the deep belief held by white Americans that private property was the path to civilization. Senator Henry Dawes of Massachusetts, who introduced the General Allotment Act in 1887[130] as a means of quickly bringing about the acculturation and eventual disappearance of distinctive indigenous identities in the American polity, had visited the Five Civilized Tribes in 1885 and utterly failed to understand the tremendous accomplishments of these mature nations:

> The head chief told us that there was not a family in that whole Nation that had not a home of its own. There was not a pauper in that Nation, and the Nation did not owe a dollar. It built its own capitol...and it built

its schools and its hospitals. *Yet the defect of the system was apparent, They have got as far as they can go, because they own their land in common.* It is Henry George's system and under that there is no enterprise to make your home any better than that of your neighbors. *There is no selfishness, which is at the bottom of civilization.* Till this people will consent to give up their lands, and divide them among their citizens so that each can own the land he cultivates, they will not make much more progress.[131]

Justice Oliver Wendell Holmes remarked in dissent in *Lochner v. New York* (1905)[132] that the Fourteenth Amendment "does not enact Herbert Spencer's Social Statics."[133] This was an accusation that the majority had incorporated Darwinian philosophy in their constitutional deliberations. Herbert Hovenkamp notes that while there is little evidence that any of the justices were social Darwinists, a close reading of many judicial opinions during this and other historical eras and an analysis of congressional policies throughout much of American history provides ample evidence that social Darwinistic racist ideas permeated American society—for example, laws aimed at the breakdown of indigenous identity, the movement to restrict immigration of Asians and Latin Americans into the United States, and the antebellum defense of slavery.[134]

Beginning in 1887 through the General Allotment Act and later amendments, Native peoples became the subject of a great social experiment in which private property became the panacea for all the government-created ills. In the Dawes Commission Report for 1894,[135] the commission justified allotment of communally held aboriginal lands by citing the alleged failure of tribal governments to exclude intruders and preserve their isolation as a people separate from others:

> As we have said, the title to these lands is held by the tribe in trust for the people. We have shown that this trust is not being properly executed, nor will it be if left to the Indians, and the question arises what is the duty of the Government of the United States with reference to this trust? While we recognize these tribes as dependent nations, the Government has likewise recognized its guardianship over the Indians and its obligations to protect them in their property and personal rights.
>
> In the treaty with the Cherokees, made in 1846, we stipulated that they should pass laws for equal protection, and for the security of life,

liberty and property. If the tribe fails to administer its trust properly by securing to all the people of the tribe equitable participation in the common property of the tribe, there appears to be no redress for the Indian so deprived of his rights, unless the Government does interfere to administer such trust.[136]

The Supreme Court, in *Stephens v. Cherokee Nation* (1899), upheld this explanation of the government's responsibility to tribal members, and the allotment of the Five Civilized Tribes was held constitutional.[137] The Court, unfortunately, did not comment on the long train of developments leading to its decision. Insofar as the legal universe was concerned, *Stephens* represented one of those rare times when both conceptions of Native peoples, as a race of uncivilized people and as domestic dependent nations, were important considerations in deciding the issue.

In his opinion in *Cherokee Nation v. Georgia*, Justice William Johnson had suggested that of the possible political rights that the Cherokee Nation might enjoy, "the alternative of departing and retaining the right of self-government may exist in them." In the turmoil of allotment and the near destruction of their governments, some of the more culturally traditional members of the Five Civilized Tribes proposed to migrate from the United States. When the Senate Select Committee on the Five Civilized Tribes visited Oklahoma in 1906, a group of Choctaw, headed by Jacob Jackson, presented them with a paper requesting their permission to sell their allotments and, with the funds secured, relocate to Central America. These traditional-minded Choctaw felt that they had but one political right remaining and they intended to exercise it. "Surely a race of people," the paper argued,

> desiring to preserve the integrity of that race, who love it by reason of its traditions and their common ancestors and blood, who are proud of the fact that they belong to it may be permitted to protect themselves, if in no other way by emigration. Our educated people inform us that the white men came to this country to avoid conditions which to him were not as bad as the present conditions are to us...All we ask is that we may be permitted to exercise the same privilege.[138]

But the United States, although it had earlier allowed the Iroquois and Kickapoo to expatriate to Canada and Mexico, respectively, refused to allow the Choctaw the same privilege. Even this basic political right had now been quashed.

New Mexico presented different problems from Oklahoma. Under the Treaty of Guadalupe Hidalgo, land titles and political rights recognized by Mexico were confirmed and the Pueblo, who lived peaceably in towns and farmed, were not legally considered Indians entitled to federal protection.[139] For nearly eighty years, the New Mexico courts systematically deprived the Pueblo of their lands and many non-Indians were illegally squatting on Pueblo territory. Questions of title and boundaries were always decided against the Indians until *United States v. Sandoval* (1913), when the treatment of the Pueblo was reversed by the US Supreme Court.[140] The case involved liquor sales to Indians within the Santa Clara Pueblo. Justice Willis Van Devanter, speaking for a unanimous Court, cited excerpts of a long history of federal problems with drinking in the various pueblos and declared "not only does the Constitution expressly authorize Congress to regulate commerce with the Indian tribes, but long continued legislative and executive usage and an unbroken current of judicial decisions have attributed to the United States as a superior and civilized nation the power and the duty of exercising a fostering care and protection over all dependent Indian communities within its borders, whether within its original territory or territory subsequently acquired, and whether within or without the limits of a State."[141]

This ruling placed the Pueblo under federal supervision and their lands and property in trust status. The Supreme Court, in defying the practice of eight decades, was, in fact, acting in a legislative capacity. Van Devanter did insist that congressional powers were limited. "Of course, it is not meant by this that Congress may bring a community or body of people within the range of this power by arbitrarily calling them an Indian tribe," he explained, "but only that in respect of distinctly Indian communities the questions whether, to what extent, and for what time they shall be recognized and dealt with as dependent tribes requiring the guardianship and protection of the United States are to be determined by Congress, and not by the courts."[142] In practice, like the conductor in *Plessy v. Ferguson* (1896), legal rights were delegated to whatever recognition the administrative agencies bestowed.

The New Deal of Franklin D. Roosevelt brought radical changes for Indian tribes.[143] John Collier, Roosevelt's commissioner of Indian affairs, was a social scientist who understood non-Western cultures better than any of his predecessors. To assist tribes in the stabilization and reconstitution of their political bases and to help them revitalize their cultural traditions, Collier, with the considerable help of Felix S. Cohen,[144] introduced the Indian Reorganization Act (IRA) in 1934.[145] Although Congress amended and dramatically reduced the breadth of the bill at the insistence of various forces, including "the fears of individual Indians owning allotments, the interests of non-Indian groups leasing Indian land or using Indian timber, the concerns of missionary groups operating on Indian reservations, and congressional beliefs about the appropriate relationship between Indians and the federal government,"[146] basic redefinitions of critical concepts produced additional changes in indigenous status. Under the IRA, as enacted, "any Indian tribe, or tribes, residing on the same reservation" had the right to organize a government and could, if they so desired, devise a constitution and bylaws to operate under that would be recognized by the federal government.[147] In practical terms, this provision meant that tracts of land called "reservations" determined the status of political entities called "recognized tribes." Some tracts of land had been set aside for individual homeless Indians classified under extremely general characteristics. Under the IRA, these tracts, designated as reservations, made the Indian inhabitants eligible for federal recognition. "Tribes," in some instances, of less than twenty people were thereby eligible to organize themselves under formal constitutions and bylaws. In other instances, two tribes sharing the same reservation, although with entirely different political and cultural backgrounds, including different treaties, were melded into one organic political entity under the act's provisions.

As important as the IRA was, it was actually through a series of subsequent solicitor's opinions, many written by Cohen or Nathan Margold, the solicitor general, that Native nations had fleshed out for them what their actual political and legal powers were. Two opinions, in particular, written in the fall of 1934, established an almost contradictory set of statuses for those nations who adopted the IRA.

On October 25, 1934, an opinion by Assistant Solicitor Cohen and signed by Solicitor Margold titled "Powers of Indian Tribes" identified and elaborated on a host of inherent powers that had vested in Native nations under existing law—for example, the power to tax, to form a government, and to regulate domestic relations, among others.[148] More importantly,

Cohen declared that Indian nations had historically exercised complete external and internal sovereign powers.

However, two months later, on December 13, 1934, another opinion was released by Solicitor Margold that then attempted to place Native nations within the structure of federal law:

> The Indian tribes have long been recognized as vested with governmental powers, subject to limitations imposed by Federal statutes. The powers of an Indian tribe cannot be restricted or controlled by the governments of the several States. *The tribe is, therefore, so far as its original absolute sovereignty has been limited, an instrumentality and agency of the Federal Government.*
>
> Various statutes authorize the delegation of new powers of government to the Indian tribes...The most recent of such statutes is the Wheeler-Howard Act, which sets up as one of its primary objectives, the purpose "to grant certain rights of home role to Indians." This Act contemplates the devolution to the duly organized Indian tribes of many powers over property and personal conduct which are now exercised by officials of the Interior Department. *The granting of a Federal corporate charter to an Indian tribe confirms the character of such a tribe as a Federal instrumentality and agency.*[149]

This conception combined John Marshall's old idea of domestic dependent nations with the contemporary idea of chartering federal corporations such as the Tennessee Valley Authority to produce a new entity with aspects of federalism and elements of aboriginal tribal status. In more abstract terms, Native governments were fully capable political entities except where they voluntarily surrendered aspects of self-government or where the Congress had eliminated certain functions of self-government. Few people, however, understood which functions had been legally divested and which had lapsed through inattention and disuse.

The courts and Congress failed to clarify the situation. Not until 1965, in *Colliflower v. Garland*,[150] did a federal judge reluctantly hold that the Blackfeet tribal court on the Fort Belknap Reservation was subject to habeas corpus from a federal district court. Judge Ben C. Duniway for the US Court of Appeals for the Ninth Circuit based his decision on the particular history of that reservation and said that tribal courts were "in part, at least, arms of the federal government" since the federal government had at least partial control over them.[151] But he further described tribal courts as functioning "in part as a federal agency and in part as a tribal agency."[152] Although the court described all indigenous courts thus, Duniway implied that this ruling was confined to the Fort Belknap Reservation's courts since "the history of other Indian courts may call for a different ruling."[153]

In *United States v. State Tax Commission of Mississippi* (1974),[154] the Mississippi Choctaw Nation, although organized under the provisions of the IRA and recognized administratively by the BIA, was thought not to have overcome the dissolution of its political integrity that the historic Treaty of Dancing Rabbit Creek (Treaty with the Choctaw) purported to effect.[155] Thus, history and federal policy continued to conflict in the courts as judges remained bewildered by which aspect should receive emphasis and be considered the determinative framework for interpretation.

Native governments and communities participated in most of the social programs established by President Lyndon B. Johnson in the 1960s—Office of Economic Opportunity, Head Start, VISTA, among others—when his administration sought to create the Great Society.[156] In almost every case, the eligibility sections of these early congressional statutes and many of those passed in the early 1970s (for example, the Indian Education Act of 1972, the Comprehensive Employment and Training Act of 1973, and the Indian Self-Determination and Education Assistance Act of 1975) contained a phrase placing Indian tribes in a position at least comparable to states and regional commissions.[157] But the wording "tribes, bands, or recognized/identifiable groups" that made the Native communities eligible for federal grants and loans did little to clarify the manner in which Native communities were conceived politically, although in practical terms such recognition carried with it the assumption of power to regulate sometimes sizable populations and to supervise activities in wide geographical areas. Since some of the social programs required that the sponsored agency—the tribal community—not discriminate on the basis of race of any program participant, some Indian programs included non-Indians, and the question of tribal jurisdiction over nontribal members achieved importance again.

The progress of Native nations as political entities exercising the functions of municipal governments expanded considerably between the passage of the IRA and the postwar world. With the expansion of tribal powers and the development of institutions such as courts and police forces, new problems arose. In the Southwest, many tribes had continued to govern themselves according to traditional structures and values, and the question of religious freedom was a major issue.

Theocratic Native nations such as the Pueblo were particularly prone to contentious situations. Thus, in *Toledo v. Pueblo de Jemez* (1954),[158] Protestant Indians attacked the exclusivity of the Pueblo government and its power to exclude them from certain tribal privileges, like refusing them the right to bury their dead in the community cemetery, and denying them the right to build a church of their own on Pueblo land, among others, on religious grounds. But the federal court dismissed their complaint, announcing that "at least since the *Sandoval* decision in 1913, it has been clear that the Pueblos do not derive their governmental powers from the State of New Mexico. It has, indeed, been held that the powers of an Indian tribe do not spring from the United States although they are subject to the paramount authority of Congress."[159] Thus, the *Talton* doctrine—the extraconstitutional status of Native nations' governing powers—was utilized to resolve a contemporary question.

Most important in establishing a contemporary definition of the status of Indian nations was *Native American Church v. Navajo Tribal Council*, handed down in 1959.[160] This case involved the enforcement of an ordinance adopted by the Navajo tribal council making it an offense to introduce peyote in Navajo country. At the time, the council was led by Paul Jones, the Chairman, who was overseeing the Navajo peoples' emergence at the national level. The members of the Native American Church attempted to get the tribal ordinance declared unconstitutional but were turned aside. The Tenth Circuit Court of Appeals introduced the unusual idea that the tribe could not be sued without the permission of Congress, which made tribal sovereignty immunity a tenuous and confused proposition. But the court also declared that "Indian tribes are not states. They have a status higher than that of states. They are subordinate and dependent nations possessed of all powers as such only to the extent that they have expressly been required to surrender them by the superior sovereign, the United States."[161] After a century and a quarter of fluctuating definitions, the conception of a Native nation returned to its fundamental origin in *Worcester* as a political entity higher than states but a degree below fully independent national status, which would be recognized by the other nations of the world. Still, the domestic dependent nation theory was now greatly handicapped by the extraneous historical and theoretical encrustations that it had accumulated in the interim.

The idea of the domestic dependent nation did not sit well with federal judges and justices in the 1970s, although the idea of captive and colonized peoples in other countries of the world received great emphasis by American political leaders. Thus, in *McClanahan v. State Tax Commission of Arizona* (1973),[162] while the court preserved the integrity of the tribal government by refusing to allow Arizona to tax Navajos living and earning income on the reservation, Justice Thurgood Marshall, delivering the opinion of the Supreme Court, declared:

> The Indian sovereignty doctrine is relevant, then, not because it provides a definitive resolution of the issues in this suit, but because it provides a backdrop against which the applicable treaties and federal statutes must be read. It must always be remembered that the various Indian tribes were once independent and sovereign nations, and that their claim to sovereignty long predates that of our own Government.[163]

However, the case was decided on other grounds so that the sovereignty issue, while important, remained too politically controversial to be considered the major point of contention.

Less than a year later, the Supreme Court was confronted with a case that required it to assess the constitutionality of the BIA's preferential hiring policy of Indians for employment purposes. In the wake of the 1972 Equal Employment Opportunity Act (EEOA), which prohibited racial discrimination in nearly all federal employment situations, a group of non-Indian BIA employees, led by Carla Mancari, filed a class action lawsuit.[164] They argued that the bureau's Indian preference policy, in existence since 1934, violated the due process clause of the Fifth Amendment and that it had been effectively repealed by the EEOA.

But the Supreme Court in *Morton v. Mancari* (1974) unanimously rejected both these arguments and dramatically upheld the BIA's preference policy.[165] It declared that Congress had not explicitly repealed the bureau's policy in the EEOA; that the federal government's policy of Native self-determination supported the perpetuation of the bureau's hiring policy; that the preference policy was not based on racial discrimination; and that it was, in fact, moored in the unique diplomatic history of indigenous/federal relations and affirmed the political status of federally recognized Native nations. In affirming tribal sovereignty, the Court declared that the "preference, as applied, is granted to Indians not as a discrete racial group, but, rather, as members of quasi-sovereign tribal entities whose lives and activities are governed by the BIA in a unique fashion."[166] The Court went on to note that "in the sense that there is no other group of people favored in this manner, the legal status of the BIA is truly *sui generis.*"[167]

In *United States v. Mazurie* (1975), the Court again upheld the idea of tribal sovereignty, describing Native nations as "a good deal more than private, voluntary organizations."[168] In this case, the right of the Wind River Tribal Council to police liquor-related activities of a non-Indian business operating within the reservation boundary were upheld. Again, the Court referred back to *Worcester* as precedent.

The controversial nature of Native nations as domestic dependent polities was clearly manifested in the report of the American Indian Policy Review Commission, which, after a two-year study of the conditions of American Indians in the United States in 1977, advocated a large number of specific reforms that Congress should make to resolve some of the perennial Indian problems. There were two distinctive and fundamentally contradictory views expressed in the final report to Congress. The majority, represented by most of the commission, contended that:

> The relationship of the American Indian tribes to the United States is founded on principles of international law. It is a political relation: a relation of a weak people to a strong people; a relationship founded on treaties in which the Indian tribes placed themselves under the protection of the United States and the United States assumed the obligation of supplying such protection. It is a relationship recognized in the law of this Nation as that of a domestic, dependent sovereign.[169]

Consequently, the majority argued, from this basic position two fundamental concepts emerge that should be considered guidelines for any future development of Indian policy: (1) "That Indian tribes are sovereign political bodies, having the power to determine their own membership and power to enact laws and enforce them within the boundaries of their reservations," and (2) "That the relationship which exists between the tribes and the United States is premised on a special trust that must govern the conduct of the stronger toward the weaker."[170]

These principles seemed reasonable, well within the historical declarations of national responsibility issued by a succession of presidents, congresses, and justices, and yet sufficiently flexible and general to enable the tribal nations and the federal government to negotiate the difficult questions. But the members of the commission preferred to place the legal status of American Indians still within the emotional dimension of law, relying upon the goodwill and good faith of the nation and its Congress, and failing to insist that new federal laws be enacted that would finally vest property and political rights in the Indian nations themselves. Goodwill and good faith are clearly assumptions that underlay political institutions, but they are profoundly inadequate as a means of protecting and ensuring the exercise of legal rights, particularly rights as distinctive and historically rooted as are aboriginal rights.

The minority report of the American Indian Policy Review Commission, conversely, originated in the politics of the moment. Native nations had been winning significant cases in the federal courts involving large land claims in Maine[171] and the affirmation of treaty fishing rights in the Pacific Northwest.[172] Indian activists and the Red Power movement, however, had created an unfavorable image for Native peoples in midwestern states because of their protests and the occupation of Wounded Knee, South Dakota.[173] Much previous white sympathy for Native peoples and issues vanished in the wake of organized backlash in the western states and in Maine by people who, for the most part, had enjoyed privileges at the expense of Indian rights because the federal government had failed to enforce treaties and laws protecting tribal rights and resources. The presidential election of 1976 saw aboriginal issues become important in several western states and particularly in the congressional districts of Washington State's Lloyd Meeds, cochairman of the review commission.

Realizing that he had to switch sides in order to keep his seat in Congress, Meeds, with the assistance of an attorney, prepared a minority report for the review commission. Accusing commission members and staff of deliberately slanting the report to favor Indian interests, Meeds's dissent misrepresented both history and law but proved immensely popular with his political constituency and the growing anti-Indian movement. Meeds's position well summarized the longstanding arguments used by anti-Indian interests by contending that the majority report contained a fundamental error: "It perceives the American Indian tribe as a body politic in the nature of a sovereign as that word is used to describe the United States and the States, rather than as a body politic which the United States, through its sovereign power, permits to govern itself and order its *internal* affairs, but not the affairs of others."[174]

Legal rights by sufferance of the larger political entity, as Meeds suggested here, are, in fact, no rights at all but mere privileges dependent upon the whims of the majority, a condition that the political theorists of the western condition, the Founding Fathers, and the succession of Indian political leaders all disavowed and attempted to avoid by requiring treaties and statutes to govern the relationship.[175]

Meeds's second premise asserted that "in our Federal system, as ordained and established by the United States Constitution, there are but two sovereign entities: the United States and the States. This is obvious not only from an examination of the Constitution, its structure, and its amendments, but also from the express language of the 10th amendment."[176] Meeds cited the delegation of powers phraseology, adding in his concluding sentence that the Fourteenth Amendment made all citizens of the United States citizens of the state in which they reside, making the non sequitur the standard of rationality. This view clearly overlooked the two centuries of American existence and the entire history of American constitutional law. Of course there would be no sections or clauses in the Constitution expressly dealing with Indian sovereignty because the Indian nations, at the time of the adoption of the Constitution, were regarded as independent nations with whom the United States had already and would continue to engage in relations of conflict and cooperation. It must be noted that neither France nor Spain, two countries as intimately involved with Indians at the time the American Constitution was adopted, did not have Indian sovereignty included within their organic documents either.

Nevertheless, Meeds concluded:

> The blunt fact of the matter is that American Indian tribes are not a third set of governments in the American federal system. They are not sovereigns. The Congress of the United States has permitted them to be self-governing entities but not entities which would govern others. American Indian tribal self-government has meant that the Congress permits Indian tribes to make their own laws and be ruled by them. *The erroneous view adopted by the Commission's report is that American Indian tribal government is territorial in nature. On the contrary, American Indian tribal self-government is purposive.*[177]

Meeds's attitude demonstrated the belief that law did not apply, or had no significance with respect to Indians; Congress had plenary powers that could overwhelm historical promises, legal theories, and even the best moments of congressional wisdom and insight in favor of expedient political solutions. The distinction between *territorial* and *purposive* is, of course, a rhetorical sleight of hand and explains little, for it means nothing in this particular context.

Meeds's dissenting opinion might deserve respect had it reflected the studied opinion of a scholarly mind. Since it was the desperate effort of a politician hoping to assuage a political constituency at home by appealing to the baser instincts of a non-Indian interest group, it had little substance and the perpetual twisting of historic fact and doctrines of law, while emotionally satisfying to the anti-Indian forces, had little to recommend it except as a testimony to the lack of personal integrity that Meeds then exemplified. As a line of reasoning that lurks in the hidden and half-conscious recesses of the mind, however, Meeds's argument holds considerable weight. The anti-Indian forces—ranchers, states' rights activists, corporate interests, and environmental groups, among others—that organized in the late 1970s gained additional power and prestige when Ronald Reagan was elected president in 1980. The two Reagan administrations precipitated profound cultural, legal, intergovernmental, and economic changes in indigenous status. But Reagan left his most indelible mark in the judicial arena, where his many appointments of conservative judges and justices to the federal bench would lead to a welter of court decisions that powerfully dampened tribal self-governance and sovereignty just as it was beginning to gain strength after the previous century of oppressive rulings.

Reagan (followed by presidents George H. W. Bush, Bill Clinton, George W. Bush, and Barack Obama), increasing numbers of federal and state lawmakers, and an ever-fickle American public acted upon the stereotypical belief that Native peoples had a favored status in American law. When the Indian gaming phenomenon began to blossom in economic and political importance in the early 1990s and fully exploded in the first decade of the 2000s, and as some Native nations finally began to emerge from their devastating socioeconomic depressions, this seemingly positive step was frequently greeted by angry non-Indian politicians who were intent on challenging the tribal nations' efforts to secure a measure of sustainable economic independence and exercise their right to politically participate in the American democratic process.[178]

Thus, it appears that Native nations can never rest assured that their basic rights as preexisting nations or as individual citizens in three polities will not come under assault by an always suspicious set of forces in the larger society who believe they have the inherent power to maintain their preeminent perch atop indigenous peoples. Should these anti-Indian forces ever succeed in their efforts to terminate indigenous sovereignty, self-governance, and territorial distinctiveness it would be tragic because the next generation of Americans, once again discovering the history of their country, would simply reserve their gains as a means of salving their consciences. Thus it is that "history" totally dominates all efforts to resolve the status of Native peoples in law.

Indigenous peoples are shadowy inhabitants of the legal universe. They carry with them not simply the emotional prejudices attached to the other racial minorities, but a contradictory image of both nobility and savagery that most people, observing Indians, prefer them as larger-than-life symbols of the American past rather than a diverse set of living peoples. African Americans and women had aspects of this image and, in large measure, they retain some potency in their capability to provoke emotional responses. In the case of both these groups, their legal rights had to be secured by constitutional amendment to ensure that succeeding Congresses would not bow to political pressures of the moment and reduce their rights to mere sufferance given at the whim of the majority. This solution may be the only sensible course of action for Native peoples as well. A new, comprehensive definition of what characteristics constitute a Native nation, how Indian land title is defined, what treaties are and what affects their legal or moral potency, and what the relationship of Native nations should be to the other polities in the United States could be included within such an amendment so that indigenous legal rights and the conception of Native peoples might be, at least theoretically, stabilized once and for all.

Tocqueville, discussing Americans, marveled at their naive attitude about the nature of law. "It has never come into their heads that one cannot apply the same law uniformly to all parts of one state and all men living in it," he observed.[179] Americans have still not perceived that a variety of laws specifically designed for particular situations is the most intelligent manner of handling certain issues. In view of the tremendous conflicts between the various indigenous nations and the descendants of the European immigrants that have raged with little respite for five centuries, the just solution to bring these problems to a close, or at least make them more manageable, would be the realization that law cannot and probably should not be made a universal structure into which human beings must be fitted. This attitude, however, requires a maturity that American society does not yet have and may not possess for several more generations.

Wards of the Government

The idea that Native nations were domestic dependent nations and that as individuals Indians owed allegiance first to their tribal government and only secondarily, if at all, to the United States long dominated legal thinking about the rights of Native peoples. In the eastern states, where many tribal nations had suffered devastating depopulation crises and had lost much of their political and legal status—with important exceptions like the Iroquois Nations, the Eastern Band of Cherokee, and the Seminole of Florida— many individual Indians had generally merged into the non-Indian population. Aside from a few cases that defined the civil rights of eastern tribes still under state control and trusteeship, there was little effort to affirm or deny citizenship rights to individual Indians because there was virtually no way to distinguish them in society.

In the western states, however, where a number of large reservations still existed and various policy considerations made expatriation from the tribe attractive to mixed-blood Indians, the courts began to create a situation similar to that of other minority groups who suffered deprivation of citizenship because of rigid beliefs held by jurists. An easy standard was that controversies arose when individual Indians attempted to reject their Indian heritage and become indistinguishable from other citizens. Only as Indians tried to assimilate did legal theories arise to classify them distinctly as Indians incapable of enjoying the rights, protections, and immunities of citizens, a classic case of conflicting definitions excluding individuals from any legal consideration whatsoever.

Part of the confusion came from the multitude of treaty provisions that dealt with the rights and status of individual tribal members. Treaties had two types of provisions, which, because of their close similarity yet radically different orientation, proved to be extremely confusing. The first type conceived tribal membership as severe insofar as eligibility to receive tribal income and promoted a peculiar dual citizenship in which an Indian could simultaneously become a citizen of the United States and a state and yet retain tribal membership. Article 14 of the 1830 Treaty of Dancing Rabbit Creek with the Choctaws, a typical removal-period treaty, contains a common provision:

> Each Choctaw head of a family being desirous to remain and become a citizen of the States, shall be permitted to do so, by signifying his intention to the Agent within six months from the ratification of this Treaty, and he or she shall thereupon be entitled to a reservation of one section of six hundred and forty acres of land, to be bounded by sectional lines of survey... If they reside upon said lands intending to become citizens of the States for five years after the ratification of this Treaty, in that case a grant in fee simple shall issue; said reservation shall include the present improvement of the head of the family, or a portion of it. *Persons who claim under this article shall not lose the privilege of a Choctaw citizen, but if they ever remove are not to be entitled to any portion of the Choctaw annuity.*[180]

The potential for exploitation by white and Indian alike is apparent. Indians could take allotments within their original homelands, claim their intent to become citizens of the state, sell their lands after five years, move to the new location of the tribe, and take additional lands. Unscrupulous whites could quickly marry Native women, stake out claims on choice land, and, after title was confirmed, abandon their wives while keeping the land. Both situations occurred with regularity and made it extremely difficult to resolve the rights of individual Indians.[181] No one could define with certainty when an Indian had truly and finally severed tribal relations.

The second type of treaty provision was very similar. In the treaties of March 15, 1854, with the Oto and Missouri, and of March 16, 1854, with the Omaha, the federal government inserted allotment articles. The sixth article of the Omaha treaty became a prototype for other treaties signed that year and in succeeding years. It introduced allotment as a factor of cultural change, designed to gradually transform tribal members into acceptable citizens through the device of private property:

> The President may, from time to time, at his discretion, cause the whole or such portion of the land hereby reserved, as he may think proper, or of such other land as may be selected in lieu thereof, as provided for in article first, to be surveyed into lots, and to assign to such Indian or

Indians of said tribe as are willing to avail of the privilege, and who will locate on the same as a permanent home...And he may prescribe such rules and regulations as will insure to the family, in case of the death of the head thereof, the possession and enjoyment of such permanent home and the improvements thereon.[182]

This provision changed the manner in which tribal Indians lived, required permanent homes, and provided a means of inheritance. But it did not discuss citizenship. *The Kansas Indians* case illustrates the ultimate conditions to which this policy led.[183] Indians became virtually indistinguishable from their white neighbors, and the question of state control and citizenship finally returned to the unwillingness of Congress to precisely extinguish the tribal nation as a political entity. After these radical cultural changes, Indian tribal citizenship verged on a legal fiction that appeared unreasonable to undiscerning eyes.

Native individuals, we have already noted, were excluded from the provisions of the Fourteenth Amendment because they were regarded as citizens of domestic dependent nations. Not as well known is the exclusion of Indians from the protections of the Thirteenth Amendment, which forbade slavery or involuntary servitude in the United States and its territories. The first interpretations of the amendment, while prescribing Mexican peonage and Chinese labor, were silent on Indian slavery. In the early nineteenth century, an extensive trade in Indian slaves existed in the Southwest. In July 1868, Congress passed Senate Joint Resolution 83 providing:

That Lieutenant-General W. T. Sherman be, and is hereby, authorized and requested to use the most efficient means his judgment will approve to reclaim from peonage the women and children of the Navajo Indians, now held in slavery in the territory adjacent to their homes and the reservation on which the Navajo Indians have been fined.[184]

Sherman's efforts were temporary and sporadic, yet with the settlement of the Southwest it became increasingly difficult to traffic in slaves. For Indians, the importance of the Peonage Act was that they were not allowed to enjoy this basic protection.

To understand the exclusion of Indians from the civil rights amendments, we need to examine the first major case in which an Indian attempted to invoke the protections of the Fourteenth Amendment. The Ponca Indian Reservation, along the Niobrara River in Nebraska, bordered the Great Sioux Reservation established by the Treaty of 1868. The Ponca were subject to frequent depredations by the Sioux. Ponca appeals for federal assistance and protection resulted in a forced migration to Oklahoma. There, in unfamiliar lands, surrounded by other unfriendly tribes, and in a climate radically different from their homeland, the Ponca were ravaged by disease, plagued with loneliness, totally demoralized, and within a year drastically reduced in numbers. Fearing they would all perish, a group of Ponca led by Chief Standing Bear left the Indian Territory and joined their cousins, the Omaha, in northeastern Nebraska, not far from the Ponca homeland.[185]

The BIA discovered that this small group had fled from Oklahoma, and although the Ponca were living peacefully and hoping to find a permanent home among the Omaha, the bureau ordered the army to return them to Oklahoma. The task of arresting the Ponca and marching them back to Oklahoma fell upon General George Crook, a veteran soldier and a man of immense humanity and sympathy. Crook considered this task the most onerous of his career and conspired to prevent what he felt was a gross injustice against the Ponca. With the aid of Thomas Tibbles, an assistant editor of the *Omaha Herald*, Crook publicized the struggles of the Ponca and secured competent attorneys, who agreed that the proposed arrest and return to Oklahoma was an unusually cruel solution to the situation. A writ of habeas corpus was issued and served on Crook as the arresting officer. The Ponca were detained in jail at Omaha and a sympathetic federal judge, Elmer S. Dundy, immediately set hearings. In the interim, the Ponca became the cause celebre of the nation. The resulting publicity enabled Judge Dundy and General Crook to bring out their knowledge of Indian affairs and to express their feelings about the case. It had become impossible for the federal government to be deceptive.

Early in May 1879, the Ponca case was heard in a Nebraska federal district court. After the legal arguments had been made, Judge Dundy asked Standing Bear to speak. The chief's speech was simple, eloquent, emotional, and devastating. Dundy's decision to release the Ponca was viewed by the American public as a classic case of the law working to prevent injustice. Several years later, a separate presidential commission recommended that the Ponca receive part of their Nebraska reservation back. Standing Bear's band, by separating itself from the Oklahoma group, became recognized as a separate political entity, occupied the Nebraska reservations, and remained there until the mid-1960s, when the band finally dissolved. Helen Hunt Jackson, the outstanding polemicist of Indian rights, made the Standing Bear story the keystone of her classic work, *A Century of Dishonor* (1881), and created a climate of sympathy for Native peoples that lasted well into the twentieth century.

United States ex rel. Standing Bear v. Crook, in addition to its national impact, made important progress in defining the constitutional status of Indians.[186] The prosecution had closely followed the theoretical structure of *Cherokee Nation v. Georgia*, with the district attorney arguing a long historical recitation that only American citizens could avail themselves of a writ of habeas corpus in the federal courts. Judge Dundy, however, smartly turned aside this argument: "Whilst the parliament of Great Britain was legislating in behalf of the favored few, the congress of the United States was legislating in behalf of all mankind who come within our jurisdiction." Further, Dundy noted, "it must be borne in mind that the habeas corpus act describes applicants for the writ as 'persons,' or 'parties,' who may be entitled thereto. It nowhere describes them as 'citizens,' nor is citizenship in any way or place made a qualification for suing out the writ."[187] With the elimination of the citizenship requirement that had severely narrowed the issue of standing, the remaining questions in the case turned on whether Standing Bear and the Ponca were persons in the legal sense of the word.

Dundy refused to interpret *persons* narrowly and employed common understandings of the term: "the most natural, and therefore most reasonable, way is to attach the same meaning to words and phrases when found in a statute that is attached to them when and where found in general use." Citing *Webster's* definition of a person as a popular usage, Dundy concluded that it was sufficiently broad to include Indians. "I must hold, then, that Indians, and consequently the relators, are 'persons' such as are described by and included within the laws before quoted."[188] When the district attorney complained that this was the first instance in which an exceedingly broad definition of *person* had been used by a court, Dundy simply noted that perhaps the occasion had never arisen before.

Turning then to the alternatives presented to the Ponca, Dundy noted that unless the Indians were allowed to present their case before some tribunal, they were left with war as their only alternative. Since the band was so small, this was hardly a humane resolution and would have resulted in the Ponca's probable extermination. This condition made recognition of the Ponca by the court imperative. In this theoretical dilemma, the original concept of the Indian tribe as domestic dependent nation played a major role. In expanding his definition of *person* to ensure a proper context for the decision, Dundy ruled that with respect to habeas corpus, race, origin, and even political allegiance had no bearing. Habeas corpus assumed the status of natural law available to all humans as a fundamental right. "When a 'person' is charged, in a proper way, with the commission of crime," Dundy explained, "we do not inquire upon the trial in what country the accused was born, nor to what sovereign or government allegiance is due, nor to what race he belongs. The questions of guilt and innocence only form the subjects of inquiry."[189]

A serious policy problem remained. The federal government was determined to return the Ponca to Oklahoma, and even though their imprisonment was found to violate their basic human rights, the final disposition of the band could not be resolved as long as Standing Bear's group was considered part of the Ponca Nation. If, however, this group could be defined by the court as a new political entity, politically separate from the rest of the Ponca people, then the government would be forced to negotiate with Standing Bear's band as a new tribal entity. Judge Dundy, however, did not have to pursue this line of thought. To his credit, he extended the implications of the domestic dependent nation theory to make certain that the Ponca had sufficient legal status to prevent further administrative tyranny against them. Dundy reviewed the history of the Ponca "for the purpose of showing that the relators did all they could to separate themselves from the tribe and to sever their tribal relations, for the purpose of becoming self-sustaining."[190] The real question in *Standing Bear* then, as Dundy had reshaped the issue, was the determination of the status of an Indian, or Indian group, when the tribal relation was deliberately severed.

His conclusion, unfortunately, did little to clarify this basic question, and his logic took an unaccountable twist that avoided the obvious elevation of the Indian individual to American citizenship. "If Indian tribes are to be regarded and treated as separate but dependent nations," he wrote, "there can be no serious difficulty about the question. If they are not to be regarded and treated as separate, dependent nations, then no allegiance is owing from an individual Indian to his tribe, and he could, therefore, withdraw therefrom at any time."[191] The status of an Indian tribe would preclude the individual from expatriation without the permission of tribal political leaders, but such an act, as we have seen in the provisions of the treaties, would certainly have worked to expedite the change of citizenship. But the converse must certainly not follow since if Indian nations were not domestic dependent nations, they had no political status whatsoever and withdrawal would be a wholly fictional act. Dundy, however, missed the clear distinction that tribal citizenship demanded, arguing instead that "it can make but little difference, then, whether we accord to the Indian tribes a national character or not, as in either case I think the individual Indian possesses a clear and God-given right to withdraw from his tribe and forever live away from it, as though it has no further existence."[192]

Dundy then cited the Expatriation Act of July 1868, which declared:

Whereas the right of expatriation is a natural and inherent right of all people, indispensable to the enjoyment of the rights of life, liberty, and the pursuit of happiness; and whereas in the recognition of this principle the Government has freely received emigrants from all nations, and invested them with the rights of citizenship; and whereas it is claimed that such American citizens, with their descendants, are subjects of foreign states, owing allegiance to the governments thereof; and whereas it is necessary to the maintenance of public peace that this claim of foreign allegiance should be promptly and finally disavowed: Therefore, any declaration, instruction, opinion, order, or decision of any officer of the United States which denies, restricts, impairs, or questions the right of expatriation, is declared inconsistent with the fundamental principles of the Republic.[193]

General Crook's instructions, Dundy argued, fell within the prohibitions of this act and therefore inhibited the expatriation of the Ponca and provided the final justification for issuing the writ and freeing the Indians.

Although the Ponca case rectified a dreadful situation, it did not clarify the status of a Native individual with respect to US citizenship. Achieving recognition as a person within the context of the writ of habeas corpus meant only that an Indian could claim the same fundamental rights as a foreign citizen, and with respect to the expatriation statute, and could not be prohibited from leaving his former political allegiance. All the same, the Indian person did not move into emigrant status with the potential for full citizenship. Rather, the status was one simply of a stateless citizen as long as the tribal entity existed.

Standing Bear was followed five years later by *Elk v. Wilkins*, also originating in Nebraska.[194] This case also involved citizenship and determining the precise point discussed above with relation to expatriation. John Elk, an Indian whose tribal affiliation was not stated in the opinion—this fact alone precluded the Supreme Court from adequately dealing with the question since it was not known under which treaty, if any, Elk might have claimed rights—had moved to Omaha to live as a white man, in a manner indistinguishable from any other citizen of the city.[195] He paid taxes, which precluded his classification as an "Indian not taxed." When Elk attempted to register to vote in a city ward, Charles Wilkins, the ward's registrar, refused registration on the basis that Elk was an Indian. The issue reached the US Supreme Court in 1884.

Critical to the lower court decision was the Nebraska Constitution, which defined voter eligibility in two classes: citizens of the United States, and persons of foreign birth who had declared their intention to become citizens. Since some of the treaties with Indian tribes contained provisions for granting individuals American citizenship, and since the treaties were also laws of the United States, the court had to confront the specifics of Indian law and the status of Indians, individual and tribal, as well as naturalization statutes.

Although Standing Bear had been a person within the scope of the writ of habeas corpus, it was not clear whether Elk was a person within the scope of the Fourteenth Amendment, so the court first directed its attention to this question. Justice Horace Gray's majority opinion began with John Marshall's definition of an Indian tribe. He compared this status with the wording of the first section of the Fourteenth Amendment, which extended protection to "all persons, born or naturalized in the United States, and subject to the jurisdiction thereof," and found an important distinction in the amendment.[196] "The evident meaning of these last words is not merely subject in some respect or degree to the jurisdiction of the United States," Gray declared, "but completely subject to their political jurisdiction, and owing them direct and immediate allegiance."[197] Gray denied that Indians were ever subject to the complete jurisdiction of the United States in this fundamental sense:

Indians born within the territorial limits of the United States, members of and owing immediate allegiance to one of the Indian Tribes, an alien, though dependent power, although in a geographical sense born in the United States, are no more "born in the United States and subject to the jurisdiction thereof," within the meaning of the first section of the 14th Amendment, than the children of subjects of any foreign government born within the domain of that government; or the children, born within the United States, of ambassadors or other public ministers of foreign nations.[198]

For the second time, a federal court compared an individual Indian with a foreign political official rather than another emigrant seeking residence in the United States. This propensity to elevate the status of the individual Indian, admittedly an argument by analogy, increased the mystical aspect of citizenship in both Native nations and the federal government, which has not yet been completely overcome today.

Gray cited several treaties that were pending ratification during passage of the Fourteenth Amendment, observing that these treaties contained provisions for the naturalization of Indians as American citizens. For the most part, these procedures were variances in the standard way that non-Indian aliens gained admission to citizenship and therefore should have been viewed as special legislation designed to help Indians achieve citizenship. But Gray also cited statutory evidence that seemed to preclude Indians from general provisions for all citizens. The Pension Act of 1873, for example, exempted Indian claimants from the obligation to take an oath to support the Constitution; the Indian Homestead Act of 1875 required Indians wishing to become citizens to follow rules promulgated by the Secretary of the Interior. Treaties and statutes seemed to fall equally on both sides of the question.

Most favorably cited of previous state and federal cases involving the citizenship question, however, was an 1880 Oregon case, *United States v. Osborn*,[199] in which a federal district court defined the status of individual Indians attempting to secure citizenship:

An Indian cannot make himself a citizen of the United States without the consent and cooperation of the government. The fact that he has abandoned his nomadic life or tribal relations, and adopted the habits and manners of civilized people, may be a good reason why he should be made a citizen of the United States, but does not of itself make him one. *To be a citizen of the United States is a political privilege, which no one not born to can assume without its consent in some form.*[200]

The Gray opinion depended quite heavily on this definition and, for the purposes of individual Indian applicants, citizenship was said to require the acceptance of the individual through an affirmative act by the US government.

Justice John Marshall Harlan, along with Justice William B. Woods, dissented in *Elk* and in the process raised critical theoretical questions about the nature of citizenship. Harlan argued that at the adoption of the Constitution there had been Indians in many states, not members of recognized tribes, who had participated in the deliberations that led to the formation of the United States and approval of the present form of government. Furthermore, Harlan contended, the Civil Rights Act of 1866 had covered all persons except Indians not taxed, thereby for the first time bringing those Indians who were taxed within the purview of federal statutes. He then cited the congressional debates on the Fourteenth Amendment and arguments within the judiciary committee that seemed, at least to him, to support this new reclassification of Indians into constitutionally protected Indian taxpayers and otherwise alien Indians. The Indians not taxed were at birth members of a nation sufficiently foreign to preclude natural citizenship. Most critical to Harlan's interpretation was the conclusion of the 1870 Senate Judiciary Report on the Fourteenth Amendment, which noted that "when the members of any Indian tribe are scattered, they are merged in the mass of our people and become equally subject to the jurisdiction of the United States."[201]

In conclusion, Justice Harlan said of Elk:

If he did not acquire national citizenship on abandoning his Tribe and becoming subject by residence in one of the States to the complete jurisdiction of the United States, then the 14th Amendment has wholly failed to accomplish, in respect of the Indian race, what we think was intended by it; and there is still in this country a despised and rejected class of persons, with no nationality whatever; who, born in our territory, owing no allegiance to any foreign power, and subject, as residents of the States, to all the burdens of government, are yet not members of any political community nor entitled to any of the rights, privileges or immunities of citizens of the United States.[202]

Harlan's assessment of the situation accurately struck at the majority position that required that a tribal entity must be totally extinguished before any individual tribal member could be eligible for American citizenship.

A possible solution to the Court's dilemma might have been a comparison between the political status of individual states and Indian tribes. The Supreme Court had already examined federal and state citizenship in the *Slaughter-House Cases* by making federal citizenship a tenuous privilege of little substance and vesting major authority in the states. This unbalanced dual citizenship created no conceptual difficulties for the Court. An analogy between states and tribes would not have been a major logical hurdle. This line of thought would most certainly have reached the conclusion that tribal members, at least those who had willingly separated from their aboriginal nations, were American citizens, and while not immediately helpful to Elk's position, it could easily have established a rule that under the Fourteenth Amendment tribal members should not be victims of state discrimination.

Elk recited several treaties with provisions for individual Indians to gain federal citizenship. The fact that the Supreme Court rejected arguments regarding self-operating articles of treaties made no impression on Congress. Congress enacted the General Allotment Act only three years later, which outlined the policy and procedures for dividing tribal land holdings among the membership. Section 6 of the act provided:

> And every Indian born within the territorial limits of the United States to whom allotments shall have been made under the provisions of this act, or under any law or treaty, and every Indian born within the territorial limits of the United States who has voluntarily take up, within said limits, his residence separate and apart from any tribe of Indians therein, and has adopted the habits of civilized life, is hereby declared to be a citizen of the United States, and is entitled to all the rights, privileges, and immunities of such citizens, whether said Indian has been or not, by birth or otherwise, a member of any tribe of Indians within the territorial limits of the United States without in any manner impairing or otherwise affecting the, right of any such Indian to tribal or other property.[203]

This broad phraseology was intended to cure the many defects in the citizenship provisions of treaties and promulgate a major policy of assimilation that had at its root the tenacious western belief in private property as the means of "civilizing" individual Indians. The act only created more confusion. Many of the previous treaties that contained allotment provisions, particularly the major series of treaties signed in 1867 and 1868 with a number of western tribes (for example, the Kiowa, Comanche, Cheyenne, Arapahoe, Sioux, Crow, and Navajo), required the tribe to keep a "Lands Book," in which individual tribal members recorded their choice of lands within the reservation.[204] Title to these lands thus derived from the political status of the tribe rather than from federal law, and the broad policy statement of the General Allotment Act now produced a situation in which both kinds of allotments, federal and tribal, were suspect in their power to provide national citizenship for individual tribal members.

Even more critical than the conflict with treaty provisions, however, were two irreconcilable concepts contained in section 6 of the Allotment Act. All Indians were eligible for allotments, including those who had long ago abandoned tribal affiliation and become assimilated into neighboring white communities in situations comparable to John Elk's. The Allotment Act seemed to require that these people re-affiliate with their former tribal community in order to receive an allotment. In many cases, reservations being allotted experienced a rapid influx of mixed-blood former members who now saw a chance to exploit their Indian heritage to obtain lands that they could sell immediately for cash. Efforts to maintain proper tribal membership rolls were thwarted as land speculators reaped benefits to which few had previously considered themselves entitled. Federal courts, burdened with the task of reconciling conflicting legal doctrines, twisted the previously clear concepts of *tribe* and *treaty* out of recognizable shape in an effort to show that the government's policy was consistent with past efforts. In a 1905 case, *Waldron v. United States*, a federal court, in order to resolve the question of tribal membership, interpreted an agreement with the Sioux as it were a treaty ratified prior to 1871.[205]

Most allotments received under the General Allotment Act had restrictions against alienation for a period of twenty-five years. Earlier treaty allotments lacked this period of trusteeship and restriction and provided citizenship by the simple device of agreeing to take an allotment. Under this restrictive clause, the concept of individual Indians experienced another transformation.

Since Indians were theoretically citizens, they should have been able to alienate their land at will. But the restrictive clause meant that their citizenship was less complete than that of white people, and the courts, lacking statutory direction from Congress, had to resolve their legal incompetency with respect to property. The reasoning by which Indians were declared legally incompetent to sell land was mysterious but effective. *Wards of the government* was a phrase deriving from the descriptive language used by Chief Justice John Marshall in *Cherokee Nation* to explain the nature of the political relationship of Indian tribes to the United States. In respect to the migratory Native peoples, which had no apparently objective or formal tribal organization, the individual members were described as wards. Thus, the dual nature of the individual Indian began to emerge.

The Allotment Act clearly provided that the land, not the individual owner, was subject to the restriction, but the reason for the restriction was to prevent rapid and unwise sale of lands by the owners. The restriction of the deed was prima facie evidence of the legal incompetency of individual Indians. In *United States v. Debell* (1915),[206] a federal court explained that "the chief purpose and main object of the restriction upon alienation is not to prevent the incompetent Indian from selling his land for a price too low, but to prevent him from selling it at all, to the end that he shall be prevented from losing, giving away, or squandering its proceeds and thus be left dependent upon the government or upon charity for his support."[207] Citizenship, then, did not include cultural differences or propensity to squander resources; Indian individuals were burdened with the nebulous expectation that they would always be inadequate to deal with daily economic decisions in the US capitalistic economy.

With the gradual diminishment in the governing capacities of the Five Civilized Tribes in Oklahoma and the allotment of their lands, followed by Oklahoma statehood in 1906 and the extension of state court jurisdiction over the estates of individual Indians, the problems became insurmountable. Cases dealing with the distinctions of citizenship and restrictions against alienation increased spectacularly, and the question of compatibility of these two legal doctrines became critical. In 1917, in *United States v. Waller*, a case dealing with Chippewa allotment on the White Earth Reservation, in Minnesota, the confrontation between incompetency and citizenship, long anticipated, occurred.[208] The Supreme Court, perhaps recognizing that any solution would be distasteful, calmly incorporated the two ideas into one doctrine:

The tribal Indians are wards of the government, and as such under its guardianship. It rests with Congress to determine the time and extent of emancipation. Conferring citizenship is not inconsistent with the continuation of such guardianship, for it has been held that even after the Indians have been made citizens the relation of guardian and ward for some purposes may continue. On the other hand, Congress may relieve the Indians from such guardianship and control, in whole or in part, and may, if it sees fit, clothe then with full rights and responsibilities concerning their property or give them a partial emancipation if it thinks that course better for their protection.[209]

Full citizenship rights under the Constitution would be distributed to Indians at the whim of Congress, partially, wholly, or in fluctuating segments. These same rights could also be withdrawn at any time by federal lawmakers. Until very recent times, this situation has been precisely the legal condition of Indians.

The *Waller* case was decided in 1917, during World War I, and seemed to represent the final logical term of an ideology that had been developing in the courts since *Cherokee Nation* (1831) gave the concept of wardship legal airing. During World War I, Indians volunteered for service in large numbers even though, not being US citizens, they could not be drafted or required to serve in the American armed forces. The Iroquois, uncertain as to their status with respect to the drafting and unwilling to recognize any political power of the United States, declared war against Germany and authorized any of their young men to serve *with* the United States, not *for* it. Following the war, Congress awarded full citizenship to all honorably discharged Native veterans.[210]

In 1924, tired of the permutations and combinations of citizenship, Congress passed a problematic statute unilaterally bestowing citizenship to all other Indians born within the territorial limits of the United States without regard to qualifications or previous legal status.[211] But these acts were largely ineffectual because the doctrine of compatibility of indigenous legal incompetence remained good law and nullified efforts by Congress to provide Indians with constitutional protections with respect to their lands and tribal benefits.

An obscure phrase in the General Allotment Act referred to individual Indians "adopting the habits of civilized life" as part of their qualifications for citizenship. Strangely enough, little bother was made over this phrase, although in the case of relatively isolated Native nations it could have been used to distinguish legal rights or to deny citizenship. As legal doctrine developed in the direction of the restrictions on allotment deeds, it appeared there would be no court test of this cultural qualification for citizenship. In Alaska, however, habits of civilized life proved critical in determining the rights of the Natives. The major contention involved eligibility for territorial public schools.

Davis v. Sitka School Board (1908) illustrates the difficulty faced by Alaska Natives.[212] Alaska had been purchased from Russia by the United States in 1867 for $7.2 million dollars.[213] The treaty ceding the territory included a promise by the United States that Native land claims be treated fairly. After 1867, the territory remained sparsely settled, even after the Klondike Gold Rush. Natives were sometimes included in general acts of Congress intended to provide government and services for the territory; at other times they were the subject of special legislation. Their exact status, however, remained muddled.

In January 1905, as part of its continuing supervision of American territories, Congress passed an act providing for the construction and maintenance of roads and schools in Alaska.[214] Section 7 of the act required "that the schools specified and provided for in this act shall be devoted to the education of white children and children of mixed blood who lead a civilized life."[215] The mixed-bloods of Sitka felt that this included their children; when they discovered they could not enroll their children in school, they filed suit. Dora and Tillie Davis, lead plaintiffs in this case, were mixed-blood children of Fred Davis, a deceased Indian, and an unnamed mother who appeared to be of mixed racial ancestry, who lived in Sitka. The mother had remarried "a full-blood native," Rudolph Walton, who became the guardian *ad litem* of the children. Walton was a leading storekeeper in the village and a member of the local Presbyterian church. Considering the criteria for school admission under the statute, this appeared to be an ideal family.

Judge Royal Arch Gunnison, determined to bar mixed-blood children from the school, demonstrated the extent to which legal concepts can be twisted to achieve predetermined conclusions. He discovered a distinction he said was intended by Congress in the requirement that mixed-blood children "lead a civilized life." So, he argued, "from the very inception of the United States, the care and education of the Indian has been one of the problems that has vexed the government. The Indian in his native state has everywhere been found to be savage, an uncivilized being, when measured by the white man's standard."[216]

Having declared that Congress had something specifically in mind when attaching this phraseology, Gunnison then promptly negated his contention, arguing "that Congress, by the use of the words 'civilized life,' had in mind any particular or definite condition to which the 'mixed blood,' or his parents or guardians, must have attained, cannot be presumed, since the term 'civilization' is at best only relative. The standards of civilization which have been erected for today will undoubtedly 100 years hence be far behind the vanguard of progress." "The courts," Gunnison concluded, "have never essayed to define it."[217] Thus, he concluded sadly, "each generation must decide for itself what constitutes the civilized life, and each case involving the question of civilization must be decided upon its own merits, free and untrammeled by rules laid down by either philosopher, judge, or encyclopedian."[218] Having thus rejected any commonly acceptable definition of civilization that he might have shared with Congress, Gunnison announced that his criterion would be "whether or not the persons in question have turned aside from old associations, former habits of life, and easier modes of existence; in other words, have exchanged the old barbaric, uncivilized environment for one changed, new, and so different as to indicate an advanced and improved condition of mind, which desires and reaches out for something altogether distinct from and unlike the old life."[219] Exactly how this transition could be accomplished in the barrens of Alaska, where land and climate usually required white people to adopt the ways of Natives rather than the opposite, was never explained. Reciting the evidence that the Davis family had placed before him to support their convention that they lived a civilized life, Judge Gunnison remarked that "civilization, though, of course the term must be considered relative, includes, I apprehend, more than a prosperous business, a trade, a house, white man's clothes, and membership in a church."[220]

The court examined increasingly personal evidence forwarded by the Davises and the other families: their ownership and use of sewing machines, spotless homes with kitchens superior to those of their white neighbors, church attendance and membership in the choir, and other indices of social, economic, and religious integration with the white community. One family had been socially connected with the territorial governor and had attended social functions in the governor's mansion. No amount of evidence, however, qualified Indians for admission to the public school. Every cultural adaptation of the Natives was rejected out of hand by the court as incapable of establishing a claim to civilized life.

Several other cases followed *Davis* and eventually the effects of this decision were reversed. Although not an integral case of the multitude of court decisions on individual Indian rights, *Davis* eloquently demonstrated how the emotional conception of the Indian as savage still dominated the minds of Euro-Americans in 1905. Case law and legal doctrines had not progressed significantly during two centuries of American political existence. The major stumbling block to full citizenship rights was, as we have seen, the conception of Indians as citizens of another political entity. Insofar as federal courts and statutes extended the idea of wardship into the inner workings of the tribal body politic to provide a trustee relationship with respect to the property owned by individual Indians, the popular conception of Indians was that of foreigners or people with a privileged status who did not need or deserve constitutional rights and protections. Cultural differences, racial origins, and the foibles of American history combined to present such a confused concept of the rights of Indians as both national collectivities and individuals that the present posture of federal law still contains no useful landmarks for the careful articulation of Indian rights.

Two arguments summarize the barriers against which indigenous peoples are thrust: (1) A political argument states that Indians are not citizens of the United States but of Indian nations, which, although within the political jurisdiction of the United States and therefore not completely independent, are nevertheless sufficiently independent to justify their exclusion from many constitutional protections; (2) A cultural argument describes Indians as savages insufficiently schooled in the manners, customs, and values of Western civilization, and therefore incapable of properly benefitting from any common legal rights.

The cultural argument, while abandoned by the federal courts insofar as it is used to deprive Indians of ordinary legal rights, has recently reemerged to strip away or dramatically diminish Native treaty rights. Now Natives are asked to prove that they are still Indians and entitled to the benefits secured by their ancestors. In the 1999 gray whale incident involving the Makah of Washington State, Native hunters were savagely attacked by state, federal, and environmental groups for employing hunting methods—the Makah used steel harpoons and a .50-caliber assault rifle—that whites felt were not "traditional." In many fishing rights cases, courts frequently restrict Indian fishing to so-called ancient methods while non-Indian sportsmen are encouraged to use all forms of modern technology to gain the upper hand in their quest to catch fish; in land claims cases in the eastern United States, courts have frequently demanded that Indians dress, eat, and live as their ancestors did if they expect to receive judicial recognition of their aboriginal land claims. Such a crude rendering of static cultural values is no more intelligent or sophisticated than the ramblings of Judge Gunnison of Alaska. In nontreaty areas such as economic development, similar cultural arguments are used against Native peoples to weaken or crimp their efforts at self-sufficiency. This is especially true in regard to Indian gaming, with their detractors frequently arguing that gambling operations are not a traditional form of subsistence and should be regulated by the federal and state governments.[221] In a fundamental sense, this is the counterpart of the dilemma faced in *Plessy v. Ferguson*, where fair skin was treated as a property right. Cultural attributes have in many instances become the most critical evidence that defines and determines the legal and political rights of Native peoples.

Indigenous peoples remain pilgrims in the legal universe, with no sure haven from the depredations of courts, congresses, or corporations. The definitions that have been useful in determining their legal status derive more from the incidents of history than from the political philosophies or constitutional doctrines of Western civilization. Although the domestic dependent nation theory originated in the colonial period and enjoyed some status within the worldview of European and Euro-American thinkers of those days, subsequent settlement of the North American continent has generally submerged Native peoples' rights and resources beneath the threshold of a national and world consciousness and forced them into the status of semi-distinct ethnic groups, which are encouraged to function as interest groups.

Insofar as Natives participate in the social and economic programs of the federal government, in today's world they are frequently treated as racialized interest groups, albeit ones with a definite political and legal status that removes many roadblocks that would otherwise inhibit their active participation. Facing a choice of full-fledged assimilation or the restoration of a significant amount of indigenous political and economic independence, aboriginal peoples must master the technical skills necessary to survive. Thus, the critical area is education. Like African Americans, indigenous peoples are vitally interested in the perennial problems of the relationship of the federal government to the states and the opening of educational opportunities for all people without regard to origin and background. While the *Bakke* case and its progeny are not as crucial for Native nations as they are for other groups—because of the ever-increasing number of tribally run colleges and the ongoing relevance of Indian preference policies in the BIA that continue to benefit qualified Native applicants over equally qualified non-Native applicants—nevertheless they become a major point of contention in any long-term vision of the future of Indians.

CHAPTER 7
"Those of a 'Delicate' Nature: Women and the Law

UNLIKE THE SITUATION OF WOMEN in Afghanistan, Pakistan, India, China, Africa, and in other parts of the non-Western world—where brutal policies and practices are still evident in the public executions of women for prostitution, where women are denied the right to work outside the home, and where they can be publicly flogged for not wearing a veil, for talking to male shopkeepers, or even for being out on the streets at night[1]—the legal, political, and social standing of women in the United States and throughout the Western world has improved considerably. This is evident in health and life expectancy, in the securing of the most basic civil and political rights, in the attainment of a measure of economic independence, and in public education.[2]

These are, to be sure, profound differences. Since our focus, however, is on the status of women under US law, with particular attention to the role played by the Supreme Court in improving or diminishing women's status, it is important to note that while American women fare comparatively well to women in many non-western countries, they have not always been so favorably situated, and even today women in America face serious constraints not encountered by men.

In the formative years of American history under the common law doctrine of coverture, when a woman married, her legal identity became merged into that of her husband. As the authors of the famous Declaration of Sentiments put it in 1848, women were "civilly dead" in the eyes of the law. Women could not sue or be sued, enter contracts, make wills, retain their own earnings, control property, or protect her physical person. Her husband could beat her, restrain her freedom, and legally rape her. Outside of marriage, women confronted an even harsher political, social, and economic world: they were deprived of the important democratic privilege of voting, and they were prohibited from working in certain professions, including the practice of law.

Conditions improved somewhat for women by the mid-1800s, with the enactment of a number of married women's property acts in certain states, which gave women some control over their own property, but as we shall see when we move into the case law, the legal, political, and economic status of women remained unequal in many respects. By the 1990s, the federally funded Glass Ceiling Commission, which was created in 1991 under the Civil Rights Act to study and make recommendations concerning eliminating barriers to the advancement of women and minorities, reported that while two-thirds of the US population and 57 percent of the working population was female, racial minority, or both, "at the highest levels of business, there is indeed a barrier only rarely penetrated by women or persons of color."[3] One glaring fact: 95–97 percent of the senior managers of Fortune 1000 industries and Fortune 500 companies are male. And when women have gained a foothold in senior positions, their compensation was invariably lower than that of their male colleagues.

Besides the economic glass ceiling, the judicial data confirms that the absence of legal equality, quality education, freedom from sexual discrimination, protection from physical and sexual abuse, equal opportunities in military service, and reproductive freedom continue to plague women across the board, with minority women facing the double burden of race and gender.

Constitutional Neutrality or Masculinity

The Constitution is, of course, generally phrased in gender-neutral language.[4] In fact, there is no mention of gender in the original document; the word *person* is typically used. The words *male* and *sex* appear only in two later amendments: *male* is inserted in the Fourteenth Amendment, and *sex* is a part of the Nineteenth Amendment. Section 2 of the Fourteenth Amendment, adopted in 1868, declares that when the right to vote in any general election "is denied to any of the male inhabitants of such State...the basis of representation therein shall be reduced in the proportion which the number of such male citizens shall bear to the whole number of male citizens twenty-one years of age in such State." This section is now inoperative.

The Nineteenth Amendment, ratified in 1920, however, is very important for our purposes since it involves women and the right to vote. It declares that "the right of citizens of the United States to vote shall not be denied or abridged by the United States or by any State on account of sex."

The paucity of gender-based language might lead an uninformed observer to conclude that legal and political equality were the reality for all persons, including women, under the Constitution. The evidence, however, shows conclusively that far from being gender neutral, the Constitution's interpretation and the application of laws were and remain deeply masculine and patriarchal. As Robin West has noted: "Jurisprudence is 'masculine' because jurisprudence is about the relationship between human beings and the laws we actually have, and the laws we actually have are 'masculine' both in terms of their intended beneficiary and in authorship."[5]

While the law in practice and in theory is manifestly patriarchal, the Constitution's authors, by employing the words *person* rather than *man* or *male*, inadvertently made it possible for women to exercise some constitutional rights and enjoy other benefits even before they had secured the right to vote. Thus, such important rights as the freedom of expression and association proved useful to women in their pre-vote days as they rallied to complain about discriminatory treatment and voting denial. Women also took advantage of educational and teaching opportunities made available at female seminaries like Emma Willard's, Troy Female Seminary, and Catharine Beecher's Hartford Female Seminary, and other public universities.[6] In addition, since there was no question that women were at least eligible to run for political office, this made it possible for Jeannette Rankin to become the first woman elected to the House of Representatives, in 1916, four years before women as a class could actually exercise the franchise.[7]

The Difference Barrier: Gender and Stereotype

Notwithstanding the sporadic victories earned by some individual women in American history, like the other racial and ethnic groups we have studied thus far, women far more often have had their humanity masked by the law that has often relied on or created stereotypes, myths, and legal fictions to keep them disenfranchised and disempowered. As Jill Norgren and Serena Nanda put it, US law has long been based on gender stereotypes that posit the female's world as that of home and hearth. They have also been handicapped by the attitude that it is their nature to have and rear children. The lives of women were formed into a subculture whose principal criterion was gender, although race and class factored in. "The myth," say Norgren and Nanda, "of woman as fragile, dependent, childlike creatures formed the basis of laws which created and maintained a reality in which women, often under the guise of protective laws, were denied access to political power and economic resources."[8]

The notion that men and women functioned in separate spheres, with the women (as wives) being the center of the private world of the family, and the men (as husbands) the representative in the public world and the breadwinner, was certainly an improvement from the early American/English perspective of women having virtually no rights. But although women were recognized as having certain civil and property rights, they were still situated in a subservient position under the law and in society. "The public world of men was governed by law," says Wendy Williams, "while the private world of women was outside the law, and man was free to exercise his prerogatives as he chose."[9]

Judicial Entrenchment of the Separate Spheres Ideology

The women's movement reached an early apex when the Seneca Falls Convention, the first National Women's Rights Convention, was held at Seneca Falls, New York, in 1848. Conference organizers, including Elizabeth Cady Stanton and Lucretia Mott, and others, including Frederick Douglass, the prominent African American activist, challenged the "supremacy of men, the denial of a woman's right to vote, the unequal distribution of power in the state, church, and family, and the different moral expectations applied to men and women." A Declaration of Sentiments and Resolutions was approved at the end of the conference, having been modeled after the Declaration of Independence, and women continued their active campaign to obtain the ballot and gain greater employment opportunities and equality under the law.[10] However, it was not until the early 1870s that the Supreme Court got directly involved in their struggle, rendering two rulings, *Bradwell v. Illinois* (1873)[11] and *Minor v. Happersett* (1874),[12] that had debilitating and lasting effects on women—the practice of law in *Bradwell*, and the nature and meaning of citizenship, which, in the *Minor* case, did not include the right to vote.

Both cases utilized well-known stereotypes, or what Judith Olans Brown, Lucy A. Williams, and Phyllis Tropper Baumann call "mythic generalizations," which reduce women as a class to one of two archetypes: madonna or whore.[13] The madonna image holds that women are natural nurturers and pristine role models; the whore image, also referred to as jezebel, is that of a sexually vivacious slut, lacking any caregiving qualities. The Court's reliance on these archetypes allows it to legitimize rulings that deny justice to women.

Myra Bradwell, an Illinois resident and the wife of a noted attorney, and bearing all the necessary qualifications including "good character," had been denied the right to practice law in the state because she was both a woman and because of her marital status as a married woman. Bradwell sued to the US Supreme Court, arguing that the state had violated her Fourth and Fourteenth Amendment rights as a US citizen. Justice Samuel F. Miller, for the majority, in a decision showing deference to states' rights, ruled that although women were nowhere expressly excluded from practicing law, it had never been the intention of the Illinois legislature to allow women to practice law. More bluntly, Miller said that the right to practice law in states "in no way depends on citizenship of the United States."[14] The unequal dual spheres of male and female rights were here broadened and deepened by the dual spheres of state and national sovereignty, discussed previously in the *Slaughter-House Cases*, when the two sovereign entities were held to be relatively independent of the other insofar as the privileges and immunities clause of the Fourteenth Amendment was concerned.

This case, however, is better remembered for dicta in the concurring opinion by Justice Joseph P. Bradley, joined by Justices Stephen J. Field and Noah H. Swayne, that powerfully and unequivocally entrenched numerous stereotypes and legal fictions about the nature of women, their abilities or inabilities, and the actual state of conditions that would predominate in the law for nearly the next century.

In Bradley's view, the civil law "as well as nature herself" admitted to fundamental differences in the "spheres and destinies" of men and women.[15] First, men were regarded as the protectors and defenders of women, who were deemed timid and delicate and therefore not capable of doing "many of the occupations of civil life." Second, Bradley reinforced the idea that the domestic sphere was the logical and ordained place for women to fulfill their destiny. The family as an essential institution demanded that women not work outside the home. Third, this view of domesticity, according to Bradley, was clearly acknowledged in the existing laws, which, along with "recent modifications" still supported the view that "a married woman is incapable, without her husband's consent, of making contracts which shall be binding on her or him."[16]

While Bradley acknowledged that single women were not as burdened as married women, he insisted that "the paramount destiny and mission of women are to fulfill the noble and benign offices of wife and mother."[17] "This is," said Bradley, " the law of the Creator." Since Bradley had elevated himself and his brethren to be the spokesmen for God, women stood little chance of challenging this patriarchal view of the world.

Finally, Bradley, while seemingly supportive of those changes in the law that had brought some social and economic advancements for women, like the married property acts, ended his comments by reinforcing state police power when he noted that there were clearly some occupations and professions, like the practice of law, that required special qualifications not everyone possessed. It was up to state lawmakers to decide who was eligible for such positions. Bradley took this last moment, however, to inject his own opinion, which was that "in view of the peculiar characteristics, destiny, and mission of women," the legislatures would and should rightly decide that complicated and demanding professions, like the practice of law, be preserved for men because they are "the sterner sex."

Two years later, in 1875, the Supreme Court was again asked to hear a case involving one of the fundamental privileges and immunities of the Fourteenth Amendment: the right to vote. The case was brought by Virginia Minor, who was supported by the women's movement. Minor sued the local registrar in a Missouri state court for denying her the right to vote on the grounds that she was not a male citizen. She lost at the state trial and appellate levels and then appealed to the US Supreme Court. Her argument was that as a citizen of the United States, she was entitled to all of the privileges and immunities accorded to citizens. The privilege of voting, she asserted, was the "preservative of all rights and privileges" and was essential if participatory democracy was to have real meaning. Furthermore, the franchise could be denied or constrained only by language found in the Constitution of the United States.[18] And since states were forbidden by the Fourteenth Amendment from making or enforcing any laws that abridged the privileges or immunities of US citizens, it followed that Missouri was in error and had wrongly denied her the right to vote.

Chief Justice Morrison R. Waite, for a unanimous Court, went to great lengths, however, to narrowly define what citizenship entailed. For the Court, citizenship was understood as "conveying the idea of membership of a nation, and nothing more."[19] Waite went even further in crafting a bizarre legal argument to deny women, who were admittedly citizens, of the most fundamental privilege of citizenship—the right to vote—since, in his opinion, the constitutional framers had not intended to enfranchise them. He effected this by rejecting the Fourteenth Amendment as a source of a right to vote or as a federal limit on state control of the franchise.[20]

Having severely weakened the major constitutional argument of Minor, Waite then created what he said was "the direct question," which was "whether all citizens, are necessarily voters." The Court was now free to construct three conclusions that significantly hampered women's voting rights for many years to come. First, Waite stated that since nearly all women had historically been denied the franchise, it was therefore appropriate for state lawmakers to simply continue this practice. Second, the Court also held that Minor's gender was, like age, length of residency, and propertied status, a reasonable criteria states could use to extend or withhold the right to vote. And finally, and most obviously from Waite's perspective, since women were not explicitly mentioned in either the original Constitution or, more importantly, the Fourteenth Amendment, which happened to mention only male citizens, or the Fifteenth Amendment, which only referred to race, color, or condition of servitude, this absence of express language was sufficient to deny women the vote.

More damning, from women's perspective, was the Court's absolute acquiescence to the state's actions and its unwillingness to exercise any measure of judicial review over such a crucial matter. "It is not for us," said Waite, "to look at the hardship of withholding [the franchise]. Our duty is at an end if we find it is within the power of a State to withhold."[21]

Women, Wage Labor, and Economic Discrimination

Until the Industrial Revolution, most Euro-Americans, male and female, labored on farms and in family businesses. Men and women, of course, worked in different economic spheres, with women largely being concentrated in the production of goods for family life (cloth making, candle making, tending the gardens, raising children, and preserving food)[22] and men holding the economic reigns in virtually every other aspect (manufacturing, real estate, government, various trades and professions, and so forth). By 1890, however, wage and salaried positions had more than doubled over those self-employed. This remarkable transition was accompanied by the movement of production from private homes to the bustling factories.

These bustling factories, the epitome of industrialization, urbanization, and the laissez-faire view of the market economy as a self-executing system that rewarded hardworking individuals through voluntary agreement, came with horrendous work conditions for all but the most elite workers. Social reformers and unions pushed for laws to regulate conditions including work hours and wages. These legislative efforts were challenged legally by conservative leaders of the American Bar Association who resurrected the natural law notion of freedom of contract and located it in the due process clause of the Fourteenth Amendment.[23]

The result was a decision by the Supreme Court, *Lochner v. New York* (1905), that invalidated a New York regulation limiting the hours of labor males or females could work in bakeries to ten per day or sixty per week. The Court, speaking through Justice Rufus W. Peckham, reasoned that the state law, which had as its goal improving the unsanitary environmental conditions of bakers, who frequently were required to work more than 100 hours per week, was not a legitimate exercise of state police power, but was "an unreasonable, unnecessary and arbitrary interference with the right and liberty of the individual to contract in relation to his labor." The liberty protected by the Fourteenth Amendment, Peckham stressed, included the right to purchase and sell labor. Thus, any statute interfering with that right would be deemed invalid unless circumstances dictated otherwise.

Three years later, in *Muller v. Oregon* (1908) the Supreme Court was faced with a challenge to a 1903 Oregon statute that prohibited women from working more than ten hours in laundries, factories, or other "mechanical establishments."[24] In response to the *Lochner* majority's claim that it was not "reasonable" to believe that maximum-hours legislation promoted public health, an amicus brief was filed by Louis Brandeis (a future Supreme Court justice), and two leading women reformists, Josephine Goldmark and Florence Kelly, that provided voluminous pseudoscientific data purporting to analyze the negative relationship between long hours of labor on the health, safety, child-bearing capacity, and morals of women. A mere 2 pages of the more-than-100-page brief followed the typical pattern of explaining legal precedents as they related to the case.[25]

The Brandeis brief view was adopted by a unanimous Court, which upheld the challenged legislation. The same Court that had vigorously enriched the freedom of contract and the constitutional right to labor in an unregulated economy in *Lochner* now with even more vigor denied women the same right and justified this denial on powerful myths about motherhood, women's alleged dependency, and so forth. Excerpts from the case reveal the stereotypical assumptions accepted by the Court about the nature of women. This language was used to justify a variety of sex-based discrimination laws, or so-called protective legislation that barred women from certain types of employment for the next sixty years.

Justice David J. Brewer, for a unanimous Court, noted unequivocally "that women's physical structure and the performance of maternal functions place her at a disadvantage in the struggle for subsistence is obvious."[26] As the "weaker" of the two sexes, yet endowed with the distinctive ability to bear children, women had a special obligation, said Brewer, to not overwork themselves since "healthy mothers are essential to vigorous offspring."[27] Such needs were enough to invoke public interest and state action to provide the necessary care and protection women required. "History," noted Brewer, shows that women have always been "dependent upon men," physically, economically, and educationally. Because of this alleged subservient status and childbearing capacity, women may be "properly placed in a class by herself," and the states were "free to enact legislation for her protection even though such legislation would not stand for men."[28]

In short, the Court concluded that women constituted a special category of dependent citizens and it was therefore permissible to place special restrictions on them when such restrictions were done for the well-being of women and the future well-being of the human race.[29]

Commerce and Female Sexuality

Coincidentally, the enshrinement into law of the mythic generalization of the maternal functions of women and the need to protect the health and well-being of such "dependents" clashed vigorously with another of the mythic archetypes, that of woman as whore, in another Supreme Court decision rendered the same day as *Muller v. Oregon, United States v. Bitty*.[30] Clarifying the whore archetype and its relationshp to the marketplace, Norgren and Nanda observe: "On the one hand, society demands chastity and innocence of women; at the same time, it creates a ready and profitable market for their sexual services. Thus, prostitution and pornography—and more recently, surrogate motherhood—have permitted women to find opportunities to earn through the commercialization of those aspects of their nature and biology with which the dominant culture has insisted upon identifying them."[31]

Thus, in *Bitty*, Justice John Harlan, for a unanimous Court, upheld a 1907 federal law that criminalized the importation of an alien woman for the purpose of prostitution or any other "immoral purpose," including living with a man sans a valid marriage certificate. Any woman willing to engage in such activities was deemed to be acting in ways that "would be hurtful to the cause of sound private and public morality and to the general well-being of the people."[32] The criminalization of prostitution, the unequal enforcement of laws against prostitutes (since female prostitutes are arrested more often than male prostitutes), and, of course, the fact that prostitutes and not their male customers are prosecuted are "all ways in which American law demonstrates the moral hypocrisy which underlies it."[33]

Such mythic generalizations as expressed in the law—madonna or whore—broadly reflect Euro-American women. But white society has created similar mythologies for African American women and other minority women as well. For African American women, the two dominant archetypes are the mammy, the childless Eve, patient and wise caregiver who dotes on a white family; and the jezebel, the sexually energized woman who tempts white men with her sexual favors.[34] Similarly, American Indian women are portrayed as tender and lifesaving Pocahontas types or conversely as dirty and lecherous squaws, which, not coincidentally happens to be a derogatory word for *vagina*. While the overt use of such crass terms has lessened over time, it is clear that such myths are still pervasive in society and the law.

Women, Voting, and Employment

Although stymied in their effort to vote by the 1875 *Minor* decision, women activists had continued unabated in their desire to secure the franchise. Their activism was clearly evident in the temperance movement, Indian affairs, and other reform crusades. Taking advantage of the changing social and political climate of the Progressive period and in the wake of World War I, the suffragist movement succeeded in convincing Congress to enact the Nineteenth Amendment in 1919. It was ratified August 26, 1920, culminating a bitter seventy-year struggle.

This important constitutional victory prompted feminist leaders to pursue other rights for women, including an equal rights amendment to the Constitution. While these constitutional debates were raging, the subject of economic rights for women was also a major topic. In fact, between 1912 and 1922, some fifteen states enacted minimum-wage laws for women and children. This brief period of apparent economic rationality, however, was radically curtailed by the Supreme Court in a 1923 case, *Adkins v. Children's Hospital*.[35] This was the first case to address minimum-wage legislation. It involved the constitutionality of a District of Columbia minimum-wage law for women. In a 5–3 decision, Justice George Sutherland, for the majority, declared the law unconstitutional because it was an arbitrary determination that a certain income was necessary for health and safety and that minimum-wage laws constituted "undue" interference with the "liberty to contract." Thus, the Court had revived *Lochner*, which most observers thought had been silently overruled in *Bunting v. Oregon* (1917).[36]

Surprisingly, the Court asserted that recent developments, including the Nineteenth Amendment, did more than just confer the right to vote to women, but indicated an awareness that women had made real improvements in the law and in society. "In view of the great—not to say revolutionary—changes which have taken place since that [*Muller*] utterance in the contractual, political, and civil status of women, culminating in the Nineteenth Amendment, it is not unreasonable to say that these differences have now come almost, if not quite, to the vanishing point."[37] Sutherland went on to say that while physical differences between the sexes could still be acknowledged in appropriate circumstances, he could find no basis for "women of mature age" to be restricted in their right to contract when men were not similarly restrained. Such discriminatory treatment would "ignore all the implications to be drawn from the present day trend of legislation, as well as that of common thought and usage, by which woman is accorded emancipation from the old doctrine that she must be given special protection or be subjected to special restraint in her contractual and civil relationships."[38]

While the Court appeared to be making an effort to step away from the harsh and deeply prejudicial stereotypical language of the *Muller*-era cases, there is language in the case that confirms that sex-based discrimination based on physical differences would still be found constitutional; and of equal importance, the Court, in stressing that women could negotiate wages but not hours, perpetuated the appearance that it was still unmoved by the severe economic constraints women workers faced. This was evident in the fact that women's earnings were, on average, at the bottom of the pay scale. They had less take-home pay because of the fewer hours worked, and they were still denied access to certain jobs that required longer hours or evening work.[39]

The *Muller* legacy, in muted form, continued. In fact, when the Supreme Court expressly overruled *Adkins* fourteen years later in *West Coast Hotel Co. v. Parrish* (1937), the majority relied heavily on *Muller*'s description of women as a class of people who were "disadvantaged" because of their physical structure and childbearing functions.[40] As such, the state could enact legislation to "protect" women—in ways that would not pass constitutional muster if applied to men.[41]

Long before *Adkins* was overturned, however, the Court was already making exceptions to the economic opportunities available to women, ostensibly on the grounds that they were too delicate to handle long hours. Thus, in *Radice v. New York* (1924), Mr. Radice, a restaurant owner in New York City, challenged a state law that prohibited women from working the night shift between the hours of 10 PM and 6 AM in restaurants in large cities.[42] Ironically, while they could not engage in restaurant work per se, due to the alleged difficulties of said work that might "impair their peculiar and natural functions" and expose them to "the dangers and menaces incident to night life in large cities," they could still entertain in the same establishment as "singers and performers of any kind" and could serve as cloakroom and parlor attendants. Moreover, women were still permitted to work in dining rooms and kitchens of hotels and in restaurants "conducted by employers solely for the benefit of their own employees."[43]

This economically discriminatory statute, in effect, reserved the most lucrative restaurant positions for men. The state defended the discriminatory legislation on the grounds that night employment was detrimental to the health and welfare of women. Justice Sutherland, for a unanimous Court, said the Court was without power to review the legislation, but did agree that the evidence offered by the state was sufficient to warrant such a measure. Stressing that women were "the most delicate organism," Sutherland found that *Muller*'s declarations of women's physical limitations were controlling in the case. As such, the Court distinguished the *Adkins* case on the grounds that it was a wage-fixing law, while the present case focused on hours and conditions of labor.

What the Court never explained, however, was how working at night as a waitress in a hotel-related restaurant or, more to the point, performing as a singer or dancer would have a less harmful impact on women's health or welfare than working at the same job in a nonhotel restaurant. The Court effectively denied Radice's due process challenge and addressed the equal protection argument by claiming that "if the law presumably hits the evil [nighttime employment in a major city restaurant] where it is most felt, it is not to be overthrown because there are other instances to which it might have been applied."[44]

Of Imbecility, Eugenics, and Female Reproductivity

During the Progressive Era that prospered in the United States in the first two decades of the twentieth century, there arose a powerful, nearly fanatical eugenics movement, which claimed that the human population could be improved by controlled breeding. Eugenical sterilization, as it came to be called, would shortly become the most common practice aimed at breeding out so-called undesirable hereditary defects, like mental illness, physical disabilities, and others, that allegedly weakened the vitality of the white race. Typically, these sterilizations of women—men, of course, were not subject to vasectomies—were performed without informed consent on state hospital inmates. Nationally, nearly 60,000 eugenic sterilizations were done between 1927 and 1964, spread across twenty states. In Virginia alone, where the practice had its ignominious beginning, more than 8,300 female inmates at state mental institutions were sterilized between 1927 and 1972.[45]

The eugenics campaign in general, and the sterilization of female hospital inmates in particular, received legal sanction by the Supreme Court in the 1927 case, *Buck v. Bell*.[46] In this decision, the Court was called upon to determine whether it was in the state's police power to craft a law that provided for the sterilization of state inmates who were allegedly affiliated with "hereditary forms of insanity or imbecility."[47] Certain procedural safeguards were included in the statute: the superintendent of the institution had to present a petition to a board of directors exploring the facts and grounds for his opinion; the intended victim was given notice of the hearing and could attend; if the inmate was a minor then her parents were notified of the hearing; the hearing's evidence was written down and could be used as the basis of an appeal to the current court of the county; and appeals could also be taken to the Virginia Supreme Court of Appeals.[48]

Carrie Buck, a poor eighteen-year-old from Charlottesville, Virginia, and a rape victim who had become pregnant from the attack was committed to the Virginia State Colony for Epileptics and Feeble Minded in 1924 by the family she lived with. Her mother had previously been committed to the same institution. Both were alleged to be mentally incompetent and morally delinquent, although available records indicate that Carrie was a normal child in every respect, save one: she had been violently impregnated against her will. It appears, then, that the fact of her unwed pregnancy and subsequent birth of a daughter was enough to convince Albert Priddy, the superintendent of the state colony, that Carrie was not only morally deficient but mentally imbecilic and thus in need of sterilization.[49]

Before proceeding with the procedure, however, Priddy "as a matter of precautionary safety" and with the board's approval, decided to bring a test case to be sure of the sterilization law's constitutionality. Aubrey E.

Strode represented Priddy, while Irving Whitehead, a former member of the colony's board and a friend of Strode, was retained to represent Ms. Buck.

At the trial before the Amherst County Court, Strode produced witnesses who sought to portray Carrie as socially inadequate, feeble-minded, and as part of a family characterized as "shiftless, ignorant, and [a] worthless class of anti-social whites." Whitehead, on the other hand, called no witnesses to dispute the dubious allegations of Carrie's undesirable character or her immorality, and the evidence from the trial record indicates that his cross-examination of the witnesses "was so weak that it was often unclear which side he was representing."[50]

When the case went before the Virginia Supreme Court of Appeals, that body affirmed the Circuit Court of Amherst ruling. The case was then appealed to the US Supreme Court on equal protection and due process grounds. In an 8–1 decision, written by Justice O. W. Holmes (Butler dissented without an opinion), the Supreme Court rejected Whitehead's Fourteenth Amendment due process and equal protection arguments that sterilization would violate Carrie's bodily integrity. In stunningly frank and ominous language for all women and poor people, Justice Holmes accepted the eugenics arguments that Carrie was indeed a "feeble minded white woman," that she was the child of a "feeble minded mother," and that in recent years she had given birth to an "illegitimate feeble minded child."[51]

Convinced that Carrie's procedural rights had not been abridged during her fight over sterilization, Holmes confidently and callously exploited the efforts of those who had made sacrifices during World War I to conclude that if the "best citizens" were willing to give their lives "it would be strange if it [public welfare] could not call upon those who already sap the strength of the State for these lesser sacrifices, often not felt to do such by those concerned, in order to prevent our being swamped with incompetence."[52]

Writing as if it were inevitable that the offspring of poor and unwed mothers, even those who had been raped, would be degenerates responsible for untold amounts of criminal activity or subject to utter dependency because of their imbecility, Holmes concluded his remarkable assault on poor, allegedly mentally handicapped women and their reproductive rights by uttering one of the most-quoted lines in constitutional history: "Three generations of imbeciles are enough."[53]

Carrie was sterilized five months later, setting in motion a chain of national events that would culminate in many states passing similar laws and the singular international event—Nazi Germany's genocidal policy against the Jews. Although Carrie was later released from the institution, she remained, like that of the multitude of other sterilized colony women, subject to the institution's jurisdictional control and could have been forcibly returned if her behavior veered in an unacceptable direction. According to Paul Lambardo, Carrie showed intelligence and kindness that contradicted the alleged feeble-mindedness and immorality that had been used as an excuse to sterilize her.[54]

Of Bars, Conspiracies, and Juries

Over the next four decades, women continued their struggle for justice. At the individual level, women took prominent positions on issues like prohibition and violence against African Americans, and they fought hard, if unsuccessfully, to secure an equal rights amendment. And they also played a crucial economic role during World War I, adopting the motto "Use it up, wear it out, make it do." Women also attained prominent social and political positions—Jane Addams became the first women to win the Nobel Peace Prize, in 1931; Haltie Wyatt Caroway (D-AZ) was the first woman elected to the US Senate, in 1932; and Eleanor Roosevelt was appointed as a delegate to the United Nations.[55]

While improvements were occurring, the Supreme Court continued to be a hostile environment for women as a class in their efforts to challenge the rank sexual discrimination they still endured. Two mid-twentieth-century cases, *Goesaert v. Cleary* (1948) and *Hoyt v. Florida* (1961), powerfully confirmed that women still faced a decidedly uphill battle to gain access to economic and institutional roles long denied them.

In *Goesaert*, which involved a Michigan statute that prohibited a woman from serving as a bartender unless she was the wife or daughter of a male bar owner, Justice Felix Frankfurter, for the majority, ruled that although there had been "vast changes" in the social and legal status of women in recent years, it was still the state's prerogative to make sexual distinctions between men and women, especially when it came to regulating "vices" like alcohol traffic.[56] Frankfurter circumvented the fact that Michigan was treating some groups of women—in this case wives or daughters of male bar owners—differently than others by asserting that a female barmaid's husband or father "minimizes hazards [moral and social problems associated with liquor] that may confront a barmaid without such protective oversight."[57]

He was convinced that "beguiling as the subject is," the case was an easy one since the state was not "playing favorites" but had made what he thought was a rational distinction between the classes of women involved. Frankfurter also disputed the contention that the real motive behind the statute was "an unchivalrous desire of male bartenders to try to monopolize" this profitable occupation.[58]

This case, however, generated a strong dissent from three justices—Wiley B. Rutledge, William O. Douglas, and Frank Murphy. They argued that Michigan law created "invidious distinction and was arbitrarily discriminatory and further suggested that it was not male chivalry that animated the state, but rather an action designed to curtail women's access to bartending, a fairly lucrative job, and was thus a means to protect men's monopoly of that profession.[59]

Judith Baer's analysis of this case provides compelling evidence that an effort, spearheaded by the International Union of Hotel and Restaurant Employees and Bartenders, to return this profession to male monopoly at the conclusion of World War II was indeed a major reason for the statute. The union had adopted a resolution urging the ban of women and then lobbied the Michigan legislature to adopt it, which it did in 1945, setting the stage for this litigation.[60] The conclusion of Frankfurter's stereotyping of women as ever in need of protection from immorality, except for the wives and daughters of bar owners, arguably the very ones who would most need such "protection," and the more subtle yet equally impressive economic motives—male dominance of a profitable occupation—were sufficient to deny women this opportunity.

By 1960, in the area of family law, women had attained certain successes; they could sign contracts and could keep property they owned before marriage, and men could no longer legally punish their wives. But in general, men were still lawfully the head of household, which meant that men remained the principal controller of jointly owned property, that women still took their husband's name at marriage, that husbands had the exclusive power to determine the couple's domicile, and that wives still had the legal duty to submit to their husband's sexual demands.[61]

Since family law is essentially the province of states, the Supreme Court rarely decides cases involving these matters. But in 1960, in *United States v. Dege*, the Court heard a case involving a criminal conspiracy charge between a wife and a her husband, who had tried to fraudulently bring goods into the United States in violation of a 1948 federal statute.[62] In *Dege*, Justice Frankfurter, for the majority, reinstated the conspiracy indictment despite the common law doctrine that held that conspiracy between husband and wife was impossible since "man and wife are one." Frankfurter said such "medieval views" on the legal status of women and the way the common law understood their status would "enthrone an unreality into a rule of law to suggest that man and wife are legally incapable of engaging in illicit enterprises and therefore, forsooth, do not engage in them."[63]

Continuing, and contrary to his more stereotypical views of frail women in need of constant male protection expressed in *Goeseart*, Frankfurter declared that it was not in the province of the Court to read into the conspiracy statute a "medieval notion of women's submissiveness to the benevolent coercive powers of a husband" to relieve the women of her obligation to follow the law.[64]

Despite the Court's favorable rhetoric on women's status, a vigorous three-person dissent, led by Chief Justice Warren, served up ample judicial language that kept the traditional institution of marriage in place by referring to the solidarity and confederated nature of marriage, a relationship that the dissenting justices felt the Court should tenaciously adhere to since it is "predicated upon underlying policies unconnected with problems of women's suffrage or capacity to sue."[65] In fact, it would not be until 1979, in *Orr v. Orr*, which transformed the alimony award by holding unconstitutional an Alabama law that permitted wives to get alimony from husbands but denied the courts from awarding alimony to husbands in appropriate cases.[66]

A year after *Dege*, the Supreme Court returned to the subject of jury service for women in *Hoyt v. Florida* (1961)[67] and handed down the last of a number of opinions that categorically denied women opportunities expressly made available to men.[68] In this case, the denial challenged by Gwendolyn Hoyt was the historically rooted custom that excluded women from jury duty unless they had specifically requested to be added to the jury list. White males, by contrast, had been legally mandated to perform this duty since the ratification of the Sixth and Seventh Amendments to the Constitution, in 1791.

Arising in the wake of the Warren Court's critically important desegregation case in 1954, *Brown v. Board of Education*, and other cases attacking racial segregation and oppressive criminal justice issues, women may have sensed a solid opportunity to challenge the juror selection system, which had effectively denied them an opportunity to serve from the 1789 Judiciary Act to the Civil Rights Act of 1957. Ironically, although the 1957 civil rights law made women eligible for federal jury service, they remained ineligible under state laws. And since Florida statutes did not expressly exclude women from jury duty, since it gave them the "privilege" of registering their willingness to serve, the Court concluded that Florida's action was a "reasonable classification" that did not violate the Fourteenth Amendment's equal protection clause.

Equally important to Justice John Harlan and the unanimous Court was the sexist notion that "woman is still regarded as the center of home and family life."[69] As such, the state, according to the courts, was well within its right to conclude that "in pursuit of the general welfare" a woman "should be relieved from the civil duty of jury service unless she herself determines that such service is inconsistent with her own special responsibilities."[70]

Women's Reproductive Rights in the Modern Era: Steps Forward, Strides Backward

A number of important events, personalities, and developments began to coalesce in the 1960s that would eventually lead to tangible improvements in the political, legal, sociocultural, and economic rights of women: the Vietnam War; labor unrest; student activism; the civil rights movement; the Black Power movement; the increasing number of women securing law and graduate degrees; women's political and social activism culminating in the birth of feminism in 1966—with both a radical branch (led by former members of the Student Non-Violent Conducting Committee) and an integrationist branch (epitomized by the establishment of the National Organization for Women [NOW]); the US Congress's enactment of the Equal Pay Act of 1963, which forbade sex discrimination in wages, and Title VII of the Civil Rights Act of 1964, which prohibited sex discrimination in employment; and two 1963 books, Betty Friedan's *The Feminine Mystique* and the summary report of the Commission on the Status of Women, which had been established by President John F. Kennedy. In addition, an equal rights amendment, first proposed in the 1920s, also gained considerable cache in the 1960s, and in 1972 the amendment overwhelmingly passed both houses of Congress.[71]

While these broader events were dynamically unfolding, the US Supreme Court was also active and produced a spate of generally positive opinions in this period that reflected the dramatically altered state of affairs in the area of women's rights regarding social security, welfare, worker's compensation, child-care allowances, and the like.[72] As Laura Otten noted, what was critical about the numerous decisions in the late 1960s and 1970s was the Court's "growing recognition of exactly what it had claimed in *Hoyt* to be unable to see: an unfortunate atmosphere of prejudice and a long history of discriminatory administrative practice against women."[73]

One of the most important cases of this era was *Griswold v. Connecticut*,[74] handed down in 1965. A number of commentators assert that this ruling, in establishing a new constitutional right of privacy, provided the legal rational and philosophical foundation for the Court's powerful *Roe v. Wade* opinion in 1973, which legalized abortion.

In *Griswold*, the constitutionality of Connecticut's birth-control law was being tested. The state statute, enacted in 1879, declared that "any person who uses any drug, medical article or instrument for the purpose of preventing conception," would be subject to a fine or imprisonment or both. It further stated that any person assisting another in committing any such offense could be prosecuted as if they were the primary offender. The statute had been challenged previously, but without success. The situation had ripened by 1965, and a suit was filed by members of Connecticut's Planned Parenthood League, led by Estelle Griswold, the executive director. Griswold had been convicted at trial of violating the law by providing information and medical advice to married couples about how to prevent conception. Her conviction was affirmed by the state's Supreme Court of Errors.

The US Supreme Court, in a 7–2 decision, reversed and held that (1) Griswold, et al., had standing to raise the constitutional issue because they were accessories to violation of the statute insofar as they were advising married persons about how to prevent conception; and (2) the statute was invalid because it infringed on the constitutionally protected right to privacy of married individuals. In Justice William O. Douglas's words: "The present case, then, concerns a relationship lying within the zone of privacy created by several fundamental constitutional guarantees. And it concerns a law which, in forbidding the use of contraceptives...seeks to achieve its goals by means having a maximum destructive impact upon that relationship."[75]

After *Griswold*, a factor leading to the next series of cases was the more rigorous standard of review—intermediate scrutiny to gender-based classifications that the Court first began to apply to sex-discrimination cases starting in 1971 in *Reed v. Reed*.[76] Intermediate scrutiny was higher than the rational basis standard that had been used heretofore, but it was short of the strict scrutiny that until very recently was applied to suspect classifications such as those based on race. This lower standard essentially reflected the Court's ideological view that racial discrimination was a more serious social problem than sexual discrimination.[77]

This perspective is most vividly evidenced in regard to the failure of the Equal Rights Amendment to be ratified and constitutionally entrenched, the lack of equality of opportunity in education and employment, continuing sexual discrimination in the military, where most jobs are set aside for men, physical and sexual violence against women, discrimination in insurance rates for women, and particularly in the area of reproductive freedom.[78]

While each of these issues is important, not least of which is the fact that the Supreme Court has "never held that the Constitution's equality guarantee applies fully to women or to gender-based discrimination,"[79] for many, the legal and social challenges women face in their quest for equal protection of their reproductive rights is most emblematic both of how far women have come, yet how fragile and tenuous their rights remain.

Two cases in particular merit attention here: *Roe v. Wade* (1973) and *Geduldig v. Aiello* (1974). In *Roe*, the Court, by a 7–2 vote, with Justice Harry Blackmun writing for the majority, issued a highly controversial ruling that legalized a woman's right to obtain an abortion within the guidelines developed by the Court of viability and trimesters. The opinion, however, did not address the issues of abortion as gender discrimination, although it was blatantly obvious that questions of gender were fundamentally involved since the burden of unwanted pregnancy falls exclusively on women and since all abortion laws have been enacted by male-dominated legislatures. Rather, the Court relied on the newly created constitutional right to privacy to justify a woman's right to decide to terminate her pregnancy.

Blackmun, as well as the rest of the justices, was keenly aware that this decision would be problematic, regardless of the rationale or the holding. As he noted:

> We forthwith acknowledge our awareness of the sensitive and emotional
> nature of the abortion controversy, of the vigorous opposing views, even
> among physicians, and of the deep and seemingly absolute convictions
> that the subject inspires. One's philosophy, one's experiences…and the

moral standards one establishes and seeks to observe, are all likely to influence and to color one's thinking and conclusions about abortion... Our task, of course, is to resolve the issue by constitutional measurement, free of emotion and predilection.[80]

But Blackmun's own previous words contradicted him; no one, least of all the Supreme Court justices, was "free of emotion" in discussing and analyzing this issue. And the Court's compromise ruling—that women should not be criminalized for seeking an abortion; that women must consult with their physician prior to the "compelling" point (prior to the end of the first trimester); that the state then had a compelling right to protect maternal and prenatal life in the second and third trimester of pregnancy and could even deny abortion altogether after viability; only served to foretell a troubled, violent, and deeply political post-*Roe* era.

Roe was dramatically weakened, though not explicitly overruled, as a rabid right-to-life movement erupted and began an intense lobbying campaign aimed at electing policy makers and having judges and justices appointed who have vowed to overturn *Roe*. Several cases have eroded the *Roe* precedent: *Harris v. McRae* (1980) held that Congress, in enacting the Hyde Amendment, had not violated the Constitution when it prohibited the use of Medicaid funds to pay for nontherapeutic abortions; *Webster v. Reproductive Health Services* (1989) eliminated the trimester formula outlined in *Roe* and authorized states to adopt virtually any regulations they desired to promote the interest in protecting potential life, including criminal bans on performing or obtaining abortions; *Rust v. Sullivan* (1991) essentially removed from doctors the right to discuss abortion at federally funded clinics; and *Planned Parenthood v. Casey* (1992) supported the states in their efforts to persuade women not to have abortions and imposed a twenty-four-hour waiting period before the abortion could proceed. Teenagers seeking abortions were also required to secure a parent or judge's consent prior to the procedure.

Thus, while *Roe* has not been overturned, a woman's right to abortion, especially the rights of pregnant indigent women, have been seriously curtailed and *Roe*'s permanence is most unstable in the second decade of the 2000s. For while public support for legal abortion remains quite strong, the antiabortion campaign is extremely active, and depending on the decisions made by the president regarding judicial nominees for the Supreme Court, it is possible that *Roe*'s days are indeed numbered.

A year after *Roe*, the Supreme Court accepted another case, *Geduldig v. Aiello*, involving a woman's reproductive power—pregnancy. Specifically, four female California state employees, Carolyn Aiello, Augustina Armendariz, Elizabeth Johnson, and Jacqueline Jaramillo, each of whom had paid sufficient amounts of money into the disability fund, became pregnant and suffered employment disability as a result of their pregnancies. They challenged California's otherwise comprehensive disability benefits system, which excluded from coverage any hospitalization resulting from a "normal pregnancy."

They claimed that the denial of pregnancy benefits amounted to sexual discrimination, thus violating the Fourteenth Amendment's equal protection clause. Justice Potter Stewart for the Court, in a remarkable and befuddling 6–3 decision, focused on the solvency of California's social insurance plan and said that the state's policy benefits met the required rational relationship to its legitimate goal of reducing costs. "The essential issue," said Justice Stewart, "is whether the Equal Protection Clause requires such policies to be sacrificed or compromised in order to finance the payment of benefits to those whose disability is attributable to normal pregnancy and delivery."[81]

The short answer, of course, was no. This was because the exclusion of pregnancy from coverage, according to the Court, did not amount to "invidious discrimination" or even a direct case of sex discrimination, since most women most of the time were classed as nonpregnant persons, which entailed a group merely distinguished from pregnant women. In short, discrimination on the basis of pregnancy, the Court declared, was somehow not discrimination on the basis of sex.

Stewart's explanation for this bizarre holding—pregnancy discrimination is not sex-based discrimination—is lodged in footnote 20. Here Stewart sought to distinguish this case from recent cases such as *Reed v. Reed* and *Frontiera v. Richardson* (1973) involving gender discrimination. Stewart declared that the California plan did not exclude women on the basis of gender but simply removed one physical condition, pregnancy, as an approved disability. Although admitting that "it is true that only women can become pregnant," Stewart declared that lawmakers retained the right to include or exclude pregnancy from coverage since the California plan divided potential recipients into two groups—pregnant women and nonpregnant persons. "While the first group is exclusively female, the second includes members of both sexes. The fiscal and actuarial benefits of the program thus accrue to members of both sexes."[82]

But the dissenting opinion, written by Justice William J. Brennan and joined by Douglas and Thurgood Marshall, saw through this sophistry and pointedly noted that by singling out a gender-linked status "peculiar to women," California had, in effect, established a double standard for disability compensation. While women thus faced explicit limitations for one of their "disabilities," men, on the other hand, were entitled to receive full compensation for all disabilities, "including those that affect only or primarily their sex, such as prostatectomies, circumcision, hemophilia, and gout."[83] This, said Brennan, inevitably constituted sex discrimination since two different sets of rules were applied to males and females. That type of unequal treatment of men and women purely on the basis of physical characteristics associated with one's gender denied equal protection. Congress overturned this case's discriminatory precedent in 1978 with the passage of the Pregnancy Discrimination Act.

A subsequent case, *Dothard v. Rawlinson* (1977), provided further evidence that the Supreme Court's perspective on social norms continued to regard a woman's biological capacity to reproduce—a fundamental difference from men—"as a deviation from the standard conception of a rational, adult person entitled to the full respect of the law."[84] Such a deviation, in the court's view, could still imperil a woman's rights under the law.

In *Dothard*, the Supreme Court upheld an Alabama state prison regulation that prohibited hiring female guards in maximum-security prisons for men if the job description required "close physical proximity" to prisoners. The Court said that the exclusion of women guards from those positions was not a violation of the equal employment opportunity principle specified in Title VII of the Civil Rights Act of 1964. Although agreeing that federal law now prohibited the use of sex stereotypes in determining employment standards, Justice Stewart effectively relied on one of the oldest of such stereotypes when he stated that a woman's ability to keep order in a male, maximum-security facility "could be directly reduced by her womanhood."[85] The majority supported this stereotyping even though prison experts had testified that female guards could be effective and safe in such an environment. In fact, there was evidence of this very fact from California's prison, where women guards operated in male prisons.[86]

The perspective of this stereotype was also not lost on the dissenters, led by Justice Marshall, who observed that "the fundamental justification for the majority's ruling was that women as guards would create a situation leading to sexual assaults."[87] But this rationale, said Marshall, "regrettably perpetuates one of the most insidious of the old myths about women that women, wittingly or not, are seductive sexual objects."[88] Marshall said it was wrongheaded to deprive women of employment opportunities because of the potential threatening behavior of male convicts. Once again, the alleged pedestal that women were being placed upon in an effort to protect them from convicted felons, according to Marshall, turned out to more closely resemble a cage that limited their job opportunities.

Notwithstanding the continuing legal struggles women had regarding their reproductive capacity, feminist interpretations of gender differences combined with the civil rights movement, the Vietnam War, labor unrest, and a surge of social and cultural activism by racial and ethnic minorities had a powerful effect on American society. For our purposes, the multiple levels of activity aimed at women's liberation led to state and societal changes that helped ease some of the overwhelming burdens women had faced in politics, career choices, education, sports, and sexual freedom.

In 1972, for instance, Congress overwhelmingly passed the Equal Rights Amendment (ERA) (House 354 to 23; Senate 84 to 8), and amended the Civil Rights Act by adding Title IX, which prohibited any college or university that received federal aid from discriminating against women. This act also required that collegiate athletic programs provide an equal number of scholarships to women as to men.[89]

But even as these positive developments were occurring, a significant antifeminist movement was already brewing. The ERA and *Roe v. Wade* helped galvanize the forces that would lead to the gradual dismantlement of some of the historic changes that had only just begun. Ronald Reagan's two presidential terms (1980–1988), followed by George H. W. Bush's single term (1988–1992), oversaw a series of debilitating judicial losses for women. As Susan Faludi reported in her powerful polemic *Backlash: The Undeclared War Against Women*, the 1980s was a decade of reversal of women's fledgling gains:

> Just when women's quest for equal rights seemed closest to achieving its objective, the backlash struck it down. Just when a "gender gap" at the voting booth surfaced in 1980, and women in politics began to talk of capitalizing on it, the Republican Party elevated Ronald Reagan and both political parties began to shunt women's rights off their platforms. Just when support for feminism and the Equal Rights Amendment reached a record high in 1981, the amendment was defeated the following year.[90]

Women and the Military

Although women had made real gains in the areas of family law, employment, voting, jury selection, and, to a lesser degree, reproductive rights, in regard to their right to serve unencumbered in the military they still lagged far behind their male counterparts. The view that women should not be allowed to serve unencumbered was reaffirmed enthusiastically in 1981 in *Rostker v. Goldberg*, which held that a congressional law requiring only males to register for a possible draft conformed to the due process clause.[91] Such a view, precluding women from having to register, thus rejecting President Jimmy Carter's earlier request that women also register, only served to reinvigorate the popular and belittling stereotypes that women were physically frail and in constant need of male protection.[92]

Showing significant deference to Congress's authority on matters of national defense and military affairs, and expressing the belief that Congress had given the question of whether or not to register women considerable attention through the hearings process, floor debate, and in committee discussions, Justice William Rehnquist, for the majority, said that the existence of combat restrictions for women found in the navy, air force, army, and Marine Corps statutes and policies "clearly indicates the basis for Congress' decision to exempt women from registration."[93]

Because of this history, Rehnquist maintained that this was a case of Congress arbitrarily acting to burden one of two "similarly situated groups, such as would be the case with an all-black or all-white registration."[94]

Because of the preexisting combat restrictions on women, men and women "are simply not similarly situated for purposes of a draft or registration for a draft."[95] Rehnquist further declared that the "heightened scrutiny that developed in *Craig v. Boren* [1976] for ascertaining the constitutionality of gender discrimination was satisfied in this case because the military's need for flexibility was a vital goal." Rehnquist thus sidestepped the controversial policy and gender issues raised by the Congress's barring of women troops from combat since the constitutionality of that policy was not before the Court. Interestingly, while Justices Byron White and Marshall wrote separate dissents, insisting in part that the government had not sufficiently proved that barring women from registration furthered any compelling governmental interest, neither dissent challenged the general rule that excluded women from combat roles.

The outstanding performance of female soldiers in the Gulf War, in

1991, and the wars in Afghanistan and Iraq in the first decade of the 2000s, many of them in indirect combat roles, prompted the Department of Defense and congressional members to reexamine the combat restrictions confronting women soldiers. However, women are still banned from serving in direct combat positions in the infantry, armor, and other field artillery positions that are important precursor steps to promotion to higher military ranks.[96]

Subsequent to this case, and even as the Court became increasingly conservative, fewer constitutional cases involving sex discrimination come before the Court. In part, this can be attributed to the fact that most of the easier cases had already been resolved and there was general consent on the intermediate standard of review in the lower courts. Blatant sex discrimination is generally unacceptable now, even to the Rehnquist, now Roberts, Court's conservative majority. Feminist groups also contribute to this altered litigative environment as they remain ever vigilant and use their resources in an effort to preserve the right to abortion that is still being assaulted by some conservative political and religious groups.

Two contemporary cases indicate that while the legal situation for women has certainly improved, there is still much room for advancement. In *United States v. Virginia*, decided in 1996, the Supreme Court ruled that the Commonwealth of Virginia's all-male military academy, Virginia Military Institute (VMI), unjustifiably violated the equal protection clause by categorically denying women from attendance.[97] Although it was a 7–1 victory for women, with Justice Ruth Ginsburg writing for the majority, and with even Rehnquist filing a concurring opinion, Nadine Taub and Elizabeth M. Schneider point out that the Court failed to consider the degree to which the assessment of qualifications were influenced by gender.[98] Rather, the majority, except for Justice Antonin Scalia, who wrote a scathing dissent that emphasized the tradition of male honor, still failed to treat gender-based classifications as violating the Constitution to the same extent as race-based classifications. Gender classifications, in other words, receive a lessened presumption of unconstitutionality.[99]

Our final case centers on an issue that has plagued women since time immemorial: the violence they often endure at the hands of men. In 2000, a divided Court ruled in *United States v. Morrison*[100] that Congress lacked authority under the commerce clause to enact a civil rights remedy in the Violence Against Women Act, passed by Congress in 1994, which stated in part that "all persons within the United States shall have the right to be free from crimes of violence motivated by gender."[101] This case, part of the Rehnquist Court's broader and largely successful constitutional campaign to redefine federalism in favor of states and to curb Congress's commerce clause power vis-à-vis states, reaffirmed the fragility of women's status on the grounds that states, and not Congress, as one of their retained powers, had the right to suppress violent crimes. "The Constitution," said Chief Justice Rehnquist, "requires a distinction between what is truly national and what is truly local."[102] And in the majority's interpretation of the commerce clause, the regulation and punishment of intrastate violence was and had always been in the province of the states.

Justice David Souter, in dissent, concentrated on the "mountain of data" that had been gathered from doctors that, in his opinion, showed that violence against women did indeed constitute interstate commerce and therefore was within Congress's power to regulate. Here are a few facts from that data: three out of four women will suffer violent crimes in the course of their lifetime; violence causes more injuries to women ages 15–44 than any other cause; some 50 percent of homeless women and children are put in that condition because they are fleeing male violence.[103] Based on the gross accumulation of data, Congress found that gender violence adversely affects interstate commerce because it deters potential victims from "traveling interstate, from engaging in employment in interstate business,…and decreasing the supply of and the demand for interstate products."[104] More distressing still was the fact that violence against women in the 1990s appeared to operate in a way similar to the racial discrimination experienced by minorities in the 1960s. Such discrimination had clearly had negative impact on minority mobility and their production and consumption of goods.[105]

While significant strides have been made in the pursuit of life expectancy, healthcare, educational opportunities, and constitutional protections for women, the Supreme Court, in particular, still wrestles with status of women, as evidenced by women's problems in pursuing equal opportunity in education and employment, reproductive freedom, the military, and violence against women. The backlash against women appears to be part of a larger assault on civil liberties, human rights, and environmental issues by the Court, now led by Chief Justice John Roberts, and confirms the fundamental lack of constitutional equality for women and the other groups we are discussing.

CHAPTER 8
"Alien Friends and Alien Enemies": Mexican Americans and the Law

SETTLEMENT OF THE VAST WESTERN INTERIOR BY THE UNITED STATES produced relations with two major racial and ethnic groups. In addition to the various aboriginal nations who attached themselves politically and economically to the United States by treaties, the western expansion brought into the Union a large number of citizens of Spanish Mexican descent, who also forged unique connections to the United States. The history of Mexican/US relations is fascinating because the question of whether Mexican Americans* are an ethnic group or a racial minority is complicated. Their experience, as Peter Skeery has noted, is complicated because it contains "*both* a history of territorial conquest and racial subjugation (particularly in the Southwest) *and* a pattern of massive, ongoing immigration and subsequent upward mobility." Mexican Americans, according to Skeery, more than nearly every other racial, ethnic, or gender group, experiences what he terms a "profound ambivalence" at their standing in the country. On the one hand, they have harsh memories and experience frustrating resentment about how they have been and continue to be treated by other Americans. On the other hand, many Mexican American and Latinos in general continue to put great stock in the economic opportunities they see as being more readily available in the United States, notwithstanding the occasional outburst of xenophobia that Americans sometimes exhibit toward them. As Mexican Americans frequently say, "Some of us have been here for three hundred years, some for three days."[1]

Spain was one of the original major colonial powers, but because it concentrated its efforts in South and Central America and failed to establish a permanent foothold in the southeastern United States, Spain reached the American Southwest somewhat late in its colonial era. In 1819, Spain sold the Floridas to the United States, providing in the treaty of cession that all Spanish citizens then living in the Floridas be accepted as rapidly as possible

---

* Mexican Americans are typically grouped in the broader category of Latinos or Hispanics. But as with the situation of Asian Americans and indigenous peoples, the term *Latin American* embraces an extremely diverse set of peoples and cultures from Mexico and Central and South America, not to mention parts of Europe. Since Mexicans and Mexican Americans are the largest Latin American segment, and since virtually all of the judicial and statutory data we will be relying on focuses on Mexicans and Mexican Americans, they will be our focus in this chapter.

as American citizens.[2] Within two years, Mexicans revolted, and after three hundred years Mexico ended its relationship with the king of Spain, curtailing Spanish political influence in North America, but in turn creating a new republic, which claimed large tracts of land within the area now, or soon to be, occupied by the United States.

On February 24, 1821, even before the Treaty of Cordova, which declared the independence of the United Mexican States, the revolutionary government, inspired by French revolutionary ideas, promulgated the Plan de Iguala, which declared in article 12 that "all the inhabitants of New Spain, without distinction, whether Europeans, Africans, or Indians, are citizens of this monarchy, with a right to be employed in any post according to their merit and virtues."[3] The government was led by Agustín de Iturbide. Iturbide was exiled in 1823. Within a year, the first Constitution of Mexico was proclaimed. It was based on the US Constitution.

Following the Mexican Revolution, parties of Americans began to arrive in Texas, and although they enjoyed the benefits of the Mexican state, culturally and emotionally they were still Americans. Within fifteen years, they revolted and Texas became an independent republic. Unlike the Mexican revolutionaries, the Texans restricted their citizenship. Section 10 of the Texas Constitution, adopted on March 2, 1836, provided: "All persons (Africans, and the descendants of Africans, and Indians excepted), who were residing in Texas, on the day of the Declaration of Independence, shall be considered citizens of the Republic and entitled to all the privileges of such."[4] Apart from the obvious exclusion of Natives and blacks from citizenship, this phraseology contained a hidden problem that did not manifest itself until several years later. What of the Mexicans who supported the Mexican state during the revolution, yet were declared by the Texas Constitution to be citizens on the day of independence?

Some of the Mexicans who fled to the southern provinces left behind them large tracts of land, the titles of which had been confirmed by the Mexican Republic or the king of Spain. New settlers had arrived in Texas and, assuming that these lands were forfeited or abandoned, settled and claimed them. Then as years passed and the Mexicans saw no widespread effort to punish them for supporting the republic, many individuals returned and claimed their lands, often seeking only to clear their titles and sell, intending to return to Mexico. The newcomers naturally resented the effort to reclaim estates that appeared to have been abandoned and, often as not, they defended themselves by claiming that Mexicans were aliens incapable of holding lands in the republic.

Hardy v. De Leon (1849)[5] and *Kilpatrick v. Sisneros* (1859)[6] are representative state cases in which the question of alien citizenship proved critical to the determination of land title. De Leon had been removed from Texas by the revolutionary government, sent to Louisiana, and returned years later to claim his estate. He had sold some lands and was returning to Mexico to move his children to Texas and resume Texan citizenship when he was killed. His heirs sued to affirm their interest in his lands. Sisneros moved from Texas during the revolution but continued to hold lands there. His heirs attempted to get their claims to land confirmed. The defense, in both cases, argued that the Mexicans had become "alien enemies" upon their removal from the province during the war and hence could not hold good title to their lands.

In *Hardy*, the Texas Supreme Court rejected this argument, contending that a jury finding that De Leon was an alien enemy was a nullity. The court pointed out that even a citizen could become an alien enemy if attached to a commercial venture of another country during a time of war and if the citizen refused to support the country's effort to end the war. In *Sisneros*, the fact that the family left Texas with the Mexican army and remained away for several years was not thought critical in determining their rights. "They may have forfeited their right of citizenship and their title to their lands," the court remarked, "but until the forfeiture has been ascertained and adjudged by some proceeding, to be authorized by law for that purpose, their civil *status* is not changed, nor their rights of property divested."[7]

The critically important point in these cases, aside from the affirmation of land titles and the affirmation by Texas (as a republic) of international legal doctrines that individuals do not suffer in their property or civil rights upon a change of sovereignty created by revolution, is the characterization of Mexicans as aliens. The cultural differences between Americans and Mexicans were such that although the Texas Constitution adopted a general citizenship standard of residency that included Mexicans, the subsequent confusion regarding their status revolved about cultural distinctions as much as political loyalties. Texas, to be certain, accepted everyone who could conceivably be described as supporting the revolution. Yet there remained an underlying suspicion that Mexicans were, in fact, aliens. This notion of Mexicans, Mexican Americans, and other Latinos as alien, regardless of the length of their tenure in the United States, has largely continued until the present time. Much of the time, the term's persistence remains rooted in ethnocentric notions of so-called Latino "cultural traits," like clannishness, fatalism, or presentmindedness, which were said to hinder "the assimilation process and explained many of the social problems in the ethnic communities."[8]

In *McKinney v. Saviego* (1855) the US Supreme Court had an opportunity to comment on the interpretation of alien status with respect to Texas nearly a decade after Texas had entered the Union and declared that the Saviego family, which had removed from Texas a year prior to the revolution, had become aliens and could not inherit lands there.[9] Thus the determinative factor in Mexicans becoming Texan citizens was, as the Texas Constitution declared, simply residence in that province on the day of the declaration of independence.

The westward movement of Americans continued at a rapid pace, and it was apparent by 1846 that Mexico's territorial claims in the Southwest were the primary obstacle to American domination of the continent. On March 1, 1845, Texas was annexed by joint congressional resolution,[10] and on December 29 of that year it was formally admitted to the Union as a state.[11] Also in 1845, Thomas Larkin, US consul at Monterey, was appointed confidential agent by President Polk with instructions to encourage the Americans in California, of whom only five hundred could be counted, to seek annexation of California to the United States. By mid-March of 1846, the Americans had made apparent their hostile intentions toward Mexico, and on April 25 the first hostilities occurred. In June 1846, Americans in California revolted and established the Republic of California. The tenuous hold on the state was significantly bolstered by the discovery of gold at Sutter's Fort, and if the Americans did not in fact possess California before, the rush of people westward ensured that the occupation by Mexicans could never again be a significant factor in West Coast settlement. On February 2, 1848,[12] the Mexican War ended with the Treaty of Guadalupe Hidalgo, in which Mexico ceded its extensive holdings in the Southwest for $15 million, including territory that now forms the states of Arizona, California, Nevada, New Mexico, Utah, and half of Colorado. The United States also secured clear title to Texas.[13]

Extensive Mexican settlement existed in the ceded area, and the Treaty of Guadalupe Hidalgo attempted to define the status that former Mexican citizens would have after the United States assumed jurisdiction over the Southwest. The eighth article provided that

> Mexicans now established in territories previously belonging to Mexico, and which remain for the future within the limits of the United States, as defined by the present treaty, shall be free to continue where they now reside, or to remove at any time to the Mexican Republic, retaining the property which they possess in the said territories, or disposing thereof, and removing the proceeds wherever they please; without their being subjected, on this account, to any contribution, tax or charge whatever.[14]

And it provided that

> those who shall prefer to remain in the said territories, may either retain the title and rights of Mexican citizens, or acquire those of citizens of the United States. But they shall be under the obligation to make their election within one year from the date of the exchange of ratifications of this treaty: and those who shall remain in the said territories after the expiration of that year, without having declared their intention to retain the character of Mexicans, shall be considered to have elected to become citizens of the United States.[15]

This article appeared to assure the Mexican citizens of American citizenship. But Article 9 created severe doubts about how this status was to be accomplished. It declared that

> Mexicans who, in the territories aforesaid, shall not preserve the character of citizens of the Mexican Republic, conformably with what is stipulated in the preceding article, shall be incorporated into the Union of the United States and be admitted at the proper time (to be judged of by the Congress of the United States) to the enjoyment of all the rights of citizens of the United States, according to the principles of the Constitution; and in the mean time, shall be maintained and protected in the free enjoyment of their liberty and property, and secured in the free exercise of their religion without restriction.[16]

Astute Mexican diplomats realized all too well how this article could be interpreted. Manuel Crescencio Rejón, a liberal from Yucatán, on the occasion of signing the treaty, published his opposition to the treaty in a document titled "Observations on the Treaty of Guadalupe Hidalgo." He called it the political death of Mexico and remarked:

> Our race, our unfortunate people will have to wander in search of hospitality in a strange land, only to be ejected later. Descendants of the Indians that we are, the North Americans hate us, their spokesmen depreciate us, even if they recognize the justice of our cause, and they consider us unworthy to form with them one nation and one society, they clearly manifest that their future expansion begins with the territory they may take from us and pushing aside our citizens who inhabit the land.[17]

Congress also recognized the inconsistency between articles 8 and 9, and the Senate amended the ninth article by inserting the language from article 3 of the Louisiana Purchase Treaty, which said that "the inhabitants of the ceded territory shall be incorporated in the Union of the United States and admitted as soon as possible according to the principles of the federal constitution to the enjoyment of all these rights, advantages, and immunities of citizens of the US, and in the mean time they shall be maintained and protected in the free enjoyment of their liberty, property and the religion which they profess."[18]

The rights of Mexicans and Mexican Americans in US law established under the Treaty of Guadalupe Hidalgo and the rights of indigenous nations negotiated in various treaties with the federal government raise some interesting comparative points.

The Treaty of Guadalupe Hidalgo, said Rebecca Tsosie, acknowledged the rights of Mexican citizens to liberty and property, but also contemplated their incorporation into the United States as citizens. The treaty also recognized existing rights of Mexican citizens as equal to those of American citizens and declared that the federal government would respect this equality during the transition period before citizenship was bestowed. When the treaty began to be breached, many of the property owners first looked to the Mexican government to bring pressure on the United States to resolve their claims. But the contemporary descendants of those original landowners rely a great deal on their US citizenship to seek redress for their claims.

Indian treaties, by comparison, noted Tsosie, acknowledged the separate sovereignty of Native nations living on identifiably separate reservations, where they would continue to exercise a degree of political sovereignty under the protection of their trust partners, the United States. Native nations were entitled to beneficial ownership of their lands, and they were also entitled to self-governance. In fact, the commerce clause, according to Tsosie, sets Native peoples apart from states and foreign nations as distinctive governments and affirms that Congress alone has exclusive authority to regulate trade with Native nations. In other words, the unique constitutional relationship of indigenous people to the United States depends upon their citizenship in sovereign governments and is not based upon their identity as citizens of the United States. "Indian treaty claims," said Tsosie, "have been framed to acknowledge this trust relationship, and the courts have employed the canons of construction as interpretive aids for these agreements, to account for the language and cultural differences between the parties, and the dominant position of the United States."[19]

Despite these important differences, Tsosie acknowledged that both peoples' treaty claims were still group-based and there was a clear understanding of cultural rights that both Mexican Americans and Native peoples continue to adhere to, even in their close affiliation with the United States.

Few people understood that the Treaty of Guadalupe Hidalgo had been amended to provide for rapid assumption of citizenship by former Mexican citizens. Congress itself added to the confusion by distinguishing Mexicans from other citizens when devising territorial governments for the lands recently taken by the United States from the Mexican Republic. Section 5 of the 1850 territorial act of Utah, for example, treated Mexicans as if they were a separate category of citizens, providing

> that every free white male inhabitant above the age of twenty-one years, who shall have been a resident of said Territory at the time of the passage of this act, shall be entitled to vote at the first election, and shall be eligible to any office within the said Territory...Provided, that the right of suffrage and of holding office shall be exercised only by citizens of the United States, including those recognised as citizens by the treaty with the Republic of Mexico, concluded February second, eighteen hundred and forty-eight.[20]

Theoretically, when a territory passes from one sovereign to another, the individual citizens are not disturbed in their property and are considered to have become citizens of the new sovereign unless other provisions are made. The treaty only extended by a year this transfer of allegiance by former Mexican citizens to enable them to ponder the seriousness of the choice in surrendering their former citizenship and, perhaps, to induce sufficient numbers to depart for the Mexican provinces. There was no good reason, except perhaps clarification of Mexican rights and insurance that they would be protected as citizens, to distinguish them separately in legislation as a class of citizens.

The confusion extended beyond the confines of congressional minds, however, and made the lives of Mexican Americans very difficult, since any display of political activity on their part produced charges that they were actually aliens and encouraged American settlers to attempt to disqualify them from political rights. *People v. De La Guerra*, handed down in 1870, was typical of the problems created by the uncertainty of Mexican American political status.[21] Pablo De La Guerra was a well-known and respected figure in southern California. He had been active in California politics from the very beginning, serving as a member of the convention that framed its constitution, voting to accept it as the governing document of the state, and later being elected as a state senator. In a judicial election, De La Guerra was elected a judge of the First Judicial District of California, but the opposition challenged his election on the grounds that he was not a citizen of the United States because Congress had not acted under article 9 of the Treaty of Guadalupe Hidalgo.

The arguments raised against De La Guerra's citizenship are characteristic of the manner in which Mexican Americans were viewed in the decades following the cession of the southwestern territories. Even judges were uncertain whether the treaty had made them full citizens or whether it required Congress to perform an additional act to qualify them fully for political rights. The amended version of the treaty was not widely published and the prominent cultural differences that existed between Mexican Americans and other white Americans were considered so vast as to be considered alien to the majority of white citizens. The major argument raised by the district attorney who brought the charges against De La Guerra suggested that because there was some evidence of ill feelings between Mexican Americans and Californians after the Bear Flag Revolt in 1846[22] and the land cessions of that treaty, article 9 should be interpreted as if Congress had intended a period of calm to occur before it vested former Mexican citizens with full political rights. Thus, the attorney contended, De La Guerra could not be a citizen eligible for election to an office in California until Congress acted to give him full citizenship.

Judge Temple, delivering the opinion for the California Supreme Court, denied this interpretation of the treaty, declaring instead that "it required this special treaty stipulation to enable the inhabitants to remain in the ceded territory and owe no allegiance to the new Government. But for this provision," the judge suggested, "the Mexicans who remained would not have been considered aliens, but would have been vested with such rights of citizenship as can be conferred upon the inhabitants of a Territory who are not citizens of any of the States of the Union."[23] Those Mexicans who did not make a formal choice of political allegiance within the grace period provided in the treaty could be assumed to have become American citizens, the judge contended, since "otherwise they remained a people without a country."[24]

Answering the argument that Congress was required to pass special new legislation to perfect citizenship rights of the inhabitants of Florida, Louisiana, and the Southwest, Judge Temple stated that "they can be incorporated into this Union only as a State, and the admission of the people to the full rights as citizens of the United States follows as a consequence of that act; and this is the only way in which it was possible for Congress to confer upon them all the rights of citizens of the United States."[25] A curious synthesis of state and federal citizenship emerges with this interpretation of the provisions of the treaties of cession. Unlike the *Slaughter-House Cases*, in which the two types of citizenship were carefully distinguished to the virtual elimination of federal rights, *De La Guerra* describes an orderly flow of federal citizenship from the admission of states into the Union with a corresponding return flow back to state citizenship wherein the federal status seems to guarantee state rights. The geographical distribution of sovereignty, when applied to the new territory acquired by purchase and conquest, makes much more sense than when it is applied to the original states or when, after all states have been admitted to the Union, the question of state-federal citizenship rights arises.

De La Guerra marked the end of an era that began with the Mexican Revolution of 1821 and continued through the Texas Revolution and annexation, the Mexican War, and the first wave of settlement in the Southwest. Mexicans were originally considered aliens because they were citizens of another republic, and the cultural and social customs and values of this republic were considered so radically different than the Anglo-Saxon milieu in which the Constitution was written that the term *alien* described not simply political rights but distinguished cultural differences also. After the 1870s, there were few original settlers still alive who had been participants in the struggles of the past, and memories of Mexican rule in the Southwest faded rapidly as this pioneering generation passed away. Mexicans and Mexican Americans, however, continued to be regarded as aliens by the succeeding generations, but on an entirely different basis.

In 1897, Ricardo Rodríguez, an immigrant from Mexico who had lived for ten years in San Antonio, applied for citizenship naturalization. The federal district judge handling the case asked prominent members of the local bar to submit written briefs on the question of naturalization, because, he remarked, "Although 49 years have elapsed since the negotiation of the Treaty of Guadalupe-Hidalgo, which greatly increased our territorial area, and incorporated many thousands of Mexicans into our common citizenship,...the question of the individual naturalization of a Mexican citizen is now for the first time, so far as the court is advised, submitted for judicial determination."[26] The problem of naturalization was unnecessarily complicated because the immigration laws had been amended to provide that only free white men could become citizens, and the judge had to decide whether Mexicans were members of the white race.

The attorneys submitting briefs in the case *In re Rodríguez* were generally hostile to Rodríguez and described him as an Aztec Indian rather than a Mexican citizen, reaching the conclusion that he was, because of his Indian blood, ineligible for naturalization. Judge Thomas Sheldon Maxey carefully reviewed the treaties and statutes that had previously been used to describe the status of Mexican citizens and rejected the arguments of the local bar. Although recognizing that Rodríguez did not read or write English and was inarticulate in the area of constitutional rights, Maxey concluded that he was eligible for naturalization, writing that "whatever may be the status of the applicant viewed solely from the standpoint of the ethnologist, he is embraced within the spirit and intent of our laws upon naturalization, and his application should be granted if he is shown by the testimony to be a man attached to the principles of the constitution, and well disposed to the good order and happiness of the same."[27]

Rodríguez, although perhaps too broadly decided by the recognition of the moral qualities of the applicant, enabled the individual Mexican immigrant to escape the discriminating interpretations then given to the immigration acts and suggested that Mexican Americans were at least members of the majority race, and not a minority group that discriminatory legislation was designed to exclude. But when this new image was combined in the realm of half-conscious ideas, the product was devastating. Mexican Americans were still conceived as aliens because of their cultural heritage, and the continuing stream of Mexicans immigrating to the United States across the Rio Grande did nothing to dispel the idea that all Mexicans, including Mexican Americans, were alien to the American style of life. Apparently, no one could distinguish a native-born Mexican American from a newly arrived immigrant, a scenario that is still not satisfactorily resolved, and Mexican Americans (and other Latino subgroups) became, until very recently, an invisible minority group subject to severe discrimination but conceived to be indistinguishable from Anglo-Saxon and northern European peoples. Mexican Americans and other Latinos had no status in the legal universe as a protected group or as members of a distinct racial group because they were frequently conceived to be a part of the white race. Still, they experienced serious practical difficulties because they were so easily distinguished by culture and language.

A typical example of the manner in which Mexican Americans were excluded from virtually all political and legal rights is *Independent School District v. Salvatierra* (1930), a case involving discriminatory segregation of Mexican American children in the schools of Del Rio, Texas.[28] The segregation was explained by the school authorities as necessary because

> as much as or more than half of those pupils go each autumn with their families to other localities where they engage in picking cotton or other farm work until the school terms are well advanced. Other pupils, entering at the beginning of the term, have thus progressed materially into the year's work, and it is the theory of the school authorities that the late comers will be handicapped in their morale and work if allocated with those having one to four months' advantage over them in attendance, training, and progress.[29]

While this program superficially seemed designed to meet the needs of Mexican American children, the school authorities did admit that non–Mexican American children came to school late under somewhat identical conditions but were not placed in the Mexican American schools; the excuse given was that they already knew how to speak English and did not have the adjustment problems the Mexican American children had. The question posed no little difficulties since the court remarked that it should be added that "this segregation or classification is restricted to the lower grades, and does not extend to higher grades, where all the scholastics mingle in play and work indiscriminately, in the same rooms and on the same playgrounds."[30] Unmentioned was the fact that few Latino children remained in school until the latter grades, the discrimination experienced in the elementary grades being sufficient to convince them that education held few benefits for them.

"It is a matter of pride," the court said, "and gratification in our great public educational system and its administration that the question of race segregation, as between Mexicans and other white races, has not heretofore found its way into the courts of the state."[31] Following this line of thought, the court then concluded:

> In this case this court can say no more than that the school authorities have no power to arbitrarily segregate Mexican children, assign them to separate schools, and exclude them from schools maintained for *children of other white races*, merely or solely because they are Mexicans. An unlawful discrimination will be effectuated if the rules for the separation are arbitrary and are applied indiscriminately to all Mexican pupils in those grades without apparent regard to their individual aptitudes or attainments, *while relieving children of other white races from the operation of the rule*, even though some of them, as for instance those who tardily enter the terms, may be subject to the classification given the Mexican children. To the extent that the classification is arbitrarily imposed upon those of one race, but relaxed in its application to those of the other races so as to exclude the latter from its operation, it constitutes an unlawful racial discrimination.[32]

In 1930, of course, segregation of blacks was still considered good constitutional law, so the references to "other white races" was really a means of describing the ethnic groups that composed the white majority, not a general statement that segregation was unconstitutional or unlawful. Thus, while recognizing Mexican Americans as members of the majority, the court supported and continued the de facto segregation by refusing to recognize that classification by language was discriminatory. The result was to endorse a situation in which Mexican Americans existed for administrative purposes but not for constitutional protections.

Mexican Americans differed from African Americans in the legal universe, then, because of the presence of language, which acted as a stalking horse for the larger issue of racial discrimination. As long as Mexican Americans were regarded by and described by the courts as members of the white race, there could be no appeal on the basis of racial prejudice alone, although it most certainly existed. In a California case in 1946, *Mendez v. Westminister School District*, the language barrier was broken.[33] *Mendez* dealt with a nearly identical set of facts as *Salvatierra*. Mexican American children were systematically excluded and segregated while in the early grades but were not excluded in the higher grades. The Mexican American plaintiffs based their complaint on a violation of the Fourteenth Amendment but, realizing that claims of racial prejudice would not carry the argument, conceded that no question of race discrimination existed. However, the court noted, all parties had "admitted that segregation per se is practiced in the above-mentioned school districts as the Spanish-speaking children enter school life and as they advance through the grades in the respective school districts."[34]

The magnitude of the difficulty facing the Mexican American plaintiffs in this case cannot be underestimated. Article 7 of the 1849 California Constitution directed the legislature to "encourage, by all suitable means, the promotion of intellectual, scientific, moral, and agricultural improvement"[35] of the people and article 9 provided for the election of a superintendent of public instruction. Only four other states—Michigan, Iowa, Wisconsin, and Vermont—had similar provisions in their constitutions.[36] The California Education Code was a partial response to these constitutional provisions. The code, however, was rich in racial prejudice, and the court opted to ignore this since it was "not pertinent to this action."[37] Section 8003, for example, authorized the governing board of any school district to "establish separate schools for Indian children, excepting children of Indians who are wards of the United States Government and children of other Indians who are descendants of the original American Indians of the United States, and for children of Chinese, Japanese, or Mongolian parentage."[38] And the following section, 8004, provided that "when separate schools are established for Indian children or children of Chinese, Japanese, or Mongolian parentage, the Indian children or children of Chinese, Japanese, or Mongolian parentage shall not be admitted into any other school."[39]

Clearly, the California legislators were still using outmoded racial classifications based on a nearly obsolete social science. Yet when the code dealt with Mexican American children, their old identification as being part of the white race emerged so that Section 16004 of the Education Code read: "Any person, otherwise eligible for admission to any class or school of a school district of this State, whose parents are or are not citizens of the United States and whose actual and legal residence is in a foreign country adjacent to this State may be admitted to the class or school of the district by the governing board of the district."[40]

School districts wishing to discriminate against Mexican Americans then, had to devise a different criterion than race to justify their exclusion from the schools since the non-Aryan races had already been excluded and Section 16004 obviously referred to Mexican Americans and allowed their full participation in the educational program. The school districts of Westminister, Garden Grove, and El Modeno were equal to the task, providing that all non-English-speaking children be required to attend schools designated by the school boards separate and apart from the schools attended by English-speaking children.[41] Language and culture, thought to have been protected by the Treaty of Guadalupe Hidalgo, became the means of enforcing discriminatory treatment against Mexican American children.

The federal district court in interpreting the California Educational Code would not accept the school board's regulations regarding the language barriers. In referring to these laws, the court noted that they dealt specifically with Mexican American children and forbade discrimination against them. "We perceive in the laws relating to the public educational system in the state of California a clear purpose to avoid and forbid distinctions among pupils based upon race or ancestry except in specific situations not pertinent to this action" (the laws regarding Indians, Chinese, Japanese, and Mongolian children).[42] "The evidence clearly shows," the court held,

> that Spanish-speaking children are retarded in learning English by lack
> of exposure to its use because of segregation, and that commingling of
> the entire student body instills and develops a common cultural attitude
> among the school children which is imperative for the perpetuation of
> American institutions and ideals. It is also established by the record that

the methods of segregation prevalent in the defendant school districts foster antagonisms in the children and suggest inferiority among them where none exists.[43]

It is fascinating that a federal court in 1946 could understand the debilitating effects of segregation when made on the basis of language and culture, but not when it was made on the basis of race alone. It was precisely this handicap that African Americans emphatically demonstrated in *Brown v. Board of Education of Topeka* some eight years later.

Striking down the segregation of Mexican American children, the court referred to the evidence of linguistic handicaps that the school boards presented in an effort to justify their school system. With reference to the Santa Ana City Schools, the court remarked that

the omnibus segregation of children of Mexican ancestry from the rest of the student body in the elementary grades in the schools involved in this case because of language handicaps is not warranted by the record before us. The tests applied to the beginners are shown to have been generally hasty, superficial, and not reliable. In some instances, separate classification was determined largely by the Latinized or Mexican name of the child. Such methods of evaluating language knowledge are illusory and are not conducive to the inculcation and enjoyment of civil rights which are of primary importance in the public school system of education in the United States.[44]

Although the court mentioned the "public system of education in the United States" as the arena in which discriminatory practices should not be allowed, it restricted its decision to an interpretation of the application of the Fourteenth Amendment to the California school system, remarking that equal protection of the laws "is not provided by furnishing in separate schools the same technical facilities, text books and courses of instruction to children of Mexican ancestry that are available to the other public school children regardless of their ancestry."[45] Although dealing with Mexican Americans, *Mendez* had the potential to become a premier case in race relations. Unfortunately, the question of race had been explicitly precluded by agreement, so that the decision produced the bizarre doctrine that the Fourteenth Amendment protected cultural and linguistic differences but did not affect discrimination based on racial characteristics alone.

Despite this, in 2008 the California legislature, realizing the importance of the case, adopted a bill that mandated teaching *Mendez* as part of the state's social studies curriculum. Governor Schwarzenegger, however, vetoed the bill, claiming that lawmakers should not be involved in curriculum matters.[46]

The problem of emergence from the vague generality of the "white race" continued to plague Mexican American and other Latino efforts to achieve full political equality. In *Sanchez v. State* (1951), when a murder conviction was appealed on the basis that Mexican Americans were systematically excluded from the selection of grand jury commissioners and grand jurors, the Court of Criminal Appeals of Texas blithely dismissed the contention.[47] "Appellant has filed quite an exhaustive brief on the subject in which he discusses decisions of other jurisdictions which, either intentionally or loosely, refer to Mexican people as a different race. *They are not a separate race but are white people of Spanish descent, as has often been said by this court. We find no ground for discussing the question further.*"[48] Three years later, however, the US Supreme Court, in *Hernandez v. Texas* (1954), decided to address this question.[49] And as Ian Haney Lopez and Michael A. Oliver reported, this case, rather than *Brown*, actually "deserves the honor of being recognized as the first civil rights decision of the Warren Court." They argued further that it was the first Supreme Court ruling to extend the Fourteenth Amendment's protections to Mexican Americans and was clearly one of the most far-reaching victories in their quest for civil rights.[50]

"The State of Texas," Chief Justice Earl Warren said, "would have us hold that there are only two classes—white and Negro—within the contemplation of the Fourteenth Amendment."[51] Speaking for a unanimous Court, Warren noted:

> Throughout our history differences in race and color have defined easily identifiable groups which have at times required the aid of the courts in securing equal treatment under the laws. But community prejudices are not static, and from time to time other differences from the community norm may define other groups which need the same protection. Whether such a group exists within a community is a question of fact. When the existence of a distinct class is demonstrated, and it is further shown that the laws, as written or as applied, single out that

class for different treatment not based on some reasonable classification, the guarantees of the Constitution have been violated. *The Fourteenth Amendment is not directed solely against discrimination due to a "two-class theory"—that is, based upon differences between "white" and Negro.*[52]

Looking at the evidence, the Court concluded: "Circumstances or chance may well dictate that no persons in a certain class will serve on a particular jury or during some particular period. But it taxes our credulity to say that mere chance resulted in there being no members of this class among the over six thousand jurors called in the past 25 years."[53]

Mendez had provided Mexican Americans protection against discrimination based on linguistic and cultural differences; *Hernandez* had identified them as an occasional class that might be singled out for discriminatory attention by a community. But no case had clearly identified Mexican Americans or other Latinos as an ongoing group that suffered continuing prejudice, so their status in the legal universe remained nebulous. Many courts still preferred to pass over their problems in the same manner as the *Sanchez* case, affirming, with some piety, that Latinos were simply white people who happened to speak Spanish. The major problem, then, was to break the stranglehold of the conception held by many jurists that they were simply a variant group of the majority. Instead, an effort had to be made to show that they were clearly an identifiable group that had suffered prolonged, systematic, and institutionalized discrimination. In *Cisneros v. Corpus Christi Independent School District* (1970) the question of racial status was attacked directly.[54]

The classification of Mexican Americans as whites served many purposes in the southern states. They and African Americans could be segregated in public schools in cities and in county school systems, and when charges were leveled against the system claiming discriminatory practices, the school board had only to announce the racial balance of the target schools and show that they were indeed integrated. If, however, Mexican Americans were understood by the courts as a racial group that also suffered prejudicial treatment, then integrating them and blacks was not constitutional but simply a more sophisticated manner of continuing discriminatory practices. *Cisneros* is notable for the great amount of social science research and evidence introduced into the record to prove that Mexican Americans were an identifiable group. The court expressed admiration at the manner in which such evidence was presented, remarking that "one great advantage and help to the court was the way and manner all the statistical evidence was worked and catalogued at the beginning of the trial, and which was offered and stipulated to early in the trial, and which was available to the court for study for these three (3) weeks."[55]

Although Judge Woodrow Seals identified five distinct issues in the case, each related to dual systems and comparing Mexican Americans to African Americans, the first, "can *Brown v. Board of Education*…and its progeny apply to Mexican-Americans in the Corpus Christi Independent School District; or, stated in another way, is *Brown* limited to Negroes only?" was the most important.[56] Judge Seals suggested that if Mexican Americans as a group had certain identifiable characteristics that were used to degrade them, then they were a group protected by *Brown*. And, as Seals stated, "Occasionally you hear the word 'Mexican' still spoken in a derogatory way in the Southwest—it is clear to this court that these people for whom we have used the word Mexican-Americans to describe their class, group, or segment of our population, are an identifiable ethnic-minority in the United States, and especially so in the Southwest, in Texas and in Corpus Christi."[57]

It was not surprising that Mexican Americans could be so identified, the court continued, since "we can notice and identify their physical characteristics, their language, their predominant religion, their distinct culture, and, of course, their Spanish surnames."[58] And based on the statistical evidence presented, the court concluded that "the Mexican-American students in the Corpus Christi Independent School District are now separated and segregated to a degree prohibited by the Fourteenth Amendment."[59] Not only were Mexican Americans discriminated against at that time, Seals said, but "it is obvious to the court from the evidence that the Mexican-Americans have been historically discriminated against as a class in the Southwest and in Texas, and in the Corpus Christi District."[60] This extension of the findings to include historical discrimination was critical to the articulation of Fourteenth Amendment rights since it eliminated arguments that discrimination was only a contemporary phenomenon.

Judge Seals then attacked Corpus Christi's integration plan, whereby Mexican Americans and blacks were placed in the same schools. "The court is of the opinion that by placing Negroes and Mexican-Americans in the same school does not achieve a unitary system as contemplated by law. A unitary school district can be achieved here only by substantial integration

of the Negroes and Mexican-Americans with the remaining student population of the district."[61] This finding provided the final step in the process of
recognition of legal rights that Mexican Americans needed. Thereafter they
would not be classified as simply another group of whites that happened to
speak Spanish, attend the Catholic Church, and have Spanish surnames;
they were now a specific racial minority whose rights would be protected.
The district court followed the Warren opinion of *Brown* in describing the
function of the public school system, leaving no doubt that it considered the
case crucial to the solution of social problems:

> While many of our institutions have a tendency to divide us—religious
> institutions, social institutions, economic institutions, political institu-
> tions—the public school institution, as I see it, is the one unique institu-
> tion which has the capacity to unite this nation and to unite this diverse
> and pluralistic society that we have. We are not a homogenous people;
> we are a heterogeneous people; we have many races, many religions,
> many colors in America. Here in the public school system as young
> Americans, they can study, play together and interact. They will get
> to know one another, to respect the others' differences and to tolerate
> each other even though of a different race or color, or religious, social
> or ethnic status.[62]

Integration, then, was a way of exploring that hidden recess of emotions and
symbols that constituted the legal universe. Common educational experiences, the court felt, would do much to banish the conceptual demons and
stereotypes that contributed to racial discrimination in American society.

The court asked the two parties to recommend fifteen individuals
they felt would fairly represent their interests, and from that list the judge
appointed a human relations committee to help it supervise implementation
of the desegregation plans. It kept a continuing supervisory role for itself in
the matter, and two years later, the Fifth Circuit Court of Appeals ruled on
the trial court decision.[63] The circuit court clarified the importance of the
original decision by describing the case as a novel one, commenting that
although Mexican Americans

> are now and have been historically separated in fact from Anglos in
> the schools of the city, this separation has never had a statutory origin.

Therefore, unlike cases involving the traditional black-white dual systems, the question is whether the segregation of Mexican-American children who are not the victims of statutorily mandated segregation is constitutionally impermissible. We hold that it is, and affirm the district court's finding that the Mexican-American children of Corpus Christi are segregated in violation of the Constitution.[64]

There could not have been, of course, statutory authority for the segregation of Mexican Americans since they had been submerged within the category of white citizens during most of their legal existence. In more precise legal terms, the court said, "we discard the anodyne dichotomy of classical de facto and de jure segregation. We find no support for the view that the Constitution should be applied antithetically to children in the north and south, or to Mexican Americans vis-à-vis Anglos, simply because of the adventitious circumstance of their origin or the happenstance of locality."[65]

"*Brown*," said the court, "prohibits segregation in public schools that is a result of state action. It requires simply the making of two distinct factual determinations to support a finding of unlawful segregation. First, a denial of equal educational opportunity must be found to exist, defined as racial or ethnic segregation. Secondly, this segregation must be the result of state action."[66] After a long struggle with de facto discrimination, Mexican Americans had finally become an identifiable inhabitant of the legal universe with discernible characteristics and rights.

The old nemesis of classification was raised by Judge James Coleman, who concurred with the procedures outlined in the remedy but dissented on other grounds. Rather, he attempted to confuse the issue of race and citizenship. "I am compelled to say that I am unable to agree, as a legal proposition, that the United States is a Country which is composed of 'many nations within a nation.' We have Americans of Mexican extraction, of Polish extraction, of Irish extraction, of many other extractions, and we have Americans who are either poor or rich."[67] Recognition of cultural, racial, or ethnic differences created divisions in American society, Judge Coleman naively explained, as if no divisions had been experienced prior to the filing of the *Corpus Christi* suit.

Americans of Mexican ancestry are members of the white race. Therefore, if any children of Mexican ancestry are being required to attend a school which by comparison is deficient in faculty, or curriculum, or school plant, then the school board should be mandatorily required to correct the deficiencies right where they exist. This should be done not because the children are of Mexican ancestry but because *all children* in these United States are entitled to the equal protection of the law.[68]

Coleman sought to generalize the situation to such a trivial proposition that there would be no justiciable issue for the court. The majority, however, rejected his argument. The Corpus Christi school board, of course, had always had the responsibility to provide for all children, but it had not provided for either black or Mexican American children.

The Treaty of Guadalupe Hidalgo was signed in 1848, and Mexican diplomats worried that in ceding the southwestern region they were dooming their fellow citizens to centuries of discrimination and prejudice. In large measure their fears were realized, but in a manner entirely different than they originally envisioned. Instead of being regarded as quasi-Indians and therefore racially inferior, Mexican Americans became objects of discrimination because their Spanish, Mexican, and indigenous heritage, although largely western European in origin and principles, was too far removed from the Anglo-Saxon tradition that dominated New England and the eastern United States and colored legal perceptions of human rights. Mexican Americans and other later-arriving Latino immigrants never have fully escaped the *alien* label that had been attached to them early in their contact with Anglo-Americans. As the twentieth century melded into the twenty-first and Mexican Americans and other Latin Americans were brought into the United States to perform migratory labor or entered on their own accord in search of improved socioeconomic conditions, the image of the alien was broadened and deepened in the minds of other Americans. The problem of Latino immigrants has remained an explosive social, economic, cultural, and political issue since the 1970s. But no satisfactory solution has yet been presented to this problem.

The Mexican American community and other Latin Americans present the United States with a fundamental problem inherent in the original patterns of settlement of former centuries, when England, France, and Spain contested with each other for dominance in North America. What culture base should the United States really have? Was it bound to follow the narrow worldview of Anglo-Saxon culture and that particular culture's political and social institutions, or would it broaden itself and transform its identity into a truly diversified North American expression? These more basic questions lie at the root of any discussion of the legal rights and status of Latinos. This diverse collection of peoples pose the most serious cultural and philosophical questions of the present because collectively they have been able to preserve their distinct ethnic identity in spite of all efforts to benignly submerge them beneath the waters of Anglo-Saxon uniformity, where prejudice and discrimination are abstract things that do not happen to people.

Mexican Americans and more recent Latino arrivals have only recently become inhabitants of the legal universe. In some respects, they are in danger of again becoming conceptually hidden by the larger question of the legal rights of the poor, since poverty remains a distinguishing mark of this diverse set of peoples. A dangerous movement in this direction was *San Antonio Independent School District v. Rodriguez, et al.* (1973) in which the Supreme Court essentially held that while education was an important interest, it was not constitutionally guaranteed.[69]

Specifically, the Court upheld the constitutionality of the Texas school-financing system that favored the rich districts over the poor districts in the distribution of school funds. In a concurring opinion, Justice Potter Stewart said that "the method of financing public schools in Texas, as in almost every other State, has resulted in a system of public education that can fairly be described as chaotic and unjust. It does not follow, however, and I cannot find, that this system violates the Constitution of the United States."[70] The plaintiffs in this case were obviously Mexican Americans, yet in becoming part of the more prevalent poor class, they temporarily lost their hard-won identity as a distinct group with constitutionally protected rights.

Despite this judicial setback, it is important to note that Mexican Americans, like African Americans, achieved their entrance into the American political system and their status in the legal universe in litigation over the right to an equal education, thereby continuing to affirm the critical role of education in the political life of the nation.

As important as education has been and remains, other issues also figure prominently in the efforts of Latinos to make further inroads into the American social contract. Language, exacerbated by the significant political actions of Chicanos in the 1960s and 1970s, and the surge in the growth of the US Latino population since the 1960s, is one such topic. As Jill Norgren and Serena Nanda note, for ethnic groups, a common language has important functions: It affirms the group's ethnic identity and provides an important boundary between themselves and others...As a medium of communication in economic, political, and social life, language has obvious and important instrumental functions. Language functions as a political tool, not only in disseminating information critical for political rights and obligations, but also in fashioning group solidarity and expressing relations of dominance and subordination within the civic culture.[71]

Although there is not now and has never been an official national language in the United States, English speakers have often acted as if their language were superior, and occasional English-only laws have been enacted in various states to force the members of various non-English-speaking groups—indigenous nations, Latinos, Asian Americans, and even, at certain crucial moments in history, those from certain European states like Germany—to learn English as part of a punitive assimilation campaign.

Mexican Americans and Latinos have faced conspicuous judicial efforts that have negatively affected their language rights. For instance, in 1978, in *Guadalupe v. Tempe Elementary School District*, the Ninth Circuit Court of Appeals, in a case that affected both Mexican American and Yaqui Indian elementary school children, held that the equal protection clause of the Fourteenth Amendment did not require the state to provide minority children with bilingual-bicultural educational programs.[72] Interestingly, the court interpreted the constitutional social contract in such a way that governmental institutions, like courts, were not mandated to provide anything beyond certain basic rights, privileges, powers, and immunities. Rights such as bilingual programs, said the court, "must be determined by the people acting upon the urging of their hearts. The decision of the appellees to provide a predominantly monocultural and monolingual education system was a rational response to a quintessentially 'legitimate' State interest."[73]

That "legitimate" interest of the state, the court fearfully implied, was severely threatened by Spanish/Yaqui language and cultural diversity. In Judge Joseph T. Sneed's words, "linguistic and cultural diversity within the nation-state, whatever may be its advantages from time to time, can restrict the scope of the fundamental compact. Diversity limits unity. Effective action by the nation-state rises to its peak of strength only when it is in response to aspirations shared by each constituent culture and language group."[74] In short, Latinos and Native students' right to a multicultural education were dashed by the court's determination that the state's interest in preserving a monolingual—English only—society was the only legitimate interest worthy of protection.

The merger of race, gender, and reproductive rights led to a horrific decision, also in 1978, that had devastating consequences for Latinos. Five years after *Roe v. Wade* (1973) held that women had a constitutionally protected right to choose whether to have an abortion, a federal district court, in *Madrigal v. Quilligan,* dealt with the related issue of voluntary consent for sterilization.[75] As background, Dolores Madrigal and nine other Mexican and Mexican American women asserted at trial that they had been subjected to unwanted sterilizations at the University of Southern California–Los Angeles County Medical Center. They presented evidence that "hospital staff pressured or coerced most of the women into signing consent forms during labor, presented those forms when the women were under heavy sedation, or in some cases never presented consent forms at all."[76] Although most of the women spoke Spanish as their primary language, the majority of them received forms that were printed in English.

Judge Jesse Curtis, while acknowledging the emotional and physical stress the women had endured because of the operations, expressed sympathy "for the inability to communicate clearly," but held the doctors and hospital blameless. Besides the obvious language barriers, Curtis also blamed the women's "culture" for the sterilization. He said, "the cultural background of these particular women has contributed to the problem in a subtle but very significant way."[77] The women's "extreme dependence on family" leads them, said Curtis, when faced with the decision whether to be sterilized, to confront a decision process that "is a much more traumatic event with her than it would be with a typical patient and, consequently, she would require greater explanation, more patient advice, and greater care in interpreting her consent than persons not members of such a subculture would require."[78] In other words, Judge Curtis was blaming the women for their sterilization and refused to consider how the hospital staff had violated their reproductive rights.[79]

The already complicated situation of Latino identity was exacerbated in 1980 when the US Census Bureau institutionalized the term *Hispanic* in the census of that year. This label was a result of a number of external forces that were seeking to simplify a diverse number of Latino subgroups—Mexican

Americans, Puerto Ricans, Cuban Americans, and people from various Central and South American states.[80] While it was one way for the federal government to improve the historic undercount of Latinos, it also led to a homogenization of very different ethnic communities with unique histories. As a federal court noted in a 1988 class action lawsuit, *Perez v. FBI*,[81] filed by Latino FBI agents,

> throughout the litigation, there seemed to be some question as to what is an "Hispanic." Some witnesses seemed to consider it a racial distinction. One witness for the Defense, not a member of the class and carrying a surname of Northern European origin, stated that because of a Latin maternal ancestor he "liked to think that he was Hispanic." The implication of his testimony is that he had not felt discrimination and bore Hispanic class members no ill will. No class members were in doubt that their ethnic heritage was from Spain or of Spanish origin and the Defendant does not dispute whether any individual member possesses this quality…For the purposes of this class, appellation "Hispanic" will signify ethnic and national origin categories.[82]

The Supreme Court returned to the issue of minority language rights in 1991. In *Dionisio Hernandez v. New York*, a criminal justice case, Hernandez had been convicted of murder in state court.[83] On appeal, his attorney argued that the state prosecutor during the criminal trial had wrongly removed all Spanish-speaking prospective jurors by reason of their ethnicity. Hernandez's attorney argued that such exclusion of bilingual jurors was impermissibly discriminatory and violated his client's equal protection rights.[84] The prosecutor defended his action to strike the bilingual Latino jurors by arguing that "the challenges rested neither on the intention to exclude Latinos or bilingual jurors, nor on stereotypical assumptions about Latinos or bilinguals."[85] In other words, the prosecutor alleged that his actions were "race-neutral."

A divided Supreme Court, speaking through Justice Anthony Kennedy, accepted the state's race-neutral argument and found no violation of equal protection. Seeking to soften the brunt of this finding, Kennedy noted, "Our decision today does not imply that exclusion of bilinguals from jury service is wise, or even that it is constitutional in all cases." "It is," said Kennedy, "a harsh paradox that one may become proficient enough in

English to participate in trial...only to encounter disqualification because he knows a second language as well."[86]

Three dissenters, Justices John P. Stevens, Harry Blackmun, and Thurgood Marshall, found the prosecutor's explanation insufficient for three reasons. First, the jurisdiction would lead to a disproportionate disqualification of Spanish speakers. A so-called race-neutral explanation "on its face is nonetheless unacceptable if it is merely a proxy for a discriminatory practice."[87] Second, the prosecutor could have accomplished the same task with less drastic measures. And third, had the prosecutor's concern been valid and substantiated by the record, it would have "supported a challenge for cause."[88] But since the prosecutor failed to make any challenges, this disqualified him from "advancing the concern as a justification for a peremptory challenge."[89]

In regard to voting rights, Louis Disipio says that Latinos have never faced the same degree of electoral exclusion as African Americans have.[90] That is not to say, however, that they have not experienced any discrimination in voting. Like African American and Native peoples, they have also faced barriers to political participation, such as poll taxes, racial gerrymandering, all-white primaries, restrictive registration laws, and laws that prohibit interpreters at polling places.[91]

Despite these structural and institutional constraints, studies from the 1960s show that Latino voter turnout was similar to that of the years following the 1975 extension of the Voting Rights Act (1965) to Latinos and several other language minorities. The 1975 extension provided the members of the following language groups with the identical procedural guarantees that African Americans had secured in 1965: Latinos, Asian Americans, and Native peoples and Alaska Natives. And it ensured that these language speakers "could register and vote without intimidation and that local jurisdictions could not change voting rules or procedures without Justice Department approval."[92] Additionally, bilingual election materials were also to be provided. Despite these legal changes, and even though Latinos are now the largest ethnic minority group in the United States (48.5 million in 2009, or 15.8 percent of the population—projected by 2050 to be 30 percent), they are dramatically underrepresented in elected office at both the federal and state levels.[93]

The Supreme Court became intimately involved in this issue as applied to Latinos when it heard *Bush v. Vera* in 1996.[94] This case followed the

Court's earlier ruling in 1993 of *Shaw v. Reno*, a redistricting case challenging the establishment of a new majority-minority congressional district for African Americans.[95] In *Shaw*, the Court held that the use of race must be limited because segregation by race was unacceptable.

In *Vera*, in a 4–3 ruling, the Supreme Court applied its *Reno* holding to Latinos and said that race could not be a predominant factor in redistricting. But Justice Stevens, for Ruth Bader Ginsburg and Stephen Breyer in dissent, emphatically observed that "the history of race relations in Texas and throughout the South demonstrates over evidence of discriminatory voting practices lasting through the 1970s."[96] Stevens skeptically opined:

> Perhaps the state of race relations in Texas and, for that matter, the Nation, is more optimistic than might be expected in light of these facts. If so, it may be that the plurality's exercise in redistricting will be successful. Perhaps minority candidates, forced to run in majority-white districts, will be able to overcome the long history of stereotyping and discrimination that has heretofore led the vast majority of majority-white districts to reject minority candidacies. Perhaps not.[97]

Mexican Americans and the many other Latino subgroups that now constitute the largest racial/ethnic minority group in the United States, like Native peoples, exhibit distinctive cultural, language, ideological, and economic differences that make their status in the legal universe an unstable one. And, as with most indigenous nations, Mexico had a treaty-based relationship with the United States that was closely connected to US territorial aspirations of dominance. As a result, racial discrimination, anti-immigrant fervor, physical violence, and other problems ensued and, in fact, continue to fester, thus complicating intercultural relations. As Gary Orfield and Chungmei Lee reported in 2006–2007, Latino students face, in particular, "triple segregation by race, class, and language" and are often compelled to attend schools where more than half the students are Latino.[98]

Unlike African Americans and women, who gained a measured entrance to the American social contract via constitutional amendment, Mexican Americans and Latinos in general have had to push hard at the doors of Congress and the federal courts and confront state lawmakers in their efforts to protect their always-fragile legal, economic, and political foothold in the United States. But attacks on bilingual education programs, the resurgent English-only movement, criminal justice problems, and that most vexing of issues—immigration—will likely continue to plague Mexican American efforts to stabilize and improve their standing in this country.

CHAPTER 9
"Strangers in the Land":
Asian Americans and the Law

ASIAN AMERICAN IS AN ENCOMPASSING TERM, like *Latino American* or *American Indian*, coined in the late 1960s and generally referring to a diverse set of peoples and their descendants who originally immigrated from the Far East, Southeast Asia, the Indian Subcontinent. In the last twenty years, *Asian American* is often understood to include Pacific Island ethnic groups as well, and the term is sometimes written as Asian Pacific American or Asian-American and Pacific Islander.[1]

The 2010 US Census identified twenty-four Asian groups, including Chinese, Japanese, Filipinos, Koreans, Vietnamese, Cambodians, Laotians, Hmong, Asian Indian peoples, Hawaiians, Samoans, and Guamanians, among others.[2] They had an estimated population in 2008 of over fifteen million when reporting their race as Asian or Pacific Islander alone, with some projections indicating that it will increase to about forty million by 2050.[3]

While their level of racial and ethnic diversity is comparable to that of Latino/as, their historic experiences and position within the legal universe more closely resembles that of African Americans. As Angelo N. Ancheta noted, "for most of the nation's history, Asian Americans have been treated primarily as *constructive* blacks [legal jargon for "implied" blacks]. Asian-Americans for decades endured many of the same disabilities of racial subordination as African Americans—racial violence, segregation, unequal access to public institutions and discrimination in housing, employment, and education."[4]

As a result, Asian Americans historically and today must also cope with conflicting images and stereotypes. As we shall see, they are sometimes depicted as largely unassimilable foreigners, but in more recent times they have been depicted as the "model minority" group, a racist and inaccurate phrase coined by William Peterson in 1964. He used this seemingly laudatory image of Japanese Americans to "discredit the protests and demands for social justice of other minority groups by admonishing them to follow the 'shining example' set by Asian Americans."[5]

But as Sucheng Chan observed, while the socioeconomic status of Asian Americans has improved markedly since the 1960s, the model minority thesis is flawed on several grounds, including the fact that the relatively low income rate of Asian Americans "merely camouflages high unemployment. Wary of being on welfare, many Asian American workers apparently would rather have low-paid, part-time, or seasonal jobs than receive public assistance."[6]

Moreover, the persistent model minority image distracts attention from less well-off and undereducated segments of the Asian American population, minimizes the negative impact of racial discrimination, lays heavy pressure on young Asian Americans, and generates tension and resentment against Asian Americans by other minority group members and whites as well.[7]

With this backdrop, we now move to assess how the courts have dealt with the rights and status of two of the major Asian American groups— Chinese Americans and Japanese Americans—largely because individuals in these two groups have been involved in the most litigation throughout American history.

Chinese Americans

The most astute observer of the American scene in the 1790s might well have predicted that the African slaves who toiled on the southern plantations would someday be incorporated in the political system as citizens. They might even have ventured beyond that issue to suggest that American expansion would progress so rapidly during the decades ahead that the Spanish provinces of the Southwest would fall under American domination and that within a century thousands of former Spanish citizens would pledge allegiance to the American flag. No seer of those days, however wise, could have predicted that the most explosive racial and ethnic issue at the close of the next century would revolve about the question of Chinese and Japanese immigration and citizenship. Yet as Americans pushed aside the question of black slavery in the South, the issue of Asian immigration assumed increasing importance so that as the nineteenth century gave way to the modern era, racial hatred against Asians and Asian Americans occupied the center stage of American life.

The Far East, Southeast Asia, the Indian Subcontinent, formerly and derisively known as the Orient, had always been a puzzle to European peoples. Marco Polo had spurred European commercial instincts with his stories of fabulous riches that seemed to abound in China, India, and other parts of this vast landscape. Columbus, of course, stumbled across the Western Hemisphere on the way to India, and succeeding explorers of all nations sought more direct passages to the East that would elevate their nations to the forefront of European trade and commerce. Exploitation of the peoples of the Western Hemisphere was easily justified by both church and state as the only means of bringing the savage inhabitants within the scope of enlightened civilization. Western Europeans, relying on the doctrine of discovery, secured title to lands of non-Christian peoples who did not share their common cultural heritage. On this basis, some indigenous populations were exterminated in the Americas while others were enslaved in Africa. But the Far East was a much different situation. "Unlike America and Africa, which could only provide versions of the Noble Savage to mirror the vices of Europe," Andrew Sinclair wrote in *The Savage,* "China could provide an example of a counter-civilization" and the very antiquity of Asian peoples, their great numbers, and their remote geographical location, made dealings with China, Japan, Korea, and other Asian countries a delicate matter to consider.[8]

Euro-Americans were brought into the Chinese sphere of activity in a most backward manner. Most of the European states had already been trading with China for centuries before the United States achieved independence, and the few ships that traversed the Pacific between the West Coast and China during the first decades of the nineteenth century were latecomers and hardly a matter of European concern. The United States was fortunate to have any Chinese commerce at all and until the 1840s this trade was confined to a single port.

The desire to compete with British trade on an international basis provided the first incentive to Americans to expand trade with China. In 1842, England and China, having concluded the first Opium War (1839–1842) over trade relations, signed a peace treaty, the Treaty of Nanjing (Nanking), and the provisions of this treaty gave the British, the victors in the war, rights to reside in the five principal ports of China for the purpose of carrying on mercantile pursuits.[9] China had not granted such privileges to other European powers and Congress, fearful that the United States would be completely excluded from the Far East, authorized the president to establish future commercial relations between the two countries "on terms of national equal reciprocity."[10] Caleb Cushing was appointed to head the American mission to China, and upon his arrival he discovered that the United States could receive terms as favorable and flexible as those received by Great Britain. On July 3, 1844, the United States and China concluded their first treaty, and relationships between the two governments were established.[11]

The treaty established, among other things, that there was to be "perfect, permanent and universal peace and a sincere and cordial amity between the two nations." China's five major ports were also opened to US citizens. The much-sought-after Chinese connection had been formalized.

Soon after the 1848 Treaty of Guadalupe Hidalgo was signed and California was annexed by the United States, the migration of Chinese nationals and eventually other Asians into the country via California was a foregone conclusion. In fact, Aaron H. Palmer, a policy maker, suggested that San Francisco would become a central location for Pacific commerce. He also proposed that Chinese laborers be "imported to build the trans-continental railroad as well as bring the fertile lands of California under cultivation."[12] "No people," said Palmer, "in all the East are so well adapted for clearing wild lands and raising every species of agricultural product... as the Chinese."[13]

As the Chinese foreign trade continued to expand, tensions between China and the western countries also accelerated, and by 1856 England insti-gated yet another war with China. When the war ended in 1868 with the Treaty of Tianjin (Tiantin), England wrought additional concessions from China and as a means of achieving this end asked France and the United States to join in a demand that China expand its commercial activities with the western powers, that it guarantee religious freedom for all Christians— which naturally included those Chinese who had become converts to Chris-tianity as a result of the activities of English and American missionaries— and that China legalize opium and pay an additional indemnity.[14]

The United States was fearful that it would become embroiled in the feud between China and England but anxious that it not be excluded from access to China's riches. Seeking to distinguish its aims from those of Eng-land, the United States sent another mission to China to represent its inter-ests, and in June 1858, led by William B. Reed of Philadelphia, another treaty was concluded that reinstated the desire for peace and friendship and gave the Americans the same commercial privileges accorded to Great Brit-ain. The Christian missionaries played a critical role in writing this treaty and were rewarded accordingly, with the treaty providing:

> The principles of the Christian religion, as professed by the Protes-tant and Roman Catholic churches, are recognised as teaching men to do good, and to do to others as they would have others do to them.

Hereafter those who quietly profess and teach these doctrines shall not be harassed or persecuted on account of their faith. Any person, whether citizen of the United States or Chinese convert, who, according to these tenets, peaceably teach and practice the principles of Christianity, shall in no case be interfered with or molested.[15]

While the open-door policy was a later innovation in foreign affairs, the 1858 treaty protections accorded the American missionaries made it certain that China would be opened to the west rather quickly by the intrusions of the Christian missionaries since, rather than "peaceably teach and practice" their religion, the missionaries aggressively sought to transform Chinese society and its people into accepting a set of institutions based on Western values and mores.

The place where Christianity among the Chinese might have been more welcomed was California. In 1848, gold was discovered at Sutter's Mill, and the following year thousands of adventurers from around the world descended upon California in search of the riches that seemed to lay beneath the surface of the Sacramento valley. In the first few years, only a few hundred Chinese from Toishan, a tiny district of Kwang-tung in southern China, joined this tidal wave of immigrants to the Pacific Coast.[16] But far greater numbers of Chinese began arriving in 1852, when some 52,000 made it to California.[17] Their arrival testified to the extreme courage of the first Chinese immigrants since the Ching Dynasty had made it a capital offense for Chinese to emigrate. Chinese who left the mainland were considered to be in rebellion against the emperor. The majority of these early Chinese immigrants did not seek to establish permanent homes in California but, like so many other immigrants, sought only to accumulate enough capital to return home and live a better life. California, it turned out, did not have, as many had been led to believe, gold nuggets lying in the streets, and by 1850 it was apparent that very few people were actually going to make themselves rich from the digging.

As the mining claims were taken over by large corporations and individual mining became a more competitive affair, measures began to be taken against the Chinese and Mexicans designed to eliminate them as serious competitors for the gold and silver of the mining districts. In 1850, the new state legislature, in the first of what would be many efforts by California legislatures to pass discriminatory laws clothed in innocent language, passed the Foreign Miners' License Law, which imposed a tax of twenty dollars a month on all foreign miners.[18] On its face the law was ludicrous. Outside of the Indian settlements and a few long-established Mexican families, both of whom had already been dispossessed by the wave of white immigrants, everyone could be said to be a foreign miner since they had all come from someplace else within the previous two years. Yet the law was interpreted to apply primarily to Mexicans and Chinese—those people who appeared to be linguistically, culturally, and racially different than white Americans. When this law was challenged, a state court in *People v. Naglee* (1850) held that the Mexicans were citizens under the Protocol of Queretero of 1848, a three-article agreement negotiated between the United States and Mexico upon the exchanged ratifications of the Treaty of Guadalupe Hidalgo, and thus were not foreigners under the statute.[19] The Chinese, in effect, became the only group to suffer the impact of this discriminatory legislation.

Four years later, California's Supreme Court overturned the conviction of a white man, George Hall, who had killed a Chinese man. Hall had been convicted, in part, based on the testimony of a white man and three Chinese witnesses. The Court held that Chinese witnesses were not allowed to testify against whites in criminal trials. Chief Justice Justin Murray, writing for the majority, strangely interpreted parts of two state laws that did not mention Chinese—section 394 of the Civil Practice Act, which provided that "no Indian or Negro shall be allowed to testify as a witness in any action in which a white person is a party," and section 14 of the Act of April 16, 1850, which provided that "no Black, or Mulatto person, or Indian, shall be allowed to give evidence in favor of, or against a white man"—in a way that penalized them as if they were an integral part of the laws.

Chief Justice Murray engaged in sophistry of the highest order and fashioned an argument alleging that the Chinese were meant to be included in the law's interpretation because they were racially related to American Indians since the phrase "Black person" necessarily excluded all non-Caucasian races, and because allowing Chinese to testify would constitute bad policy. It was the judge's explanation of the third element where the racism was most palpable:

> The same rule which would admit them [Chinese] to testify, would admit them to all the equal rights of citizenship, and we might soon see them at the polls, in the jury box, upon the bench, and in our legislative halls...The anomalous spectacle of a distinct people, living in our

community, recognizing no laws of this State except through necessity, bringing with them their prejudices and national feuds, in which they indulge in open violation of law; whose mendacity is proverbial; a race of people whom nature has marked as inferior, and who are incapable of progress or intellectual development beyond a certain point, as their history has shown; differing in language, opinions, color, and physical conformation; between whom and ourselves nature has placed an impassable difference, is now presented, and for them is claimed, not only the right to swear away the life of a citizen, but the further privilege of participating with us in administering the affairs of our Government.[20]

In 1855, the state legislature imposed a fifty-dollar capitation tax on "the immigration to this state of persons who cannot become citizens thereof." Three years later, the state explicitly acted to deny Chinese immigration by enacting a law titled "An Act to prevent the further immigration of Chinese and Mongolians to this State."[21]

As a result of these laws and policies, the Chinese already in California abandoned the mining districts and swarmed into San Francisco. There they took whatever jobs were available and provided a cheap and badly needed labor force for the city. Within a short time, entrepreneurial-minded Chinese had started their own businesses, generally hand laundries and restaurants. They set up their own schools and organizations, began purchasing homes and business locations, and entered into some phases of urban life while preserving as much as they could of their distinct customs and culture. New immigrants were taken into the family organizations and given support while they established themselves, and the Chinese community exercised a remarkable degree of self-discipline and orderliness considering the fact that they constituted a persecuted ghetto of alleged foreigners in a land not noted for its racial tolerance. Why the resentment? One white author, Theodore Hittell, writing in 1898, said, "As a class [the Chinese] were harmless, peaceful and exceedingly industrious; but, as they were remarkably economical and spent little or none of their earnings except for the necessities of life and this chiefly to merchants of their own nationality, they soon began to provoke the prejudice and ill-will of those who could not seen any value in their labor to the country."[22]

Despite sporadic outbursts of rage at their presence, the Chinese community in San Francisco remained remarkably stable and served as an efficient, albeit informal, port of entry for newly arriving Chinese immigrants seeking entrance into the United States. Moreover, like the political elites of the Five Civilized Tribes in Indian Territory, the Chinese did not hesitate to file their grievances in the US judicial system if they felt that their rights were being abridged or denied. In fact, between 1854 and 1882 more than one hundred Chinese-related cases were adjudicated in the California Supreme Court and in the courts of other western states.[23]

China, meanwhile, was losing ground at home with European intrusions into its important port cities and through the missionaries' activities, which were quickly spreading out into the interior of the country. Chinese subjects abroad were being abused terribly, and this treatment reflected a basic attitude of suspicion and superiority, which the Western nations exhibited toward China in their more formal dealings. In 1868, the emperor of China decided to seek better relations with the West and sent a diplomatic mission to the United States. Leading this mission was Anson Burlingame, an American citizen and entrepreneur, and the US minister to the Manchu Court in Peking. Burlingame had so impressed the emperor with his honesty and concern for Chinese-US relations that he had won the confidence of the emperor, and he was charged by the imperial court with the task of gaining for China a new and favorable treaty with the United States to replace the 1858 Treaty of Tientsin. Burlingame arranged a treaty containing very favorable terms for the Chinese, and since the articles of this treaty played so important a role in later developments in the United States, it is critical that we review some of its major provisions.[24] Article 5, for instance, dealt with immigration, and the provisions of this article contained a major concession on the part of both the United States and the emperor:

> The United States of American and the Emperor of China cordially recognize the inherent and inalienable right of man to change his home and allegiance, and also the mutual advantage of free migration and emigration of their citizens and subjects, respectively, from the one country to the other, for purposes of curiosity, of trade, or as permanent residents.[25]

The article further provided that both states would make it a penal offense for either Americans or Chinese to bring Chinese laborers to the United States against their will, eliminating, at least partially, that dreadful trade that was then taking place between southern China and the West Coast.

Article 6 forbade discriminatory practices by each nation against the citizens of the other, recognizing that the other's citizens would enjoy the status of people from a "most favored nation" while living in the other country. Article 7 built upon this theme and provided:

> Citizens of the United States shall enjoy all the privileges of the public educational institutions under the control of the government of China, and, reciprocally, Chinese subjects shall enjoy all the privileges of the public educational institutions under the control of the government of the United States, which are enjoyed in the respective countries by the citizens or subjects of the most favored nation. The citizens of the United States may freely establish and maintain schools within the Empire of China at those places where foreigners are by treaty permitted to reside, and, reciprocally, Chinese subjects may enjoy the same privileges and immunities in the United States.[26]

The provisions of this article raise certain questions about Burlingame's integrity. He surely knew that the federal government did not control schools in the United States and that, with the exception of some minor institutions on the East Coast for freedmen and Indians, such as Hampton Institute in Virginia, education in the public sector was primarily a state and local governmental function. The promise, then, to allow Chinese immigrants to enjoy the public school institutions was almost wholly fictional and would have been practically unenforceable. The educational provisions, however, were not nearly as important as the provisions allowing virtually unrestricted immigration of Chinese as laborers. Hence, article 7 might be construed as a futuristic and idealistic stance taken by Burlingame in an effort to establish Chinese cultural and social parity with the Americans.

The Burlingame treaty opened the West Coast to immigration in a fundamental sense, along with construction of the transcontinental railroad, and with the penalties imposed by the emperor now reduced somewhat in their severity, many Chinese felt that the United States could provide them with opportunities they had not experienced in their ancient homeland for millennia. Chinese immigration increased dramatically. Between 1849 and 1882, nearly 300,000 Chinese immigrated to the United States.[27] Hawaii, years from statehood, was also a destination site, but in not nearly the same numbers.

The Chinese were generally tolerated, with exceptions, as long as economic conditions on the West Coast remained expansive. Justice Stephen J. Field, describing the impact of Chinese labor during these years, wrote in *The Chinese Exclusion Case* (1889)[28] that the Chinese

> were generally industrious and frugal. Not being accompanied by families, except in rare instances, their expenses were small; and they were content with the simplest fare, such as would not suffice for our laborers and artisans. The competition between them and our people was for this reason altogether in their favor, and the consequent irritation, proportionately deep and bitter, was followed, in many cases, by open conflicts, to the great disturbance of public peace.[29]

The basic sources of racial conflict between the Chinese and white Americans, then, was simply that the Chinese were typically better and harder workers, unaffected by the pretentiousness that has often inflicted American workers when confronted with brutal physical labor.

California might have become the melting pot of a new type of society had the emperor forbidden emigration earlier in the century. If the Chinese had been encouraged to immigrate to the Pacific Coast prior to the discovery of gold, and if they had made substantial settlements during the first several decades of the nineteenth century, the history of the United States might have been entirely different. Although the Burlingame treaty opened the West Coast to Chinese immigration, the waves of Euro-American settlers arriving in California more than made up for the increasing influx of Chinese males (90 percent of the arrivals were men), so that no matter how many Chinese arrived on the West Coast, they were always in a desperate numerical minority position existing at the whim of the white majority. To give an indication, however, of the numbers of Chinese that took advantage of the free access to the United States, one need only look at the agricultural statistics for the years following the Burlingame treaty. In 1870, the Chinese made up only one-tenth of the agricultural workforce. A decade later, when California was considerably more settled, they constituted one-third of the rural labor force, and four years later they represented one-half of these workers.[30]

At the agitation of the laboring classes, riots broke out against the Chinese in many places in California. In San Francisco in July 1877, twenty-five Chinese laundries were burned, many of them with the occupants still inside. For weeks afterward, no Chinese were safe on the streets of the city, and any Chinese caught in the open was certain to be beaten and robbed. The violence spread to other places in California. In 1878, the entire Chinese population of Truckee was unceremoniously rounded up and driven from the town. During the following decade, the violence against the Chinese spread to the neighboring states. In 1885, the entire Chinese population of Rock Springs, Wyoming, came under attack and twenty-eight people were killed and the remainder driven from their homes. Log Cabin, Oregon, hardly a hotbed of Asian American intrigue, was the sight of a massacre of Chinese in 1886.[31] If the whites of the West Coast had been brutal with Native peoples in California, hunting them for Sunday afternoon's sport, or if they had disenfranchised the indigenous Mexican citizens through a variety of intrigues during the 1850s, they reached tragic proportions with their war on the Chinese during the late 1870s and early 1880s.[32]

Western whites, particularly those in unions and political parties, like the influential Working Men's Party, did not depend on statistics to convince them that they were facing a strong economic power from "cheap Chinese labor" and convinced state lawmakers to adopt a tougher stance toward the Chinese. In the revised California Constitution of 1879, article 19 contained highly discriminatory provisions against the Chinese.[33] Section 1 authorized the legislature to take all necessary measures to protect the state "from the burdens and evils arising from the presence of aliens." The succeeding sections were even less covert:

> *Section 2.* No corporation now existing, or hereafter formed under the laws of this state, shall, after the adoption of this constitution, employ, *directly* or *indirectly*, in any capacity, any Chinese or Mongolians.

> *Section 3.* No Chinese shall be employed on any state, county, municipal, or other public work, except in punishment for crime.

> *Section 4.* The presence of foreigners ineligible to become citizens is declared to be dangerous to the well-being of this state, and the legislature shall discourage their immigration by all the means within its power. Asiatic coolieism is a form of human slavery, and is forever prohibited in this State; and all contracts for coolie labor shall be void. All companies or corporation whether formed in this country or any foreign country, for the importation of such labor, shall be subject to such

penalties as the Legislature may prescribe. The Legislature shall delegate all necessary power to the incorporated cities and towns of this State for the removal of Chinese without the limits of such cities and towns, or for their location within prescribed portions of those limits; and it shall also provide the necessary legislation to prohibit the introduction into this State of Chinese after the adoption of this Constitution.[34]

There could be no doubt after 1879 that California's politicians had seized on the Chinese as a useful vehicle for popular demagoguery. The constitution of 1879 was adopted during a period of intense labor difficulties on the West Coast. The white workers, inflamed by an Irish sailor, Dennis Kearney, railed against the moguls of big business, the railroads, and mining companies, but inevitably concluded their tirades by demanding that the Chinese be expelled from the state, thinking in their simplicity that elimination of the best workers in the state would add to the marketable skills that they presumed to possess.[35]

The federal courts, to their great credit, did not approve of such brutal activities. Numerous cases were taken against the Chinese in California, Oregon, and Washington when cities attempted to enforce blatantly discriminatory ordinances that had the effect of severely restricting the activities of Chinese in their businesses and homes. In *Baker v. Portland*, an early 1877 case on the validity of the 1858 treaty with China, the federal court concluded that the treaty could not be overridden by a local ordinance and that the Chinese would have to be protected in their trades and occupations like any other people exercising commercial privileges under a treaty.[36] In an interesting "note" attached at the end of the opinion, Judge Matthew P. Deady elaborated on California's motives in enacting such discriminatory laws. He said, "But the fact is, the anti-Chinese legislation of the Pacific coast is but a poorly disguised attempt on the part of the state to evade and set aside the treaty with China, and thereby nullify an act of the national government. Between this and the 'firing on Fort Sumner,' by South Carolina, there is the difference of the direct and indirect—nothing more."[37]

In re Tiburcio Parrott (1880) was a direct challenge to the provisions of article 19 of the 1879 constitution and state law that barred any corporation from hiring any Chinese or Mongolian workers.[38] Judge Ogden Hoffman found the California law to be unconstitutional on two grounds. First, it violated the rights of corporations; second, it also violated the rights of the

Chinese.[39] Not surprisingly, corporate rights were affirmed more forcefully than Chinese individual rights. "Behind the artificial or ideal being created by the statute and called a corporation, are the corporators," Hoffman noted,

> natural persons who have conveyed their property to the corporation, or contributed to it their money, and received, as evidence of their interest, shares in its capital stock. The corporation, though it holds the title, is the trustee, agent, and representative of the shareholders, who are the real owners. *And it seems to me that their right to use and enjoy their property is as secure under constitutional guarantees as are the rights of private persons to the property they may own.*[40]

And, the judge concluded, "irrespective of the rights secured to the Chinese by the treaty, the law is void, as not being a 'reasonable,' *bonafide*, or constitutional exercise of the power to alter and amend the general laws under which corporations in this state have been formed; that it would be equally invalid if the prescribed class had been Irish, German, or Americans."[41]

Some acknowledgment was made, to be sure, of the existence of the Chinese treaty that described the subjects of China as enjoying the status of citizens of the "most favored nation," a position that they hardly enjoyed under the 1879 constitution. "No enumeration would, I think, be attempted of the privileges, immunities, and exemptions of the most favored nation, or even of man in civilized society, which would exclude the right to labor for a living," Judge Hoffman contended. "It is as inviolable as the right of property, for property is the offspring of labor. It is as sacred as the right to life, for life is taken if the means whereby we live be taken."[42]

More to the point was the comment of Judge Lorenzo Sawyer, who wrote a concurring opinion, discussing the actual state of conditions of the Chinese:

> Common experience, I think, would lead to the conclusion that the Chinese within the state, with equal opportunities, are as little likely to fall into vagrancy, pauperism, and mendacity, and thereby become a public charge, as any other class, native or foreign born. Industry and economy, by which the Chinese are able to labor cheaply and still accumulate large amounts of money to send out of the country—the objection perhaps most frequently and strenuously urged against their presence—are not the legitimate parents of "vagrancy, pauperism, mendacity and crime."[43]

Although the whites tried desperately to characterize the Chinese as the scum of California society, helpless beggars on the public treasury and therefore undesirable citizens and residents, the federal courts in these cases knew well the conditions under which the Chinese lived in America and refused to acknowledge a public policy argument to justify their exclusion from practicing their occupations. Despite this favorable ruling, however, the judge could not resist raising an alarm about the ever-increasing number of Chinese immigrants in the country. Near the end of his opinion, Hoffman opined that "the unrestricted immigration of the Chinese to this country is a great and growing evil, that presses with much severity on the laboring class, and that, if allowed to continue in numbers bearing any considerable proportion to that of the teeming population of the Chinese Empire, it will be a menace to our peace and even to our civilization, is an opinion entertained by most thoughtful persons."[44]

In addition to blatant and straightforward discriminatory language in laws and constitutions, white Californians attempted various subterfuges against the Chinese, hoping that the courts would uphold discriminatory laws if they were couched in police power or welfare clause phraseology. A typical case of this kind was *Ho Ah Kow v. Nunan* (1879), involving the practice of cutting off the queues (long hair braids) of Chinese prisoners in the county jail in San Francisco under the guise of improving the sanitary conditions of the city.[45] When the case was heard in federal district court, the two judges, Field and Sawyer, cut through the guise of sanitary concern to the real issue. "The ordinance," they reminded the parties,

> is known in the community as the "queue ordinance," being so designated from its purpose to reach the queues of the Chinese, and it is not enforced against any other persons. The reason advanced for its adoption, and now urged for its continuance, is, that only the dread of the loss of his queue will induce a Chinaman to pay his fine. That is to say, in order to enforce the payment of a fine imposed upon him, it is necessary that torture should be superadded to imprisonment. Then, it is said, the Chinaman will not accept the alternative, which the law allows, of working out his fine by his imprisonment, and the state or county will be saved the expense of keeping him during the imprisonment.[46]

The judges might have added that only if a Chinese had his queue could he hope to return safely to China, and thus cutting the queue, far from inducing him to leave California, was actually a means of ensuring that he remain in this country.

Field and Sawyer based their important decision invalidating the ordinance on the provisions of the Fourteenth Amendment and declared that the law's alleged neutrality did not immunize it from Fourteenth Amendment scrutiny. That amendment, said the judges, "further declares that no state shall deprive *any person* [dropping the distinctive term *citizen*] of life, liberty or property, without due process of law, nor deny to *any person* the equal protection of the laws."[47] Although the Chinese were forbidden from becoming citizens, like Standing Bear, they were persons within the law and therefore within the scope of legal protections. The judges continued, noting that

> the equality of protection thus assured to every one whilst within the United States, from whatever country he may have come, or of whatever race or color he may be, implies not only that the courts of the country shall be open to him on the same terms as to all others for the security of his person or property, the prevention or redress of wrongs and the enforcement of contracts; but that no charges or burdens shall be laid upon him which are not equally borne by others, and that in the administration of criminal justice he shall suffer for his offenses no greater or different punishment.[48]

Since the *Slaughter-House Cases* had separated state and federal citizenship, frequently denying constitutional protections to citizens against state actions, the courts found themselves in the uncomfortable position of interpreting the Fourteenth Amendment to protect noncitizens and corporations, but not ordinary citizens. This was an anomaly of law if ever there was one. Finally, the judge, in a rare case of frankness, also reluctantly acknowledged a real-world dimension to their status as law interpreters. As Field put it,

> When we take our seats on the bench we are not struck with blindness, and forbidden to know as judges what we see as men; and where an ordinance, though general in its terms, only operates upon a special race, sect or class, it being universally understood that it is to be

enforced only against that race, sect or class, we may justly conclude that it was the intention of the body adopting it that it should only have such operation, and treat it accordingly.[49]

Despite this impressive ruling, agitation and open violence against the Chinese continued unabated, and while the federal courts insisted on interpreting the 1868 Burlingame treaty on terms favorable to the Chinese, they left no doubt that a change in the laws would be welcomed. In 1880, a delegation of three distinguished Americans—James B. Angell, John F. Swift, and William H. Trescott—was sent to China to secure another treaty, which would allow the United States to better regulate Chinese immigration while still guaranteeing Chinese subjects the right to reside in and carry on trade with the United States. President Chester A. Arthur hoped that a revision of the immigration laws would suffice and that the rampant anti-Chinese feelings on the coast would subside. The treaty was concluded on November 17, 1880, and ratified the following May. Article 1 read:

> Whenever in the opinion of the Government of the United States, the coming of Chinese laborers to the United States, or their residence therein, affects or threatens to affect the interests of that country, or to endanger the good order of the said country or of any locality within the territory thereof, the Government of China agrees that the Government of the United States may regulate, limit, or suspend such coming or residence, but may not absolutely prohibit it. The limitation or suspension shall be reasonable and shall apply only to Chinese who may go to the United States as laborers, other classes not being included in the limitations.[50]

With discretionary powers vested in the United States and the sole criterion of limiting immigration that of the perceived "interests" of the United States, China in effect forfeited any leverage it might have exercised to protect both its citizens and its commercial interests in this country. Article 3, however, contained clauses that seemed to protect the Chinese laborers or other Chinese subjects already in this country:

> If Chinese laborers, or Chinese of any other class, now either permanently or temporarily residing in the territory of the United States, meet

with ill treatment at the hands of any other persons, the Government of the United States will exert all its power to devise measures for their protection and to secure to them the same rights, privileges, immunities, and exemptions as may be enjoyed by the citizens or subjects of the most favored nation, and to which they are entitled by treaty.[51]

But the "most favored nation" phrase had become a hollow concept given the actual, lived experiences of most Chinese in the United States, and if the Chinese had any group to fear after this treaty it was the federal officials themselves who were charged with the administration of this treaty.

In fact, agitation for a federal law banning Chinese immigration began almost immediately after the ratification of the treaty in July 1881. Within less than a year, Congress passed an immigration bill suspending Chinese labor immigration for twenty years and the establishment of an internal passport system to identify Chinese laborers. President Arthur objected to the bill's harsh terms, and it proved an international embarrassment to the president, who subsequently vetoed it, calling it unreasonable and unjustified. But Congress was intent on enacting such a law, and by reducing the suspension period to ten years and eliminating the passport provision, the legislature secured the president's consent and in 1882 the Chinese Exclusion Act became law.[52] Passage of this "temporary" law proved an intolerable hardship on many Chinese since many laborers had returned home to visit and were barred from reentry under the new treaty. The situation worsened considerably for the Chinese when Congress adopted the Scott Act in 1888.[53] Introduced by William Scott (D-PA), this law declared that no Chinese laborer, regardless of his former residence in the United States, should ever enter the country. Section 2 of the act harshly provided: "That no certificates of identity provided for in the fourth and fifth sections of the act to which this is a supplement shall hereafter be issued; and every certificate heretofore issued in pursuance thereof, is hereby declared void and of no effect, and the Chinese laborer claiming admission by virtue thereof shall not be permitted to enter the United States."[54]

Clearly the Scott amendment was an ex post facto law, particularly with respect to those Chinese laborers who, acting according to the established laws of the United States, had secured exit and reentry identification certificates and were in transit back to the United States at the time of the passage of the act. Upon arriving on the West Coast, they found themselves prohibited from entering and forbidden to contact relatives and friends, were not allowed to conclude their business, or even to appeal the provisions of the act. Lawsuits challenging the amendment were filed in nearly all of the western federal courts and were consolidated in the Supreme Court under the collective title of *The Chinese Exclusion Case* (1889).[55]

This decision was not one of the Supreme Court's finest moments. It appeared to reflect the old adage that the Court follows the election returns. "Notwithstanding the favorable provisions of the new articles of the treaty of 1868," the majority opinion announced in its historical review of Chinese-US relations,

> by which all the privileges, immunities, and exemptions were extended to subjects of China in the United States which were accorded to citizens or subjects of the most favored nation, they remained *strangers in the land*, residing apart by themselves, and adhering to the customs and usages of their own country. *It seemed impossible for them to assimilate with our people or to make any change in their habits or modes of living.*[56]

It was not all the fault of the Chinese that they remained a people apart, yet the Court acted as if they had deliberately agitated for a separatism that could no longer be tolerated. The Court, speaking through Justice Field, then lapsed into a repetition of traditional accusations—many offered by the State of California—raised against the Chinese, citing them as if they had provided the factual basis for the decision:

> that the presence of Chinese laborers had a baneful effect upon the material interests of the State, and upon public morals; that their immigration was in numbers approaching the character of an Oriental invasion, and was a menace to our civilization; that the discontent from this cause was not confined to any political party, or to any class or nationality, but was well-nigh universal; that they had retained the habits and customs of their own country, and in fact constituted a Chinese settlement within the State, without any interest in our country or its institutions.[57]

That the Court was overreacting to the magnitude of the alleged invasion of the Chinese is apparent from an examination of immigration statistics. The decline in Chinese immigration since the enactment of the Chinese

Exclusion Act had been dramatic. In 1882, some 39,000 Chinese had entered the United States.[58] But in 1884, only 279 arrived. In 1885, a mere 22 entered. In 1886, some 40 Chinese arrived, in 1887 only 10, and in 1888 just 26 came into the country. These numbers hardly constitute a deluge.[59]

Apart from the racism inherent in the case, the Court arrived at some relatively sound principles of immigration theory. "If, therefore, the government of the United States, through its legislative department, considers the presence of foreigners of a different race in this country, who will not assimilate with us, to be dangerous to its peace and security, their exclusion is not to be stayed because at the time there are no actual hostilities with the nation of which the foreigners are subjects,"[60] the Court argued. And had it restricted its reasoning solely to the proposition that a nation has an arbitrary right to determine its own constituency, it might have decided the case on more intelligent and humane grounds and reached the same decision. But the final twist was delivered by the Court, which had no sympathy for the thousands of Chinese who were unexpectedly caught in the turn of events: "Whatever license, therefore, Chinese laborers may have obtained, previous to the act of October 1, 1888, to return to the United States after their departure, is held at the will of the government, revocable at any time, at its pleasure."[61] The Court, relying on the political question doctrine it had used effectively in many Indian law cases, declared that "if there be any just ground of complaint on the part of China, it must be made to the political department of our government, which is alone competent to act upon the subject."[62]

The exclusion of Chinese possessing certificates of reentry spurred on the cities of the West Coast in their discriminatory ordinances, and within a year San Francisco passed the Bingham Ordinance, which required all Chinese to remove to a particular part of the city. The ordinance was challenged immediately in federal court, and again the court upheld the rights of the Chinese. In two consolidated cases in 1890, *In re Lee Sing*[63] and *In re Sing Too Quan*,[64] a federal circuit court voided the San Francisco ordinance, stating emphatically that

> the discrimination against Chinese, and the gross inequality of the operation of this ordinance upon Chinese, as compared with others, in violation of the constitutional, treaty, and statutory provisions cited, are so manifest upon its face, that I am unable to comprehend how this discrimination and inequality of operation, and the consequent violation

of the express provisions of the constitution, treaties and statutes of the United States, can fail to be apparent to the mind of every intelligent person, be he lawyer or layman.[65]

The hysteria that accompanied mention of the Chinese, even Chinese American citizens, did not abate with the drastic decline of Chinese immigration, and in 1892 Congress passed the oppressive Geary Act.[66] Its first major provision extended for another decade all existing laws dealing with Chinese immigration. Section 6 contained provisions more discriminatory than any previous act dealing with immigration, in effect, creating "America's first internal passport system."[67] It stated:

> And it shall be the duty of all Chinese laborers within the limits of the United States, at the time of passage of this act, and who are entitled to remain in the United States, to apply to the collector of internal revenue of their respective districts, within one year after the passage of this act, for a certificate of residence, and any Chinese laborer, within the limits of the United States, who shall neglect, fail, or refuse to comply with the provisions of this act, or who, after one year from the passage of hereof, shall be found within the jurisdiction of the United States without such certificate of residence, shall be deemed and adjudged to be unlawfully within the United States, and may be arrested...and taken before a United States judge whose duty it shall be to order that he be deported from the United States.[68]

The real meaning of this law was that apart from a certification of residence, it was now criminal to be a Chinese in the United States. Chinese resistance to this law was immediate, led by the Chinese Six Companies, the prominent coordinating council of Chinese district associations of merchants, officials, and the like that had been organized in the 1860s for mutual aid and support.[69] The council issued several proclamations in which they denounced the Geary Act. One of the proclamations declared that the act was "an unjust law and no Chinese should obey it. The law degrades the Chinese and if obeyed will put them lower than the meanest of people... In making the law the United States has violated the treaties...we hope all will work with us and then we can and will break this infamous law."[70] The law was challenged in the Supreme Court by three Chinese who were facing deportation. In *Fong Yue Ting v. United States* (1892),[71] the majority upheld the constitutionality of restrictions on Chinese immigration, arguing:

> Chinese laborers, therefore, like all other aliens residing in the United States for a shorter or longer time, are entitled, so long as they are permitted by the government of the United States to remain in the country, to the safeguards of the Constitution, and to the protection of the laws, in regard to their rights of person and of property, and to their civil and criminal responsibility. But they continue to be aliens, having taken no steps towards becoming citizens, and incapable of becoming such under the naturalization laws; and therefore remain subject to the power of Congress to expel them, or to order them to be removed and deported from the country, whenever in its judgment their removal is necessary or expedient for the public interest.[72]

Again the reasoning, if applied to general conditions and not directed specifically against the Chinese and only them, was not far removed from general principles of sovereignty exercised by all nations. But the decision, because it upheld the arbitrary exercise of judgment by minor officials and was directed at persons already residing in the United States under existing laws and ratified treaties, drew stinging dissents from Justices David J. Brewer and Field, and from Chief Justice Melville Fuller.

Justice Brewer objected quite strenuously to the arbitrary nature of the criteria under which a Chinese laborer could be deported. "Again," he wrote,

> it is absolutely within the discretion of the collector to give or refuse a certificate to one who applies therefor. Nowhere is it provided what evidence shall be furnished to the collector, and nowhere is it made mandatory upon him to grant a certificate on the production of such evidence. It cannot be due process of law to impose punishment on any person for failing to have that in his possession, the possession of which he can obtain only at the arbitrary and unregulated discretion of any official.[73]

Brewer concluded his remarks with a sardonic reference to American religious activities in China, writing, "In view of this enactment of the highest legislative body of the foremost Christian nation, may not the thoughtful Chinese disciples of Confucius fairly ask, Why do they send missionaries here?"[74]

Justice Field might be viewed as a protector of the Chinese since he upheld their treaty rights quite frequently while a judge in the lower federal courts in California, before his elevation to the Supreme Court. Yet his dissent went directly to the issue before the Court and the distinctions he drew remain a classic statement of legal reasoning. "Between legislation for the exclusion of Chinese persons—that is, to prevent them from entering the country—and legislation for the deportation of those who have acquired a residence in the country under a treaty with China," Field argued, "there is a wide difference."[75] He later added,

> Aliens from countries at peace with us, domiciled within our country by its consent, are entitled to all the guaranties for the protection of their persons and property which are secured to native-born citizens. The moment any human being from a country at peace with us comes within the jurisdiction of the United States, with their consent—and such consent will always be implied when not expressly withheld, and in the case of the Chinese laborers before us was in terms given by the treaty referred to—he becomes subject to all their laws, is amenable to their punishment and entitled to their protection.[76]

Field ended his spirited dissent with a heartrending description of the impact of the new law on the Chinese laborers in human terms:

> The punishment is beyond all reason in its severity. It is out of all proportion to the alleged offence. It is cruel and unusual. As to its cruelty, nothing can exceed a forcible deportation from a country of one's residence, and the breaking up of all the relations of friendship, family, and business there contracted. The laborer may be seized at a distance from his home, his family and his business, and taken before the judge for his condemnation, without permission to visit his home, see his family, or complete any unfinished business.[77]

The chief justice's opinion was shorter, but he, too, bemoaned the injustices Congress was leveling upon lawfully situated Chinese. The law, said Fuller, "contains within it the germs of the assertion of an unlimited and arbitrary power, in general, incompatible with the immutable principles of justice, inconsistent with the nature of our government, and in conflict with the written constitution."[78]

The Chinese were outraged at the high court's decision, and diplomatic relations that had been severed following the upholding of the constitutionality of the Scott Act were now virtually nonexistent and verging on the edge of war. American commercial ventures in China reached a critical low, and it became important that something be done about restoring some measure of sanity to the relations between the two nations. In 1894, the United States and China negotiated a new treaty on emigration between the two states.[79] The treaty was badly negotiated by China, and all of the previous restrictive laws regarding Chinese immigration were affirmed and accepted and an additional requirement was placed upon Chinese laborers by article 2: those laborers who had relatives in the United States or property worth at least $1,000 were allowed to travel back and forth between China and the United States, except

> every such Chinese laborer shall, before leaving the United States, deposit, as a condition of his return, with the collector of customs of the district from which he departs, a full description in writing of his family, or property, or debts, as aforesaid, and shall be furnished by said collector with such certificate of his right to return under this Treaty as the laws of the United States may now or hereafter prescribe and not inconsistent with the provisions of this Treaty; and should the written description aforesaid be proved to be false, the right of return thereunder, or of continued residence after return, shall in each case be forfeited.[80]

Additionally, article 4 declared that while Chinese workers were entitled to "protection of their persons and property" as citizens of a most favored nation, they were not entitled to become naturalized citizens of the United States.[81]

While highly and specifically restrictive, the terms of this treaty dealt with the increasingly difficult problem of undocumented Chinese immigration. The Chinese had been immigrating, legally at first, and then without proper documentation, to the Pacific Coast since the gold rush days. Despite the various laws passed against their immigration, the situation had become exceedingly complex. Enterprising Chinese could enter the United States from either Canada or Mexico and find immediate sanctuary in the various Chinese communities in each coastal city. Federal officials and state law enforcement officers struggled in their efforts to curb the number of Chinese arrivals in these communities. Few spoke Chinese or knew much about

Chinese culture and history. And after decades of abuse by whites, Chinese residents in the United States were not exactly welcoming state and federal officials into their communities. Many Chinese had by now been born in this country and while the ratio of women to men was always very low, still numerous families had appeared and the West Coast had a stable and continuous Chinese population.

Chinese American Population: Sex, Citizenship, and Sex Ratio, 1860–1940

Year	Male	Female	Total	Ratio	Citizen	Alien
1860	33,149	1,784	34,933	18.6:1	n/a	n/a
1870	58,663	4,556	63,199	12.8:1	n/a	n/a
1880	100,686	4,779	105,465	21.1:1	n/a	n/a
1890	103,620	3,868	107,488	26.8:1	n/a	n/a
1900	85,341	4,522	89,863	18.9:1	9,010	80,853
1910	66,858	4,675	71,531	14.3:1	14,935	56,596
1920	53,891	7,748	61,639	7.0:1	18,532	43,107
1930	59,802	15,152	74,954	3.9:1	30,868	44,086
1940	57,389	20,115	77,505	2.9:1	40,262	37,242

Source: Roger Daniels, "Asian Americans," in *Encyclopedia of American Social History*, vol. II, eds. Mary Kupiec Cayton, Elliott J. Gorn, and Peter W. Williams, 875 (New York: Charles Scribner's Sons, 1993).

Agitation against the Chinese slackened quickly after the 1890s for the most malignant of reasons. Deprived of cheap Chinese labor to work their fields, the large landowners in California and Hawaii had been importing Japanese, and the racial tensions spread from the Chinese to the Japanese as the twentieth century began. It is worthy of note that following the racial outbursts against the Japanese and the restriction of their immigration, the landowners promptly began importing Hindus until they also came under attack. Filipinos then followed. Later came the Mexicans. More recently, South Koreans, Asian Indians, Taiwanese, Vietnamese, Cambodians, Hmong, Somalis, and many others have arrived from Latin American states and former Soviet bloc Eastern European countries.

The story of Chinese immigration, then, is the paradigm of race relations on the Pacific Coast, and the severity of measures taken against the Chinese is partially because they happened to form the first identifiable group to be made a scapegoat of labor and agricultural problems in California.

Chinese as American "Citizens"

The citizenship question was an important issue in view of the history of efforts to exclude the Chinese from the West Coast. As the requirements for entrance into the United States stiffened, more Chinese began claiming citizenship rather than treaty rights as a means of entering the country. The clauses in the treaty of 1894 that require a Chinese laborer to fully describe his family, possessions, and other relationships prior to departing the country for a visit to China spoke directly to the confusion that existed when an entering Chinese, hardly speaking English and seemingly unacquainted with the United States, claimed that he had been born in this country and was therefore a natural citizen and entitled to immediate entrance. On occasion, and there were many instances of this subterfuge, individuals would switch identities and one Chinese would return to mainland China permanently but send another back to the United States to assume their place in the Chinese community.

The issue came to a head in 1895, when a twenty-four-year-old Chinese cook named Wong Kim Ark, who had been born in San Francisco, attempted to disembark in that lively port city after a trip to China.[82] Customs collectors denied him entrance into the United States and he sued for a writ of habeas corpus, saying that he had been born in the United States and was therefore a citizen. The case reached the US Supreme Court in 1897, and the decision was handed down the following year.[83] The majority upheld Wong Kim Ark's citizenship, with Chief Justice Fuller and Justice John M. Harlan dissenting. The majority opinion, written by Justice Horace Gray, examined in detail the history of citizenship statutes, beginning with the very earliest statements in common law and extending through every conceivable change in ideologies and theories. The opinion itself is a masterpiece of scholarly research on this topic, but, when all bases were covered, the decision rested upon the simple, literal interpretation of the Fourteenth Amendment. Justice Gray concluded that "the Amendment, in clear words and in manifest intent, includes the children born, within the territory of the United States, of all other persons, of whatever race or color, domiciled within the United States. Every citizen or subject of another country, while domiciled here, is within the allegiance and the protection, and consequently subject to the jurisdiction of the United States."[84] That Wong Kim Ark's parents had not been citizens, then, did not prohibit him from becoming a citizen upon birth, the Court decided, since they were, for all purposes, under the jurisdiction of the United States.

Chief Justice Fuller and Justice Harlan denied that past precedents with respect to citizenship should apply to Wong Kim Ark. "The framers of the Constitution were familiar with the distinctions between the Roman law and the feudal law, between obligations based on territoriality and those based on the personal and invisible character of origin, and there is nothing to show that in the matter of nationality they intended to adhere to principles derived from regal government, which they had just assisted in overthrowing,"[85] they stated. Using this distinction as the basis for their dissent, the two justices then argued that the former British colonies during the American Revolution "became sovereign and independent States, and when the Republic was created each of the thirteen States had its own local usages, customs and common law, while in respect of the National Government there necessarily was no general, independent and separate common law of the United States, nor has there ever been."[86]

Denying the existence of a federal common law that might control this situation, the two justices then revived the argument used in the important Indian law case *Elk v. Wilkins* (1884) regarding whether the jurisdiction possessed by the United States over Wong Kim Ark was "complete."[87] "To be 'completely subject' to the political jurisdiction of the United States," they argued, "is to be in no respect or degree subject to the political jurisdiction of any other government."[88]

Chief Justice Fuller, writing the dissent, then shifted the argument to a cultural basis:

> Generally speaking, I understand the subjects of the Emperor of China—that ancient Empire, with its history of thousands of years and its unbroken continuity in belief, traditions and government, in spite of revolutions and changes of dynasty—to be bound to him by every conception of duty and by every principle of their religion, of which filial piety is the first and greatest commandment; and formerly, perhaps still, their penal laws denounced the severest penalties on those who renounced their country and allegiance, and their abettors; and, in effect, held the relatives at home of Chinese in foreign lands as hostages for their loyalty. And whatever concession may have been made by treaty in the direction of admitting the right of expatriation in some sense, they seem in the United State to have remained pilgrims and sojourners as all their fathers were.[89]

All these things may have been true from the perspective of the Chinese emperor, but they had no relevance for the question of citizenship by birth within the confines and jurisdiction of the United States. The dissent, nonetheless, concluded its argument by weakly remarking:

> When, then, children are born in the United States to the subjects of a foreign power, with which it is agreed by treaty that they shall not be naturalized thereby, and as to whom our own law forbids them to be naturalized, such children are not born so subject to the jurisdiction as to become citizens, and entitled on that ground to the interposition of our Government, if they happen to be found in the country of their parents' origin and allegiance, or any other.[90]

Wong Kim Ark represented a significant, if little discussed or legally enforced, victory for the Chinese—and by extension all others who are native born—in that it protected their citizenship rights and made possible the recognition of Chinese as American citizens in spite of the severe restrictions placed upon them insofar as direct immigration was concerned.[91] Even then, however, restrictive decisions continued to be handed down by the courts whenever the question of Chinese entrance into the United States arose. A typical case of this kind was *United States v. Ju Toy* (1905), in which a returning Chinese American, asserting his native-born US citizenship, was denied a writ of habeas corpus.[92] The majority opinion, written by Justice Oliver Wendell Holmes, did not add to the luster of his reputation, since it accepted almost all of the allegations made by the customs officials to the detriment of the incontrovertible evidence of his US citizenship presented by Ju Toy and called forth an outraged dissent by Justices Brewer and Rufus W. Peckham. Their complaint dealt basically with the roughshod procedural tactics of the customs officials:

> It will be seen that under these rules it is the duty of the immigration officer to prevent communication with the Chinese seeking to land by any one except his own officers. He is to conduct a private examination, with only the witnesses present whom he may designate. His counsel, if under the circumstances, the Chinaman has been able to procure one, is permitted to look at the testimony, but not to make a copy of it.

He must give notice of appeal, if he wishes one, within two days, and within three days thereafter the record is to be sent to the Secretary at Washington; and every doubtful question is to be settled in favor of the Government. No provision is made for summoning witnesses from a distance or for taking depositions, and if, for instance, the person landing at San Francisco was born and brought up in Ohio, it may well be that he would be powerless to find any testimony in San Francisco to prove his citizenship. If he does not happen to have money he must go without the testimony, and when the papers are sent to Washington (three thousand miles away from the port, which, in this case was the place of landing), he may not have the means of employing counsel to present his case to the Secretary.[93]

There was no question but that these procedures were arbitrary and designed to eliminate all except the most carefully prepared Chinese Americans from reentering the country. What further outraged the dissenting justices was the fact that Ju Toy had already been declared a citizen and "the contention of the Government," the dissent pointed out, "sustained by the judgment of this court, is that a citizen, guilty of no crime—for it is no crime for a citizen to come back to his native land—must by the action of a ministerial officer be punished by deportation and banishment, without trial by jury and without judicial examination."[94] The final question of this case, then, for the dissent was the burden of proof required of citizens before administrative officers charged with performance of their duties: "Can one who judicially establishes his innocence of any offense be punished for crime by the action of a ministerial officer? Can he be punished because he has failed to show to the satisfaction of that officer that he is innocent of an offense?"[95] The question was answered in the affirmative in the first decade of the twentieth century with respect to Chinese Americans, and it would again be answered in the affirmative quite late in the century with respect to political dissidents, indicating that while the Constitution spoke of certain rights, presumptions of wrongdoing widely held by the popular mind often negated rights articulated in the abstract.

Racial hatreds and discriminatory treatment against Chinese and Chinese Americans seemed to follow them with each step of American development in the decades following the Chinese Exclusion Act. In 1898, when Hawaii was annexed as a US territory, the exclusion acts were applicable to that territory even though there had been no previous agitation against them in Hawaii.[96] Again, with the American possession of the Philippines, Chinese exclusion was made an issue even though Philippine-Chinese relationships had extended cordially for more centuries than the United States existed.[97] The Immigration Act of 1924 barred entry to those ineligible for citizenship, which effectively banned all Asians from migrating to the United States.[98] Alien land acts in the Pacific states banned Chinese Americans from landownership, although they were originally designed to preclude Japanese more than Chinese. Yet once citizenship by birth was established, Chinese Americans generally enjoyed all the benefits of other citizens. Perhaps the allegedly eternal mystery of Chinese American communities made it more difficult to pursue them once they were settled in the United States, and rather than waste time and energy harassing them, the state and federal officials preferred to leave them alone.

World War II brought on an ideological crisis that was to serve the Chinese well. Hatred against Japan and Japanese Americans escalated to epic proportions after the attack on Pearl Harbor, and the extension of the war to the Pacific meant that the United States, for better or worse, had to embrace China as its ally. Suddenly, Chinese Americans were considered "hardworking, honest, brave, religious, intelligent," whereas the Japanese were said to be "treacherous, sly, cruel, and warlike."[99] And the American public, largely oblivious for nearly a century of the discriminatory national treatment of the Chinese and the bitterness that they had experienced in their stay in America, wondered why the federal government was still prohibiting Chinese immigration. The Chinese government pushed hard for a repeal of the Chinese exclusion acts, now considered by most Americans remote relics of the past. Warren Magnuson, a House Democrat from the State of Washington, which had itself participated in some of the most virulent anti-Chinese activities, sponsored a repeal of the exclusion acts in the House, and Senator Charles Andrews of Florida, a southerner not especially in the forefront of race relations, pushed the bill through the Senate.[100]

Congress enacted a law on December 17, 1943, that effectively repealed the acts dealing with exclusion or deportation of Chinese, beginning with the original Chinese Exclusion Act of 1882 and covering all of the acts through 1913.[101] Section 2 of the act provided that "all Chinese persons entering the United States annually as immigrants shall be allocated to the quota for the Chinese computed under the provisions of section 11 of the said Act."[102] In the fervor of war, everyone thought that justice had at last been served to their loyal Asian allies. But the impact of this repeal on the Chinese seeking to immigrate to the United States was ridiculously minute. When the annual quota was finally computed, the Chinese were granted an annual quota of only 105 persons. Since Chinese immigration to the United States had declined dramatically during the previous several decades, the repeal of the exclusion acts, along with the new quota system, meant that Chinese immigrant numbers would remain low. Betty Lee Sung explained why the quota system was unfair:

> The quota of 105 was arrived at by computing one-sixth of one percent of the number of Chinese residents in the United States in 1920 as determined by the census of that year. The same formula was used to determine the quotas for all countries whose nationals were eligible for US citizenship, but as applied to the Chinese there were two inequalities. First, as the Chinese had been excluded from the country for more than sixty years, the number of Chinese residents in the United States in 1920 was insignificant—only 61,639. It was hardly a realistic base to compute a quota for a national group numbering more than 600 million.[103]

But in retrospect, the Chinese were undeterred. Despite all the restrictions and discriminations they had faced and the virtual stripping away of any constitutional protections from them even when citizens native born, they had managed to maintain a steady, if relatively low, stream of immigrants coming into the United States. At the time of the repeal of the Chinese exclusion acts, "there were approximately 78,000 persons of Chinese ancestry in this country, of which 80 percent were foreign-born."[104] It was a magnificent record of persistence and a testimony to the failure of exclusion laws based solely on racial antagonism.

The Chinese American community in the United States took advantage of the changes in immigration policy and the policies put into place at the conclusion of World War II to stabilize their situation. For instance, nearly half of the Chinese American veterans used the GI Bill to secure college degrees or to purchase homes. And when the Communists gained control in China in 1949, nearly five thousand Chinese students sought and gained political asylum in the United States. According to Sucheng Chan, "the US was willing to open its doors a crack because the Cold War was on. Perceiving itself as the leader of the 'Free World,' the US competed with the Communist bloc of countries for power and influence in the rest of the world."[105]

These developments were later joined by a major law, the Immigration Act of 1965, that entailed a dramatic reversal of historic American immigration policy.[106] This law jettisoned the quota system and set numerical limitations of 170,000 annually on the Eastern Hemisphere and 120,000 annually on the Western, with no more than 20,000 immigrants allowed from any one nation. Asian immigration has increased so significantly since this law's enactment that Asians now comprise nearly half of the total immigrant population.[107]

During the turmoil of the 1960s when other groups were protesting historical wrongs, Chinese Americans, although with moral claims of great magnitude, generally preferred to maintain a quiet dignity as befitted a people whose history and culture extended far into the remote past. The Chinese American population grew tremendously in the wake of the Immigration Act and the Vietnam War. And while they benefitted from the model minority stereotype to an extent, they also "suffered from the gangster image produced by increasingly violent crime in America's overcrowded Chinatown's."[108]

In 1973, as a means of furthering their children's education under the greatly expanded programs of the federal government, some Chinese American parents sued the San Francisco school boards to ensure that their children would receive the proper education in the English language.[109] When the case *Lau v. Nichols* went to the US Supreme Court, it did not take the justices long to decide in their favor. Citing Title VI of the Civil Rights Act of 1964, under which the case was brought, the Supreme Court said that "it seems obvious that the Chinese speaking minority receive fewer benefits than the English-speaking majority from respondents' school system which denies them a meaningful opportunity to participate in the educational program—all the earmarks of the discrimination banned by the regulations."[110] Chinese Americans, it seemed, had finally arrived as an identifiable group entitled to legal protections without the further requirement of special pleadings and evidence.

But as Edward Steinman, Lau's attorney, noted in a 1994 speech,

> The case was based on a different notion of equality. At that time, the country was focused on problems of racial segregation. A focus on segregation and the treatment of blacks, in essence, provides one notion of inequality: taking people who are the same and treating them

differently. That is only half of the coin. The other side of inequality is more subtle, less visible, and equally invidious. It is taking kids who are different and treating them the same.[111]

In other words, despite victories like *Lau*, federal laws are less effective in confronting racial and ethnic differences.

As the number of Asian immigrants to the United States surged in the wake of more liberal immigration policies in the last four decades of the twentieth century, the social, economic, political, and perceptual challenges Chinese Americans faced also mounted. Chinese American families (and other Asian American families, for that matter) appear more favorably positioned than other ethnic groups, however, to cope with many of these challenges. For instance, the average family is generally more traditionally structured than those of non-Asian families. That is to say, more than 80 percent of Asian children lived in households with two parents. Additionally, these households were significantly larger than the average American household.[112]

Data from the 2000 US Census confirms that Chinese and other Asian Americans—except for Koreans and Vietnamese—are better off socioeconomically than other minorities and whites, and had a higher percentage of students with a bachelor's degree or higher than minorities and whites.[113] Despite these facts, poverty and discrimination continue to bedevil Chinese and other Asian Americans, and nearly 12 percent of Asians were living below the poverty level.

As Timothy P. Fong pointed out, "socioeconomic 'success' for Asian Americans can be understood only within the context of: (1) a high percentage of urbanization; (2) more wage earners per family; and (3) comparing per capita income instead of median family income. By examining these factors we find that most Asian Americans are indeed advantaged relative to blacks and Hispanics, but are still disadvantaged relative to whites."[114]

Even as their economic and educational figures, in some cases and due to unique factors, rate very highly compared to members of other groups, all Asian Americans, including Chinese Americans, continue to endure high levels of violence—both physical and judicial—based on their Asian ancestry. Two events, separated by nearly two decades, Vincent Chin's tragic murder in 1982 in Detroit, Michigan, and Wen Ho Lee's arrest and indictment in 1999 for allegedly transmitting classified documents to the Chinese national government, point to the fragility of Chinese American rights, as well as the ongoing persistence of stereotypes about Asian Americans and how these continue to adversely affect all Asian Americans, regardless of their job status or educational level.

Chin, a young Chinese American engineer, was clubbed to death by two white autoworkers who felt that Japan—they assumed Chin was Japanese—was responsible for the economic recession in the country and in Detroit's auto industry in particular. Regardless of the viciousness of the crime, the two men, in a plea bargain, pled guilty to manslaughter and were given lenient three-year probationary sentences and a fine of $3,780 by a state judge. Chinese Americans and other Asian Americans, locally and nationally, were outraged by the trial judge's ruling, and they demanded that the federal government step in and do something. The Department of Justice did intervene and brought civil rights charges against the men. In 1984, however, Michael Nitz was acquitted, but Ronald Ebans was declared guilty and given a twenty-five-year sentence. Ebans appealed and in 1986 his conviction was overturned. A second trial was then initiated in Cincinnati. It ended in 1987 with Ebans again being acquitted.[115] Neither man ever served a single day in jail or prison for Chin's murder. An award-winning documentary, *Who Killed Vincent Chin?*, was later made that featured how devastated all Asian Americans were in the wake of the attack and the bizarre judicial proceedings that unfolded.[116]

Fast-forward to 1999, when Dr. Wen Ho Lee, a naturalized US citizen born in Taiwan and a nuclear scientist by training, was fired by the secretary of energy, Bill Richardson, after a three-year investigation for allegedly having engaged in spying behavior for the Peoples Republic of China at his workplace. Lee had worked at the Los Alamos National Laboratory for twenty-five years prior to his firing.[117]

In December 1999, the United States indicted Lee on fifty-nine counts of "mishandling of classified computer files."[118] Accused of being a high security risk, Lee was held in solitary confinement from December 1999 to September 2000 while awaiting trial, "despite a statutory presumption in favor of the pre-trial release of defendants and the congressional intent that very few defendants should be subjected to pre-trial detention."[119]

Major irregularities in the government's case against Lee began to appear, and eventually his case was settled through a plea agreement wherein the United States dismissed all but one of the fifty-nine counts of mishandling classified files. Lee pled guilty to a single count of improperly transferring restricted, but nonclassified, information to his personal computer. This, it turned out, was a fairly common practice among the scientists at Los Alamos, who sometimes took work-related data home to work on.[120]

As Lee suffered in solitary confinement, evidence began to mount via statements and affidavits by federal officials that racial profiling had been employed by the government in their efforts to find the culprit who had smuggled the data to China. In fact, "the federal judge overseeing Lee's case even went so far as to lambaste the prosecution for misleading him to incarcerate Lee as a security risk while awaiting trial, and issued a formal apology."[121]

The federal government and the media's emphasis on Lee's Chinese ethnicity exacerbated social and political perceptions that Chinese Americans, and all Asian Americans, for that matter, had divided loyalties that allegedly prevented them from ever being considered "real" Americans, but that they also had a "foreignness" that left them deeply suspect.[122] Frank Wu pithily put it this way:

> The perpetual foreigner syndrome that afflicts Asian Americans in general affects Lee in particular. The perpetual foreigner assumption—that Asians are sojourners, visitors, and/or guests who cannot overcome an inherent alien status—makes it easy to deprive Asian Americans of civil rights. Asian Americans are not integrated into a paradigm of civil rights because the poor treatment accorded Asian Americans is based not on their race but on their alienage, and therefore is acceptable.[123]

After his release from prison, Dr. Lee filed a lawsuit in 2000 against the departments of justice and energy and the Federal Bureau of Investigation for money damages, alleging that their actions—disclosing information to newspapers about Lee without his consent, and so forth—against him had violated his rights under the Privacy Act of 1974. In 2003, in *Wen Ho Lee v. US Department of Justice*, the district court for the District of Columbia held five journalists in contempt of court based on the view that the journalist's First Amendment interest in protecting their confidential news sources were outweighed by Lee's interest in compelling disclosure of those sources.[124] The journalists appealed this decision but it was upheld for four of the five defendants in 2005 by the court of appeals.[125]

Chinese and other Asian Americans occupy a special place in the legal universe. Unlike African Americans and Native nations, they derive from an ancient civilization that represents both philosophical and political alternatives to Western civilization. That white Americans have misunderstood their customs and traditions hardly needs repetition. The Chinese experienced the first and greatest wave of racial discrimination because they were the first Asian peoples to actively seek to live in North America. Nearly a century passed before Euro-Americans could understand that Asian customs and traditions, far from preventing assimilation into the mass of citizenry, served to develop healthy individuals who as a community contributed a great deal to American society. The story of Chinese Americans within the constitutional framework is unique because the federal courts for the most part upheld their legal rights in the face of intense opposition by the general public. The question of immigration dominated every conception of the Chinese experience, and even with the restrictive laws passed against them they managed to establish and bring some degree of growth to their own community on these shores. Perhaps the restrictive laws only served to encourage them to make the West Coast a permanent residence since the great difficulties that faced them at every turn only seem to have made them stronger.

The situation today is quite different. From the very beginning of intercourse between the United States and China, the Chinese government was weak and ineffective in protecting the rights of its citizens abroad. For many decades, it was harsh and unrelenting toward those Chinese who sought adventure abroad and failed to realize the great contributions that those immigrants were making toward their host state and their homeland. Many of the Chinese were not disloyal to their own traditions and customs, and they looked upon their stay in the United States as only a temporary means of providing economic opportunities for themselves that did not exist in their mother country. "In 1942, Lui Wei-chih, Minister of Overseas Affairs, stated that for the twenty or thirty years prior to the outbreak of the Sino-Japanese War, the annual cash remittances to China from the overseas Chinese had averaged $300,000,000 Chinese national currency—an amount far exceeding the country's unfavorable trade balance."[126] This source of income was lost to mainland China with the eradication of customs and culture by the Communist government, but it indicates the importance of Chinese living in foreign lands to the Chinese economic system.

Although China continues as a Communist state in the twenty-first century, it has seen the need to modernize economically, and the 2008

Beijing Olympics proved a showcase event for the state and society. All things considered, then, the place of Chinese Americans in the legal universe seems secure, history and practical matters having transcended the doctrines and beliefs that might have intervened to deny them their legal rights. But this security was purchased at the cost of a century and a half of dishonor and demeaning treatment rivaling and surpassing in some respects the treatment suffered by African Americans and Native peoples. Because Chinese Americans are now firmly entrenched in the American social and political system, it is doubtful that they will be dislodged since the violence and discrimination of former times, while still a potent force in American society as the recent cases attest, is increasingly that of economic class rather than racial origin. The historical track record for Chinese Americans seems to indicate that they are capable of progressing at their own pace regardless of the obstacles raised against them.

Japanese Americans:
"Persons Likely to Become a Public Charge"

Asian peoples, no matter whether they were from Japan, China, Korea, the Philippines, or elsewhere, settling in North America in the nineteenth and twentieth centuries, were derisively labeled Oriental as if they all belonged to the same society. But the differences between the peoples—whether in terms of food, architecture, music, or politics—were, of course, profound.

Besides their historic and natural tensions, the two states had very different emigration policies and immigration patterns with regard to the United States. From the early years of the seventeenth century until the middle of the nineteenth century, emigration from Japan was legally prohibited. This coincided with the country's prohibition against immigration into Japan, which was a result of the Tokugawa shogunate (1615–1867) to keep Japan isolated from the rest of the world.[127] Japan's geopolitical isolation began to ease in 1853, when Admiral Richard Perry's warship entered Edo, or Tokyo Bay. Perry's invasive action "forced the Japanese government to open up its ports to Western nations and to enter into specific trade agreements."[128] A treaty was negotiated in 1854 between the United States and Japan that gave the United States some of the same advantages it had secured against the Chinese in its treaties with that state.[129]

With regard to immigration to the United States, scholars have noted several differences between the Japanese and the Chinese. The first difference centers around the time of their arrival. The peak Chinese immigration years were between 1848 and 1862; whereas the major Japanese influx occurred from 1885 to 1920. For the Japanese, some 200,000 people left for Hawaii as plantation laborers, and 180,0000 headed toward the mainland of the United States as agricultural workers.[130] A second difference was their employment patterns. Nearly three times as many Japanese (62.2 percent) as Chinese (23.7 percent) were engaged in agricultural pursuits. And third, their settlement patterns differed. While both Japanese and Chinese initially settled on the West Coast, a greater majority of Japanese still reside in the West, whereas the Chinese have become much more dispersed across the United States.[131] Finally, a fourth difference centers on gender. As late as 1890, some fifty years after their initial immigration to the country, only 5 percent of all Chinese in the country were women. Conversely, while most Japanese migrants initially were men, this changed to eventually include a significant number of women. In fact, Ronald Takaki says that by 1920, women represented 46 percent of the Japanese population in Hawaii and 35 percent in California.[132] Although the earliest known Japanese immigrants came to the United States in 1843, it was not until the 1860s that steadier, though still smaller numbers arrived—at first in Hawaii, but also in California.[133]

The Early Years

In fact, in 1868 a small party of Japanese families arrived in California.[134] Political liberals, they had sought refuge in America like so many of the immigrants of those turbulent years of the nineteenth century. In a matter of weeks, they had leased a tract of farming land in Alameda County near San Francisco and set about learning the American methods of agriculture, for they realized full well that, having left their homeland against the explicit orders of the emperor, there was no return for them.[135] Within a few years, the small Japanese colony was prosperous and thriving, establishing early the Japanese tradition of superior agricultural abilities.

There had been other Japanese before them, to be sure. The Pacific was the scene of intense commerce during the nineteenth century and occasionally the survivors of a shipwreck would drift ashore on the western coast of America. Usually the shipwrecked sailors would seek a returning ship and immediately set sail for their native lands. One Japanese sailor, Hikozo Hamada, was adopted by the collector of customs in San Francisco and given an American education, becoming something of a celebrity in the

Bay area in the 1850s and an inspiration to the missionary-minded that the Japanese would prove eager listeners to the message of salvation.[136] But there were so few Japanese who sought permanent residence in the United States that they could hardly be considered a separate group. In 1870, only fifty-five Japanese were living in the United States and in 1890, after the pattern of immigration had been established, there were only two thousand Japanese to be found in the entire nation.[137]

While Japan was subjected to the same forcible "opening" by the western powers that China experienced in the 1850s and 1860s, the response of the two giants was radically different. Both emperors forbade their people to immigrate to other lands but the structure of Japanese society was such that the intense longing for opportunity did not produce the desperate waves of immigration that Chinese society spawned. The Japanese had one of the best and earliest educational systems, and in 1850 their literacy rate was higher than even that of Great Britain and the average Japanese citizen had sufficient opportunities to make a decent living within the confines of their own town or province.[138] In fact, the large majority of Japanese immigrants to Hawaii and California came from four districts—Kumamoto, Fukuoka, Yamaguchi, and Hiroshima—that were economically stable.[139]

More important, however, was the posture that the two nations took toward Western culture and technology. China balked at the idea of incorporating Western ideas with its ancient heritage, but Japan quickly saw that by adopting the most sophisticated technology, it could postpone the domination of Western powers almost indefinitely.[140] Thus, by the end of the nineteenth century, Japan had successfully adopted those elements of Western culture that would bolster its traditional ways, and it ranked third among the nations of the world as a naval power precluding gunboat diplomacy by the Western powers.

The passage of the Chinese Exclusion Act of 1882 produced a strong effect on Japanese immigration. With the Chinese banned from the United States and forced to employ calculating methods for entrance, a labor shortage in western agriculture quickly developed, and white farmers on the Pacific coast turned to the Japanese as their source of labor. Despite the rampant accusations of the Teamsters Union that "Oriental" labor was depriving white Americans of jobs, California's fertile fields were not exactly overflowing with Irish laborers. So Japanese immigration began as individuals heard about the opportunities for work in the United States and starting arriving in the Pacific Coast ports. Like some of the most sophisticated Chinese aliens, the Japanese went first to Hawaii, where a plantation laborer could earn six times more than they could in Japan.[141] There they made contacts with people from the mainland and, after several months of working in the pineapple fields and learning a pidgin English, they moved on to the mainland. This route of immigration proved eminently successful, for it was many decades before Congress discovered that banning direct immigration was useless if a regular immigration route existed through the American possessions.

The Chinese immigration issue, generated and supported by the yellow journalism of the Hearst papers on the West Coast, dominated the thinking about immigration in the 1890s, and each new immigration act was conceived as an additional anti-Chinese measure although fewer and fewer Chinese were taking official channels in their immigration activities. But in 1891, just prior to the discovery by the popular press that the Japanese were arriving in increasing numbers, another immigration act was passed that broadened the number of those excluded. The first section of this act provided:

> That the following classes of aliens shall be excluded from admission into the United States, in accordance with the existing acts regulating immigration, other than those concerning Chinese laborers: All idiots, insane persons, paupers or persons likely to become a public charge, persons suffering from a loathsome or a dangerous contagious disease, persons who have been convicted of a felony or other infamous crime or misdemeanor involving moral turpitude, polygamist…[142]

Presumably this statute covered all situations that might arise, but it was not the qualifying phraseology that gave the law its potency. Under section 8 of the act, inspection officers of the Department of Treasury were designated to enforce all immigration provisions and were given almost total discretionary power to determine whether or not people came under the rubrics of section 1. They had the power, among other things, to "administer oaths, and to take and consider testimony touching the right of any such aliens to enter the United States."[143]

The first test of this statute with respect to the Japanese occurred a year later, when Nishimura Ekiu, a young woman of twenty-five, attempted to come ashore at San Francisco. Ekiu had a somewhat vague story to tell: she had been married two years, her husband was in the United States, she had twenty-two dollars and was "to stop at some hotel until her husband call[ed] for her."[144] This set of facts did not inspire confidence in the immigration inspector, John L. Hatch, and he arrested her, eventually lodging Ekiu in the Methodist Episcopal Japanese and Chinese Mission in San Francisco. A writ of habeas corpus was taken and a decision, *Nishimura Ekiu v. United States* was reached by the US Supreme Court in January 1892.[145] The Court, with only Justice Brewer dissenting, found the 1891 statute constitutional and upheld the action of Congress that vested almost total discretionary power in the port inspection officers. While the facts in the case severely handicapped Ekiu in arguing her case, the impact of the decision was tremendous since it meant that port inspection officers, by merely characterizing Japanese as "persons likely to become a public charge" might thwart any effort by Japanese to immigrate to the United States. The question of Japanese immigration, however, was not yet an emotional public topic so that while the case had immense consequences, it created little public interest at the time and was not regarded as the vehicle by which Japanese might be excluded from immigrating to the United States.

Events on the world scene were moving toward a climax in the Pacific. There was every indication that the occasional abortive efforts of the United States to annex Hawaii would soon bear fruit. Japan, the United States, and Spain were cautiously circling each other in the Pacific, and the Spanish control of the Philippines and other islands looked so tenuous as to inspire dreams of empire by both the Americans and Japanese. The Russians, overconfident in the extreme, were making noises about a Pacific coastal empire, and while Japan had its flanks exposed on both east and west, it nevertheless proudly maintained its place among the world powers. On November 22, 1894, Japan and the United States concluded a treaty and protocol designed to ensure peace while the two powers flexed their muscles toward Russia and Spain, respectively.[146]

The 1894 treaty read stylistically in phraseology like some of the Chinese treaties with the United States, but was in fact a declaration by two relatively equal powers and not a set of hollow promises. Article 1 gave citizens of each nation equal treatment while in the territory of the other country. Article 2 gave reciprocal freedom of commerce and navigation between the "territories" of each nation, a certain indication that the parties intended to share a Pacific empire between themselves. Unlike the Chinese treaties, no provision existed for the promulgation and protection of missionary activities, no restrictions on immigration were included, and article 17 contained the following provision:

> The several Foreign Settlements in Japan shall, from the date this Treaty comes into force, be incorporated with the respective Japanese Communes, and shall thenceforth form part of the general municipal system of Japan. The competent Japanese Authorities shall thereupon assume all municipal obligations and duties in respect thereof, and the common funds and property, if any, belonging to such Settlements shall at the same time be transferred to the said Japanese Authorities.[147]

Japan thereafter maintained full control over foreigners within its boundaries, and this surrender of jurisdiction by the Western powers marked the final ascendancy of the Japanese as a world power. It also meant that discriminatory laws against Japanese by the Western powers would produce corresponding problems for westerners in Japan.

Although there were no expatriation provisions in this treaty and it was not certain whether Japanese could become permanent US citizens, the number of Japanese coming to the United States continued to increase. By 1900, there were 24,326 Japanese in the United States and another decade would see this number increase nearly threefold, to 72,157.[148] As the number of Japanese increased and the paranoia about the Chinese ebbed, the Japanese came under increasing pressure from immigration officials. The formula used originally in *Ekiu v. United States* became the standard method for deporting Japanese. In *United States v. Yamasaka* (1900),[149] the immigration inspector merely filed an answer to a writ of habeas corpus issued on behalf of Yamasaka, alleging his right to investigate the conditions under which Yamasaka was present in the United States, and describing Yamasaka as "a pauper,...a person likely to become a public charge,...one of the prohibited classes of aliens, under the immigration laws of the United States."[150] The US Court of Appeals for the Ninth Circuit easily upheld the inspector's decision. But it was increasingly obvious to the federal courts that this formula could not be consistently used without some further elaboration by the highest court since it contained the elements capable of producing an international incident.

In 1903, as the number of Japanese immigrants was increasing dramatically, another case, with the docketed title *Yamataya v. Fisher*, reached the

Supreme Court. Reported under the name *The Japanese Immigrant Case*, the decision affirmed the arbitrary practices of the immigration officials respecting Japanese immigrants.[151] The defense presented the question of whether the Fifth Amendment's protections of due process applied to Japanese who had arrived in the United States legally but who had thereafter been challenged by the immigration officials during the year following their arrival. The majority, led by Justice Harlan, desiring to reconcile the actions of the immigration officials with the act of Congress that authorized them to prohibit undesirable aliens, declared:

> In the case of all acts of Congress, such interpretation ought to be adopted as, without doing violence to the import of the words used, will bring them into harmony with the Constitution. An act of Congress must be taken to be constitutional unless the contrary plainly and palpably appears. *The words here used do not require an interpretation that would invest executive or administrative officers with the absolute, arbitrary power implied in the contention of the appellant.*[152]

Having denied that the statute gave the immigration officials absolute power over the immigrating aliens, the only alternative left to the Court was to deny the factual situation that gave rise to the case. In a calculated rewriting of the facts, the Court continued:

> Besides, the record now before us shows that the appellant had notice, although not a formal one, of the investigation instituted for the purpose of ascertaining whether she was illegally in this country…It is true that she pleads a want of knowledge of our language; that she did not understand the nature and import of the questions propounded to her; that the investigation made was a "pretended" one; and that she did not, at the time, know that the investigation had reference to her being deported from the country.[153]

Kaoru Yamataya was ordered deported. The Supreme Court concluded unkindly: "If appellant's want of knowledge of the English language put her at some disadvantage in the investigation conducted by that officer, that was her misfortune, and constitutes no reason, under the acts of Congress, or under any rule of law, for the intervention of the court by *habeas corpus*."[154]

Within the year following this decision, the question of nicety in discussing the Japanese question was moot.

The attention of the public was finally directed to the Japanese at the turn of the century. Between December 5, 1901, and December 11, 1905, the Idaho, Montana, and Nevada legislatures petitioned Congress for specific legislation limiting the immigration of Japanese laborers.[155] In November 1904, the American Federation of Labor (AFL), meeting in its annual convention in San Francisco, demanded that the Chinese Exclusion Act be applied to the Japanese. The California legislature, supporting the AFL, passed a resolution expressing their great alarm that the conclusion of the Russo-Japanese War would result in great waves of Japanese immigration to the United States:

> We cannot but regard with the greatest sense of danger and disaster the prospect that the close of the war...will surely bring to our shores hordes, to be counted only in thousands, of discharged soldiers of the Japanese army, who will crowd the State with immoral, intemperate, quarrelsome men bound to labor for a pittance, and to subsist on a supply with which a white man can hardly sustain life.[156]

Once again, the rigorous application of avowed American values and principles, hard work and thrift, when practiced by Asians, loomed as the most threatening of all developments facing white America.

Racial tensions now escalated swiftly. In May 1905, a mass meeting was held in San Francisco, at which the Asiatic Exclusion League was formed. The avowed purpose of this new organization was to pressure the Congress for an extension of the Chinese Exclusion Act to Japanese and to prevent the sale of land to Japanese aliens.[157] Within a year the league's membership reached nearly 80,000 members, three-quarters of which were San Francisco residents. Coincidentally, Japanese immigration actually increased with the agitation. During the first six months of 1906, nearly a thousand Japanese a month came to the United States. Most of these immigrants, unfortunately, landed in San Francisco, giving the false impression that the city was being inundated by the Japanese. As the immigrants became more noticeable, unrest continued and the labor unions and newspapers fueled the growing anti-Japanese sentiment with rumors.

In October 1906, the San Francisco school board, frightened by rumors that the Japanese students were much older than the other students, primarily male, and responsible for bringing forbidden adult knowledge of the world into the innocent schoolyards of the city, announced that they were segregating the Japanese from the other students. The action created a sensation around the world. Minor rioting broke out in San Francisco, and President Theodore Roosevelt found himself in the midst of an international crisis of no small proportion. He immediately sent a personal emissary to the Pacific Coast to determine the basis for the school board's action, with orders to apply whatever pressure might be needed to get the board to rescind its orders. Roosevelt condemned the "idiots" of the California legislature and said that "the mob of a single city may at any time perform acts of lawless violence which would plunge us into war."[158]

Thomas Bailey, describing the situation in his book *Theodore Roosevelt and the Japanese-American Crises*, pointed out the fallacies behind the school board's action, noting that "only ninety-three Japanese children, twenty-five of whom were American citizens, were enrolled in twenty-three San Francisco schools on October 11, 1906," the date when the school board directive took effect.[159] And he further noted that "only thirty-three Japanese in the San Francisco schools were over fifteen years of age, and the two oldest were twenty. Furthermore, twenty-eight of the ninety three pupils were females."[160]

War with Japan was averted by the narrowest of margins. President Roosevelt, at one time, asked for a ship-by-ship comparison between the Japanese and American navies, worried that hostilities might break out at any moment. Europeans speculated over the possible victors in the event of such a war and had the Japanese as 5–4 favorites over the Americans, primarily on the strength of Japan's recent victory over Russia and the readiness and efficiency of their navy, which had been amply demonstrated during the war.

During the winter of 1907, events became more critical. In January, two ships carrying Japanese laborers from Hawaii to San Francisco were temporarily detained in the harbor while authorities vainly sought a legal basis for excluding them. Early February saw another vessel with 250 Japanese encounter the same difficulty.[161] The Imperial Government, fearful that these incidents would force Congress to exclude Japanese in the immigration legislation then being considered, worked with Roosevelt and the American ambassador to Japan to get an informal agreement that might avert a diplomatic and military confrontation. The Immigration Act of February 20, 1907, therefore did not mention Japanese laborers specifically.[162] The United States assumed that Japan would not issue passports to laborers who attempted to travel directly from Japan to the United States, since an informal agreement of 1907, often called the Gentlemen's Agreement of 1907, between the two states had effectively prevented passports of that kind from being issued by the Japanese. The act made provision for preventing immigration from "any country other than the United States," an obvious reference to Mexico, where many Japanese stopped prior to their entrance into the United States. And the president of the United States was given discretionary power to stop all immigration of laborers. On February 25, another ship arrived in San Francisco with 600 laborers aboard, creating a considerable stir on the West Coast.

Japanese immigration to the mainland before 1908 totaled 55,000, whereas more than 150,000 had arrived in Hawaii. But between 1908 and 1924, more than 120,000 Japanese arrived at ports along the Pacific Coast.[163] This, despite the gentlemen's agreement made between President Roosevelt and the Japanese foreign office. No specific formal written agreement seems to have existed. Rather, it was a series of notes communicated between the president and Japan between 1907–1908. It was characterized by informal understandings to be read into the memoranda by informed observers. Ambassador Wright in Japan received a note from Minister Hayashi that acknowledged Japan's understanding of the pact which read:

> The Imperial Government...beg to state that they have no intention of canceling or modifying the order now in force under which no passports are granted to either skilled or unskilled Japanese laborers for the mainland of the United States other than settled agriculturists, farmers owning or having an interest or share in their produce or crops. The Imperial Government confidently believe that a strict adhesion on their part to the foregoing order coupled with the continuation of the existing practice of inserting in all labor passports the destination of the laborers will be sufficient to make the new legislation of the United States more satisfactory and obviate the necessity of adopting additional measures.[164]

In the *Report of the Commissioner General of Immigration* in 1908 the American understanding was reported. "An understanding was reached with Japan that the existing policy of discouraging emigration of its subjects of the laboring classes to continental United States should be continued, and should, by cooperation with the governments, be made as effective as possible."[165]

The gentlemen's agreement, however, was an international arrangement that did little to alleviate the immediate racial tensions in the Pacific states. In 1906, Oregon and Washington passed alien land laws, which attempted to divest both Chinese and Japanese landowners of their lands and prevent them from purchasing or even leasing new parcels of land. In 1907, the first anti-Japanese land bills were introduced in the California legislature, although both President Roosevelt and California governor James Gillett worked to kill the legislation. In 1909, seventeen anti-Japanese land bills were introduced. One assemblyman declared: "I would rather every foot of California was in its native wilderness than to be cursed by the foot of these yellow invaders, who are a curse to the country, a menace to our institutions, and destructive of every principle of Americanism." And, he added, "I want no aliens, white, red, black or yellow, to own a foot of land in the State of California."[166] How this state lawmaker determined that an indigenous landowner was an "alien" remains a mystery, but indicates how irrational the emotional response to the Japanese, other immigrants, and Native peoples was.

This anti-Japanese sentiment prompted the founding in 1908 of the Japanese Association of America (JAA), which has been called the most important institution in the Japanese American community before World War II.[167] The national headquarters were in San Francisco, but there were also several branches and many local associations formed as well. One of the main functions of the JAA, delegated to it by the Japanese foreign ministry, was to issue certificates to Japanese who wished to return to the United States after having visited Japan. The JAA was allowed to keep half of the fees charged for this important service, which provided the organization a stable income. It also gave the JAA significant control over the Japanese immigration policy.[168]

In Hawaii in 1908, Japanese laborers also organized and established the Higher Wages Association to improve their incomes to levels comparable to Euro-American workers on Hawaiian plantations. And a specialist Japanese labor union, the Fresno Rodo Domei Kai (Fresno Labor League) was organized and successfully constricted the flow of Japanese laborers to the handful of labor contractors who reduced the rate agreed upon by the Japanese labor contractors organization.[169]

While tensions continued to mount, Japan and the United States signed another treaty in 1911 in an effort to repair some of the damage to commercial relations that the racial agitation on the Pacific Coast had produced. Article 1 of the treaty provided that "the citizens or subjects of each of the High Contracting Parties shall have liberty to enter, travel and reside in the territories of the other to carry on trade, wholesale and retail, to own or lease and occupy houses, manufactories, warehouses and shops, to employ agents of their choice, to lease land for residential and commercial purposes."[170] No mention was made of free immigration or citizenship and expatriation so that the prohibition on Japanese immigration remained intact but the treaty attempted to stem the tide of alien land bills that were being considered by the legislatures of the western states. In 1911, more than twenty different anti-Japanese measures were proposed, but again these bills were thwarted by the active pressure of the president.[171]

During these years, there was no question but that the Japanese were entering the agricultural field in substantial numbers. Between 1900 and 1910, Japanese landholdings in the state increased from 4,698 to 99,254 acres, a considerable increase, but in comparison with the total acreage devoted to farming in California hardly a threat to white agriculture.[172] But the racial issue dominated all considerations, and finally in 1913 the California legislature passed the Alien Land Law. It denied "aliens ineligible to citizenship" the right of purchasing agricultural land and restricted their right to lease farming lands to a term of no more than three years. The legislation was drawn to avoid the obvious meaning of the 1911 treaty, which allowed leasing and occupancy of land for residential and commercial purposes but made no mention of agricultural lands. The law, however, had little immediate practical effect because district attorneys refused to enforce it strenuously during World War I because of the nation's food production needs.[173]

After the war ended, the anti-Japanese groups pushed vigorously to see that the law was implemented. The attorney general of California, one of the authors of the law, when addressing the Commonwealth Club of San Francisco in August 1913, left no doubt about the racial prejudice behind the statute: "The fundamental basis of all legislation upon this subject, State and Federal, has been, and is, race undesirability. It is unimportant and foreign to the question under discussion whether a particular race is inferior. The simple and single question is, is the race desirable...?"[174] The Alien Land

Law, he explained, sought to restrict the Japanese "by curtailing their privileges which they may enjoy here; for they will not come in large numbers and long abide with us if they may not acquire land. And it seeks to limit the numbers who will come by limiting the opportunities for their activities when they arrive."[175]

White Californians, however, did not anticipate the Japanese determination or ingenuity in circumventing the law. As Masakazu Iwata noted, the Japanese got around the ownership provision of the law "by purchasing agricultural land in the names of their minor children born in the United States or by paying American citizens to buy land and hold it for them or their children."[176] The California State Board of Control statistics for 1920 indicate the ineffectiveness of the restrictions. Of the total of 27,931,444 acres of farmland in the state, Chinese Americans owned 12,076 acres, Japanese Americans 74,769 acres, and Hindu Americans, the latest Asian group to arrive as agricultural laborers to feed the insatiable need for workers, 2,099 acres. The Japanese leased 383,287 acres, while the Chinese leased only 65,181 acres, and the Hindus 86,430 acres.[177] In the decade during which the most virulent agitation against Japanese farmers occurred, they increased their agricultural activities nearly fourfold.

When the nature of immigration was considered, there was no question but that the Japanese were becoming a significant factor in West Coast agriculture. Unlike the Chinese, who were specifically named in exclusion and immigration acts, the Japanese were informally controlled through the restrictions placed on their passports by their own government. Many, as noted earlier, went first to Hawaii, the Philippines, or Mexico and worked on plantations to accumulate some financial security before making the second step of the journey to the United States. The Japanese typically came as families, not individually as workers as did many of the Chinese. And while the first wave of Japanese farmers could not own land or become citizens, any children they might have while living in the United States were, of course, American citizens and eligible to all constitutional rights including that of property ownership.

Inevitably, since Japanese were not specifically excluded in any immigration statute, a case was taken to determine whether the Japanese were legally prohibited from immigrating with the intent of becoming citizens. Takao Ozawa was born in Japan but had moved to San Francisco when he was nineteen.[178] After he graduated from the Berkeley, California, high school and spent the next three years at the University of California–Berkeley, he returned to the territory of Hawaii in 1906. On October 15, 1914, Ozawa applied for admission as an American citizen to the US District Court for the Territory of Hawaii. The district court ruled against him on the grounds that having been born in Japan, he was Japanese by race and not white. Ozawa had argued that while his name was not American, at heart he was "a true American" because he had culturally separated himself from Japanese culture and was proud of his proficiency in the English language and the fact that he and his family were Christians.[179] He appealed this decision to the Ninth Circuit Court of Appeals, which certified several questions to the Supreme Court, which court finally gave its opinion in 1922.[180]

The Supreme Court rephrased the questions originally certified to it and assumed that the case revolved around section 2169 of the Revised Statutes, which dealt with immigration and specifically applied to "aliens, being free white persons, and to aliens of African nativity and to persons of African descent."[181] This phraseology, of course, was originally found in the act of March 26, 1790, which defined a uniform rule of naturalization and which had been carried forward as the definitive clause in subsequent immigration statutes. Ozawa argued, with considerable force, that the Japanese could not be excluded from the United States since that would violate the treaties with Japan, and that therefore the Japanese must be presumed to fall under the eligibility requirements as "free white persons." The case thus placed racial definitions and considerations in the foreground of the opinion and sharpened the popular perception of federal laws and their relationship to Asian immigration.

The Court, in a unanimous opinion by Justice George Sutherland, worked through a tortuous chain of logic, beginning with the 1790 act, and concluded that "the provision is not that Negroes and Indians shall be *excluded* but it is, in effect, that only free white persons shall be *included*." Hypothesizing backward to rewrite American history, Sutherland continued, arguing that "it is not enough to say that the framers did not have in mind the brown or yellow races of Asia. It is necessary to go farther and be able to say that had these particular races been suggested the language of the act would have been so varied as to include them within its privileges."[182] Sutherland then turned to the great body of ethnographic evidence introduced by the two parties and concluded that the actual pigmentation of the skin itself had no bearing on the statutory definition. "Manifestly, the test afforded by the mere color of the skin of each individual is impracticable, as that differs greatly among persons of the same race, even among Anglo-Saxons, ranging by imperceptible gradations from the fair blond to the swarthy brunette, the latter being darker than many of the lighter hued persons of the brown or yellow races."[183]

Relying more upon the classifications of the human species then popular with scientific authorities, Sutherland maintained that "the words 'white person' are synonymous with the words 'a person of the Caucasian race' simplifies the problem, although it does not entirely dispose of it." But, the Court asserted that "the effect of the conclusion that the words 'white person' means a Caucasian is not to establish a sharp line of demarcation between those who are entitled and those who are not entitled to naturalization, but rather a zone of more or less debatable ground outside of which, upon the one hand, are those clearly eligible, and outside of which, upon the other hand, are those clearly ineligible for citizenship."[184] This reasoning, however, is illusory since the final determination of eligibility must inevitably resolve itself on an arbitrary criterion with respect to skin color, cultural background, and other factors.

With respect to Ozawa, however, the Court ruled that he was "clearly of a race which is not Caucasian and therefore belongs entirely outside the zone on the negative side."[185] Arguing that a large number of state and federal courts had already so ruled, although refusing to admit that they had based their decisions on purely racial grounds, which this case was designed to resolve, the high court certified all of the questions posed by the Ninth Circuit in the negative, thus effectively precluding Japanese from eligibility for citizenship. "The briefs filed on behalf of appellant refer in complimentary terms to the culture and enlightenment of the Japanese people, and with this estimate we have no reason to disagree," the opinion read. "But, these are matters which cannot enter into our consideration of the questions here at issue. We have no function in the matter," the Court said in pretended innocence, "other than to ascertain the will of Congress and declare it."[186] Sutherland concluded by gratuitously and insincerely adding that the decision in no way implied Ozawa's "unworthiness or racial inferiority."[187]

If the attitude of the Supreme Court was one of benign racism, the whites of the Pacific Coast provided a violent counterpart. In 1920, a vigorous campaign was conducted to amend the Alien Land Law by popular referendum to exclude ineligible aliens from leasing lands. The Japanese, although they constituted a statistically insignificant portion of California's overall population, through their efficient farming methods developed in their native land where farming land was at a premium, constituted a real economic presence in California agriculture, and the local white farmers did not wish to be confronted by this kind of sophisticated competition. The campaign featured some of the most despicable tactics ever seen in American political contests. The American Legion produced and distributed an extremely racist movie called *Shadows in the West*, which alleged that Japanese controlled the statewide vegetable market and that there were Japanese spies moving in and out of American cities. The Japanese were also depicted as sexual predators, with two white girls being abducted by a group of Japanese men. In the climax of the film, the girls are rescued by a stalwart band of Legionnaires.[188] In this atmosphere of irrational racial hatred, fueled by the vast majority of California's media outlets, the proposal to prohibit leasing of lands by ineligible aliens passed by a majority of 668,483 to 222,086.[189] This measure also denied "aliens" from purchasing land through corporations where they held more than half of the stock or in the names of their children, who, by birth, were American citizens.[190]

Closing this provision of the Alien Land Law had devastating effects on Japanese Americans. Of the total number of farms in California in 1920, Japanese controlled or worked 4.4 percent, which represented 1.2 percent of the total acreage under cultivation. A decade later, they controlled only 2.9 percent of the farms and 0.6 percent of the acreage, and in 1940 they controlled 3.9 percent with 0.7 percent of the acreage.[191] The figures do not tell the complete story since these decades saw small farms consolidated into larger, more economical units and a great deal of farmland adjoining the expanding urban areas taken for housing developments. So the erosion of the Japanese American land base was actually more dramatic than these statistics indicate. Yet the efficiency of the small Japanese truck farm cannot be underestimated. In 1941, Japanese farmers produced more than 90 percent of California's snap beans, 50 to 90 percent of the state's artichokes, and almost half of the asparagus, cabbage, cantaloupes, onions, watermelons, carrots, and lettuce produced in the state.[192]

Facing such severe legal and economic restrictions on their agricultural activities, many Japanese had to pursue other vocations. Many entered the cities and established restaurants and other small businesses. Even in these areas, racial discrimination against them flourished, although the courts sometimes sided with Japanese litigants. For example, in *Asakura v. Seattle* (1924), the Supreme Court ruled that a city ordinance that forbade pawnbroking without a license and restricted licenses to "citizens" was in violation of the 1911 Japanese-US treaty.[193] And in *In re Naka's License* (1934), a state case, the court upheld the right of a Japanese man, a subject of the Empire of Japan and therefore not a citizen of the United States, to engage in the retail liquor business in Alaska since this activity was found to be clearly contemplated by the 1911 treaty.[194] But in a case with almost the same fact situation, *Tokaji v. State Board of Equalization* (1937), a California state court ruled that the inclusion of the word *generally* in the 1911 treaty meant that exceptions in trade were contemplated and that the state restrictions placed upon the Japanese were clearly within this exception.[195]

Japan and World War II

In 1941, there were approximately 280,000 persons of Japanese birth living in the United States—130,000 lived on the mainland, 150,000 lived in Hawaii. Some 70 percent of the overall figure were native-born American citizens, while their parents remained ineligible for US citizenship, largely because of their race.[196]

The United States and Japan, for reasons discussed earlier, had lived on the brink of war for most of the twentieth century, so there should have been no surprise when war finally erupted between the two nations. In retrospect, one might conclude that the Japanese had been remarkably patient. Beginning with the Gentlemen's Agreement of 1907 and continuing through the San Francisco school board crisis and the various immigration and alien land law acts, Japan and Japanese Americans had been systematically insulted, and they experienced numerous discriminatory laws and policies by federal lawmakers and rank discrimination from many American citizens. A less mature nation might have seized any of these provocations as an excuse for hostilities. Even in relatively peaceful times the Japanese had suffered from the libelous campaigns of the West Coast newspapers, such as the Hearst chain, which engaged in race-baiting and rumor mongering against them. When Japan attacked Pearl Harbor on December 7, 1941, all of the hatred and misinformation bore fruit. The newspapers, allied with economic interests who had been seeking the removal of the Japanese for years, stirred public hysteria over the Japanese to a fever pitch.[197] While the status of other Asian Americans, especially the Chinese, Koreans, Filipinos, and Asian Indians, improved during the war, the situation of most Japanese Americans plummeted precipitously.

One of the first rumors to be widely accepted concerned the possibility of Japanese sabotage in conjunction with the attack on Pearl Harbor. Stories circulated that the Japanese had cleverly infiltrated critical industrial areas over the years and had assisted the Japanese navy in providing information and creating confusion. An impartial examination of the facts revealed that the Japanese lived near coastal facilities because they were primarily fishermen, that they farmed near and under high-power electrical lines because that was the only land that the whites would lease to them in certain areas, and that they remained exclusive and concentrated in ghettolike communities because they were not allowed to assimilate freely in all parts of the West Coast. As to sabotage, the Alien Registration Act of June 28, 1940, had required that all aliens (some one million Italian, German, and Japanese individuals) register with the police, and federal security agencies had already investigated individuals suspected of sympathetic leanings toward the Axis powers.[198] The attorney general of the United States, describing the actions taken during the confusion of Pearl Harbor in his *Annual Report* for 1942, reported that "on the night of December 7, 1941, the most dangerous of the persons in this group were taken into custody; in the following weeks a number of others were apprehended. Each arrest was made on the basis of information concerning the specific alien taken into custody. We have used no dragnet techniques and have conducted no indiscriminate, large-scale raids."[199] Presumably, then, the threat of internal subversion by people of German (314,715), Italian (695,363), and Japanese (91,858) ancestry, whether citizen or alien, was quickly eliminated in the weeks following the war's beginning.

There were, to be certain, individuals of Japanese ancestry taken into custody during this period. The population of Hawaii at that time was in excess of 500,000 and 32 percent, or 160,000, of these people were Japanese. But less than 0.5 percent—some 700 to 800—were taken into custody. During the entire war, only 1,100 Japanese, citizens and aliens, were taken from Hawaii to internment camps in the United States.[200] In contrast to Hawaii, the Japanese in the United States, concentrated primarily in the Pacific states, composed an infinitesimal percentage of the population, there being only a little over 112,000 Japanese Americans in the Western Military Command District, which consisted of Washington, Oregon, California, and parts of southern Arizona. Although there were instances of white sabo-teurs working for Japan, there was no instance where an individual Japa-nese, motivated by thoughts of the emperor or the homeland, committed any subversive act against the United States. Against this background, then, the subsequent events that occurred with respect to the mainland Japanese, 70,000 of which were native-born American citizens, must be evaluated.

Within weeks after the attack on Pearl Harbor, the army was asked to make recommendations concerning the defense of the West Coast. On February 14, 1942, General John L. DeWitt, later to command the Western Military District, filed his final recommendation to the secretary of war. This report was filled with distortions and racial prejudice and reflected the falsehoods and misinformation that the yellow journalism of the West Coast had inculcated in the public mind in the preceding decades. In char-acterizing the war, General DeWitt reported:

> In the war in which we are now engaged racial affinities are not sev-ered by migration. The Japanese race is an enemy race and while many second and third generation Japanese born on United States soil, pos-sessed of United States citizenship, have become "Americanized," the racial strains are undiluted. To conclude otherwise is to expect that chil-dren born of white parents on Japanese soil sever all racial affinity and become loyal Japanese subjects, ready to fight and, if necessary, to die for Japan in a war against the nation of their parents. That Japan is allied with Germany and Italy in this struggle is no ground for assuming that any Japanese, barred from assimilation by convention as he is, though born and raised in the United States, will not turn against this nation when the final test of loyalty comes.[201]

Overlooking the fact that the Japanese state as a political entity had gone to war with the United States, DeWitt conceived the war as one between the Japanese people, wherever located, and the United States. "It, therefore, follows" the general reported, "that along the vital Pacific Coast over 112,000 potential enemies, of Japanese extraction, are at large today. There are indications that these are organized and ready for concerted action at a favorable opportunity." And, the general claimed, "the very fact that no sabotage has taken place to date is a disturbing and confirming indication that such action will be taken."[202]

With evidence and reasoning such as DeWitt's to support his action, President Franklin D. Roosevelt on February 19 issued Executive Order Number 9066, which provided that certain military commanders, in their discretion, might prescribe military areas and define the extent to which any or all persons may be excluded and the restrictions under which any persons could remain or leave the area so designated. The following day, DeWitt was named commander of the Western District. On March 2, he issued Public Proclamation Order Number 1, which described the Pacific Coast as an area "particularly subject to attack, to attempted invasion" and "subject to espionage and acts of sabotage." The proclamation established Military Areas 1 and 2 and announced that subsequent orders would be issued that would exclude persons and classes of persons from these areas. The order required that any person of German, Italian, or Japanese ancestry residing in Area 1 who wished to change his residence had to execute and deliver to the military commander a change of residence notice.

In late March, events began to move with alarming swiftness. On March 21, Congress enacted a statute that provided that anyone who knowingly "shall enter, remain in, leave or commit any act in any military area or military zone prescribed...by any military commander...contrary to the restrictions applicable to any such area or zone" would be guilty of a misdemeanor and if convicted subject to a fine up to $5,000 and imprisonment for up to one year.[203] On March 24, DeWitt instituted a curfew for certain areas applicable to all aliens and issued the first of a series of 108 Civilian Exclusion Orders, which would systematically exclude aliens from designated areas on the West Coast, eventually covering almost all of the western states. Three days later, in Proclamation Order Number 4, DeWitt announced that "it is necessary to provide for the welfare and to insure the orderly evacuation and resettlement of Japanese voluntarily migrating from Military Area No. 1, to restrict and regulate such migration" and ordered that beginning on March 29, "all alien Japanese and persons of Japanese ancestry who are within the limits of Military Area No. 1, be and they are hereby prohibited from leaving that area for any purpose until and to the extent that a future proclamation or order of this headquarters shall so permit or direct." Finally on May 19, 1942, DeWitt issued Civilian Restriction Order Number 1, which prohibited evacuees from leaving assembly or relocation centers without an authorization from his headquarters.

Thus, during the winter of 1942, when the crisis of war had started to become routine, in the complete absence of sabotage or disloyalty by the Japanese, and as the American forces were beginning their successful counteroffensive in the Pacific, which was daily making the threat of invasion a remote possibility, about 110,000 civilian Japanese Americans of all ages and sexes—two-thirds of whom were American citizens by birth—were forced from their homes and imprisoned in ten concentration camps in California, Arizona, Utah, Colorado, Wyoming, Idaho, and Arkansas because of their racial ancestry. One dare not contemplate what their fate might have been had the war continued to go against the United States. There were ominous parallels between the treatment of the Jews by Nazi Germany and the Japanese Americans by the United States. Fortunately, we have no evidence in the United States of anything resembling the Final Solution that was being carried out by the Fascist regime against the Jews; but those forced to the detention camps were allowed no hearings or appeals processes.[204]

Japanese Americans suspected of disloyalty or requesting expatriation to Japan at the end of the war were sent to the camp at Tule Lake, California, and "loyal" Japanese citizens were scattered in the other camps. No effort was made to round up the Japanese in Hawaii, nor was there any attempt to gather up comparable Americans of German or Italian descent who also lived in the coastal cities. Eugene V. Rostow, writing in protest in the *Yale Law Journal* in 1945, while most of the Japanese were still behind barbed wire, criticized the standard explanation offered by military and civilian authorities that the Japanese had to be gathered up because it was impossible to interrogate them individually. He argued that

> the exclusion program was undertaken not because the Japanese were too numerous to be examined individually, but because they were a small enough group to be punished by confinement. It would have been physically impossible to confine the Japanese and Japanese Americans in Hawaii, and it would have been both physically and politically impossible to undertake comparable measures against the 690,000 Italians or the 314,000 Germans living in the United States.[205]

Because they were a small group, targets of perennial race-baiting by whites on the West Coast who feared them as social and economic equals, the Japanese became the first racial group since Geronimo's Chiricahua Apaches to be systematically imprisoned because of their racial status.

The forced evacuation, although described as "voluntary" and justified at least partially by the excuse that they were being moved for their own protection, was devastating to the Japanese. Families were disrupted, careers terminated, schooling postponed, farms lost or sold for pennies on the dollar, and businesses destroyed or bankrupted as the evacuation ripped entire communities apart and transported them inland to bleak relocation camps.[206] The sentiment against the Japanese was kept high by newspaper accounts of supposed subversive activities that rumors attributed to them. Rich farming valleys, developed by several generations of Japanese from stark and unproductive lands, fell into the hands of white farmers, and these people, fearful that their ill-gotten gains might be negated by the return of the Japanese, continued to spread racial hatred well beyond the point of rationality.

The Japanese American response was not one of raw emotion, however. They began planning a means of testing the constitutionality of the curfew, the evacuation orders, and their detainment, and soon four cases were headed for the US Supreme Court, where the Japanese hoped there would be more intelligent discussion of the issues.[207] In June 1943, nearly a year after their initial confinement, the Supreme Court handed down two companion decisions, *Hirabayashi v. United States*[208] and *Minoru Yasui v. United States*,[209] that sought to test the proposition that Congress could delegate broad powers to the military that obviously violated Fifth Amendment rights of American citizens. The cases were well presented and well briefed in the law but, to the chagrin of the Japanese, the Supreme Court found the actions of General DeWitt and the military to be constitutional. Chief Justice Harlan F. Stone delivered the majority opinion and made it evident that the cases were so controversial as to force the Supreme Court to dodge the constitutional issues and to accept without inquiry all of the allegations made by General DeWitt concerning the state of military conditions on the West Coast the year before.

The *Hirabayashi* decision, Jerry Kong has argued, is more important than the more celebrated *Korematsu* case of the following year because it provided the procedural basis for that later case.[210] In this opinion, to the discredit of the Supreme Court, the justices simply recited the rumors and misinformation of the preceding year as if these allegations were facts. Distortion became history as, for example, in the characterization of the purported danger of sabotage and espionage posed by the Japanese, the opinion stated as fact that "the German invasion of the Western European countries had given ample warning to the world of the menace of the 'fifth column.' Espionage by persons in sympathy with the Japanese Government had been found to have been particularly effective in the surprise attack on Pearl Harbor."[211] There was virtually no evidence apart from DeWitt's visceral hatred of the Japanese for this statement. In respect to the behavior of the Japanese, the Court repeated DeWitt's reasoning contained in his *Final Recommendations* report:

> There is support for the view that social, economic and political conditions which have prevailed since the close of the last century, when the Japanese began to come to this country in substantial numbers, have intensified their solidarity, and have in large measure prevented their assimilation as an integral part of the white population. In addition, large numbers of children of Japanese parentage are sent to Japanese language schools outside the regular hours of public schools in the locality. Some of these schools are generally believed to be sources of Japanese nationalistic propaganda, cultivating allegiance to Japan. Considerable numbers, estimated to be approximately 10,000, of American-born children of Japanese parentage have been sent to Japan for all or a part of their education.[212]

The Japanese, as we have seen in the San Francisco school board crisis and the Alien Land Law, were forbidden from assimilating with the white population, and numerous political, legal, and economic roadblocks to full citizenship had been placed in their path, yet now the Supreme Court was citing the effects of four decades of such discrimination as an indication that Japanese Americans were clannish and owed their loyalties to another nation and political system.

This reasoning, in fact, became the basis for suspecting disloyalty on the part of the Japanese, an offhand admission that they certainly had every conceivable reason for not supporting the American war effort. There was, however, no real evidence of their disloyalty, so the court treated DeWitt's unreasoned and biased reporting as the matured and considered judgment on the matter. "Whatever views we may entertain regarding the loyalty to this country of the citizens of Japanese ancestry, we cannot reject as unfounded the judgment of the military authorities and of Congress that there were disloyal members of that population, whose number and strength could not be precisely and quickly ascertained."[213]

In response to the argument that segregating the Japanese was a violation of the Fifth Amendment protections regardless of the military judgment, the Court countered by insisting that "because racial discriminations are in most circumstances irrelevant and therefore prohibited, it by no means follows that, in dealing with the perils of war, Congress and the Executive are wholly precluded from taking into account those facts and circumstances which are relevant to measures for our national defense and for the successful prosecution of the war, and which may in fact place citizens of one ancestry in a different category from others."[214] The logical circle was complete and expediency became the criterion of constitutional rights.

Justice William O. Douglas, concurring in an opinion of which he later expressed the utmost shame, attempted to reemphasize the idea of urgency that the military faced. "The point is that we cannot sit in judgment on the military requirements of that hour," Douglas argued. "Where the orders under the present Act have some relation to 'protection against espionage and against sabotage,' our task is at an end."[215] But what relation actually existed between the situation of peaceful and loyal Japanese American citizens and the paranoia of an American general who exhibited virulently racist views toward Japanese Americans? Justice Frank Murphy also concurred, but with the greatest hesitation, for he saw the obvious and painful parallels between the government's treatment of the Japanese and the activities of the Fascist states that the United States fighting:

> Today is the first time, so far as I am aware, that we have sustained a substantial restriction of the personal liberty of citizens of the United States based upon the accident of race or ancestry. Under the curfew order here challenged no less than 70,000 American citizens have been placed under a special ban and deprived of their liberty because of their particular racial inheritance. In this sense it bears a melancholy resemblance to the treatment accorded to members of the Jewish race in Germany and in other parts of Europe.[216]

Even with this devastating similarity drawn between the actions of the Nazis and the US Army, the Court could not bring itself to uphold the constitutional rights of the Japanese while the Pacific war raged. The years of yellow journalism were bearing a bitter fruit for civilized existence.

The next year, two additional cases were heard by the Supreme Court,

Korematsu v. United States[217] and *Ex parte Mitsuye Endo*.[218] With some variations, these cases attempted to test the constitutionality of the further humiliations to which the Japanese had been subjected after the curfew order, their relocation, and continued confinement for no good cause. *Korematsu* seemed to provide the turning point in the Japanese internment cases, for although the Court upheld the legality of the Civilian Exclusion Order under which Fred Korematsu and thousands of other Japanese had been forced from their homes, Justices Owen J. Roberts, Robert H. Jackson, and Murphy issued powerful dissenting opinions.[219] Justice Hugo Black delivered the majority opinion. The majority did not take a new tack in its reasoning, depending heavily upon the *Hirabayashi* case of the previous year and extending its logical implications to cover the activities of the military commander then under attack.

Black's opinion dealt gingerly with the question of constitutional rights. He cited evidence, since made available to the government, that nearly 5,000 Japanese Americans had refused to swear allegiance to the United States and requested expatriation to Japan as proof that DeWitt's fears had some substance. Totally lacking was the recognition that after two years in concentration camps, some of the Japanese might have been less than impressed with the substance of their constitutional rights and now sought to return to their ancestors' homeland. Concerning the hardships placed on the loyal citizens, Black was something less than specific regarding the legality of their sufferings. He admitted that they had suffered great hardships. "But hardships are part of war," he argued, "and war is an aggregation of hardships. All citizens alike, both in and out of uniform, feel the impact of war in greater or lesser measure. Citizenship has its responsibilities as well as its privileges, and in time of war the burden is always heavier."[220] Disruption of homes, educations, and family relationships, violations of constitutional rights, and the palpable loss of property were certainly not equivalent to the rationing of foodstuffs and other minor sacrifices other Americans were making, but Black only drew the analogy; he did not wish to develop the point more fully since it obviously constituted the weakest part of his reasoning.

Black's treatment of the racial theme left much to be desired and must certainly provide a classic example for future students of judicial logic. He suggested:

Korematsu was not excluded from the Military Area because of hostility to him or his race. He *was* excluded because we are at war with the Japanese Empire, because the properly constituted military authorities feared an invasion of our West Coast and felt constrained to take proper security measures, because they decided that the military urgency of the situation demanded that all citizens of Japanese ancestry be segregated from the West Coast temporarily, and finally, because Congress, reposing its confidence in this time of war in our miliary leaders—as inevitably it must—determined that they should have the power to do just this.[221]

The fallacy throughout this series of cases, however, was the attempt by the justices to make urgency and emergency the criteria of constitutionality, and if Justice Louis Brandeis once established the "clear and present danger test" for freedom of speech, the justices in the Japanese cases brought that concept to its ultimate technical use by projecting backward into a historical situation a danger that existed primarily in the minds of minor bureaucratic functionaries.

The dissenting justices' views contained a good deal more substance than did the majority opinion. Justice Roberts reviewed the sequence of events leading to Korematsu's conviction and pointed out that the situation made it impossible for Korematsu to obey the law since the orders dealing with the Japanese conflicted. "The two conflicting orders," Roberts noted, "one which commanded him to stay and the other which commanded him to go, were nothing but a cleverly devised trap to accomplish the real purpose of the military authority, which was to lock him up in a concentration camp."[222] Justice Jackson dealt specifically with the Civilian Exclusion Order and showed how it was drawn to deal exclusively with the Japanese. "Had Korematsu been one of four—the others being, say, a German alien enemy, an Italian alien enemy, and a citizen of American-born ancestors, convicted of treason but out on parole—only Korematsu's presence would have violated the order. The difference between their innocence and his crime would result, not from anything he did, said, or thought different than they, but only in that he was born of different racial stock."[223]

Justice Murphy had been uncomfortable with the reasoning of the *Hirabayashi* case, warning that it approached the limits of constitutionality when applied to a specific group. In *Korematsu* he was less kind, announcing that the exclusion of the Japanese "goes over 'the very brink of constitutional power' and falls into the ugly abyss of racism."[224] Citing the stereotypes in DeWitt's *Final Recommendation* report, Murphy argued that "Justification for the exclusion is sought…mainly upon questionable racial and sociological grounds not ordinarily within the realm of expert military judgment, supplemented by certain semi-military conclusions drawn from an unwarranted use of circumstantial evidence."[225] "A military judgment," he wrote, "based upon such racial and sociological considerations is not entitled to the great weight ordinarily given the judgments based upon strictly military considerations."[226] "All residents of this nation are kin in some way by blood or culture to a foreign land," Murphy reminded his fellow justices. "Yet they are primarily and necessarily a part of the new and distinct civilization of the United States. They must accordingly be treated at all times as the heirs of the American experiment and as entitled to all the rights and freedoms guaranteed by the Constitution."[227]

Justice Jackson, who had accepted that the military had the authority to arrest citizens, nevertheless echoed Murphy's theme, warning that

> once a Judicial opinion rationalizes such an order to show that it conforms to the Constitution, or rather rationalizes the Constitution to show that the Constitution sanctions such an order, the Court for all time has validated the principle of racial discrimination in criminal procedure and of transplanting American citizens. The principle then lies about like a loaded weapon ready for the hand of any authority that can bring forward a plausible claim of an urgent need.[228]

Reviewing the *Korematsu* decision in light of the persistent struggle by Justices Black and Douglas to protect the freedom of speech a decade later, and recognizing that a switch of two votes would have reversed Korematsu's conviction, we can see the tragedy that slow intellectual growth often visits upon defendants appealing to the highest court in the land. Nevertheless, when *Ex parte Mitsuye Endo* (1944) was decided, the conservative dam broke and Mitsuye Endo's conviction was overturned on little more evidence and the same basic reasoning that had convicted Hirabayashi and Korematsu. All four cases were tied together with a monstrous chain of reasoning that accepted the military definition of crisis and solutions as a realistic appraisal of the situation and then sought to justify by logical implication the measures used against the Japanese. With *Endo*, the majority discovered that they could not endlessly extend their reasoning to include all the fact situations that the Japanese cases presented.

The *Endo* case was designed to test the final step in the Japanese internment issue. Having lost the questions of curfew and detention, the next step was to test the continued confinement of the Japanese after they had been found to be loyal citizens. Mitsuye Endo was an internee first at Tule Lake, then at Topaz, Utah. She had been cleared for an indefinite leave by the War Relocation Authority but was not given permission to depart. In the meanwhile, she filed a writ of habeas corpus asking that she be released and restored to full liberty as a citizen. In the trial court, the government admitted everything that Endo alleged concerning her status as a loyal citizen and her eligibility for release. Their only excuse for detaining her, a typical bureaucratic response to human needs, was that "detention for an additional period after leave clearance has been granted is an essential step in the evacuation program."[229] The loyal Japanese were thus detained simply to enable the War Relocation Authority to perform its paperwork in a systematic manner.

This situation was too much for the now largely sympathetic justices. The decision to release Endo was unanimous, although Justices Murphy and Roberts, who had led the fight to release the Japanese, felt compelled to write concurring opinions in the hope that the constitutional issues could be clarified for the record. They urged that the decision be based on the constitutional ideas they had provided in *Korematsu* and not solely on the statutory interpretation that Justice Douglas relied on.[230]

Justice Douglas, slow to adopt the Japanese position, wrote the majority opinion. The history of the Japanese detention was quickly summarized by Douglas, and its tone took on a decided note of apology. No longer was the urgency of the moment emphasized. Douglas cleverly shifted the discussion away from the blanket powers of Executive Order Number 9066 to an analysis of the program of the War Relocation Authority, noting that it had three basic missions: "l) the maintenance of Relocation Centers as interim places of residence for evacuees; 2) the segregation of loyal from disloyal evacuees; 3) the continued detention of the disloyal and so far as possible the relocation of the loyal in selected communities."[231] Taking refuge in the Fifth and Sixth Amendments, Douglas then embarked on a paean of patriotism to cover what was obviously a difficult situation: "Loyalty is a matter of the heart and mind, not of race, creed, or color. He who is loyal is by definition not a spy or a saboteur. When the power to detain is derived from the power to protect the war effort against espionage and sabotage, detention which has no relationship to that objective is unauthorized."[232]

This conclusion could have been reached prior to the confinement of the Japanese since there were no incidents in which the Japanese were involved that would justify interning them in concentration camps. But the Court and the nation had accepted without examination General DeWitt's claim that the lack of evidence meant that the Japanese were planning to engage in espionage and sabotage activities against the United States. Douglas's opinion represents a belated effort to bring rationality to the issue.

Justice Roberts, philosophically and constitutionally far ahead of the rest of the justices in comprehending the implications of these four decisions, objected to the casual way that Douglas shifted the blame away from the army and the president and toward the War Relocation Authority. In a prophetic concurring opinion, Roberts declared that Douglas overlooked the patent facts of the case. "As the opinion discloses, the executive branch of the Government not only was aware of what was being done but in fact that which was done was formulated in regulations and in a so-called hand-book open to the public. I had supposed," the justice satirically wrote, "that where thus overtly and avowedly a department of the Government adopts a course of action under a series of official regulations the presumption is that, in this way, the department asserts its belief in the legality and validity of what it is doing."[233] Anticipating the Nuremberg and Watergate defenses, Roberts argued that it was "inadmissible to suggest that some inferior public servant exceeded the authority granted by executive order in this case. Such a basis of decision," he warned, "will render easy the evasion of law and the violation of constitutional rights, for when conduct is called in question the obvious response will be that, however much the superior executive officials knew, understood, and approved the conduct of their subordinates, those subordinates in fact lacked a definite mandate so to act."[234]

The *Endo* decision marked the beginning of a new period for Japanese Americans. Some non–Japanese Americans, now fully aware of the actions of their government with respect to their fellow citizens, were ashamed of the situation and began to speak up on behalf of the Japanese. Many Japanese were now being released from relocation camps and moved to new homes all over the United States. Of course, some of those who still owned property returned to find their homes dilapidated and vandalized, their personal belongings either stolen or destroyed.[235] Nevertheless, the Japanese proved to be outstanding citizens and their appearance in cities and towns that had never seen a Japanese before served to emphasize the constructive image that was beginning to emerge. The 442 Regimental Combat Team, an all-Japanese unit, participated in the invasion of Italy, distinguished itself, and received a great deal of favorable publicity. As the Allies moved into parts of Germany and discovered the ghastly products and unimaginable number of deaths meted out by the Nazis and their Final Solution to the Jewish "problem," efforts were quickly made to distinguish between the conditions of these camps and the treatment of the Japanese in America.

Japanese Americans survived their internment with dignity but learned quickly to evaluate their precarious political position in America. Recognizing that they could easily become the scapegoats for another American failure, they were determined to eliminate the remaining barriers that prevented them from enjoying full citizenship. Over the years, numerous state laws had been passed in an effort to reject and isolate any Japanese effort to assimilate into American society. Intermarriage with Japanese was prohibited in several of the western states. The Issei, the first-generation Japanese immigrants, were still ineligible for naturalization. No equality existed under the law for immigration quotas and procedures and hostilities against the Japanese still existed in many West Coast areas.

Two issues dominated the agenda of reform, however, and Japanese Americans were determined to secure justice in these areas first. All property held by the Japanese was subject to escheat to the states under the alien land laws, and these enactments made it virtually impossible for the Japanese to accumulate tangible property. Those who had been able to purchase lands had lost most of their property during the forced evacuation. Believing they had a good case, the Japanese raised $325,000 to lobby in Washington for indemnification.[236] On July 2, 1948, the Congress passed the Japanese Evacuation Claims Act, providing persons of Japanese ancestry the right to claim from the government for real and personal property losses (homes, stock, or land, for example).[237] They could not, however, seek monetary compensation. From 1948 to 1965, when the last payment was made, Congress paid out $38 million. However, the Commission on Wartime Relocation and Internment of Civilians estimated that Japanese Americans lost between $1.2 billion and $3.1 billion because of their evacuation, relocation, and internment.[238]

As 1948 began, an important case, *Oyama v. California*, was decided in the US Supreme Court that declared the California Alien Land Law to be in violation of Fifth Amendment rights.[239] The composition of the Court had changed somewhat in the period between *Oyama* and *Endo*, and while Black and Douglas were now solidly on the side of the Japanese, three justices—Stanley F. Reed, Harold H. Burton, and Jackson—filed dissenting opinions in the case. *Oyama* represented an important part of the Japanese adaptation to the severe discriminatory conditions that had faced them before the war. Kajiro Oyama was a Japanese farmer ineligible under the California statute to purchase or lease agricultural land, but his son, Fred, was a citizen of the United States, having been born in California and therefore eligible to become a landowner. Kajiro, as had been the Japanese custom, invested his savings in land, eight acres to be exact, and had the land purchased in the name of his son, Kajiro being named as Fred's guardian.

In 1942, when Fred Oyama and his family were still interned in a relocation camp, the state of California filed a petition to declare an escheat on the lands, claiming that the conveyances to Fred had been made with intent to evade the alien land laws. The state trial court upheld the prosecution's contention and declared that the parcels had vested in the state as of the date of the attempted transfers in 1934 and 1937. California's Supreme Court upheld this decision and it was appealed to the US Supreme Court.

Chief Justice Fred M. Vinson, who had replaced Stone as head of the Court, delivered the opinion for the majority on January 19, 1948. Vinson carefully narrowed the holding to a Fifth Amendment ruling that in this particular case, the California law violated Fred Oyama's constitutional rights. "In the light most favorable to the State," the chief justice declared, "this case presents a conflict between the State's right to formulate a policy of landholding within its bounds and the right of American citizens to own land anywhere in the United States. When these two rights clash, the rights of a citizen may not be subordinated merely because of his father's country of origin."[240] Indeed, the chief justice argued, "the only basis for this discrimination against an American citizen, moreover, was the fact that his father was Japanese and not American, Russian, Chinese, or English. But for that fact alone, Fred Oyama, now a little over a year from majority, would be the undisputed owner of the eight acres in question."[241] The chief justice, of course, was conveniently forgetting that only half a decade before, the Chinese had been excluded from the alien land laws.

Justice Black wrote a concurring opinion in which Justice Douglas joined, attacking the discriminatory nature of the California laws as applied to the Japanese:

> We are told, however, that, despite the sweeping prohibition against Japanese ownership or occupancy, it is no violation of the law for a Japanese to work on land as a hired hand for American citizens or for foreign nationals permitted to own California lands. And a Japanese man or woman may also use or occupy land if acting only in the capacity of a servant. In other words, by this Alien Land Law California puts all Japanese aliens within its boundaries on the lowest possible economic level. And this Land Law has been followed by another which now bars Japanese from the fishing industry.[242]

Justice Murphy, who had been the most aggressive member of the Court in defending the rights of Japanese Americans, used his concurring opinion to review the history of the Japanese in America, to remind the Court of its acceptance of racist views in the earlier relocation cases, and to draw the question to a finely honed argument against discrimination. "The Constitution of the United States, as I read it, embodies the highest political ideals of which man is capable. It insists that our government, whether state or federal, shall respect and observe the dignity of each individual, whatever may be the name of his race, the color of his skin, or the nature of his beliefs. It thus renders irrational, as a justification for discrimination, those factors which reflect racial animosity."[243]

In effect, Murphy used the occasion to lecture his fellow justices that when racial factors were involved, their duty to justice, fairness, and humanity was clear and unmistakable. The Japanese were not totally accepted on the West Coast after the war, but they had secured the respect of many Americans and a majority of the justices by their quiet dignity under the most trying conditions and by the example of their bravery in the war.

Pursuing Reparations

As the political activism of virtually every racial, ethnic, and gender group intensified in the 1960s, so, too, did it expand within the Japanese American community. Calls began for the federal government to provide reparations for those Japanese and their descendants who had been imprisoned or who had lost property during World War II. The Japanese American Citizens League in 1970 passed a resolution calling for reparations.[244] Gradually, the pressure mounted, and in 1980 Congress created the Commission on Wartime Relocation and Internment of Civilians. This body held hearings in several cities and over time collected many documents and the testimony of over seventy people. The commission concluded that Japanese incarceration had been a "grave injustice" and declared that the entire thrust of federal policy toward Asian Americans during the war had resulted from "race prejudice, war hysteria and a failure of political leadership."[245]

In 1988, Congress enacted the Civil Liberties Act, which contained a formal apology to Japanese Americans and a token payment of $20,000 for each living internee.[246] Despite its passage, Congress waffled on appropriating the money until an entitlement program was devised the following year.[247] Payments were made to 81,974 Japanese American citizens at a cost to the government of about $1.6 billion.[248]

Although Japanese Americans have experienced a remarkable degree of structured assimilation in the United States since World War II, given the scope of discriminatory policies and laws before and during the war, they, and other Asian ethnic groups, continue to cope with high levels of discrimination. Paula McClain and Joseph Stewart report that data from the pilot study of the National Asian American Political Survey "found that about one-third, 36 percent, of all Asian respondents reported that they have been discriminated against," with Koreans and Japanese, at 42 and 40 percent respectively, reporting the highest level of discrimination.[249] And although the Japanese American intermarriage rate has increased significantly since World War II, and while Japanese are not immigrating to the United States in large numbers—about 5,000 enter per year—they still "look different"and will have to endure stereotypical burdens like other Asian groups.[250]

The Japanese entrance into the legal universe was perhaps more prophetic than they might have dreamed. In almost all of the discriminatory laws passed to exclude them from citizenship, including most of the military proclamations and orders, they were not mentioned by name—but there was no question that the vague references to "aliens" dealt specifically with the Japanese. That they were first excluded from citizenship and immigration as "persons likely to become a public charge"; that they became one of the major racial groups in the twentieth century to become subjects of massive and institutionalized group discrimination and the only large group to have its members forcibly interned—and therefore in the most intimate sense a public charge—is irony enough. That, because of extreme racial prejudice, they were reduced to being paupers before making a profound economic and cultural recovery in the late twentieth and early twenty-first centuries was the added insult.

CHAPTER 10
"In Their 'Best Interests'":
Children and the Law

ON MAY 8, 2002, GABRIELA AZURDY ARIETA, a thirteen-year-old Bolivian, stood before sixty heads of state, several thousand members of nongovernmental organizations, and hundreds of children at the opening session of the United Nations General Assembly three-day Special Session on Children and delivered these insightful remarks: "We are street children. We are the children of war. We are the victims and orphans of HIV/AIDS...We want a world fit for children because a world fit for us is a world fit for everyone."[1]

Arieta and a seventeen-year-old from Monaco, Audrey Cheyant, were delivering a message that had been drafted by a three-hundred-member children's delegation, including US youth, to the special session. Special indeed. This was the first time children had ever been allowed to speak at the United Nations, a telling fact given the historic and contemporary problems of poverty, labor, disease, abuse, and so forth that children have endured for millennia. The meeting also was the first time the UN General Assembly had devoted an entire session to children and their issues, and it arose thirteen years after the United Nations, in 1988, adopted without a vote a landmark human rights treaty on children called the Convention on the Rights of the Child.

This convention, which the United States still has not officially ratified, provides formal international legal recognition of the human rights of children and is unique in that it protects not only the child's civil and political rights but also extends protection to the child's economic, social, cultural, and humanitarian rights. Despite the treaty, then secretary general Kofi Annan pointed out that although some improvements had been made regarding children's health and education, some 10 million children still died each year from preventable diseases and more than 100 million received no formal education.

The United States' adult delegation, for its part, expressed disappointment with the draft conference documents because they did not contain strong enough language on sexual abstinence and were apparently weak regarding protecting children under age eighteen from prostitution and pornography. This seemed a strange and tepid complaint, given that the United States was the only country in the world at the time that continued to officially sanction the death penalty for juveniles.[2]

The United States' fundamentally ambivalent views expressed above—supporting protecting children from prostitution and pornography but also (until 2005) supporting state-sanctioned capital punishment of convicted juveniles—indicates that children in American society, institutional life, and under the law are still confronted by conflicting norms, values, policies, and legal doctrines. On the one hand, Americans speak of doing what is in the "best interest" of the child because of their "childlike innocence and immaturity," their "tender years," their utter dependency on either their family or the state, or because they represent the "future generation."

On the other hand, in a bevy of issues, religion, education, criminal jurisdiction, abuse (sexual, physical, emotional), social welfare, abortion, harmful products (tobacco and other drugs, for example), immigration, and pornography, children in the United States face concentrated poverty and embedded political and economic constraints, popular and policy-maker attitudes, and institutional barriers that deny or diminish their basic human, civil, cultural, and other rights.

Examples abound:

- The high level of poverty of young people, which constitutes the gravest factor for their welfare since poverty-stricken children experience malnutrition, poor housing, inadequate healthcare, substandard schools, and higher levels of crime. Children are the poorest of all Americans and, as Barry Feld reported, "more children live in poverty in the United States, one in five, than in any other western industrialized nation."[3]
- The widespread, if until recently, underreported sexual abuse of children by Catholic priests and nuns.
- The significant levels of physical abuse of children. In 1996, Child Protective Service agencies in the United States received three million reports of alleged child maltreatment.[4]
- The US Constitution's silence on the subject of children. While parents have constitutional rights against children in the area of corporal punishment and child support, children have no constitutional rights against parental physical assaults or to their parent's financial support.[5]
- Children lack the basic right of liberty to come and go at will between the ages of six and seventeen.
- Children face compulsory education, while adults are not similarly compelled to attend school.

- Parents wield plenary (virtually absolute) power over all aspects of child rearing.
- Children lack property and are therefore economically and politically powerless. In fact, while children are not legally the property of their parents, American culture "makes assumptions about children deeply analogous to those it adopts in thinking about property."[6]
- Children, by definition, are underage and may not wield the franchise. Lacking the power to vote inhibits them from defending or generating any of their rights.
- US law and society tends to speak of children's "interests" rather than of their "rights," thus their needs and desires are oftentimes trumped or subsumed by the state's rights or parental rights.[7]
- Children's interests/rights are often conceptualized in a prospective form, that is, they are said to represent the "future generation" or they are "our future." But this futuristic approach denies the real significance of the current child's rights or needs by concentrating on an image of an adult-to-be who may one day have an important role to play.[8]
- Children endure conflicting and fundamentally irreconcilable images—as innocent, immature, incompetent; or as vigorous, autonomous, self-determining, and adultlike. This is evident in statements like, "Children, the insane, and those who are irreversibly ill with loss of brain function, for instance, all retain 'rights,' to be sure, but often such rights are only meaningful as they are exercised by agents acting with the best interests of their principles in mind."[9]

The following quotes provide further illustration of the ambivalence adults display toward children:

> When I was a child, I spoke as a child, I understood as a child, I thought as a child: but when I became a man, I put away childish things. (I Corinthians 13:11)

> It is…absurd to think that one must be mature enough to drive carefully, to drink responsibly, or to vote intelligently, in order to be mature enough to understand that murdering another human being is profoundly wrong, and to conform one's conduct to that most minimal of all civilized standards. (*Stanford v. Kennedy* [1989])

In short, children in the United States face perceptual, physical, age, and socioeconomic barriers and conditions that arguably leave them more vulnerable to state and societal powers than any of the groups under discussion in this book. Historically, women were often compared to children by lawmakers; and indigenous peoples were frequently treated as wardlike entities in a dependent relationship to their federal guardians. But over time, women's status has improved measurably and Native nations are rarely spoken of as wards.

Children, however, rather than being able to effectively mobilize and wage battles to improve their status under the law, find that while they have gained some rights in the last few decades, they still retain and must cope with numerous and vacillating statuses that make it difficult for them to protect themselves from the very forces—media, local, state, and federal policy makers, or their parents—that are supposed to nurture and guide them.

Barry C. Feld, in *Bad Kids: Race and the Transformation of the Juvenile Court*, traced how the social construction of childhood and adolescence (a period of life spanning age seven to seventeen) evolved through at least four distinct phases.[10] First, before the European Renaissance, in Western societies children after infancy were treated as "miniature adults, smaller versions of their parents, rather than as qualitatively different from their elders."[11] Second, during the Progressive Era, between the late 1890s and 1920s, in the United States a view of childhood and adolescence emerged that held that adults must protect and nurture their young in preparation for the future. Such a perspective evidenced itself in the construction of schools, child labor laws, and juvenile courts, which supported the separate status of children and adolescents from adults. Third, the Warren Court's "due process revolution" included *Brown v. Board of Education* (1954) and *In re Gault* (1967), major cases that sought to effectuate fundamental social reform by supporting civil rights, protecting minorities, and limiting states' powers. Finally, the 1980s–2000s reflect an era in which poverty, drug abuse, racial and youth crime, industrial decline, and eroded family and community social contacts generated new public and policy-maker attitudes about young people that view them as incorrigible adultlike individuals in need of harsh punishment when they commit wrongs. Let us chart the ebb and flow of children's status in the law by examining a select group of cases for each of the three American eras.

The Birth of "Best Interests" and *Parens Patriae*

American jurists struggled from the very beginning of the development of US law with how best to treat children as children and in their relation to their parents and the state. Were they rights holders, like their parents? Or did their physical, emotional, and legal dependency mean they were not entitled to the exercise of rights? Frequently, the judicial response emphasized the needs of the child and not their rights. This attitude was epitomized by a legal phrase that came to dominate the discussion about children's statuses in the law until late in the twentieth century: "The best interests of the child."[12]

This expression, not unlike the doctrine of plenary power as applied to Indian tribes, is indeterminate and is jurisprudentially unsound. Judges, justices, and federal lawmakers have vast discretionary power to define what the "best interests" of the children are and use it to judge the fitness of parents to retain custody.[13] More importantly, the best interests standard does not address the interests of any actual child or of children as a group. Instead, it "implements adult agendas, in part by assuring that courts fail to examine the interests of the real, individual children whose custody is disputed."[14]

The traditional state power to determine the child's best interest is rooted in the legal doctrine of *parens patriae* (literally, "parent of the country"), with the state acting as a surrogate parent when it is determined that the natural parents are unable or refuse to meet their responsibilities or if a child is considered a "problem" for the community.[15] This legal doctrine first appeared in US juvenile law in a Pennsylvania Supreme Court ruling, *Ex parte Crouse* (1838).[16] In *Crouse*, the court rejected a father's habeas corpus petition that his daughter was entitled to due process rights, and thus her involuntary confinement in the Pennsylvania House of Refuge by her mother without a trial was illegal. In providing a legal basis for the state's ability to incarcerate seemingly incorrigible children as well as children who had committed crimes, the court justified its decision by elevating the state's legislative power over parental rights regarding their children when it was deemed necessary for the dependent child's interests:

> The object of the charity is reformation, by training its inmates to industry; by imbuing their minds with principles of morality and religion…
> To this end, may not the natural parents, when unequal to the task of education, or unworthy of its, be superseded by the *parens patriae*, or common guardian of the community?[17]

In effect, the court was citing from an ideology that viewed children as essentially rights-less physical and social dependents in need of universal and compulsory education. The deprivation of their liberty by confinement at the refuge house was permissible, according to the court, because the state was assumed to know what was in the "infant's welfare." Parents, especially poor parents, were held to have natural rights regarding control of their children, but this was not an "unalienable right," and it could be overridden by the state if it was determined that the parents' moral character was suspect. *Crouse* established state plenary power over family sovereignty and children's needs under the guise of paternalism and *parens patriae.* This legal reality would remain an integral part of the law until late in the twentieth century.

By the later part of the nineteenth century, the subject of children's needs/rights gained considerably more attention. This was an era of social and economic uncertainty, with the United States transitioning from an agricultural to an urban industrialized society. New technology and massive immigration further complicated the status of children in society. Despite *Crouse*'s articulation of *parens patriae*, children throughout the nation continued to suffer horrendous levels of maltreatment, whether at the hands of teachers, parents, employers, or state institutions.[18]

The heightened level of child abuse, delinquency, and neglect led reformers to turn to the state for corrective action. "Emphasizing the differences between children and adults, they and their legislative allies filled state codes with new regulations that substantially enlarged the legal definition of children at risk and focused on the newly labeled years of adolescence."[19]

Another stimulant to the growing movement to better protect children from cruelty centered on the 1874 case of Mary Ellen Wilson, a ten-year-old who had been physically abused for years by Mary Connolly. In April 1874, a jury convicted Connolly of assault and battery for the physical harm she had inflicted on Wilson. The ten-year-old had been placed in Connolly's care eight years earlier by the Department of Charities. This case attracted a great deal of attention and served as a catalyst for a movement against child abuse, "initiating the use of the criminal justice system as a weapon in the movement's armamentarium and stimulating the founding of the first society against cruelty to children."[20]

Progressive-Era Child Politics

As the Progressive Era evolved, those interested in improving the lot of children's lives, the so-called Child Savers, or the Child Study movement, led a surge in institutional changes that culminated in three major developments: the creation of a juvenile court, prohibition of child labor, and compulsory school laws. These reforms constitute what Feld has called the "trinity of the legal and social construction of childhood."[21] They reflected certain core Progressive assumptions regarding the need to augment the nuclear family, protect the child from adult roles, delay the child's/adolescent's integration into the economy, provide a necessary education for social mobility, and provide the state with the right to intrude upon family sovereignty if necessary to assume a brighter future.[22]

The Child Savers continued to articulate for children's rights and made significant headway in regard to healthcare, education, and protection from economic exploitation, arguing that parents had a trusteeship responsibility to care for their children. Simultaneously, equally compelling societal forces were at work that focused on the exploitation of children, particularly in the workplace. By the late 1800s and into the early 1900s, the number of children age ten to fifteen entering an increasingly hazardous workplace increased dramatically.[23]

Child reformers turned their attention to Congress to enact laws to regulate child labor. But in 1918, the Supreme Court, in *Hammer v. Dagenhart*, ruled that Congress, in passing the Keating-Owen Child Labor Act of 1916, which relied on the commerce power to bar goods made by children from interstate commerce, had overstepped its constitutional authority by intruding upon a power that rested solely in the states' hands.[24] The 5–4 majority opinion by Justice William Rufus Day focused on federalism and said little about the exploited child laborers whose plight had prompted the legislation. Justice Oliver Wendell Holmes, in a trenchant dissent, observed that "if there is any matter upon which civilized countries have agreed…it is the evil of premature and excessive child labor."[25] Congress was undaunted and tried again by enacting a measure under its taxing power. Again, however, the Supreme Court rebuffed the legislature, insisting that the subject matter was a "local" issue.[26]

Child reformers and concerned federal lawmakers then took the penultimate step and proposed a constitutional amendment in 1924 that read:

Section 1. The Congress shall have the power to limit, regulate, and prohibit the labor of persons under 18 years of age.

Section 2. The power of the several States is unimpaired by this article except that the operation of State laws shall be suspended to the extent necessary to give effect to legislation enacted by Congress.

This amendment, like the equal rights amendment for women, is one of the few proposed amendments that was never ratified.[27] The Court's refusal in these cases to sanction legislation aimed at curtailing labor's exploitation of children may have stemmed in part from its fear of parental loss of control over children to a burgeoning national government.

This attitude of parental right to control and virtually dominate every aspect of a child's life was further evidenced in two powerful cases in the 1920s, *Meyer v. Nebraska* (1923) and *Pierce v. Society of the Sisters* (1925). Both cases involved disputes between parents and state authorities about the limits of the government's right to determine the character of public schooling.

In *Meyer*, the Court nullified a Nebraska law that prohibited the teaching of modern language, in this case German, to children who had not passed the eighth grade. While many have hailed this case as an important precedent for a constitutional right of privacy and as an expression supporting pluralism and family autonomy, the case can also be read as one that views the school-age child as the family patriarch's private property, subject to virtually absolute control and custody of both the parents and the state.[28]

A case can be made that instruction in more than one language provides a pupil with an assortment of tangible and intangible benefits. But a close reading of the text reveals that the Court was more interested in recognizing the "liberty" of the teacher to instruct in a language other than English and in providing support for the parents and state to compel education of their children. In the Court's words: "Corresponding to the right of control, it is the natural duty of the parent to give his children education suitable to their station in life; and nearly all the States, including Nebraska, enforce this obligation by compulsory laws."[29]

The state's rights to compel attendance and prescribe curriculum materials is duly acknowledged, as is the teacher's "fundamental rights" to provide instruction in languages they are comfortable with. What is missing in the Court's analysis, however, is any opinion from the students themselves as to how they view their instruction. They remain essentially anonymous, blank slates, the virtual property of both the state and their parents, awaiting whatever decision is made for them.

In *Pierce*, the Supreme Court unanimously held that an Oregon initiative that required practically every parent to send a child between the ages of eight and sixteen to public school unreasonably interfered with a parent's or guardian's liberty to choose an upbringing and education path for their children of their own choosing.[30] Justice James C. McReynolds, in affirming a parent's right to send their children to private school, categorically declared that "the child is not the mere creature of the State; those who nurture him and direct his destiny have the right, coupled with the high duty, to recognize and prepare him for additional obligations."[31]

As in *Meyer*, children are here denied any voice in the matter of educational preference. If the child was not a "creature of the state," one could plausibly reply that they were, in fact, creatures of paternalistic parents or guardians, until such time as they grow into their "additional obligations" as adults.

Continuing this trend of cases in support of broad family autonomy, but with an increased recognition that the state as *parens patriae* could step in to protect the helpless child if it had substantial justification, the Court, in *Prince v. Massachusetts* (1944), reaffirmed that its prior decisions "have respected the private realm of family life which the State cannot enter," while also acknowledging that the state has an authority over some children's activities, in this case, employment, that is far greater than over adult employment.[32]

Echoing a view of children as essentially helpless dependents who need state oversight and protection in order to attain "full maturity as citizens," the Court stated that while adults enjoyed the right to distribute religious literature as part of their tradition, such solicitation by children was "wholly inappropriate" because of their "tender years" and the potential psychological and physical injuries they might endure.[33] Justice Wiley B. Rutledge noted that while martyrdom was permissible for adults, parents were not at liberty "to make martyrs of their children before they have reached the age of full and legal discretion when they can make that choice for themselves."[34] The Court concluded by declaring that this ruling was not to be viewed as authorizing state intervention in the lawful right of parents to impose religious training and indoctrination on their children. This constitutionally protected parental right was wholly unaffected by this decision.

Meyer, *Pierce*, and *Prince* were evidence of a judiciary steeped in rank paternalism. The justices acted from an ideology that assumed that the parents' rights were congruent with their children's interests or that only the parents' opinions should be considered. Importantly, "children did not bring these cases. In the era that invented paternalistic rights for children, it was parents, social workers, judges, and other protectors who spoke for the young and fought over them."[35]

Brown, Gault, and Children's Reform

The movement to effectuate reforms aimed at extending basic social and constitutional rights to children was constructed on the foundations laid out by two landmark Supreme Court decisions: *Brown v. Board of Education* (1954) and *In re Gault* (1967). *Brown*, which struck down the separate but equal doctrine and eventually aimed to dismantle state-imposed racial segregation in education, contained a good amount of language describing children's rights to an equal education:

> Today it is a principal instrument in awakening the child to cultural values, in preparing him for later professional training, and in helping him to adjust normally to his environment. In these days, it is doubtful that any child may reasonably be expected to succeed in life if he is denied the opportunity of an education. Such an opportunity, where the state has undertaken to provide it, is a right which must be made available to all on equal terms.[36]

The notion of equality in education for all children was one thing. But *In re Gault* dramatically declared that children were persons under the Constitution. At issue was whether the State of Arizona could deprive Gerald Gault, a fifteen-year-old, of his liberty without affording him due process rights provided under the Fourteenth Amendment of the Constitution.

Justice Abe Fortas, for an 8–1 majority, wrote a detailed opinion that not only questioned the wisdom of *parens patriae* as the guiding doctrine of juvenile adjudication, but also extended a host of constitutional rights previously available only to adult criminal defendants: the right to confront and cross-examine witnesses; protection against self-incrimination; and adequate and timely notice of charges and hearing, among others. As Fortas said, "it would be extraordinary if our Constitution did not require the procedural regularity and the exercise of care implied in the phrase 'due process.' Under our Constitution, the condition of being a boy does not justify a kangaroo court."[37]

Gault reflected the Court's valiant effort to provide juveniles with a measure of constitutional equality previously unavailable to them in the form of due process rights for juvenile offenders since, in the Court's words, "neither the Fourteenth Amendment nor the Bill of Rights is for adults alone."[38] The Court sought to strike a difficult balance by respecting children as constitutional persons entitled to basic protections, while at the same time still recognizing that children are and should still be treated differently than adults.[39]

Feld, however, believes that the balance has tipped in a way that unfavorably treats children as adults. By endorsing the adversarial model, the privilege against self-incrimination, and so forth, he suggests that "the Court redefined delinquents as a subgroup of criminal defendants, rather than as a category of dependent children in need of services."[40]

Thus, while *Gault* is rightly hailed as a constitutional landmark for children's rights, in a practical sense it also fundamentally altered the essence of delinquency proceedings from an examination about a juvenile's social welfare and turned it into a criminal prosecution. This has proven to be a most problematic issue for juveniles, and the Supreme Court's subsequent case law has reflected a deep cultural ambivalence about children—vacillating between dependency and incompetence to full responsibility and virtual autonomy.[41]

The 1970s and Beyond: The Criminalization of Children

In the four decades since *Gault*, American society has changed dramatically in many respects—immigration, globalization, new technology and communication, racial and demographic changes in cities and rural America, a tremendous increase in gun violence, and a blurring of the historically bright line between children and adults, with children, for certain purposes, being treated as virtually indistinguishable from adults. While each of these topics has fostered sweeping alterations, our focus remains on how the Supreme Court, in reacting to all the above forces, generated increasingly contradictory views of children that have acted to severely disadvantage children's status in society and under the law.

There emerged a genuine ideological splintering in the Court's attitude toward children. On the one hand, in the wake of ample evidence of increasing risks facing American youth—parental physical and sexual abuse, teenage pregnancy, increased suicide rates, and higher drug addition—the Court, in two major opinions (*Ginsburg v. New York* [1968], dealing with obscenity; and *Wisconsin v. Yoder* [1972], dealing with religious freedom and education), acted to defuse the children's rights movement by reinvigorating parental control, fearing that such rights-based activity had "undermined child welfare by fostering adversarial relations and undermining necessary parental and school authority."[42]

On the other hand, other cases were handed down that expanded the constitutionally based language of children's rights unleashed in the *Gault* decision: *Tinker v. Des Moines* (1969), dealing with free speech in education; *Goss v. Lopez* (1975), which addressed the Fourth Amendment and education; and *Planned Parenthood of Central Missouri v. Danforth* (1976), an abortion case. These cases, in applying an adult model of rights to children who faced risks, built upon a range of legal developments, including a younger legal drinking age and the Twenty-sixth Amendment, that lowered the voting age to eighteen and lessened the differences between adults and children.

There was another line of cases, however, that erupted in the 1990s and has continued into the twenty-first century, focused on the criminal context, particularly drug use and abuse, that more starkly dealt with juvenile offenders, especially minority youth, as essentially incorrigible adultlike persons. As Janet Dolgin reported,

> Increasingly, the law abandons familial metaphors in understanding and dealing with such children and defines them as autonomous individuals. As a result, the justification for treating children who commit crimes differently from adults who commit crimes erodes. The redefinition of children within this context is as startling as that of children within dysfunctional families. The very children who seem most in need of adult help are being denied even the pretense of such help.[43]

These three different trends in Supreme Court precedent, while occasionally acknowledging that children and adolescents are entitled to some constitutional protections, have not, in fact, fully recognized children as constitutional persons, and our notion of constitutional personhood still does not include children qua children.[44] This is evident in the following Supreme Court cases. In *McKeiver v. Pennsylvania* (1971), Justice Harry Blackmun wrote that juveniles were not entitled to jury trials, but merely to a standard of "fundamental fairness." "The imposition," said Blackmun, "of the jury trial on the juvenile court system would not strengthen greatly, if at all, the fact finding function, and would contrarily, provide an attrition of the juvenile court's assumed ability to function in a unique manner."[45] This case has frequently been criticized, but it is still the dominant interpretive framework. States have the option to insist upon juries in juvenile cases, but so far none has done so.[46]

Six years later, in *Ingraham v. Wright* (1977), the Court found that corporal punishment of students did not violate the Eighth or the Fourteenth Amendments and that school officials were not even required to provide the students a hearing before administering punishment. "We are reviewing here a legislative judgement," said Justice Lewis Powell, "rooted in history and reaffirmed in the laws of many States that corporeal punishment serves important educational interests."[47]

In *Parham v. J.R.* (1979), parental plenary authority over children was reaffirmed with regard to their right to involuntary commit children to institutions without even providing the child with a due process hearing before their loss of liberty. "Appellees argue that the constitutional rights of the child are of such magnitude and the likelihood of parental abuse is so great that the parents' traditional interests in and responsibility for the upbringing of their child must be subordinated at least to the extent of providing a formal adversary hearing prior to a voluntary commitment." "Our jurisprudence," said Chief Justice Warren Burger, "historically has reflected western civilization concepts of the family as a unit with broad parental authority over minor children."[48]

Neither has the Constitution's Fourth Amendment's prohibition on unreasonable searches and seizures been of much use to young people. School officials, based on reasonable suspicion alone, may search student lockers and personal belongings looking for contraband items. This was the Court's decision in *New Jersey v. T.L.O.*, in 1985. There the Court said that

> we join the majority of courts that have examined this issue in concluding that the accommodation of the privacy interests of schoolchildren with the substantial need of teachers and administrators for freedom to maintain order in the schools does not require strict adherence to the requirement that searches be based on probable cause to believe that the subject of the search has violated or is violating the law. Rather, the legality of a search of a student should depend simply on the reasonableness, under the circumstances, of the search.[49]

As drug abuse continued to proliferate throughout American society, particularly for athletes, it was only a matter of time before juvenile student athletes came under the glare of officials. Thus, in *Vernonia School District v. Acton* (1995), the Supreme Court upheld random drug tests of student athletes. James Acton and his parents had argued that such tests violated the Fourth Amendment's search and seizure clause. But Justice Antonin Scalia said, "Traditionally at common law, and still today, unemancipated minors lack some of the most fundamental rights of self-determination—including even the right of liberty in its narrow sense, i.e., the right to come and go at will." "They are," said Scalia, "subject, even as to their physical freedom, to the control of their parents or guardians…the necessity for the State to act is magnified by the fact that this evil is being visited not just upon individuals at large, but upon children for whom it has undertaken a special responsibility of care and direction."[50]

Finally, in 2007, the Supreme Court held, in *Morse v. Frederick*,[51] a case that combined the First Amendment's free speech clause with the drug issue, that a school principal did not violate a student's right to free speech by confiscating a banner carrying the phrase "Bong HiTs 4 Jesus," since the principal had, in the words of Chief Justice John Roberts, "reasonably concluded that the banner promoted illegal drug use in violation of established school policy."[52] Justice Stevens, writing for David Souter and Ruth Bader Ginsburg, cast a vigorous dissenting opinion. In Stevens's view, "the First Amendment protects student speech if the message itself neither violates a permissible rule nor expressly advocates conduct that is illegal and harmful to students." Stevens stressed that the student's "nonsense banner" did neither of these things and therefore the Court was grossly overreaching and doing "serious violence to the 1st Amendment in upholding the school's actions."[53]

The Supreme Court, with its plenary interpretive power to decide cases, has played a pivotal role in defining the status of children, childhood, and juveniles on their own terms and in relation to the family unit, parental or guardian authority, and the state as *parens patriae*. But of all the groups being analyzed, children face political, social, cultural, legal, attitudinal, and economic barriers uniquely their own. These barriers leave children in a virtually powerless and defenseless position in relation to those institutions—family, courts, religious, and educational—that have the power to determine what a child's status is and what they may or may not do.

Lacking property, the franchise, basic self-determination or personal autonomy, and dependent on adults until late in adolescence, children are at the mercy of many forces, with little means to lobby for themselves. In the face of constitutional silence, the Supreme Court has crafted vacillating and ambivalent visions of children and adolescents that sometimes provide them with abbreviated doses of procedural rights, while more often establishing or reaffirming precedents that are vastly more supportive of parents' rights or that sanction state power to invade children's privacy, have them institutionalized without hearings, and dealt with harshly in criminal contexts. This situation is not likely to change unless children and childhood status is respected as a distinct, though not unrelated, human era and not employed as a chronological ploy to deny personhood to those in that age group.

Children, by definition and actual fact, are different in a number of fundamental respects, and the law should acknowledge and appreciate children's perspectives as simply different.[54] The Court should neither rely on their differences to diminish their right to and need of family love and support, and state social welfare when called upon; nor should it deny their differences by defining them as autonomous adultlike persons who should be treated to similar harsh penalties as adults.

Finally, there is the issue of rights talk for children and whether or not this helps or harms their status. Barbara Woodhouse spoke eloquently to this topic, summarizing :

> Perhaps children, as the least powerful members of both the family and the political community, are also the least dangerous of rights-bearers and the most in need of an affirmative rights rhetoric in order to be heard. By defining children's rights as flowing from their needs, we can affirm rather than undermine an ethic of care for others. By listening to children's voices and experiences as evidence of their needs, and by trying to come to terms with the children's reality, we can confront our own adult ambivalence and conflicts of interest regarding children's rights.[55]

CHAPTER 11
"The State of Nature":
The Natural World and the Law

Wealth or value is created by culture and by society;
it is culture that makes a diamond valuable and a pueblo worthless.
Property, on the other hand, is the creation of law. A man who has property
has certain legal rights with respect to an item of wealth;
property represents a relationship between wealth and its "owner."[1]

ON JULY 28, 2010, SPANISH LAWMAKERS IN CATALONIA made a decision involving the natural world that may be a harbinger of a new relationship being forged between human beings and nonhuman species. They voted to ban bullfighting, long considered a crucial part of Spanish cultural identity. The ban was lauded by animal rights groups who have long considered bullfighting to be a vicious and barbaric practice.[2] Two years earlier, the environmental committee of the Spanish parliament introduced resolutions that extended basic human rights to several species of the great apes—chimpanzees, bonobos, gorillas, and orangutans.[3] The resolutions followed the principles outlined in the Great Ape Project, started in 1993 by Peter Singer, a prominent ethicist, and Paola Cavalieri, a philosopher, who argue that the great apes, who are close genetic relatives to human beings, deserve the right to life, freedom, and to be exempt from torture. The measures made it illegal in Spain to kill apes, except in self-defense, and they would not be subject to medical experiments or arbitrary imprisonment.[4] Ironically, the 315 apes currently being held in Spanish zoos would not be freed. However, their living conditions will be improved dramatically.

In Switzerland, Antoine Goetschel, who represents nearly two hundred animals a year, is the official animal lawyer for the Swiss Canton of Zurich. Although he is officially the only lawyer in the nation representing animals, and while the Swiss in March 2010 rejected a plan that would have led to the appointment of lawyers for abused animals, Switzerland nevertheless remains at the forefront of the process of providing a degree of legal recognition of animal and plant life.[5]

A provision in Switzerland's constitution, for example, recognizes the dignity of animals, plants, and other organisms, and in April 2008 the Federal Ethics Committee on Non-Human Biotechnology issued a detailed report,

The Dignity of Living Beings With Regard to Plants, which emphasized that vegetation has "inherent worth," and unanimously concluded that arbitrary harm to plants was "morally impermissible." One example of arbitrary harm would be "decapitation of wildflowers at the roadside without rational reason."[6]

These three examples hint at a minuscule, though clearly discernible, breach in the veritable wall that has long divided Western-based humanity from nonhuman animals, other biological species, lands, trees, and vegetation, as well as the atmosphere, oceans and rivers, and so forth. But it is, indeed, a minuscule breach because the dominant legal and political paradigm in the United States still generally hews to the attitude that non-human beings and the natural world are still not entitled to a consistent measure of dignity and respect. In fact, the most extravagant pretense of Western civilization is its tenaciously held belief that only humans matter in the scheme of things. The origin of such arrogance is unknown, but it is clearly one of Western culture's greatest inflations. In this tradition, humans were created and given the privilege of naming the other creatures, thereby gaining ascendancy over them.[7]

Singer, one of the founders of the animal rights movement, referred to this arrogance as speciesism, which, he said, entails "a prejudice or attitude of bias in favor of the interests of members of one's own species and against members of other species."[8] As Singer and other commentators have noted, speciesism has existed for the four thousand years that law has been evident.[9] In fact, Western attitudes toward animals and the natural world have their origins in several Western traditions: Aristotelianism, Stoicism, and biblical or Judeo-Christian beliefs.

While each of these intellectual traditions are distinctive, they share a vision of the world in which humans are situated atop the hierarchy of life-forms known as the Great Chain of Being. As Derek W. St. Pierre notes, "the Great Chain of Being is the idea that there is a natural hierarchy, in essence a ladder, which designates a place for everything. Location on the ladder is ordained by a designed and ordered universe. Plants occupy the lowest rungs, non-human animals are further up the ladder, humans are even higher up and the upper rungs are occupied by angelic forms with God atop the whole."[10]

In this view, nonhuman animals and all the other beings in the natural world are presumed not to have souls, free will, or the ability to reason and exercise rational thought. Lacking these "human" attributes entitles human beings, the argument goes, to treat all other species as property and denies them legal personhood. In theory, our present view of the natural world provides no room for natural entities themselves. Physical forces that support life, such as air, water, and land, are conceived in a legal sense as if they had no existence apart from the human legal rights that have been attached to them. Strangely, humans could destroy all vestiges of natural life without ever violating the constitutional provisions regarding the protection of property. According to the dominant Western paradigm, the present conception of property revolves around our use of it, not around its existence as an element of the universe in its own right. Nature, in short, has virtually no rights of its own in the present legal system.[11]

In the United States, the denigration of the natural world is deeply rooted in Christianity, in particular, in the Old Testament account of how the earth and human beings were created. According to the Bible, God created humans in his own image. This initial act explicitly elevated human beings above the rest of creation. Besides being fashioned in the Creator's image, humans were also, according to the Bible, given dominion over all living beings. But when Adam and Even disobeyed God in the Garden of Eden, that act of disobedience was "so profound that the whole creation suffers a cataclysmic moral fall and eventually only God himself can redeem humanity is his eyes."[12] God then clothed Adam and Eve in animal skins before banishing them from the Garden of Eden. As a result, they came to view the natural world as a hostile and alien environment, a place they hoped to flee from eventually, once they worked their way back into God's grace.[13] This biblical version retains a powerful hold on the ideology and behavioral patterns of many Americans, including federal and state policy makers.

Charles Darwin's path-breaking research on evolution, however, represented a profound challenge to the biblical account of creation. When he published *The Descent of Man* in 1871, a key tenet in his theory was that "human beings now knew that they were not the special creation of God, made in the divine image and set apart from the animals; on the contrary, human beings came to realize that they were animals themselves."[14] But even the arrival of Darwin's theory of evolution did not herald a positive sea change in attitude toward the dignity of the natural world, especially nonhuman animals. For as St. Pierre described it, "the use of non-human animals in vivisection placed those animals somewhere in a state of limbo. Modern science presumes that non-human animals are genetically similar enough to humans that experiments on them will help to predict human reaction. Yet it is also simultaneously posited that non-human animals are so different that they do not merit ethical consideration or legal protections."[15]

Status Without Standing

Despite the power of the ideological paradigm discussed above, there have been sporadic moments where nature and nonhuman animals received a measure of recognition—not of their inherent right to be, but at least, in the case of certain animals species, a recognition that they should not be treated abusively or cruelly. For example, in 1641 the Puritans of the Massachusetts Bay Colony introduced the first animal protection law in the nation. A section of Massachusetts Body of Liberties declared that "no man shall exercise any Tirrany or Crueltie towards any bruite Creature which are usuallie kept for man's use."[16] Notwithstanding the progressive nature of this legislation, the Puritans, as Steven M. Wise pointed out, never deviated from the Old Testament view that animals were "made subject to man by the creation... [and] were created for the beneficial use of mankind."[17]

Noted English political theorist John Locke, who had significant discussion about social contract theory, the state of nature, and property in his *Two Treatises of Government*, did not have much to say about animals or the natural world, for that matter, but since animals were viewed as being owned and therefore part of the property of their homeowners, this entitled them to at least a modicum of rights, according to his philosophy. But as Roderick Frazer Nash points out, those rights "derived from the rights of the owner, not the animal, and were otherwise related to human interests."[18]

In his 1693 work *Some Thoughts Concerning Education*, Locke raised an important point about animals that would later be echoed by Jeremy Bentham—the ability to suffer accords animals some moral status that should be respected by human beings.[19] Over the next century, anticruelty statutes were enacted throughout the United States, but courts generally assumed that these laws embraced the biblical view that human interests trumped nonhuman interests and that "their purpose was to protect human morals, not animal bodies."[20]

Along with anticruelty measures, several states and the federal government began to institute laws and policies aimed at protecting specific species. For example, several states enacted statutes that benefited fish and wildlife, and Congress, in 1870, asked President Grant to study why the nation's fisheries were in decline.[21] While certain species received the attention of advocates who sought to shield them from unbridled cruelty and extermination, the environment—the earth, air, water, and the various natural elements inhabiting the environment—only more gradually came to receive some limited attention and protection from policy makers.

In the first six decades of the Republic's existence, there was virtually no protection for the environment for the reasons discussed above, and because it was presumed that the country contained virtually unlimited natural resources. In fact, the establishment of the Department of the Interior in 1849, the Homestead Act of 1862, and the Mining Act of 1872 signaled that the federal government was more than willing to allow private parties to secure title to federal and tribal land, including the waters, minerals, and timber thereon.[22]

But even as these developments were taking place, the beginnings of a conservation movement was already under way as artists, writers, and others acknowledged the grandeur, diversity, and scale of the West and sought to influence lawmakers and jurists to protect the same. Thus, in 1872 Congress enacted legislation that established Yellowstone as the first national park; the Adirondacks were set aside by New York in 1885, and Yosemite was congressionally established in 1890. These were important actions, to be sure, but as Nash points out, each of these measures was enacted through "a very anthropocentrically defined national park ideal" and were set aside largely "for peoples' pleasure and for utilitarian purposes such as water and game supply."[23]

Even as federal and state lawmakers were setting aside land, several interest groups began to organize as part of a growing conservation movement. The Sierra Club was founded in 1892 by John Muir and others. In 1901, the American Scenic and Historic Preservation Society was created to protect nature and culture. And in 1905, the National Association of Audubon Societies for the Protection of Wild Birds and Animals was established by George B. Grinnell.[24]

The members of these groups were no doubt pleased when Theodore Roosevelt became president in 1901. He used his executive order power fifty-three times to establish national wildlife refuges and is credited, along with his chief forester, Gifford Pinchot, with having made conservation a central theme of Progressive politics.[25]

As important as these land preservations and species protections were, with conservationists having introduced into American social thinking the idea that nature and nonhuman animals have more than a commercial or economic use, they were still not able to go much deeper than to argue that the natural world has more than aesthetic or recreational value. While this mind-set is certainly more beneficial than a strictly economic or property understanding, it still did not entail "a profound philosophical or religious movement that recognized a value in natural entities themselves."[26] It was this inability to recognize and affirm the inherent dignity of nature that moved Aldo Leopold to draft his now classic work, *A Sand County Almanac*, in 1948.[27]

As Leopold put it in several choice passages: "We abuse land because we regard it as a commodity belonging to us. When we see land as a community to which we belong we may begin to use it with love and respect."[28] "That land is a community is the basic concept of ecology, but that land is to be loved and respected is an extension of ethics."[29] And in one of his more cited passages: "There is as yet no ethic dealing with man's relation to land and to the animals and plants which grow upon it. Land, like Odysseus' slave girls, is still property. The land-relation is still strictly economic, entailing privileges but not obligations."[30]

Following Leopold, Rachel Carson published her powerful exposé, *Silent Spring*, in 1962, which detailed how various plant- and insect-killing chemicals had contaminated great swaths of the environment and were wreaking profound harm to the natural world and many species of plant and animal life.[31] As she noted, "Future historians may well be amazed by our distorted sense of proportion. How could intelligent beings seek to control a few unwanted species by a method that contaminated the entire environment and brought the threat of disease and death even to their own kind? Yet this is precisely what we have done."[32]

Harking back to the land ethic that Leopold had discussed, Carson observed that "the earth's vegetation is part of a web of life in which there are intimate and sensual relations between plants and the earth, between plants and other plant's, between plants and animals. Sometimes we have no choice but to disturb these relationships, but we should do so thoughtfully, with full awareness that what we do may have consequences far remote in time and place."[33]

These studies and a burgeoning environmental movement compelled Congress to act, and in the 1960s a series of laws were written that began to pay heed to the profound distress the environment and various nonhuman species were under. For example, air pollution was addressed with the passage of the Clean Air Act in 1963.[34] In 1964, Congress enacted the Wilderness Act, which declared that areas so designated were to have their "primeval character" protected.[35] Also in 1964, Congress established the Land and Water Conservation Fund, which provided funding for state and federal land acquisitions.[36] And in 1965, Congress enacted the Solid Waste Disposal Act to address the burgeoning problem of waste disposal.[37]

Nature: Standing or Falling in the Courts

As the environmental movement gained traction throughout the nation in the 1960s and early 1970s, it was still grossly evident to those who worked in the conservation and environmental movements that nonhuman animals and other natural entities lacked legal personhood and could still be treated arbitrarily, capriciously, and even be destroyed by their "owners" without having their distinctive persona recognized in the courts. Natural beings and entities, unlike corporations, ships, municipalities, universities, infants, states, Subchapter R partnerships, joint ventures, and trusts, lacked legal "rights" under the law and therefore did not have "standing."[38] A party who seeks to "bring a claim must demonstrate that they are a proper individual to challenge the government action"—to seek judicial relief of their own accord.[39]

Nature's lack of standing and the need for that status to be dramatically altered was powerfully and eloquently raised by a young law professor, Christopher Stone, who took it upon himself to draft a law review essay in the fall of 1971, "Should Trees Have Standing? Toward Legal Rights for Natural Objects," in an effort to influence the Supreme Court justices who had been asked to review a US Court of Appeals for the Ninth Circuit decision, *Sierra Club v. Hickel*. In this case, the Sierra Club was challenging a US Forest Service–approved plan by Walt Disney Enterprises to build a $39 million resort, including restaurants, motels, and recreational facilities, in the Mineral King Valley of California, a largely pristine wilderness area in the Sierra Nevada mountains.

The Sierra Club, a leading conservation organization, vigorously opposed the resort's construction on the grounds that the Forest Service's approval of the plans violated several federal statutes and because the project would profoundly affect the area's esthetic and ecological balance.[40] Importantly, the Sierra Club did not claim that its members would be directly injured by the project. Rather, it used its status as a public interest group that had long fought to protect and preserve the natural world. The federal district court in California had sided with the Sierra Club but on appeal, the court of appeals reversed on the grounds that the Sierra Club's legal defense team had no standing to bring the question to the court.

Stone's essay entailed a nuanced and unique theoretical framework on the rights of nature that he hoped would influence the justices to think hard about the status of the Mineral King park itself. "Perhaps," he said,

> the injury to the Sierra Club was tenuous, but the injury to Mineral King—the park itself—wasn't. If the courts could be persuaded to think about the park itself as a jural person—the way corporations are "persons"—the notion of nature having rights would here make a significant operational difference...In other words, if standing were the barrier, why not designate Mineral King, the wilderness area, as the plaintiff "adversely affected," let the Sierra Club be characterized as the attorney or guardian for the area, and get on with the merits?[41]

Stone's pithy and novel analysis showed how many other minority groups, including women, had also once been considered outside the law. These groups—African Americans, Asian Americans, indigenous peoples, children, women, prisoners, aliens, fetuses, and others—had once been considered either subhuman or to have such different temperaments and values as to preclude them from exercising the same corpus of rights of white men. "The fact is," said Stone, "that each time there is a movement to confer rights onto some new 'entity,' the proposal is bound to sound odd or frightening or laughable. This is partly because until the rightless *thing* receives its rights, we cannot see it as anything but a *thing* for the use of 'us'—those who are holding rights at the same time."[42]

When the Supreme Court handed down its decision in *Sierra Club v. Morton*, the Sierra Club and Mineral King Valley had lost the case but had gained a moral victory of sorts. Three justices—Harry Blackmun, William J. Brennan, and William O. Douglas—thought highly of Stone's theory and, in fact, Justice Douglas, an environmentalist himself, began his dissent with a strong statement supporting Stone's theory:

> The critical question of "standing" would be simplified and also put neatly in focus if we...allowed environmental issues to be litigated... in the name of the inanimate object about to be despoiled, defaced,

or invaded…Contemporary public concern for protecting nature's ecological equilibrium should lead to the conferral of standing upon environmental objects to sue for their own preservation…This suit would
therefore be more properly labeled as *Mineral King v. Morton*.[43]

Stone's article received a significant amount of attention, both among
environmentalists and even some federal lawmakers—it was printed in the
Congressional Record by Senator Philip Hart of Michigan. In fact, there was
excitement "at the ease with which the justices had received the new theory
within the conceptual boundaries of the federal court system and the precepts
of Anglo-Saxon law."[44] But was Stone's theory and the Court's reaction so
revolutionary? What had previous jurists had to say about the natural world?

Judicial Efforts to Address Natural Entities

Earlier, we mentioned two laws: the Body of Liberties, enacted in 1641 by
the Puritans of Massachusetts Bay Colony, and a Maine statute in 1822,
both of which were anticruelty measures designed to accord animals a modicum of protection. The Maine law was the first act of its kind in the United
States.[45] Forty-four years later, in 1866, Henry Bergh, a New Yorker who
established the Animal Society for the Prevention of Cruelty to Animals
(ASPCA) in the United States, the first of its kind, secured the passage of a
similar anticruelty statute in the state legislature. This act outlawed cruelty
to both domesticated and wild animals.

Federal and state courts, however, were much slower in acknowledging the dignity of natural forces and nonhuman animals, particularly when
those entities were viewed as property containing valuable resources (for
example, gold) that were in high demand. An important Supreme Court
case affirming the superiority of a California miner's private rights involving
mineral resources and water was an 1879 decision, *Jennison v. Kirk*.[46] In this
case, the Court said that the Mining Law of 1866, which had declared "open
to exploration" the mineral lands of the public domain to citizens subject to
those regulations established by law and the local customs or rules of mines,
was a recognition by the federal government of its obligations "to respect
private rights which had grown up under its tacit consent and approval."[47] In
effect, the ditches, appropriated waters, and mining claims of the defendant,
Kirk, which predated the ditch built by the encroachers, plaintiff's testator
ditch, Jennison, were superior under the prior appropriation doctrine—first

in time, first in right—and Kirk had the right to destroy a portion of Jennison's ditch to eliminate the interference it was causing his operation.

Justice Stephen J. Field's opinion contained interesting, if largely mythical language, on the history and settlement of California by whites during the gold rush era, a history that ignored the genocide unleashed by the miners against the Natives and the environmental catastrophes that were heaped upon the land, rivers, and mountains by the miners. "The discovery of gold in California was followed," said Field,

> as is well known, by an immense immigration into the State...The lands in which the precious metals were found belonged to the United States... Into these mountains the emigrants in vast numbers penetrated...and probing the earth in all directions for the precious metals. Wherever they went, they carried with them that love of order and system and of fair dealing which are the prominent characteristics of our people.[48]

The Court, in essence, held that Congress, under the mining act had opted not to interfere with either "local laws, customs, and decisions" or to challenge the private property rights of the earliest mining settlers. Such a precedent set a stark tone for the natural world.

A few years later, the Colorado Supreme Court, in the case *Coffin v. The Left Hand Ditch Co.* (1882),[49] had opportunity to address why the prior appropriation system of water law[50] was more appropriate for Colorado than the riparian system,[51] which had developed in the eastern United States. Judge Joseph Church Helm, who wrote the opinion, elaborated as to why prior appropriation was the more logical system for the arid and semiarid state. "Water," said Helm, "in the various streams thus acquires a value unknown in moister climates. Instead of being a mere incident to the soil, it rises, when appropriated, to the dignity of a distinct usufructuary estate, or right of property."[52]

Echoing Locke's description of the importance of mixing one's labor to produce meaningful property, Helm went on to say that to "deny the doctrine of priority or superiority of right by priority of appropriation, and a great part of the value of all this property is at once destroyed."[53]

While all the western water sources were being dammed, ditched, and otherwise appropriated as the area was settled by Euro-Americans, nonhuman animals also began to receive the attention of jurists. In 1887, the Supreme

Judicial Court of Massachusetts was called upon to decide whether Elmer Turner, who had been tried and convicted of cruelty to animals for permitting a captive fox to be released and subsequently hunted down and killed by his dogs, had been wrongly convicted. Turner's attorney's argued that what he had done was not a punishable offense because, they said, "the common law warrants the hunting of ravenous beasts of prey, as badgers and foxes, because the destroying of such creatures is said to be profitable to the public."[54]

Judge Charles Allen, however, interpreted the 1869 state statute that provided that "every owner, possessor, or person having the charge or custody of an animal, who cruelly drives or works it when unfit for labor, or cruelly abandons it...in an unnecessarily cruel or inhuman manner, or knowingly and willfully authorizes or permits it to be subjected to unnecessary torturre, suffering, or cruelty of any kind, shall be punished," in a way that applied to both domesticated and wild animals in the "custody of man."[55]

While seemingly supportive of the captive fox's right to be protected from cruel treatment, Judge Allen's opinion contained other language much less beneficial to animals. Thus, the 1869 statute would not have applied to those foxes living in "their natural free condition," the word *animal* was said to include "all irrational beings," and most emphatically "the statute does not define an offense against the rights of property in animals, nor against the rights of the animal that are in a sense protected by it. *The offense is against the public morals*, which the commission of cruel and barbarous acts tend to corrupt."[56]

A year later, Mississippi's Supreme Court heard a case, *Stephen v. State*, involving hogs, that contained an even more elaborate, if related, description of the relationship between human beings and animals.[57] Stephen, a farmer, had shot and killed several of a neighbor's hogs that had gotten into his fields a second time and caused damage to his crops. He had been found guilty of a criminal offense at the trial level for having killed the hogs in violation of a statute that made it an offense to "cruelly beat, abuse, starve, torture, or purposefully injure, certain animals."[58]

The supreme court, however, overturned the lower court's decision on the grounds that Stephen's actions had not been "actuated by a spirit of cruelty, or a disposition to inflict unnecessary pain and suffering on the animals."[59] With the case settled, Judge Arnold, in dicta, then took the liberty to express his own views about the importance of protecting "dumb brutes" from cruel treatment. "Speaking for myself," said Arnold, "I wish to say that laws, and the enforcement or observance of laws, for the protection of dumb brutes from cruelty, are, in my judgment, among the best evidence of the justice and benevolence of men."[60] Those laws were not meant, he believed, to interfere with the "discipline and government of such animals, or place any unreasonable restriction on their use or the enjoyment to be derived from their possession."[61] Arnold matter of factly pointed out that the common law "recognized no rights in such animals, and punished no cruelty to them, except insofar as it affected the rights of individuals to such property."[62]

Finally, and building upon the biblical admonition to be good stewards of the earth and to act kindly to "inferior" beings, Arnold magnanimously intoned:

> Animals whose lives are devoted to our use and pleasure, and which are capable, perhaps, of feeling as great physical pain or pleasure as ourselves, deserve, for these considerations alone, kindly treatment. The dominion of man over them, if not a moral trust, has a better significance than the development of malignant passions and cruel instincts. Often their beauty, gentleness, and fidelity suggest the reflection that it may have been one of the purposes of their creation and subordination to enlarge the sympathies and expand the better feelings of our race. But, however this may be, human beings should be kind and just to dumb brutes; if for no other reason than to learn how to be kind and just to each other.[63]

Hunt v. State, handed down in 1892, continued this line of tests for state anticruelty statutes for animals—this time in Indiana.[64] In this case, one Arthur Hunt had killed a dog owned by Clinton Bicknell. Hunt said Bicknell's dog had killed several of his sheep. Hunt had been tried and convicted in circuit court of violating the state's anticruelty statute, and he appealed his conviction.

Appellate judge Edgar Crumpacker expressed support for the state's anticruelty law by emphasizing that it had been created "to inculcate a humane regard for the rights and feelings of the brute creation by reproving the evil and indifferent tendencies in human nature in its intercourse with animals."[65] However, the law was not intended to "limit man's proper dominion 'over the fish of the sea, and over the fowl of the air, and over every living thing that moveth upon the earth.'"[66]

In other words, while unjustified infliction of pain on animals had been tempered by anticruelty laws, Judge Crumpacker found justification where it had nearly always been found—protection of person or property. As he noted: "if one destroys the life of an animal for the honest purpose of protecting his person or property, and the circumstances are of such a character as to reasonably justify the belief that the measure is necessary to that end, the act would not be in violation of the statute under consideration, though it turned out that the apprehensions were in fact groundless and the destruction of life not necessary."[67]

In fact, the appellate court could only find one justification that might lead to a conviction under the law—the human culprit would have to be found acting with a "malevolent purpose or a spirit of wickedness or cruel wantonness, or a reckless disregards of the rights and feelings of the brute creation."[68] Stephen Wise says that proving malevolency, cruelty, or reckless disregard has never been easy, and as a result humans can justify to themselves virtually everything they do to animals, leaving them without genuine recognition of their own inherent right to a dignified life.[69]

In 1896, the question of game ownership came before the US Supreme Court in *Geer v. Connecticut*.[70] Here, Geer, who had lawfully killed several birds during the open season, sought to transport the animals outside the state's territorial limits in violation of a state law. The question before the Court was whether it was legal under the US Constitution's commerce clause for the state to not allow properly killed wild game to be transported beyond the state's borders.[71]

Drawing upon both Athenian and Roman law, Justice Edward D. White declared that "from the earliest traditions the right to reduce animals *ferae naturae* [of a wild nature or disposition] to possession has been subject to the control of the law-giving power." In other words, since wild animals had no owner per se, they were "considered as belonging in common to all the citizens of the State."[72] Thus, White concluded, the state's police power allowed it to regulate wild game as "property" because such animals constituted "a food supply" that belonged in common to all the people in the state. The doctrine of state ownership of wild animals established in *Geer* remained a fixture of judicial precedent until it was explicitly overruled in 1979 by *Hughes v. Oklahoma*, which held that this doctrine was a legal fiction that had outlived its usefulness.[73]

While the US Supreme Court in *Geer* was recognizing in states a police power to regulate the ownership of wild game as the food supply of all citizens, the Supreme Court of Louisiana in *State v. Karstendiek* remarkably adopted a much more liberal approach to animals, acknowledging in them a measure of rights.[74] In upholding the convictions of two men for abusing animals under a city council anticruelty ordinance, the court said that the city's statute "relating to animals is based on 'the theory, unknown to the common law, *that animals have rights*, which, like those of human beings, are to be protected.'"[75] Animal rights, according to the statute, were akin to children's rights vis-à-vis their parents. "A horse," it was stated, "under its master's hands, stands in a relation to the master analogous to that of a child to a parent."[76] Arguing from that novel basis, Judge Breau stated that the city's ordinance in no way interfered with the "private right of property," as Karstendiek had urged. The stunning use of the term "animal rights" has been referenced several times by commentators who consider it one of the earliest state judicial mentions of such right,s[77] and it has been cited once and mentioned in numerous state court rulings.[78]

As positive as *Karstendiek* was in its recognition of a measure of rights for animals, a city magistrate's court in New York in 1911 returned to the more common understanding of animals without any rights in yet another cruelty case.[79] In *People ex. rel. Freel v. Downs*, the court was called to hear a case in which two men, Cleveland Downs and Walter Smith, had transported sixty-five green turtles from Cuba in conditions that Thomas Freel, the superintendent of the ASPCA, had alleged amounted to torture for the turtles.

Judge Freschi heard the case and noted that the first order of business was deciding whether turtles were animals under the penal law of the city. That law stated that "the word 'animal,' as used in this article, does not include the human race, but includes every other living creature."[80] Freschi found this definition "far-fetched and somewhat strange," not because human beings were exempted from the meaning, but because he thought it far too broad. Still, he acknowledged that he was bound by the definition and therefore had to hold that turtles were, indeed, animals.

He next had to ascertain whether or not the turtles' treatment constituted torture, which the penal code had defined as "every act, omission, or neglect whereby unjustifiable physical pain, suffering or death is caused or permitted."[81] Freschi answered this in the negative and went so far as to say that "certain physical pain may be necessary and justifiable in some cases."[82] The judge rationalized such treatment by invoking biblical language that humans had been given "'dominion over the fish of the sea, over the fowls of the air and the beasts, and the whole earth and every creeping creature that moveth upon the earth.'"[83] "Man," said Freschi unsurprisingly, "is superior to animals, and some of them he uses for food and is permitted to slaughter them. Many are the means he employs for such purposes, and in such cases the incidental pain and suffering is treated as necessary and justifiable."[84]

Anticruelty cases involving nonhuman animals, as we have seen, occupied more of the state and federal court's interest than the broader issue of whether or not animals, rivers, trees, or other natural entities had standing to sue of their own accord. It was not until the 1960s that the paradigm of nonstanding for nonhuman beings began to be challenged with a modicum of success. In fact, Christopher Stone pointed to a 1965 Second Circuit Federal Appellate decision, *Scenic Hudson Preservation Conference v. Federal Power Commission*,[85] as one of the cases that evidenced a "marked liberalization of traditional standing requirements."[86]

In this case, the Federal Power Commission had granted Consolidated Edison, a New York–based power company, a license to build a pumped storage hydroelectric project on the west side of the Hudson River, at Storm King Mountain, near Cornwall, New York. The issuance of that license had been vigorously challenged by several conservation groups and several towns on the grounds that the transmission lines and facilities would decrease the value of publicly held land, reduce tax revenue, adversely affect the unique beauty and historical significance of the area, harm the spawning grounds of the Hudson River striped bass, and cause severe environmental problems for other species as well.

Despite the claim that the Scenic Hudson Preservation Conference, an alliance of two conservation groups, had no standing to sue because it had not made the traditional claim of "a personal economic interest," the petitioners were heard and the case was sent back to the commission.[87] With regard to standing, Circuit Judge Hays, having moved beyond the economic injury argument, noted that section 313 (b) of the Federal Power Act provided a right of instituting review to any party including "those who by their activities and conduct have established a special interest" in areas of "aesthetic, conservational, and recreational" importance.[88] Hays thus rejected the Federal Power Commission's licensing order and remanded the case because it had not established a compelling rationale for the project, because it had failed to provide any alternatives, and because any future projects would have to include studies on how to preserve the natural beauty of the area and the historic shrines, and properly address the fisheries issue.[89]

Earlier in the chapter we discussed the Supreme Court's important *Sierra Club v. Morton* case, which had precipitated Christopher Stone's searching essay "Should Trees Have Standing?"[90] And while Stone's argument had been warmly endorsed by Justice Douglas in his dissent, it was unclear what, if any, impact the Douglas dissent would have on the future as the environmental and animal rights movements intensified their efforts to gain substantive respect and understanding for the rights of nature. Their efforts began to bear fruit, particularly in the 1970s with the enactment of various congressional statutes like the Clean Air Act (1970), the National Environmental Policy Act (1970), the Federal Water Pollution Control Amendments (now known as the Clean Water Act, 1972), the Federal Insecticide, Fungicide, and Rodenticide Act (1972), the Endangered Species Act (1973), the Safe Drinking Water Act (1973), the Resource Conservation and Recovery Act (1976), the Toxic Substances Control Act (1976), the Surface Mining Control and Reclamation Act (1977), the Federal Land Policy Management Act (1976), and the National Energy Act (1978).

Each of these acts addressed specific elements of the natural world in a way intended to have positive environmental and human consequences. The courts were also called upon to resolve various environmental and nonhuman species conflicts. In *Cappaert v. United States* (1970), a water law case that also involved a rare species of fish, the Devil's Hole pupfish, the Supreme Court emphasized that the federal government had a superior interest in water law, especially when Congress had acted by setting aside land at a particular site, in this case the Devil's Hole, Death Valley National Monument.[91] Within Devil's Hole is a pool of water, home to the pupfish, which are located nowhere else in the world.

The Cappaerts, a ranching family, had been pumping groundwater from the pool to aid their livestock. But in so doing, they had reduced the pool's water level to a degree that endangered the pupfish. Rather than focus on the rights of the pupfish, the Supreme Court, via Chief Justice Warren E. Burger, said that the question presented was whether "the reservation of Devil's Hole as a national monument reserved federal water rights in appropriated water."[92] The Court unanimously held that the presidential proclamation establishing the site as a national monument effectively reserved the necessary underground water to fulfill the purpose of the reservation—one purpose of which included preserving the pool and the pupfish residing therein.[93]

In 1976, John Lilly, an advocate of dolphins and other cetaceans, adopted Stone's thesis on legal rights for nonhuman entities and declared in a manifesto that "individual dolphins and whales are to be given the legal rights of human individuals. Human individuals and groups are to be given the right to sue in behalf of…cetacean individuals placed in jeopardy by other humans."[94]

In 1978, another small fish species, the endangered snail darter, was in the news. This time the fish species was confronted by a more formidable foe, the Tennessee Valley Authority (TVA), a public-owned corporation of the United States. The TVA had begun constructing the Tellico Dam and Reservoir Project in 1967 on the Little Tennessee River after Congress had appropriated funds for its construction. The Tellico Project was a "multipurpose regional development project designed principally to stimulate shoreline development, generate sufficient electric current to heat 20,000 homes, and provide flatwater recreation and flood control."[95]

After the project was well under way, Congress, in 1973, enacted the Endangered Species Act (ESA), and in 1975 the recently discovered snail darter—which lived in the Little Tennessee River—was added to the list of endangered species. Section 7 of the ESA titled, "Interagency Cooperation," compels consultation to ensure that agency actions do not jeopardize any endangered species. Several environmental groups then filed a lawsuit to prevent completion of the $116 million dam.

When the case, *Tennnessee Valley Authority v. Hull* was heard in the Supreme Court in the spring of 1978, a 6–3 majority, led by Chief Justice Burger, accepted the environmentalists' argument that the completion of the massive dam project would, indeed, threaten the newly classified snail darter fish and granted the injunction. The chief justice declared that

> it may seem curious to some that the survival of a relatively small number of three-inch fish among all the countless millions of species extant would require a permanent halting of a virtually completed dam for which Congress has expended more than $100 million. The paradox is not minimized by the fact that Congress continued to appropriate large sums of public money for the project, even after congressional Appropriations Committees were apprised of its apparent impact upon

the survival of the snail darter. We conclude, however, that the explicit provisions of the ESA required precisely that result.[96]

The Court majority made a point of observing that the ESA was the most comprehensive legislation adopted by any nation for endangered species since it aimed to protect not only the threatened species but their ecosystems as well.

The three dissenting justices—Lewis F. Powell, Blackmun, and William Rehnquist—seemed stunned at their colleagues' opinion and thought this "absurd result"—stopping construction of a nearly completed dam—made no sense as it violated the canons of statutory construction.[97] In a statement that anticipated Congress's response, Justice Powell expressed the view that Congress would need to amend the ESA to prevent the consequences made likely by this decision, namely that there would be "little sentiment to leave this dam standing before an empty reservoir, serving no purpose other than a conversation piece for incredulous tourists."[98]

Not long after the decision, Congress did act to amend the ESA. The amendment, introduced by Representative John Duncan of Tennessee, created a process, via a seven-member committee of federal officials, that could grant exemptions to the requirement to protect threatened species where doing so would clash with required economic interests. This "God committee's" first action was a ruling that led to an exemption of the Tellico Dam from the ESA's provisions.[99] Once again, in balancing the interests of a nonhuman species—the snail darter—against state government, economic, and public interests, the nonhuman species suffered, even when Congress, at least initially, and the Court said otherwise.

A year later, and for the first time in US legal history, a nonhuman species, a six-inch finch-billed bird, the palila (*Psittirostra bailleui*), an endangered species found only in Hawaii, became a plaintiff in a federal court and standing was granted.[100] The palila was not the only plaintiff, however. The other plaintiffs included the Sierra Club, the National Audubon Society (NAS), the Hawaiian branch of the NAS, and Alan C. Ziegler, who were suing as "next friends and on their own behalf."

This case and a series of subsequent cases through the 1990s, brought in the interest and often the name of various nonhuman species, signaled an important recognition of the standing status of these species.[101] Importantly, the fact that human plaintiffs were also involved shows that the attorneys remained nervous because, according to Stone's theory, they were covering their bets "with one or more conventional plaintiffs whose standing is less vulnerable to challenge. As a consequence, the species' standing in its own right has usually gone unchallenged by the defendant and not dwelt upon by the court."[102]

Standing was granted to each of the species in the federal court cases with one important exception, *Hawaiian Crow v. Lujan* (1991).[103] In this case, the 'alala, an endangered bird native to Hawaii, and several environmental groups filed suit against the Secretary of Interior and the Director of the Fish & Wildlife Service under the ESA, alleging that the federal officials had failed to protect the bird by not implementing a recovery plan to save it from extinction.

The first question addressed by Judge David Ezra was whether the 'alala was a proper plaintiff with standing to sue. Under the ESA, enforcement suits can be filed by any person, which is defined as "an individual, corporation, partnership, trust, association, or any other private entity." The defendants argued that under this definition, the 'alala was not a person under the ESA. The environmental groups also had to concede that "no court has addressed expressly whether an animal may constitute a 'person' within the meaning of the ESA's citizen suit provisions," although they pointed out that in several recent cases animals had appeared as identifiable parties.[104]

After reviewing these cases, Judge Ezra concluded that he could find no language in the ESA that authorized the 'alala to sue. "The 'Alala," he went on, "is clearly neither a 'person'…nor an infant or incompetent person."[105] The judge thus granted the defendant's motion to dismiss the 'alala as a plaintiff, and the bird's name was deleted from the caption of the case. Interestingly, while the court also concluded that although the environmental groups attorneys had cited no case law supporting the 'alala's right to appear as a normal plaintiff, it was also held that there was "no evidence plaintiffs named the 'Alala for an improper purpose."[106]

The denial of standing for the 'alala was a stark reminder of how fragile animal status remained under the law. But in 1994, in *Marbled Murrelet v. Pacific Lumber Co.*,[107] another federal district court approvingly cited the *Palila* ruling and held that the marbled murrelet, an endangered seabird living along the Pacific Coast, did, in fact, have standing to sue "in its own right."[108]

Contemporary Judicial Thoughts on the Natural World
While the Supreme Court has yet to definitively address the issue of standing for animals or natural entities, since 2000 it has handed down several important rulings that ambivalently address critical environmental issues.

In 2001, in *Whitman v. American Trucking Associations, Inc.*, the Supreme Court unanimously rejected the efforts by the US Chamber of Commerce and the American Trucking Associations to weaken the 1970 Clean Air Act.[109] The Court, in an opinion written by Justice Antonin Scalia, ruled on two major issues. First, that the EPA in establishing national air quality standards must consider only the requirements of public health and safety and may not use the cost-benefit analysis that the industry groups tried to import into the statute. Second, the Court declared that the EPA's broad authority to create standards for two pollutants—ground-level ozone (which causes smog) and fine airborne particles (also known as soot)—did not amount to an unconstitutional delegation by Congress of legislative power to an executive agency.[110]

The delegation and cost-benefit issues were both significant and all related, but it was the cost-benefit topic that appeared to be decisive to the justices. The industry groups urged that the EPA should have taken economic factors into account in establishing new air quality standards in 1997. But as Scalia noted, "the EPA…is to identify the maximum airborne concentration of a pollutant that the public health can tolerate, decrease the concentration to provide an 'adequate' margin of safety, and set the standard at that level. *Nowhere are the costs of achieving such a standard made part of that initial calculation.*"[111]

In 2007, the EPA was once again front and center before the Supreme Court. But unlike in the *Whitman* case, the EPA, having now been led by President Bush's appointees for seven years, had generally adopted anti-environment positions that typically favored business and corporate interests over natural interests, including the dismantling of various environmental and regulatory safeguards (lobbied to weaken the Clean Air Act, for example), and largely ignored global warming concerns expressed by the scientific and environmental communities (pulled the United States out of the Kyoto environmental agreement, for example).[112]

In *Massachusetts v. Environmental Protection Agency*, the EPA, which had abandoned its mandate under the Clean Air Act to regulate the emission of four greenhouse gases, including carbon dioxide, supported by ten states (Alaska, Idaho, Kansas, Michigan, Nebraska, North Dakota, Ohio, South Dakota, Texas, and Utah) and six large trade associations, was challenged by twelve states (including California), a number of local governments, and several environmental organizations, who urged the Court to remind the

EPA that it did, indeed, have the authority to regulate heat-trapping gases in automobile emissions.[113]

In a closely monitored 5–4 decision, the Court said that the Clean Air Act authorized the EPA to regulate greenhouse gases and that the only way the agency could avoid taking action was if it could provide a scientific basis for its refusal to act. The decision was a powerful rebuke of the Bush administration, which had argued that it lacked the authority to regulate harmful gas emissions under the Clean Air Act.[114]

Justice John P. Stevens, writing for the majority, graphically began his opinion by saying, "a well-documented rise in global temperatures has coincided with a significant increase in the concentration of carbon dioxide in the atmosphere."[115] He then carefully, yet sternly, dismantled the EPA's position on why it had chosen not to act. "The EPA," said Stevens, "has refused to comply with this [Clean Air Act] statutory command. Instead, it offered a laundry list of reasons not to regulate."[116] None of the agency's rationale amounted to a "reasoned explanation for its refusal to decide whether greenhouse gases cause or contribute to climate change," and therefore the agency's action was "arbitrary, capricious,…or otherwise not in accordance with law."[117]

Interestingly, the dissent, written by Chief Justice John Roberts, joined by the three archconservatives, Scalia, Clarence Thomas, and Samuel Alito, focused completely on the lack of standing of those who had initiated the suit—states, cities, and environmental groups. This, as Linda Greenhouse pointed out, was the issue on which the broad coalition of forces had appeared most vulnerable, given the recent cases where the Court has increasingly raised the barrier to standing, particularly in the area of environmental cases.[118] While acknowledging that global warming "may" be a "crisis," Roberts argued that the petitioners' challenges were "nonjusticiable." He said that the redress for grievances such as those alleged by the coalition was the province of the political branches and not the courts.

Two 2008 rulings, *Exxon Shipping v. Baker*[119] and *Winter v. Council of Natural Resources Defense Council*,[120] further signaled that the apparent improvements that had been taking place in the judiciary insofar as nonhuman animals and the natural world were concerned were more illusory than real. In the *Exxon Shipping* case, the long legal battle that dated to 1989, when the *Exxon Valdez*, an oil supertanker, collided with a reef in the Prince William Sound in Alaska, spilling more than eleven million gallons of crude oil into that pristine area's waters, came to a dramatic conclusion.

In the wake of the spill, vast ecological carnage was unleashed: pollution of 1,300 miles of shoreline; profound disruption of the lives of thousands of people, including many Alaska Natives; and the deaths of hundreds of thousands of birds and other animals, all caused by the incompetent actions of the tanker's drunken captain, Joseph Hazelwood. Exxon Mobile Corporation spent some $2.1 billion for cleanup efforts, pled guilty to criminal violations (violating, for example, the Clean Water Act, Refuse Act, and the Migratory Bird Treaty Act), and was fined $150 million, later reduced to $25 million, plus restitution of $100 million. The company settled a civil action by the United States and Alaska for environmental harms for approximately $900 million, and it paid out $303 million in voluntary payments to property owners, fishermen, and private parties.[121]

The remaining civil cases were consolidated into the present one that had been filed against Exxon, Hazelwood, and others by Grant Baker and other respondents—including Alaska Natives, commercial fishermen, and landowners—who sought to recover for the massive economic losses they had sustained due to the severe ecological damage to Prince William Sound. A three-phase district trial ensued. In phase one, the jury found Hazelwood and Exxon "reckless" and thus potentially liable for punitive damages. In phase 2, the jury awarded $287 million in compensatory damages to the commercial fishermen. After the court took account for what had already been paid out in the form of settlements, released claims, and other payments, the balance was a little over $19 million. The majority of Alaska Native compensatory claims were settled for $20 million. And in phase 3, the jury awarded $5,000 in punitive damages against Hazelwood and $5 billion against Exxon.[122] On appeal, the US Court of Appeals for the Ninth Circuit upheld the phase one verdict, but reduced the punitive damages against Exxon to $2.5 billion.

The Supreme Court, in a 5–3 decision written by Justice David Souter, went even further than the Ninth Circuit and reduced the $5 billion in punitive damages against Exxon to a little more than $506 million, holding that the punitive damages were "excessive as a matter of maritime common law."[123] In Souter's opinion, a punitive-to-compensatory ratio of 1:1 was appropriate in this case, and since Exxon had already paid out about $507 million as compensation to the 32,000 affected parties, it should not have to pay more in punitive damages.

Justices Stevens, Ruth Bader Ginsburg, and Stephen Breyer each wrote separate dissents. Stevens said that empirical judgments in maritime law should be left to Congress, and quoting from *Maragne v. States Marine Lines, Inc.* (1970),[124] he noted that he would abide by the principle that "it better becomes the humane and liberal character of proceedings in admiralty to give than to withhold the remedy, when not required to withhold it by established and inflexible rules."[125]

Justice Ginsburg was more forceful in her dissent. As she acerbically noted, "assuming a problem in need of solution, the Court's lawmaking prompts many questions. The 1:1 ratio is good for this case, the Court believes, because Exxon's conduct ranked on the low end of the blameworthiness scale: Exxon was not seeking 'to augment profit,' nor did it act 'with a purpose to injure.'" She continued, and pointed out the fundamental flaw in the Court's decision-making calculus: "What ratio will the Court set for defendants who acted maliciously or in pursuit of financial gain?...Should the magnitude of the risk increase the ratio and, if so, by how much?"[126]

The Court's decision was greeted with frustration, anger, and disbelief by many of the local communities and fishermen. Garland Blanchard, a third-generation fisherman who had hoped to get $1.2 million in the settlement, said he now expected less than $100,000. "This decision," he angrily declared, "is a giant cold slap in the face."[127]

In the wake of 2010's BP oil gusher in the Gulf of Mexico, the largest spillage of oil into marine waters in US history—nearly five million barrels poured into the Gulf between April 20 and July 15—it will be interesting to see how BP and the federal government carry out the cleanup responsibilities.[128]

Five months after the *Exxon* case, in a suit pitting US military interests against marine mammals and their human advocates, the Supreme Court sided with the military. In *Winter v. Natural Resources Defense Council* (2008), the Court held, in a 5–4 decision written by Chief Justice Roberts, that the navy's submarine training exercises that required the use of midfrequency sonar outweighed the "possible injury" to an "unknown number" of marine mammal species identified by the environmental groups, led by the Natural Resources Defense Council, Jean-Michel Cousteau, and others.[129]

But the possible injuries Roberts mentioned were anything but possible. As Justice Ginsburg stated in her vigorous dissent, "the Navy's own EA [environmental assessment] predicted substantial and irreparable harm to marine mammals. Sonar is linked to mass strandings of marine mammals, hemorrhaging around the brain and ears, acute spongiotic changes in the central nervous system, and lesions in vital organs."[130] Moreover, she drew from the Ninth Circuit's decision and noted that the EA also predicted that the navy's use of this sonar in its Southern California training exercises would "result in 564 instances of physical injury including permanent hearing loss (Level A harassment) and nearly 170,000 behavioral disturbances (Level B harassment), more than 8,000 of which would also involve temporary hearing loss."[131]

Ginsburg unquestionably believed that the navy's actions violated the National Environmental Policy Act of 1969, which called for a thorough environmental impact statement to be conducted by any agency embarking on actions that would impact the environment. Such a statement was required so that environmental concerns were properly integrated into decision making, and one of those concerns included "potential mitigation measures and alternatives to the proposed course of action."[132]

Roberts, however, gave great deference to the navy's position and decided that "forcing the Navy to deploy an inadequately trained antisubmarine force jeopardizes the safety of the fleet" since active sonar is the most reliable technology for identifying enemy submarines.[133] He said that while national security needs were paramount in this case, "military interests do not always trump other considerations," though in this instance there was no question which interest should rule the day—the navy's right to employ sonar clearly trumped the thirty-seven species of marine mammals that would be adversely affected by the same.

In April 2010, in *US v. Stevens*, a decision that focused on animal cruelty videos, the Court, in an 8–1 ruling, invalidated a 1999 federal law that made it a crime to create, sell, or possess dogfight videos and other depictions of animal cruelty as overly broad on First Amendment grounds.[134] Congress had enacted the Depiction of Animal Cruelty Act in December of 1999.[135] It criminalized the interstate trafficking of "crush" videos, in which "a living animal is intentionally maimed, mutilated, tortured, wounded, or killed," if that conduct is illegal under state or federal law where the creation or sale takes place. And anyone engaged in generating, selling, or possessing such depictions for purposes of commercial gain could be fined or imprisoned for up to five years or both. Several exceptions were, however, authorized: depictions for religious, scientific, political, educational, or artistic value were allowed.

Robert Stevens had been indicted for selling dogfighting videos. He was convicted in district court, but on appeal, the Third Circuit in 2008 overturned his conviction and declared the 1999 law to be unconstitutional, holding that the act violated Stevens's First Amendment rights and that the government did not have a compelling interest in preventing such animal cruelty acts.

Chief Justice Roberts, writing for an 8–1 majority, affirmed the Third Circuit's decision. The high court found that the 1999 statute was invalid under the First Amendment's free speech clause. In his dissent, Justice Alito, echoing the views of the Humane Society, which had filed a vigorous amicus brief, said that his colleagues, by striking down the law on free speech grounds, had misunderstood Congress's intent. Congress, Alito opined, had sought to prevent horrific acts of animal cruelty, what he saw as "a form of depraved entertainment" that lacked any redeeming value.

Within two months of this decision, Congress responded by introducing several bills that were more narrowly focused, like the Prevention of Interstate Commerce in Animal Crush Videos Act of 2010 (HR 5566), that assert the government's compelling interest in preventing animal cruelty by stymying the creation and sale of crush videos for economic purposes.

Nature, and all the nonhuman species and entities—waters, mountains, space—that constitute the broader natural world we necessarily depend upon for our very existence, continues to bear the brunt of human actions, fueled by attitudes and ideologies that far too often disregard, severely minimize, or distort the integrity of natural beings. And while there have been some important recognitions of the rights and standing of some nonhuman species at certain historical junctures, the data analyzed in this chapter confirms that in the United States, neither the federal or state governments nor, in particular, the courts of those two polities have been willing to consistently consider the essential integrity of the vast majority of nonhuman species in a way that would fundamentally alter the existing hierarchy that still situates human beings and their interests on a level superior to that of all other living and natural beings.

The fact that national policy makers overseeing natural resources on public lands rely on a "multiple use" paradigm in which "federal officials seek to balance the contemporary demands of ranchers and farmers, timber and mining companies, fishers, hunters, hikers, and other recreational users" does not bode well for the natural world, as the marine mammals learned in the 2008 *Winter* case.[136]

The multiple-use policy paradigm as it affects nature under the rubric of public lands is then compounded when private property owners chime in, asserting that animal rights interests and environmental regulations that negatively impact their property are unfair and wrongly target them in ways, they argue, that violate their Fifth Amendment constitutional rights. Finally, the increasingly catastrophic effects of global warming, deforestation, pollution, and related issues add both an urgency and an uncertainty to the natural world and the human beings who continue to act in generally discordant ways with the environment.

As evidence of this, environmental groups, such as the Earth Liberation Front (ELF) and the Animal Liberation Front (ALF), have begun taking a much more vigorous position in defense of animals and the environment, sometimes resulting in violent acts and demonstrations intent on drawing attention to forests, river systems, and the horrific conditions that farm animals, research animals, and other beings endure at the hands of various scientific firms that conduct animal research and businesses that have relationships with such firms, like banks, insurance companies, pharmaceutical businesses, and universities. Their activities led the Committee on the Judiciary in the House of Representatives to hold hearings in 2006 on a bill, HR 4239, the Animal Enterprise Terrorism Act, that had been introduced in the fall of 2005 by several congressmen. The lead sponsor was Representative Petri of Wisconsin.

The Animal Enterprise Terrorism Act was introduced to address what its sponsors called "a growing threat commonly referred to as ecoterrorism." Representative Howard Coble of North Carolina, who conducted the hearing, began the day's proceedings by quoting from professor Tom O'Connor, who teaches a course on the various types of terrorism. O'Connor said that "ecoterrorism involves extremist views on environmental issues and animal rights, and is a fringe-issue form of terrorism aimed primarily at inflicting economic damage on those seen as profiting from the destruction and exploitation of the environment." The professor sought to distinguish between the general environmentalist community and the "more extreme ecoterrorists" by declaring that "environmentalists work within the system for preservation, and ecoterrorists seem to want to destroy civilization as we know it in order to save the planet."[137]

The legislation, according to Representative Coble, was designed to prohibit the intentional damaging of property of a person or entity "having a connection to, relationship with or transactions with an animal enterprise, and make it a criminal act to intentionally place a person in reasonable fear of death or serious bodily injury to that person or his or her family because of his or her relationship with the animal enterprise."[138] There was immediate concern expressed by a number of environmental groups who feared that their First Amendment rights might be violated for engaging in otherwise lawful protests, such as boycotts and the like. They worried that they, too, might be labeled as ecoterrorists and wanted to ensure that this did not take place.

Congress moved forward quickly and enacted the Animal Enterprise Terrorism Act on November 27, 2006.[139] The act gives the Department of Justice the authority to apprehend, prosecute, and convict any individuals or organizations who engaged in "animal enterprise terror." Since the act's passage, various individuals have been arrested, tried, and convicted for having violated its tenets. But there is increasing concern among many in the environmental movement that the act's provisions and particularly the term *terrorist* are being expanded and applied to individuals and organizations in ways that grossly exceed the need.

As Caroline Paul pointed out in the article "Does the 'Terrorist' Label Fit the Crime?" in the *Los Angeles Times*, the federal government now defines *terrorism* so broadly, especially when so-called terroristic acts are committed by the members of so-called ecoterrorist groups like ELF or ALF, that it even encompasses property damage. The fact that the Federal Bureau of Investigation considers ELF and ALF to be the "No. 1 domestic terrorist threat" is a stark reminder of how far the government is willing to go to ensure that groups who advocate for animals and the natural world—groups that have never hurt or intended to hurt a single human being—are kept under harsh and intimidating control.[140]

CHAPTER 12
Expanding the Legal Universe

WE HAVE SUGGESTED THROUGHOUT THIS WORK that the philosophical framework within which the social contract ideas originated was never rigorously or comprehensively developed so that, had it been properly understood, much of the conflict of the past 225 years might have been avoided. We need but return to the original proposition of the individual and primordial nature to test this idea. The problem originates in the failure to give careful consideration to the manner in which a person creates property. The social contract theorists, determined to find the philosophical basis for protecting property, did not properly examine the process of reducing nature to the useful and valuable thing upon which the organization of human society could be built.

Let us return to the aboriginal Garden of Eden, an ordinary meadow, perhaps, and parade a number of persons through it, observing how they might appropriate nature and what use they could make of it. The first character is an indigenous person who sees the animals and plants exemplifying the cycle of life. She observes that the land is fruitful and can provide sustenance forever if it is not disturbed unsustainably. So that person makes their home there, careful not to disrupt nature's balance. That person has appropriated the meadow and made it her property.

A farmer looks at the same meadow and sees dozens of small family farms, a church, and a town with a square and stately courthouse. That person marks off part of the land and begins building a farm, fencing in that portion of the meadow that he can best use and encouraging his neighbors to do likewise. In no time there is a small, rural, Rockwellian American village where once there was only a fruitful natural meadow. The farmer has also created property.

Next, a land developer discovers the meadow. That individual imagines a large city with tall buildings, good transportation facilities, and cultural and business centers with a well-endowed financial district. When that person begins to fulfill this vision, surveying blocks and encouraging large industries to settle there, she has also made an appropriation and created property.

The secretary of defense and his Pentagon colleagues drive by the meadow. They are impressed by its isolation. No one knows that the meadow exists, making it a perfect spot for a missile complex. They return to Congress, obtain funds to purchase the meadow, and build a massive intercontinental missile base. They, too, have also appropriated nature and created property.

The meadow, or nature, cannot itself change. Each person sees the meadow in unique ways because they are different individuals with radically different views of the world. They consequently create different kinds of property that have value in different social contexts. But each value can be used as the basis of a social contract. All uses have value only within a particular social context, however. No particular use is necessarily better than any other because each use has an essential relationship to a human society and is acceptable to that society. John Locke, Baron de Montesquieu, Thomas Hobbes, and the constitutional creators failed to credit human genius for the role it plays in the creation of property. The real property of the social contract is the genius of human personality, the creative realm of possibilities existing in the minds of individuals, not the product of their labors.

It is no accident that when Charles Reich focused on the modern problem of person and property, he perceived that property was not a tangible product but a particular set of relationships that produced value and income. Property, in his contemporary formulation of the concept, is the license granted by the state to perform certain services for society. The license is recognition of the capacity of the person to perform valuable acts; only secondarily is it an admission that the person owns physical property. The primary function of property, in Reich's view, was to draw "a circle around the activities of each private individual or organization. Within that circle, the owner has a greater degree of freedom than without. Outside, he must justify or explain his actions, and show his authority. Within, he is master, and the state must explain and justify any interference."[1] Reich implied that the person was ultimately described in terms of the status of his property. When property is defined as a relationship that produces an income, determining eligibility for that income becomes an ethical matter affecting the person since the image of the individual must be recast in morally and politically acceptable terms to those in government who confirm and guarantee the income.

Constitutional law, despite its initial commitment to protect tangible physical property and not persons, has incrementally moved toward the view that property is a function of person and personality. We had already recognized the product of personality as property when we devised copyright and trademark laws. In composing a tune, painting a picture, developing a manufacturing process, creating a computer program, or advertising a product, we are taking the nonphysical aspects of nature, its sounds, shapes, and energies, to create property. We provide legal protection for the product, thereby securing an income to the individual who has arranged these natural things in a specific and valuable way. We recognize that individual's appropriation of nature and confirm the value of that person's work. Even instruments of business, including stocks, bonds, and options, are predicated upon a kind of nonphysical arrangement of future possibilities that depend upon the regularity of nature for their value. While the Constitution's creators may have believed that property was physical, subsequent experience indicates that the *most valuable* property is human personality because it constantly creates new uses for nature.

If the social contract is designed to protect property and person, and they have the intimate relationship we have suggested, there is no need to distinguish between them and favor the wholly physical representation of property. Simple protection of physical property with a corresponding denial of status to persons is a crude and inefficient way of operating the social contract. Government, instead of devising more complicated procedures for protecting physical property and its individual use, should instead develop the institutions and conditions within which human personality can reach its full potential. Every fully developed personality produces new and more significant kinds of property and helps to create the new conditions under which more property can be produced. Since the creation of property depends upon individual minds looking at nature in new and unsuspected ways, the proper and primary role of the social contract should be education, creating the conditions under which the maximum number of minds and personalities can be developed most completely.

If this view of the social contract is correct, then we could expect to find considerable friction between the majority and the minorities in the field of education where the real property, human personality, is developed. And we should find that the significant progress of minorities also occurs in this subject area. Initially, all the minorities except aboriginal peoples were excluded from education wherever possible. Native individuals were initially compelled to participate in educational settings primarily as a means of destroying their communal integrity. Many of the important cases in the development of minority rights, as we discussed above, have been in the field of education: *Brown v. Board of Education,*[2] *Cisneros v. Corpus Christi Independent School*

District,[3] and *Lau v. Nichols.*[4] The reaction against minority progress can also be represented by educational cases such as *DeFunis v. Odegaard*[5] and *Regents of the University of California v. Bakke,*[6] to name but a few.

It is certainly time for the American judicial system to move completely away from a materialistic interpretation of property and adopt a more comprehensive perspective on property and the social contract. Indeed, educational cases reaching the Supreme Court seem to be increasing, giving evidence that in addition to deciding the configuration of educational opportunity and procedures, the people seem to want clarification and articulation of the role of government in assisting them in fulfilling their lives. In his argument in *Pollock v. Farmers' Loan & Trust Co.,*[7] counsel for the appellants declared that "one of the fundamental objects of all civilized government is the preservation of the right of private property. I have thought that it was the very keystone of the arch upon which all civilized government rests, and that this once abandoned, everything was at stake and in danger."[8] If this view was proper and correct with respect to physical property, how much more important it is when applied to the property that we individually represent in ourselves.

NOTES

INTRODUCTION

1. *Dred Scott v. Sandford*, 60 US 393 (1857).
2. Ibid. at 404–05.
3. Ibid. at 410.
4. Ibid. (emphasis added).
5. Ibid.
6. See Baron de Montesquieu, *The Sprit of Laws*, in vol. 38 of *Great Books of the Western World*, eds. Robert Maynard Hutchins, et al. (Chicago, IL: Encyclopedia Britannica, 1952). Montesquieu writes: "In this state every man, instead of being sensible of his equality, would fancy himself inferior. There would therefore be no danger of their attacking one another; peace would be the first law of nature" (ibid. at 2). As this shows, he can also be understood as wholly emotional.
7. John Locke, 1632–1704: *Of Civil Government; Two Treatises* (London: J. M. Dent & Sons; New York, E. P. Dutton & Co., 1924): See section 49.
8. Ibid., section 13.
9. Ibid., section 4.
10. Ibid., section 26.
11. The doctrine of discovery is most clearly articulated in *Johnson* v. *McIntosh*, 21 US 543 (1823). This powerful doctrine still undergirds federal Indian law and was reaffirmed in a recent Supreme Court decision, *City of Sherrill v. Oneida Indian Nation of New York*, 544 US 197 (2005). Citing an earlier case involving the Oneida, Justice Ginsburg noted in her opinion that "under the 'doctrine of discovery,'…fee title to the lands occupied by Indians when the colonists arrived became vested in the sovereign—first the discovering European nation and later the original States and the United States" (p. 5, footnote 1). This doctrine has received considerable scholarly attention over the years. See, for example, Vine Deloria Jr., *Behind the Trail of Broken Treaties: An Indian Declaration of Independence* (Austin: Univ. of Texas Press, 1985), chapter 5; David E. Wilkins and Tsianina Lomawaima, *Uneven Ground: American Indian Sovereignty and Federal Law* (Norman: Univ. of Oklahoma Press, 2001), chapter 1; Lindsay G. Robertson, *Conquest by Law: How the Discovery of America Dispossessed Indigenous Peoples of Their Lands* (New York: Oxford Univ. Press, 2005); and Steven T. Newcomb, *Pagans in the Promised Land: Decoding the Doctrine of Christian Discovery* (Golden, CO: Fulcrum Publishing, 2008).
12. The government established a court to provide for the settlement of private land claims under the Act of March 3, 1891, ch. 539, 26 Stat. 854.
13. See, for example, *Oyama v. California*, 332 US 633 (1948).
14. See Act of Feb. 19, 1887, ch. 397, 24 Stat. 634, and the case upholding its constitutionality, *The Late Corp. of the Church of Jesus Christ of Latter-Day Saints v. United States*, 136 US 1 (1890).
15. US Constitution, art. 1, sec. 2, cl. 3.
16. US Constitution, art. 1, sec. 9, cl. 3.
17. *Dred Scott* (emphasis added).
18. Ibid. at 422.
19. *Minor v. Happersett*, 88 US 162 (1875).
20. Ibid. at 170.
21. Ibid. at 178.
22. *Standing Bear v. Crook*, 25 F. Cas. 695 (C.C.D. Neb. 1879) (No. 14,891).
23. *Elk v. Wilkins*, 112 US 94 (1884).
24. *People v. Hall*, 4 Cal. 399 (1854).
25. *Gong Lum v. Rice*, 275 US 78 (1927).
26. *Ozawa v. United States*, 260 US 178 (1922).
27. *United States v. Thind*, 261 US 204 (1923).
28. *Trustees of Dartmouth College v. Woodward*, 17 US 518 (1819).
29. *Santa Clara County v. Southern Pacific Railroad Co.*, 118 US 394 (1886).

30.   See *Berea College v. Kentucky*, 211 US 45 (1908).

31.   *Citizens United v. Federal Election Commission*, 130 S. Ct. 876 (2010).

32.   Ibid. at 52.

33.   See, especially, Russel Lawrence Barsh and James Youngblood Henderson's *The Road: Indian Tribes and Political Liberty* (Berkeley: Univ. of California Press, 1980).

34.   For Canada, see John Borrows, *Canada's Indigenous Constitution* (Toronto, ON: Univ. of Toronto Press, 2010), 11. For Latin America, see S. James Anaya's *Indigenous Peoples in International Law*, 2nd ed. (New York: Oxford Univ. Press, 2004), 206, footnote 51.

CHAPTER 1: THE MAJESTY OF LAW

1.   Richard C. Cortner, *A Mob Intent on Death: The NAACP and the Arkansas Riot Cases* (Middleton, CT: Wesleyan Univ. Press, 1988), 15. And see Robert Whitaker's recent account, *On the Laps of Gods: The Red Summer of 1919 and the Struggle for Justice That Remade the Nation* (New York: Crown, 2008).

2.   Ibid., 97 (emphasis added).

3.   *Moore v. Dempsey*, 261 US 86 (1923).

4.   Wanda D. McCaslin, ed., *Justice as Healing: Indigenous Ways* (St. Paul, MN: Living Justice Press, 2005).

5.   Thurman Arnold, *The Symbols of Government* (New Haven, CT: Yale Univ. Press, 1935), 34–5.

6.   Theodore F. T. Plucknett, *A Concise History of the Common Law*, 2nd ed. (Rochester, NY: The Lawyers Cooperative Publishing, 1956).

7.   Ibid., 227.

8.   Benjamin N. Cardozo, *The Nature of the Judicial Process* (New Haven, CT: Yale Univ. Press, 1949).

9.   Ibid., 19.

10. Benjamin N. Cardozo, "The Paradoxes of Legal Science," in *Selected Writings of Benjamin Nathan Cardozo*, ed. Margaret E. Hall, 254 (New York: Fallon Publications, 1947).

11. Arnold, *Symbols of Government*, 77.

12. Cardozo, "The Paradoxes of Legal Science," 298.

13. Christopher Stone, "Should Trees Have Standing? Toward Legal Rights for Natural Objects," *Southern California Law Review* 45, no. 2 (1972): 464.

14. Ibid., 453.

15. In theory, the court's rulings are said to be value free, unbiased, impartial. But the very word *opinion* means anything but impartial—it is counterintuitive for the court to claim that it is objective and unbiased yet insist on using the word *opinion* to describe its rulings.

CHAPTER 2: THE SOCIAL CONTRACT

1.   Baron de Montesquieu, *The Spirit of Laws*, ed. David Wallace Carrithers (Berkeley: Univ. of California Press, 1977), 101–2.

2.   John Locke, *Two Treatises of Government*, rev. ed. (New York: New American Library, 1963), 343 (emphasis his).

3.   Ibid., 307–08 (emphasis his).

4.   James Fenimore Cooper wrote four major novels that depicted the lifestyle of Native peoples in northeast America in a manner that was hardly accurate—historically or anthropologically: *The Deerslayer*, *The Last of the Mohicans*, *The Pathfinder*, and *The Pioneers*. See William A. Starna's "Cooper's Indians: A Critique," in *James Fenimore Cooper: His Country and His Art*, ed. George A. Test (Oneonta: State Univ. College of New York), 63–76.

5.   Ibid., 309 (emphasis his).

6.   Ibid., 312.

7.   Ibid., 316.

8.   Ibid., 317 (emphasis his).

9.   Ibid.

10. Hanna Pitkin, "Obligation and Consent," *American Political Science Review* 59, no. 4 (Dec. 1965): 994.

11. Locke, *Two Treatises*, 321.

12. Ibid., 328–9.

13. Andrew Sinclair, *The Savage: A History of Misunderstanding* (London: Weidenfeld & Nicolson, 1977), 71.
14. Locke, *Two Treatises*, 332.
15. Ibid., 395–6 (emphasis his).
16. Charles Reich, "The New Property," *Yale Law Journal* 73, no. 5 (April 1964): 739.
17. Locke, *Two Treatises*, 340.
18. Ibid., 430.
19. Reich, "The New Property," 771.
20. Ibid.
21. Ibid.
22. John Rawls, *A Theory of Justice* (Cambridge, MA: Harvard Univ. Press, 1971); *Political Liberalism* (New York: Columbia Univ. Press, 1993); *Collected Papers* (Cambridge, MA: Harvard Univ. Press, 1999); *The Law of Peoples* (Cambridge, MA: Harvard Univ. Press, 1999); and *Justice as Fairness: A Restatement*, edited by Erin Kelly (Cambridge, MA: Harvard Univ. Press, 2001).
23. Rawls, *A Theory of Justice*, 12.
24. Ibid., 522.
25. Ibid., 584.
26. Dan Lacy, *The Meaning of the American Revolution* (New York: New American Library, 1964), 278.
27. Jack N. Rakove, *Original Meanings: Politics and Ideas in the Making of the Constitution* (New York: Alfred A. Knopf, 1996), 203, quoting John Adams in *Thoughts on Government* in *American Political Writings*, I, 403.
28. Pitkin, "Obligation and Consent," 996–97.
29. Ibid., 999.
30. Hugo L. Black, "The Bill of Rights–James Madison Lecture," in *One Man's Stand for Freedom: Mr. Justice Black and the Bill of Rights*, 48 (New York: Alfred A. Knopf, 1963).
31. *Morse v. Frederick*, 551 US 393 (2007).
32. *Federal Election Commission v. Wisconsin Right to Life*, 551 US 449 (2007).
33. Raymond Polin, "The Rights of Man in Hobbes and Locke," in *Political Theory and the Rights of Man*, ed. D. D. Raphael, 22 (Bloomington: Indiana Univ. Press, 1967).
34. D. D. Raphael, "Human Rights, Old and New," in *Political Theory and the Rights of Man*, ed. D. D. Raphael, 60–61 (Bloomington: Indiana Univ. Press, 1967).

CHAPTER 3: CERTAIN INALIENABLE RIGHTS

1. Baron de Montesquieu, *The Spirit of Laws*, ed. David Wallace Carrithers (Berkeley: Univ. of California Press, 1977), 105.
2. Dan Lacy, *The Meaning of the American Revolution* (New York: New American Library, 1964), 94. Also see Edward Countryman, *The American Revolution* (New York: Hill and Wang, 1985).
3. Lacy, *The Meaning of the American Revolution*, 149.
4. Ibid., 124.
5. Dean Alfange, *The Supreme Court and the National Will* (New York: Doubleday, Doran & Co., 1937), 8.
6. Lacy, *The Meaning of the American Revolution*, 28.
7. F. S. C. Northrop, *The Taming of the Nations: A Study of the Cultural Bases of International Policy* (New York: MacMillan, 1952), 320.
8. Don K. Price, *The Scientific Estate* (Cambridge, MA: Belknap Press of Harvard Univ. Press, 1965), 24. See also Price's *America's Unwritten Constitution: Science, Religion, and Political Responsibility* (Baton Rouge: Louisiana State Univ. Press, 1983).
9. Alexis de Tocqueville, *Democracy in America*, edited by J. P. Mayer (New York: Doubleday, 1969), 152.
10. Alexander Hamilton, James Madison, John Jay, *The Federalist Papers* (New York: New American Library, 1961), no. 51, Hamilton, 322.
11. Hugo L. Black, "The Bill of Rights–James Madison Lecture," in *One Man's Stand for Freedom: Mr. Justice Black and the Bill of Rights*, 41 (New York: Alfred A. Knopf, 1963).
12. Hamilton, Madison, Jay, *The Federalist Papers*, no. 39, 246.
13. Ibid., no. 45, 292–93.

14. Ibid., no. 17, 119.

15. James Brown Scott, *James Madison's Notes of Debates in the Federal Convention of 1787 and Their Relation to a More Perfect Society of Nations* (New York: Oxford Univ. Press, 1918), 59.

16. Alfange, *The Supreme Court and the National Will*, 41.

17. Hamilton, Madison, Jay, *The Federalist Papers*, no. 2, 38.

18. Tocqueville, *Democracy in America*, 164.

19. William F. Swindler, *Court and Constitution in the Twentieth Century* (Indianapolis: Bobbs-Merrill, 1974), 234–5.

20. Alfange, *The Supreme Court and the National Will*, 22.

21. Price, *The Scientific Estate*, 272.

22. Tocqueville, *Democracy in America*, 374.

23. Ibid., 66.

24. Hamilton, Madison, Jay, *The Federalist Papers*, no. 10, 81.

25. Montesquieu, *The Spirit of Laws*, book VIII, chapter 2, 171.

26. Northrop, *The Taming of the Nations*, 318.

27. Charles Reich, "The New Property," *Yale Law Journal* 73, no. 5 (April 1964): 771.

28. Price, *The Scientific Estate*, 170.

29. John Adams, quoted in Lacy, *The Meaning of the American Revolution*, 229.

CHAPTER 4: "EXISTING IN CONTEMPLATION OF LAW": CORPORATIONS AND THE LAW

1. Don K. Price, *The Scientific Estate* (Cambridge, MA: Belknap Press of Harvard Univ. Press, 1965), 15.

2. Alfred North Whitehead, *Adventure of Ideas* (New York: The MacMillan, 1933), 91.

3. Thurman Arnold, *The Symbols of Government* (New Haven, CT: Yale Univ. Press, 1935), 86.

4. Ibid., 100.

5. *Trustees of Dartmouth College v. Woodward*, 17 US 518, 636 (1819) (emphasis added).

6. Ibid.

7. Ibid., 667.

8. Benjamin F. Wright, *The Growth of American Constitutional Law* (Chicago: Univ. of Chicago Press, 1967), 154.

9. *Bank of Augusta v. Earle*, 38 US 519.

10. *Louisville, Cincinnati and Charleston Railroad Co. v. Letson*, 2 How. (43 US) 497.

11. *Paul v. Commonwealth of Virginia*, 75 US 168.

12. *Paul v. Commonwealth of Virginia*, 19 Law. Ed. 357 (1869), 359.

13. Ibid., 360.

14. Ibid., 361.

15. *Slaughter-House Cases*, 16 Wall. (83 US), 36.

16. *Slaughter-House Cases*, 83 US 36 (1872), 72.

17. Ibid., 78.

18. Ibid., 90.

19. Ibid., 123.

20. *Chicago, Burlington and Quincy Railroad Company v. Iowa*, 94 US 155 (1877), 155.

21. Wright, *The Growth of American Constitutional Law*, 100–01.

22. *Sinking Fund Cases*, 99 US 700 (1879), 718–19 (emphasis added).

23. *San Mateo County v. Southern Pacific Railroad Company*, 116 US 138 (1885). This case originated in state court in April 1882 and was argued before the Supreme Court on December 19, 1882. But before a decision was reached, a stipulation was entered into between the parties and the proceedings were postponed until certain other cases were heard. The Court's final decision was handed down several years later, on December 21, 1885.

24. William F. Swindler, *Court and Constitution in the Twentieth Century* (Indianapolis: Bobbs-Merrill, 1974), 37.

25. *Santa Clara County v. Southern Pacific Railroad Co.*, 118 US 394 (1886).

26. James W. Ely Jr., *Railroads and American Law* (Lawrence: Univ. Press of Kansas, 2001), 283.

27. *Connecticut General Life Insurance Co. v. Johnson*, 303 US 77 (1938).

28.   Ibid.
29.   Dean Alfange, *The Supreme Court and the National Will* (New York: Doubleday, Doran & Co., 1937), 151.
30.   Charles A. Reich, "The New Property," *Yale Law Journal* 73, no. 5 (April 1964): 772.
31.   Ibid., 773.
32.   Thurman Arnold, *The Symbols of Government* (New Haven, CT: Yale Univ. Press, 1935), 239.
33.   Ibid.
34.   Reich, "The New Property," 772.
35.   Arnold, *The Symbols of Government*, 239.
36.   Ibid., 126.
37.   Whitehead, *Adventures of Ideas*, 34 (emphasis added).
38.   Wright, *The Growth of American Constitutional Law*, 111.
39.   Ibid., 255.
40.   *Wabash, St. Louis and Pacific Railway Co. v. Ilinois*, 118 US 557 (1886).
41.   *Chicago, Milwaukee and St. Paul Railroad Co. v. State of Minnesota* 134 US 418 (1890).
42.   Ibid., 462–63.
43.   Richard W. Stevenson, "Capitalism After the Fall," *The New York Times*, April 19, 2009.
44.   Wright, *The Growth of American Constitutional Law*, 237.
45.   Price, *The Scientific Estate*, 36.
46.   Ibid.
47.   Ibid., 44–45.
48.   Ibid., 74.
49.   Adam Liptak, "The Most Conservative Court in Decades," *The New York Times*, July 25, 2010.
50.   *Leegin Creative Leather Products Inc. v. PSKS Inc.*, 551 US 877 (2007).
51.   Adam Cohen, "Last Term's Winner at the Supreme Court: Judicial Activism," *The New York Times*, July 9, 2007.
52.   *Citizens United v. Federal Election Commission*, 130 S. Ct. 876 (2010).
53.   *Austin v. Michigan Chamber of Commerce*, 494 US 652 (1990).
54.   *McConnell v. Federal Election Commission*, 540 US 93 (2003).
55.   Adam Liptak, "Dissenters Argue That Ruling Will Corrupt Democracy," *The New York Times*, January 22, 2010.
56.   Editorial, *The New York Times*, "The Court's Blow to Democracy," January 22, 2010.
57.   Reich, "The New Property," 772.
58.   Louis O. Kelso and Patricia Hetter, *Two Factor Theory: The Economics of Reality* (New York: Vintage Books, 1967), 3.
59.   Ibid., 8.
60.   Ibid.
61.   Ibid., 74–75.
62.   Leo Hindery Jr. and Donald W. Riegle Jr., "The Jobs Solution," *The Nation* 288, no. 15 (April 20, 2009): 13.
63.   Ibid., 15–16.
64.   As quoted in Richard W. Stevenson's "Capitalism After the Fall," *The New York Times*, April 19, 2009.
65.   Alexis de Tocqueville, *Democracy in America,* edited by J. P. Mayer (New York: Doubleday, 1969), 554.

CHAPTER 5: "THREE-FIFTHS OF ALL OTHER PERSONS": AFRICAN AMERICANS AND THE LAW

1.   Alexis de Tocqueville, *Democracy in America*, edited by J. P. Mayer (New York: Doubleday, 1969), 340.
2.   Peter Kolchin, *American Slavery: 1619–1877* (New York: Hill and Wang, 1993), 4.
3.   Tocqueville, *Democracy in America*, 361.
4.   Ibid., 362.
5.   Kolchin, *American Slavery*, 5.
6.   See Winthrop D. Jordan, *White Over Black: American Attitudes Toward the Negro, 1550–1812*

(Baltimore,: Penguin Books, 1968), 56.

7.   James Oakes, "Slavery," in *Encyclopedia of American Social History*, vol. II, eds. Mary Kupiec Cayton, Elliott J. Gorn, and Peter W. Williams, 1407 (New York: Charles Scribner's Sons, 1993).

8.   Kolchin, *American Slavery*, 22.

9.   Andrew Sinclair, *The Savage: A History of Misunderstanding* (London: Weidenfeld & Nicolson, 1997), 48.

10. Oakes, "Slavery," 1410.

11. Kolchin, *American Slavery*, 186.

12. Jordan, *White Over Black*, 300.

13. Donald G. Nieman, *Promises to Keep: African Americans and the Constitutional Order, 1776 to the Present* (New York: Oxford Univ. Press, 1991), 8.

14. Alexander Hamilton, James Madison, John Jay, *The Federalist Papers* (New York: New American Library, 1961), no. 54, Madison, 337.

15. Ibid.

16. Ibid.

17. Ibid. (emphasis his).

18. Ibid., 339.

19. Ibid., no. 42, Madison, 266.

20. Jack N. Rakove, *Original Meanings: Politics and Ideas in the Making of the Constitution* (New York: Alfred A. Knopf, 1996), 87–88.

21. Tocqueville, *Democracy in America*, 618.

22. Alfred North Whitehead, *Adventures of Ideas* (New York: The MacMillan, 1933), 27.

23. Tocqueville, *Democracy in America*, 360.

24. Ibid., 344.

25. *Dred Scott v. Sandford*, 60 US 393 (1857). Sandford's name is actually spelled Sanford, but it was misspelled in the official report of the case.

26. See Don E. Fehrenbacher, *The Dred Scott Case: Its Significance in American Law and Politics* (New York: Oxford Univ. Press 1978).

27. *Dred Scott v. Sandford*, 60 US 393, 407 (1857) (emphasis added).

28. Ibid., 409 (emphasis added).

29. Ibid., 533.

30. Ibid., 624.

31. Ibid., 426.

32. Ibid., 405.

33. Ibid., 452 (emphasis added).

34. Ibid., 446.

35. Ibid.

36. Tocqueville, *Democracy in America*, 342.

37. Nieman, *Promises to Keep*, 67–68.

38. Kolchin, *American Slavery*, 209–210.

39. Benjamin F. Wright, *The Growth of American Constitutional Law* (Chicago: Univ. of Chicago Press, 1967), 253.

40. Raoul Berger, *Government by Judiciary* (Cambridge, MA: Harvard Univ. Press, 1977), 46.

41. W. E. B. DuBois, *Black Reconstruction in America, 1860–1880* (New York: Atheneum, 1935 [1973]), 691.

42. *Slaughter-House Cases*, 83 US 36 (1872).

43. Ibid., 90.

44. Ibid., 123.

45. Ibid., 74.

46. Ibid.

47. *United States v. Cruikshank*, 92 US 542 (1875).

48. Nieman, *Promises to Keep*, 95.

49. *United States v. Cruikshank*, 92 US 542, 552.

50. Ibid., 554.

51. Ibid., 556.

52. David Kairys, *With Liberty and Justice for Some: A Critique of the Conservative Supreme Court* (New York: The New Press, 1993), 187.

53. *United States v. Cruikshank*, 92 US 542, 550.

54. *Hall v. De Cuir*, 95 US 485 (1877).

55. Ibid., 487.

56. Ibid., 489–490.

57. Ibid., 490 (emphasis added).

58. Richard Bardolph, ed. *The Civil Rights Record: Black Americans and the Law, 1849–1970* (New York: Thomas Y. Crowell, 1970), 54.

59. *Hall v. De Cuir*, 95 US 485, 508–509.

60. Ibid., 509.

61. Bardolph, *The Civil Rights Record*, 63.

62. *Civil Rights Cases*, 109 US 3 (1883); and see C. Herman Pritchett, *The American Constitution* (New York: 1959), for a good analysis of these important cases.

63. *Civil Rights Cases*, 109 US 3, 11 (1883).

64. Ibid., 13.

65. Ibid., 25.

66. See Kairys, *With Liberty and Justice for Some,* and Lani Guinier and Gerald Torres, *The Miner's Canary: Enlisting Race, Resisting Power, Transforming Democracy* (Cambridge, MA: Harvard Univ. Press, 2002).

67. *Civil Rights Cases*, 109 US 3, 34 (emphasis his).

68. Ibid., 39 (emphasis his).

69. Ibid., 41.

70. Ibid., 48.

71. Ibid., 53.

72. See Charles A. Lofgren, *The Plessy Case: A Legal-Historical Interpretation* (New York: Oxford Univ. Press, 1987).

73. *Plessy v. Ferguson*, 163 US 537, 543 (1896).

74. Ibid., 544.

75. Ibid.

76. Ibid., 549.

77. Ibid.

78. Ibid., 551–552.

79. Ibid.

80. Ibid., 555.

81. Ibid., 556–557.

82. Guinier and Torres, *The Miner's Canary* and John D. Skrentny, *The Minority Rights Revolution* (Cambridge, MA: The Belknap Press of Harvard Univ. Press, 2002).

83. *Plessy v. Ferguson*, 163 US 537, 559 (1896).

84. See David M. O'Brien, *Storm Center: The Supreme Court in American Politics*, 7th ed. (New York: W. W. Norton, 2005), 30.

85. *Plessy v. Ferguson* 163 US 537, 560.

86. Bardolph, *The Civil Rights Record*, 285.

87. *Morgan v. Virginia*, 328 US 373, 377 (1946) (emphasis added).

88. Ibid., 386.

89. Ibid., 390.

90. Ibid., 394.

91. *Brown v. Board of Education of Topeka*, 347 US 483 (1954).

92. *Brown v. Board of Education of Topeka*, 349 US 294 (1955).

93. See Richard Kluger, *Simple Justice: The History of Brown v. Board of Education and Black America's Struggle for Equality* (New York: Knopf, 1977) and Mark Tushnet, *The NAACP's Legal Strategy Against Segregated Education: 1925–1950* (Chapel Hill: Univ. of North Carolina Press, 2004).

94. Dennis J. Hutchinson, "*Brown v. Board of Education*" in *The Oxford Companion to the Supreme Court of the United States*, ed. Kermit L. Hall, 94 (New York: Oxford Univ. Press, 1992).

95. *Brown v. Board of Education of Topeka*, 347 US 483, 489.

96. *Brown v. Board of Education of Topeka*, 347 US 483, 489–90.

97.   Ibid., 493.

98.   Baron de Montesquieu, *The Spirit of Laws*, ed. David Wallace Carrithers (Berkeley: Univ. of California Press, 1977), book IV, chapter 5, 130.

99.   Tocqueville, *Democracy in America*, 12.

100. Lucas A. Power Jr., *The Warren Court and American Politics* (Cambridge, MA: The Belknap Press of Harvard Univ. Press, 2000), 37–39.

101. *Brown v. Board of Education of Topeka*, 349 US 294, 301 (1955).

102. See Daryl Michael Scott, *Contempt and Pity: Social Policy and the Image of the Damaged Black Psyche, 1880–1996* (Chapel Hill: Univ. of North Carolina Press, 1997).

103. Skrentny, *The Minority Rights Revolution*, 201.

104. Jeffrey D. Schultz, et al., *Encyclopedia of Minorities in American Politics*, vol. 1, *African Americans and Asian Americans* (Phoenix: Oryx Press, 2000), 20.

105. Manning Marable, "Staying on the Path to Racial Equality," in *The Affirmative Action Debate*, ed. George E. Curry (Reading, MA: Addison-Wesley, 1996), 4.

106. Herman Belz, "Affirmative Action," in *The Oxford Companion to the Supreme Court of the United States*, ed. Kermit L. Hall, 19 (New York: Oxford Univ. Press, 1992).

107. See *Griggs v. Duke Power Co.*, 401 US 424, which established the disparate impact principle of discrimination as the theoretical framework for civil rights.

108. *Regents of the University of California v. Bakke*, 438 US 265 (1978).

109. Barbara A. Bergman, *In Defense of Affirmative Action* (New York: Basic Books, 1996), 192, note 7.

110. Ibid., 170.

111. *Shaw v. Reno*, 509 US 630 (1993).

112. Ibid., 657.

113. *Gratz v. Bollinger,* 539 US 244 (2003).

114. *Grutter v. Bollinger,* 539 US 306 (2003).

115. Ibid., 343.

116. Melanye T. Price and Gloria T. Hampton, "Linked Fates, Disconnected Realities: The Post-Civil Rights African American Politics," in *Perspectives on Race, Ethnicity, and Religion: Identity Politics in America*, eds. Valerie Martinez-Ebers and Manochehr Dorraj, 126 (New York: Oxford Univ. Press, 2010).

CHAPTER 6: "ALIENS," "INDEPENDENT PEOPLES," OR "DOMESTIC DEPENDENT NATIONS": INDIGENOUS NATIONS AND THE LAW

1.   John Locke, *The Two Treatises of Government*, book II, chapter 11, 313.

2.   Baron de Montesquieu, *The Spirit of Laws*, ed. David Wallace Carrithers (Berkeley: Univ. of California Press, 1977), book I, chapter 3, 3.

3.   See, for example, Roy Harvey Pearce, *Savagism and Civilization: A Study of the Indian and the American Mind* (Baltimore, MD: Johns Hopkins Press, 1953); Robert F. Berkhofer Jr., *The White Man's Indian* (New York: Vintage Books, 1978); Robert A Williams Jr., *The American Indian in Western Legal Thought: The Discourses of Conquest* (New York: Oxford Univ. Press, 1990); and John Mohawk, *Utopian Legacies: A History of Conquest and Oppression in the Western World* (Santa Fe, NM: Clear Light Press, 1999).

4.   Locke, *Two Treatises*, book II, chapter 5, 328.

5.   See, for example, Patricia Seed, *American Pentimento: The Invention of Indians and the Pursuit of Riches* (Minneapolis: Univ. of Minnesota Press, 2001), 13; David E. Wilkins and Tsianina Lomawaima, *Uneven Ground: American Indian Sovereignty and Federal Law* (Norman: Univ. of Oklahoma Press, 2001), especially chapter 1; and Lindsay G. Robertson, *Conquest by Law* (New York: Oxford Univ. Press, 2005).

6.   See, Wilkins and Lomawaima, *Uneven Ground*, chapter 1; and Indian Law Resource Center, "Native Land Law Project: Draft General Principles of Law Relating to Native Lands and Natural Resources," General Edition (Little Canada, MN: Indian Land Tenure Foundation, 2010), especially chapter 2, "Native Land Ownership and the Doctrine of Discovery."

7.   William N. Fenton, *The Great Law and the Longhouse: A Political History of the Iroquois Confederacy* (Norman: Univ. of Oklahoma Press, 1998).

8.   Conrad E. Heidenreich, "Huron," in *Handbook of North American Indians: Northeast*, vol. 15, ed. Bruce G. Trigger (Washington, DC: Smithsonian Institution, 1978), 368–388.

9.   H. B. Cushman, *History of the Choctaw, Chickasaw, and Natchez Indians*, edited by Angie Debo (1899; reprint, Norman: Univ. of Oklahoma Press, 1999).

10.   Alexis de Tocqueville, *Democracy in America*, edited by J. P. Mayer (New York: Doubleday, 1969), 322.

11.   Ibid., 29.

12.   Richard Slotkin, *Regeneration Through Violence: The Mythology of the American Frontier, 1600–1860* (Middletown, CT: Wesleyan Univ. Press, 1973).

13.   In Robert Odawi Porter, *Sovereignty, Colonialism and the Indigenous Nations: A Reader* (Durham, NC: Carolina Academic Press, 2005), 371–372.

14.   Tim Alan Garrison, *The Legal History of Removal* (Athens: Univ. of Georgia Press, 2002), 21.

15.   Making Provision for the Civilization of the Indian Tribes, March 3, 1819, 3 Stat. 516.

16.   Tocqueville, *Democracy in America*, 326.

17.   Hazel W. Hertzberg, *The Search for an American Indian Identity: Modern Pan-Indian Movements* (Syracuse, NY: Syracuse Univ. Press, 1971).

18.   Tocqueville, *Democracy in America*, 331.

19.   See, for example, Vine Deloria Jr. and Raymond DeMallie, *Documents of American Indian Diplomacy: Treaties, Agreements, and Conventions, 1775–1979*, vol. 1, chapter 2, which discusses the treaties signed between 1775 and 1779 between the Americans and the Iroquois, Delaware, Cherokee, Winnebago, and other nations.

20.   Hamilton, James Madison, John Jay, *The Federalist Papers* (New York: New American Library, 1961), no. 3, Jay, 44.

21.   Ibid., no. 42, Madison, 268–269 (emphasis added).

22.   Ibid., 269.

23.   Ibid., no. 22, Hamilton, 150 (emphasis his).

24.   Ibid., no. 80, Hamilton, 477.

25.   Ibid., no. 64, Jay, 394 (emphasis his).

26.   Ibid., no. 24, Hamilton, 161.

27.   Vine Deloria Jr. and David E. Wilkins, *Tribes, Treaties, and Constitutional Tribulations* (Austin: Univ. of Texas Press, 1999), 80.

28.   *Johnson v. McIntosh*, 21 US 543 (1823).

29.   Ibid., 591–592.

30.   Lindsay G. Robertson, *Conquest by Law: How the Discovery of America Dispossessed Indigenous Peoples of Their Lands* (New York: Oxford Univ. Press, 2005).

31.   See Jill Norgren's outstanding analysis of this and the follow-up case, *Worcester v. Georgia*, in her book *The Cherokee Cases: Two Landmark Federal Decisions in the Fight for Sovereignty* (Norman: Univ. of Oklahoma Press, 2004).

32.   *Worcester v. Georgia*, 31 US 515, 585 (1832).

33.   See Tim Alan Garrison's work *The Legal Ideology of Removal: The Southern Judiciary and the Sovereignty of Native American Nations* (Athens: Univ. of Georgia Press, 2002). Chapter 4 provides an excellent analysis of *Georgia v. Tassels*, the case that set the legal stage for the more famous Cherokee cases.

34.   *Cherokee Nation v. Georgia*, 30 US 1 (1831).

35.   Ibid., 6.

36.   Ibid., 10.

37.   Ibid., 17.

38.   Ibid.

39.   Ibid.

40.   Ibid., 20 (emphasis added).

41.   See Robert T. Coulter, "The Denial of Legal Remedies to Indian Nations Under United States Law," *American Indian Journal* 3 (1977): 5–11, and Nell Jessup Newton, "Federal Power Over Indians: Its Sources, Scope and Limitations," *University of Pennsylvania Law Review* 132 (1984): especially 235–236 for two accounts of the political question doctrine and how it has been used by the Supreme Court to deny justice to Native peoples.

42.   Ibid., 25.

43.   Ibid., 26–27.
44.   But see Deloria and DeMallie's *Documents of American Indian Diplomacy*, vol. 1, chapter 3, titled "Treaties Between Indian Nations and Foreign Nations," which documents the various treaties negotiated by certain tribes with Mexico and Russia after this decision.
45.   *Cherokee Nation v. Georgia*, 30 US 1, 27 (1831).
46.   Ibid., 30.
47.   Ibid., 53.
48.   Ibid.
49.   Ibid., 55 (emphasis his).
50.   Ibid.
51.   Ibid., 58–59.
52.   Ibid., 60.
53.   Ibid.
54.   Ibid., 68–69.
55.   *Worcester v. Georgia*, 31 US 515, 544.
56.   Ibid., 544–545.
57.   Ibid., 545.
58.   Ibid.
59.   Ibid., 551.
60.   Ibid., 552.
61.   Ibid., 554.
62.   Ibid., 556–557.
63.   Ibid., 557.
64.   Ibid., 559–560.
65.   Ibid., 582.
66.   Ibid.
67.   Ibid.
68.   Ibid.
69.   Paul W. Gates, *History of Public Land Law Development* (Washington, DC: Government Printing Office, 1968)
70.   *The Kansas Indians*, 72 US 737 (1867).
71.   Ibid., 755–756.
72.   Ibid., 756.
73.   To Reduce and Modify the Rates of Postage and for Other Purposes, March 3, 1851, 9 Stat. 587.
74.   *United States v. Lucero*, 1 N.M. 422, 425 (1869).
75.   Ibid.
76.   Ibid., 426.
77.   To Establish Peace with Certain Hostile Indian Tribes, July 20, 1887, 15 Stat. 17.
78.   Institute for the Development of Indian Law, *Proceedings of the Great Peace Commission of 1867–1868* (Washington, DC: Institute for the Development of Indian Law, 1975), 107.
79.   Ibid.
80.   Treaty with the Sioux, April 29, 1868, II Kappler, 998, 15 Stat. 635.
81.   Ibid.
82.   See Annie Heloise Abel's three-volume study, *The American Indian in the Civil War, 1862–1865* (Lincoln: Univ. of Nebraska Press, 1992); *The American Indian Under Reconstruction* (New York: Johnson Reprint Corporation, 1970); and *The American Indian as Slaveholder and Secessionist* (Lincoln: Univ. of Nebraska Press, 1992), for excellent analysis of the important role played by these nations during and after the Civil War.
83.   Deloria and DeMallie, *Documents of American Indian Diplomacy: Treaties, Agreements, and Conventions, 1775–1979*, 2 vols. (Norman: Univ. of Oklahoma Press, 1999). See especially chapter 11 in vol. 1, titled "Treaties between Indian Nations and the Confederate States," which contains several of these fascinating documents.
84.   Treaty with the Creeks, June 14, 1866, II Kappler, 932, 14 Stat. 785.
85.   Treaty with the Seminole, March 21, 1866, II Kappler, 911, 14 Stat. 755.
86.   Treaty with the Creeks, II Kappler, 932, 936, 14 Stat. 785.

87. Treaty with the Choctaw and Chickasaw, April 28, 1866, II Kappler, 921, 14 Stat. 469, Article 7.
88. Treaty with the Cherokee, July 19, 1866, II Kappler, 944, 14 Stat. 799, Article 7.
89. Treaty with the Seminole, March 21, 1866, II Kappler, 914, 14 Stat. 755, Article 7.
90. Making Appropriations for the Indian Department, July 15, 1870, 16 Stat. 335.
91. Senate, *Proceedings of the Council of Indian Tribes*, Senate Ex. Doc. 26, Serial Set #1440, 41st Congress, 3rd Session (January 30, 1871), 4.
92. Ibid.
93. Ibid., 5.
94. Senate Committee on the Judiciary, *A Report to the Senate of the Effect of the Fourteenth Amendment to the Constitution Upon the Indian Tribes of the Country,* Senate Report No. 268, 41st Congress, 3rd Session (December 14, 1870), 9.
95. Ibid., 11 (emphasis added).
96. Making Appropriation for the Indian Department, March 3, 1871, 16 Stat. 544, 566.
97. *Ex Parte Crow Dog*, 109 US 556 (1883).
98. See Sidney L. Harring's excellent treatment of this case, *Crow Dog's Case: American Indian Sovereignty, Tribal Law, and United States Law in the Nineteenth Century* (New York: Cambridge Univ. Press, 1994).
99. *Ex Parte Crow Dog*, 109 US 556, 571 (1883).
100. Ibid.
101. Major Crimes Act, March 3, 1885, 23 Stat. 385.
102. *United States v. Kagama*, 118 US 375 (1886).
103. Ibid., 378–379.
104. Ibid., 379.
105. Ibid., 381–382 (emphasis added).
106. Ibid., 383–384 (emphasis his).
107. *Lone Wolf v. Hitchcock*, 187 US 553 (1903). This important case has been examined by Blue Clark in *Lone Wolf v. Hitchcock: Treaty Rights and Indian Law at the End of the Nineteenth Century* (Lincoln: Univ. of Nebraska Press, 1994).
108. Ibid., 564.
109. Ibid. (emphasis added).
110. David Kairys, *With Liberty and Justice for Some: A Critique of the Conservative Supreme Court* (New York: The New Press, 1993), 188.
111. *Lone Wolf v. Hitchcock*, 187 US 553, 565.
112. Ibid., 565–566.
113. Ibid., 568.
114. Felix S. Cohen, *Handbook of Federal Indian Law* (Washington, DC: Government Printing Office, 1942), reprint ed. (Albuquerque: Univ. of New Mexico Press, 1972), xxviii.
115. Ibid., xxvii.
116. Morris Raphael Cohen, *Reason and Law* (Glencoe, IL: The Free Press, 1950): 24.
117. Major Crimes Act, March 3, 1885, 23 Stat. 385 (1885).
118. Andrew Sinclair, *The Savage: A History of Misunderstanding* (London: Weidenfeld & Nicolson, 1977), 118.
119. *Talton v. Mayes*, 163 US 376 (1896).
120. Ibid., 379–380.
121. Ibid., 384.
122. See Larry C. Skogen's *Indian Depredations Claims, 1796–1920* (Norman: Univ. of Oklahoma Press, 1996) for a detailed treatment of these fascinating and exasperating claims cases.
123. Indian Depredation Act, March 3, 1891, 26 Stat. 851 (1891).
124. *Dobbs v. the United States and the Apache Indians*, 33 Ct. Cls. 308 (1898).
125. Ibid., 315–316.
126. Ibid., 316.
127. *Montoya v. United States*, 180 US 261 (1901).
128. Ibid., 266 (emphasis added).
129. See Angie Debo, *And Still the Waters Run: The Betrayal of the Five Civilized Tribes* (Norman: Univ. of Oklahoma Press, 1984) and Clara Sue Kidwell's *The Choctaws in Oklahoma: From Tribe to Nation, 1855–1970* (Norman: Univ. of Oklahoma Press, 2007).

130. General Allotment Act, 24 Stat. 388 (1887).
131. Cited in D. S. Otis, *The Dawes Act and the Allotment of Indian Lands*, ed. Francis P. Prucha (Norman: Univ. of Oklahoma, 1973), 11 (emphasis added).
132. *Lochner v. New York*, 198 US 45 (1905).
133. Ibid., 75.
134. Herbert Hovenkamp, "Due Process," in the *Oxford Companion to American Law*, ed. Kermit L. Hall, 235 (New York: Oxford Univ. Press, 2002).
135. Senate Select Committee on the Five Civilized Tribes, Senate Report No. 377, 53rd Congress, 2nd Session, 1894.
136. Ibid., 12.
137. *Stephens v. Cherokee Nation*, 174 US 445 (1899).
138. Cited in Angie Debo, *A History of the Indians of the United States* (Norman: Univ. of Oklahoma Press, 1973), 261.
139. Treaty of Guadalupe Hidalgo, 9 Stat. 922 (1848).
140. *United States v. Sandoval*, 231 US 28 (1913).
141. Ibid., 45–46.
142. Ibid., 46.
143. See, for example, Vine Deloria Jr. and Clifford M. Lytle, *The Nations Within: The Past and Future of American Indian Sovereignty* (Austin: Univ. of Texas Press, 1984) and Elmer R. Rusco, *A Fateful Time: The Background and Legislative History of the Indian Reorganization Act* (Reno: Univ. of Nevada Press, 2000) for two sterling accounts of this critical period.
144. See Dalia Tsuk Mitchell's biographical treatment of Cohen, *Architect of Justice: Felix S. Cohen and the Founding of American Legal Pluralism* (Ithaca, NY: Cornell Univ. Press, 2007), and see Felix S. Cohen's own *On the Drafting of Tribal Constitutions,* ed. David E. Wilkins (Norman: Univ. of Oklahoma Press, 2006) for insights into the types of governments tribal nations might wish to consider establishing.
145. Indian Reorganization Act, June 18, 1934, 48 Stat. 984 (1934).
146. Tsuk Mitchell, *Architect of Justice*, 99.
147. Indian Reorganization Act, 48 Stat. 984, section 16 (1934).
148. Solicitor's Opinion, "Powers of Indian Tribes," 55 I.D. 14, October 25, 1934. *Decisions of the Department of the Interior,* ed. George A. Warren, 14–67 (Washington, DC: Government Printing Office, 1938).
149. Solicitor's Opinion, M. 27810, December 13, 1934. See *Opinions of the Solicitor of the Department of the Interior Relating to Indian Affairs, 1917–1974,* vol. 1 (Washington, DC: Government Printing Office, 1974), 484–494 (emphasis added).
150. *Colliflower v. Garland*, 342 F.2d. 369 (1965).
151. Ibid., 379.
152. Ibid.
153. Ibid.
154. *United States v. State Tax Commission of Mississippi*, 505 F.2d. 633 (1974).
155. Treaty with the Choctaw, September 27, 1830, 7 Stat. 333.
156. See George Pierre Castile, *To Show Heart: Native American Self-Determination and Federal Indian Policy, 1960–1975* (Tucson: Univ. of Arizona Press, 1998).
157. See Paul H. Stewart, "Financing Self-Determination: Federal Indian Expenditures, 1975–1988," *American Indian Culture and Research Journal* 14, no. 2 (1990): 1–18.
158. *Toledo v. Pueblo de Jemez*, 119 F. Supp. 429 (1954).
159. Ibid., 432.
160. *Native American Church v. Navajo Tribal Council*, 272 F.2d. 131 (1959).
161. Ibid., 134.
162. *McClanahan v. State Tax Commission of Arizona*, 411 US 174 (1973).
163. Ibid., 181.
164. Along with Mancari, the other plaintiffs were Anthony Franco, Wilbert Garrett, and Jules Casper. Interestingly, two of these individuals were minorities—one was African American, the other was Latino. See Carole Goldberg's article "What's Race Got to Do With It? The Story of *Morton v. Mancari*" for a thorough account of the history of this important case.
165. *Morton v. Mancari*, 417 US 535 (1974).

166. Ibid., 554.

167. Ibid.

168. *United States v. Mazurie*, 419 US 544 (1975).

169. US Congress, American Indian Policy Review Commission, *Final Report* (Washington, DC: Government Printing Office, 1977), 4.

170. Ibid.

171. See, for example, *Passamaquoddy Tribe v. Morton*, 528 F.2d 370 (1975).

172. See, for example, *United States v. Washington*, 384 F. Supp. 343 (1974).

173. See, for example, Vine Deloria Jr., *Behind the Trail of Broken Treaties* (New York: Dell Books, 1974) and Robert Burnette, *The Road to Wounded Knee* (New York: Bantam Books, 1974).

174. US Congress, *Final Report*, 573 (emphasis theirs).

175. See the published debate between Vine Deloria Jr. and Lloyd Meeds, "Sovereignty, Fact or Fiction," in "Indian Tribal Sovereignty and Treaty Rights," *La Confluencia* (Albuquerque, NM: 1978), S33-S45.

176. US Congress, *Final Report*, 573.

177. Ibid. (emphasis added).

178. N. Bruce Duthu, *American Indians and the Law* (New York: Penguin Books, 2008), 133.

179. Tocqueville, *Democracy in America*, 669.

180. Treaty with the Choctaw, 7 Stat. 333 (emphasis added).

181. See, for example, Samuel T. Wells and Rosanna Tubby, eds., *After Removal: The Choctaw in Mississippi* (Jackson: Univ. Press of Mississippi, 1986).

182. Treaty with the Omaha, March 16, 1854, 10 Stat. 1043.

183. *The Kansas Indians*, 72 US 737 (1866).

184. To Aid in Relieving from Peonage Women and Children of the Navajo Indians, July 27, 1868, 15 Stat. 264.

185. See Thomas Henry Tibbles, *The Ponca Chiefs: An Account of the Trial of Standing Bear*, ed. Kay Graber (Lincoln: Univ. of Nebraska Press, 1972).

186. *United States ex rel. Standing Bear v. Crook*, 25 F. Cas.14, 891 (1879).

187. Ibid., 696–697.

188. Ibid., 697.

189. Ibid.

190. Ibid., 699.

191. Ibid.

192. Ibid.

193. US Congress, "An Act Concerning the Rights of American Citizens in Foreign States," 40th Congress, Session II, Chapter 245, 249, July 27, 1868, 223–224.

194. *Elk v. Wilkins*, 112 US 94 (1884).

195. Although we do not know Elk's tribal affiliation from the court record, the Omaha, Oboe, Ponca, Pawnee, and Sioux nations all lived in Nebraska at the time. However, one researcher found evidence that John Elk was probably from another state. The 1880 Census shows a John Elk who had been born in Iowa. His parents were listed as being from Wisconsin. In1860, Wisconsin tribes included Chippewa, Menominee, Stockbridge, and Oneida. The census data also shows that at the time, Elk was thirty-five years old, employed as a laborer, and that he "lived with his wife, Louise, in a 'wigwam' along the Missouri land banks in Omaha in 'dwelling no. 282.'" See Anna Williams Shavers, "A Century of Developing Citizenship Law and the Nebraska Influence: A Centennial Essay," *Nebraska Law Review* 70 (1991): 480.

196. *Elk v. Wilkins*, 112 US 94, 101.

197. Ibid., 102.

198. Ibid.

199. *United States v. Osborn*, 2 F. 58 (1880).

200. Ibid., 61 (emphasis added).

201. Cited at Ibid., 119.

202. Ibid., 122–123.

203. General Allotment Act, 24 Stat. 388 (1887).

204. See, for example, Treaty with Kiowa and Comanche, October 21, 1867 (15 Stat. 581). Article 6 gave individual heads of families the opportunity to select, with the assistance of the Indian

agent, 320 acres of land that would become that person's "exclusive possession" so long as they cultivated it. Such selections were to be certified and then recorded in what was to be called the "Kiowa and Comanche Land Book" that would be kept in the Indian agent's office.

205.   *Waldron v. United States*, 143 Fed. 413 (1905).

206.   *United States v. Debell*, 227 Fed. 775 (1915).

207.   Ibid., 776.

208.   *United States v. Waller*, 243 US 452 (1917).

209.   Ibid., 459–460.

210.   Granting Citizenship to Certain Indians, 41 Stat. 350 (1921).

211.   Indian Citizenship Act, 43 Stat. 253 (1924). We say "problematic" because this act was thrust upon individual Indians without their express consent. And as we noted in an earlier work, "because Indians were in a treaty relationship with the United States and because the Senate Judiciary Committee's report firmly announced that the Fourteenth Amendment would not and could not be applied to Indians without their consent and ratification, is the bestowing of citizenship through the Indian Citizenship Act, *without the consent of the Indians*, applicable to Indians without some additional and specific act on their part indicating consent?" (emphasis added). See Vine Deloria Jr. and David E. Wilkins, *Tribes, Treaties, and Constitutional Tribulations* (Austin: Univ. of Texas Press, 1999), 147.

212.   *Davis v. Sitka School Board*, 3 Alaska 481 (1908).

213.   Treaty with Russia, 15 Stat. 539. See Donald Craig Mitchell, *Sold American: The Story of Alaska Natives and Their Land, 1867–1959* (Hanover, RI: Univ. Press of New England, 1997) for a good account of the Alaska Natives' unique historical situation.

214.   To Provide for the Construction of Roads of Alaska, January 27, 1905, 33 Stat. 616.

215.   Ibid.

216.   *Davis v. Sitka School Board*, 3 Alaska 481, 484.

217.   Ibid., 487–488.

218.   Ibid., 488.

219.   Ibid.

220.   Ibid., 490.

221.   See Renee Ann Cramer, *Cash, Color, and Colonialism: The Politics of Tribal Acknowledgment* (Norman: Univ. of Oklahoma Press, 2005) and Paul Pasquaretta's *Gambling and Survival in Native North America* (Tucson: Univ. of Arizona Press, 2003).

CHAPTER 7: "THOSE OF A 'DELICATE' NATURE": WOMEN AND THE LAW

1.   Nicholas D. Kristof and Sheryl W. DuDunn, "Why Women's Rights Are the Cause of Our Time," *The New York Times Magazine*, August 23, 2009.

2.   Mary Ellen Gale, "Unfinished Women: The Supreme Court and the Incomplete Transformation of Women's Rights in the United States," *Whittier Law Review* 9 (1987): 448.

3.   US Department of Labor, "A Solid Investment: Making Full Use of the Nation's Human Capital: Recommendations of the Federal Glass Ceiling Commission" (Washington, DC: November, 1995), iii.

4.   Judith Baer, *Women in American Law: The Struggle Toward Equality from the New Deal to the Present*, 2nd ed. (New York: Holmes & Meier, 1996), 19.

5.   Robin West, "Jurisprudence and Gender," in *Feminist Legal Theory: Readings in Law and Gender*, eds. Katharine T. Bartlett and Rosanne Kennedy, 231 (Boulder, CO: Westview Press, 1991).

6.   Natalie Zoman Davis and Jill Ker Conway, "The Rest of the Story," *The New York Times Magazine*, May 16, 1999.

7.   Baer, *Women in American Law*, 20.

8.   Jill Norgren and Serena Nanda, *American Cultural Pluralism and Law*, 2nd ed. (Westport, CT: Praeger, 1996), 197.

9.   Wendy W. Williams, "The Equality Crisis: Some Reflections on Culture, Courts, and Feminism," in *Feminist Legal Theory*, eds. Katharine T. Bartlett and Rosanne Kennedy, 16 (Boulder, CO: Westview Press 1991).

10.   The Declaration of Sentiments is reproduced in Mary Beth Norton and Ruth M. Alexander, eds., *Major Problems in American Women's History*, 2nd ed. (Lexington, MA.: D.C. Heath &

Co., 1996), 167–168.

11. *Bradwell v. Illinois*, 83 US (16 Wall.) 130 (1873).

12. *Minor v. Happersett*, 88 US (21 Wall.) 162 (1874).

13. Judith Olans Brown, Lucy A. Williams, and Phyllis Tropper Baumann, "The Mythogenesis of Gender: Judicial Images of Women in Paid and Unpaid Labor," *UCLA Women's Law Journal* 6 (Spring 1996): 461.

14. *Bradwell v. Illinois*, 83 US (16 Wall.) 130, 139.

15. *Bradwell v. Illinois*, 83 US (16 Wall.) 130, 141.

16. Ibid.

17. Ibid.

18. *Minor v. Happersett*, 88 US (21 Wall.) 162, 164 (1874).

19. Ibid., 166.

20. Ibid., 170.

21. Ibid., 178.

22. Harriet Sigerman, "An Unfinished Battle: 1848–1865," in *No Small Courage: A History of Women in the United States*, ed. Nancy F. Cott (New York: Oxford Univ. Press, 2000).

23. Nadine Taub and Elizabeth M. Schneider, "Women's Subordination and the Role of Law," in *The Politics of Law: A Progressive Critique*, 3rd. ed., ed. David Kairys, 342–43 (New York: Basic Books, 1998).

24. *Muller v. Oregon*, 208 US 412 (1908).

25. Leslie Friedman Goldstein, *The Constitutional Rights of Women*, 2nd ed. (Madison: Univ. of Wisconsin Press, 1988), 20.

26. *Muller v. Oregon*, 208 US 412, 421 (1908).

27. Ibid.

28. Ibid., 422.

29. Laura A. Otten, *Women's Rights and the Law* (Westport, CT: Praeger, 1993), 71–72.

30. *United States v. Bitty*, 208 US 393 (1908).

31. Norgren and Nanda, *American Cultural Pluralism and Law*, 214.

32. *United States v. Bitty*, 208 US 393 (1908).

33. Norgren and Nanda, *American Cultural Pluralism and Law*, 215.

34. Brown et al., "The Mythogenesis of Gender," 461–62.

35. *Adkins v. Children's Hospital*, 261 US 525 (1923).

36. In *Bunting v. Oregon*, 243 US 426 (1917), a 5–3 court upheld a 1913 Oregon law that had imposed a ten-hour maximum workday for men and women in factories, mills, and manufacturing plants. The justices determined that the law was useful for protecting the health of employees and was not discriminatory, even though it only applied to workers in certain industries.

37. *Adkins v. Children's Hospital*, 261 US 553.

38. Ibid.

39. Otten, *Women's Rights and the Law*, 72.

40. *West Coast Hotel Co. v. Parrish*, 300 US 379 (1937).

41. Ibid., 375.

42. *Radice v. New York*, 264 US 292 (1924).

43. Ibid., 293, note 3.

44. Ibid., 298.

45. Judith Baer, *Our Lives Before the Law: Constructing a Feminist Jurisprudence* (Princeton, NJ: Princeton Univ. Press, 1999), 237, note 1.

46. *Buck v. Bell*, 274 US 200 (1927).

47. Ibid.

48. Ibid., 207.

49. Paul A. Lambardo, "Three Generations, No Imbeciles: New Light on *Buck v. Bell*," *New York University Law Review* 60 (April 1985): 53.

50. Ibid., 51.

51. *Buck v. Bell*, 274 US 200, 205 (1927).

52. Ibid., 207.

53. Ibid.

54. Lambardo, "Three Generations," 61.
55. See the "Timeline" in Jeffrey D. Schultz and Laura Van Assendelft, eds., *Encyclopedia of Women in American Politics* (Phoenix, AZ: Oryx Press, 1999), 302–320.
56. *Goesaert v. Cleary*, 335 US 464, 466 (1948).
57. Ibid.
58. Ibid., 467.
59. Ibid., 468.
60. Baer, *Women in American Law*, 28.
61. Ibid., 132.
62. *United States v. Dege*, 364 US 51 (1960).
63. Ibid., 52.
64. Ibid., 55.
65. Ibid., 57.
66. *Orr v. Orr*, 440 US 268 (1979).
67. *Hoyt v. Florida*, 368 US 57 (1961).
68. *Hoyt* was implicitly overruled in *Taylor v. Louisiana* (419 US 522 [1975]), which held that the Sixth Amendment could not be interpreted to deny women from jury selection.
69. *Hoyt v. Florida*, 368 US 57, 62 (1961).
70. Ibid.
71. Baer, *Women in American Law*, 58.
72. Wendy W. Williams, "The Equality Crisis: Some Reflections on Culture, Courts, and Feminism," in *Feminist Legal Theory: Readings in Law and Gender*, eds. Katharine T. Bartlett and Rosanne Kennedy, 17 (Boulder, CO: Westview Press, 1991).
73. Otten, *Women's Rights and the Law*, 86.
74. *Griswold v. Connecticut*, 381 US 479 (1965).
75. Ibid., 485.
76. *Reed v. Reed*, 404 US 71.
77. Taub and Schneider, "Women's Subordination and the Role of Law," 345.
78. Susan Faludi, *Backlash: The Undeclared War against American Women* (New York: Crown Publishers, 1991), xiii–xix.
79. Nadine Strossen, "Women's Rights Under Seige," *North Dakota Law Review* 73 (1997): 210.
80. *Roe v. Wade*, 410 US 113, 116.
81. *Geduldig v. Aiello*, 417 US 484, 49 (1974).
82. Ibid., 497, note 20.
83. Ibid., 501.
84. *Dothard v. Rawlinson*, 433 US 321.
85. Ibid., 321, 335.
86. Kenneth L. Karst, "Woman's Constitution," *Duke Law Journal*, no. 3 (1984), 456.
87. *Dothard v. Rawlinson*, 433 US 321, 345.
88. Ibid.
89. Colette Dowling, *The Frailty Myth: Redefining the Physical Potential of Women and Girls* (New York: Random House, 2001), see chapter 5 for discussion of Title IX.
90. Faludi, *Backlash*, xix.
91. *Rostker v. Goldberg*, 453 US 57.
92. Norgren and Nanda, *American Cultural Pluralism and Law*, 198–199.
93. *Rostker v. Goldberg*, 453 US 57, 77.
94. Ibid., 78.
95. Ibid.
96. Norgren and Nanda, *American Cultural Pluralism and Law*, 199.
97. *United States v. Virginia*, 518 US 515 (1996).
98. Taub and Schneider, "Women's Subordination and the Role of Law," 351.
99. Strassen, "Women's Rights Under Seige," 210.
100. *United States v. Morrison*, 579 US 598.
101. Violence Against Women Act, 108 Stat. 1941.
102. *United States v. Morrison*, 579 US 598, 618.
103. Ibid., 631.

104. Ibid., 634.
105. Ibid., 636.

CHAPTER 8: "ALIEN FRIENDS AND ALIEN ENEMIES": MEXICAN AMERICANS AND THE LAW

1. Peter Skeery, "The Ambivalent Minority: Mexican Americans and the Voting Rights Act," *Journal of Policy History* 6, no. 1 (1994): 75. See also Skeery's *Mexican Americans: The Ambivalent Minority* (Cambridge, MA: Harvard Univ. Press, 1993). Evidence of contemporary xenophobic activity includes Arizona's enactment of a law in 2010, SB 1070, that essentially sought to criminalize all Mexicans and Mexican Americans, as well as any other Latinos, by mere suspicion alone. The Obama administration filed a successful lawsuit that invalidated the most egregious parts of that law, but the state is challenging that ruling.
2. L. H. Gann and Peter J. Dugan, *The Hispanics in the US: A History* (Boulder, CO: Westview Press, 1986), 3.
3. Plan of Iguala, February 24, 1821, www.tamu.edu/ccbn/dewitt/iguala.htm#annul.
4. Constitution of the Republic of Texas, http://tarlton.law.utexas.edu/constitutions/text/ccGP.html.
5. *Hardy v. De Leon*, 5 Tex. 211 (1849).
6. *Kilpatrick v. Sisneros*, 23 Tex. 113 (1859).
7. Ibid., 125.
8. David G. Gutierrez, "Introduction," in *Between Two Worlds: Mexican Immigrants in the United States,* David G. Gutierrez, ed., xvi (Wilmington, DE: Scholarly Resources, Inc., 1996).
9. *McKinney v. Saviego*, 59 US 235 (1855).
10. Joint Resolution for Annexing Texas, March 1, 1845, 28th Cong., Stat. vol. V, 797–798.
11. Texas Statehood, December 29, 1845, S. Con. Res. 1, 29th Cong. (1845).
12. Treaty of Guadalupe Hidalgo, 9 Stat. 922. And see Jack L. Bauer, *The Mexican War: 1846–1848* (Lincoln: Univ. of Nebraska Press, 1974) for a good discussion of this conflict.
13. Matt S. Meier and Feliciano Ribero, *Mexican Americans/American Mexicans: From Conquistadors to Chicanos*, rev. ed. (New York: Hill and Wang, 1993), 65–68.
14. Treaty of Guadalupe Hidalgo, 9 Stat. 922.
15. Ibid.
16. Ibid.
17. Cited in Richard Griswold del Castillo, "The Treaty of Guadalupe Hidalgo," in *US-Mexico Borderlands: Historical and Contemporary Perspectives,* Oscar J. Martinez, ed., 5–6 (Wilmington, DE: Scholarly Resources, 1996).
18. The Louisiana Purchase Treaty, http://avalon.law.yale.edu/19th_century/louis1.asp.
19. Rebecca Tsosie, "Sacred Obligations: Intercultural Justice and the Discourse of Treaty Rights," *UCLA Law Review* 47, no. 6 (August 2000): 1634–1635.
20. Territorial Act of Utah, 9 Stat. 453–454 (September 9, 1850).
21. *People v. De La Guerra*, 40 Cal. 311 (1870).
22. This conflict between a group of white adventurers and Mexicans arose near Sacramento and became known as the Bear Flag Revolt because the banner used by the whites featured a bear. This conflict quickly melded in with the Mexican War, and the whites were soon led by John Charles Fremont, a US Army captain, "who was illegally in the province on a reconnaissance expedition for the government." (Meier and Ribera, *Mexican Americans/American Mexicans*, 63).
23. *People v. De La Guerra*, 40 Cal. 311, 341 (1870).
24. Ibid.
25. Ibid.
26. *In re. Rodriguez*, 81 F. 337, 348 (D.W.D. Tex. 1897).
27. Ibid., 354–355.
28. *Independent School District v. Salvatierra*, 33 S.W.2d 790 (Sup. Ct. 1930).
29. Ibid., 791.
30. Ibid., 793.
31. Ibid., 794.
32. Ibid., 795 (emphasis added).
33. *Mendez v. Westminister School District*, 64 F. Supp. 544 (1946).

34. Ibid., 546.
35. Constitution of the State of California, www.sos.ca.gov/archives/ collections/1849/full-text. htm. But see Sucheng Chan and Spencer Olin, eds., *Major Problems in California History: Documents and Essays* (Boston: Houghton Mifflin, 1997) which has a good cross-section of articles and documents on some of the serious issues that have dogged California throughout its history.
36. Irving G. Hendrick, *California Education: A Brief History* (San Francisco: Boyd & Fraser Publishing, 1980), 7.
37. *Mendez v. Westminister School District*, 64 F. Supp. 544, 548.
38. Ibid., 548, note 5.
39. Ibid.
40. Ibid., 548, note 3.
41. Ibid., 546.
42. Ibid., 548–549.
43. Ibid., 549.
44. Ibid., 550.
45. Ibid., 549.
46. Philippa Strum, *Mendez v. Westminster: School Desegregation and Mexican-American Rights* (Lawrence: Univ. Press of Kansas, 2010), 162.
47. *Sanchez v. State*, 156 Tex. Crim. 468 (1951).
48. Ibid., 469 (emphasis added).
49. *Hernandez v. Texas*, 347 US 475 (1954).
50. In Rachel F. Moran and Devon W. Carbado, eds., *Race Law Stories* (New York: Foundation Press, 2008).
51. *Hernandez v. Texas*, 347 US 475, 477 (1954).
52. Ibid., 478 (emphasis added).
53. Ibid., 482.
54. *Cisneros v. Corpus Christi Independent School District*, 324 F. Supp. 599 (1970).
55. Ibid., 601.
56. Ibid., 604.
57. Ibid., 607–608.
58. Ibid., 608.
59. Ibid.
60. Ibid., 614.
61. Ibid., 616.
62. Ibid., 627.
63. *Cisneros v. Corpus Christi Independent School District*, 467 F.2d 142 (1972).
64. Ibid., 144.
65. Ibid., 148.
66. Ibid.
67. Ibid., 156.
68. Ibid. (emphasis added).
69. *San Antonio Independent School District v. Rodriguez, et al.*, 411 US 1 (1973).
70. Ibid., 59.
71. Jill Norgren and Serena Nanda, *American Cultural Pluralism and Law*, 2nd ed. (Westport, CT: Praeger, 1996), 225.
72. *Guadalupe v. Tempe Elementary School District*, 587 F.2d 1022 (1978).
73. Ibid., 1027.
74. Ibid.
75. *Madrigal v. Quilligan*, No. CV-75-2057-JWC (1978) (C.D. Cal.) This unreported case was reprinted in Dorothy A. Jones, *Critical Race Theory: Cases, Materials, and Problems* (St. Paul, MN: Thomson West, 2007), 98–107. This case was affirmed on appeal, 639 F.2d 789 (9th Cir., 1981).
76. Reynaldo Anaya Valencia, Sonia R. Garcia, Henry Flores, and José Roberto Juárez Jr., *Mexican Americans and the Law* (Tucson: Univ. of Arizona Press, 2004), 43.
77. As quoted in Jones, *Critical Race Theory*, 100.
78. Ibid.

79. See Carlos G. Velez, "The Nonconsenting Sterilization of Mexican American Women in Los Angeles," in *Twice a Minority: Mexican American Women,* ed. M. B. Melville (St. Louis, MO: C. V. Mosby, 1980).

80. John A. Garcia, *Latino Politics in America: Community, Culture, and Interests* (Lanham, MD: Rowman & Littlefield, 2003), 75.

81. *Perez v. FBI*, 707 F. Supp. 891 (1988).

82. Ibid., 900.

83. *Hernandez v. New York*, 111 S. Ct. 1859.

84. Ibid., 1864.

85. Ibid.

86. Ibid., 1872.

87. Ibid., 1877.

88. Ibid.

89. Ibid.

90. Louis DeSipio, "Latino Voters: Lessons Learned and Misunderstood" in *The Unfinished Agenda of the Selma-Montgomery Voting Rights March,* ed. Dara N. Byrne, 135 (Hoboken, NJ: John Wiley & Sons, 2005).

91. Valencia, et al., *Mexican American and the Law*, 115.

92. DeSipio, "Latino Voters," 136.

93. Alvaro Bedoya, "The Unforeseen Effects of *Georgia v. Ashcroft* on the Latino Community," *Yale Law Journal* 115 (2006): 2146.

94. *Bush v. Vera*, 517 US 952 (1996).

95. *Shaw v. Reno*, 509 US 630 (1993).

96. *Bush v. Vera*, 517 US 952, 1040–1041.

97. Ibid., 1041.

98. Strum, *Mendez v. Westminster*, 162.

CHAPTER 9: "STRANGERS IN THE LAND": ASIAN AMERICANS AND THE LAW

1. Don T. Nakanishi and James S. Lai, eds., *Asian American Politics: Law, Participation, and Policy* (Lanham, MD: Rowman & Littlefield, 2003), 2. And see Angelo N. Ancheta, *Race, Rights, and the Asian American Experience*, 2nd ed. (New Brunswick, NJ: Rutgers Univ. Press, 2006), xvii.

2. Terrance J. Reews and Claudette E. Bennett, "We the People: Asians in the United States" (Washington, DC: US Bureau of the Census, 2004).

3. Facts for Features: Asian/Pacific American Heritage Month: May 2010, www.census.gov/news room/releases/archives/facts_for_features_special_editions/cb10-ff07.html; and Nakanishi and Lai, *Asian American Politics*, 2.

4. Ancheta, *Race, Rights, and the Asian American Experience*, 5.

5. Bob H. Suzuki, "Education and the Socialization of Asian Americans: A Revisionist Analysis of the 'Model Minority' Thesis," *Amerasia* 4, no. 2 (1977): 24.

6. Sucheng Chan, *Asian Americans: An Interpretive History* (New York: Twayne Publishers, 1991), 169.

7. Timothy P. Fong, *The Contemporary Asian American Experience: Beyond the Model Minority* (Upper Saddle River, NJ: Prentice Hall, 1998), 68.

8. Andrew Sinclair, *The Savage: A History of Misunderstanding* (London: Weidenfeld & Nicolson, 1977), 84.

9. Chan, *Asian Americans*, 2.

10. *The Chinese Exclusion Case*, 130 US 581, 590 (1888).

11. Treaty with China, July 3, 1844, 8 Stat. 592.

12. Ronald Takaki, *A Different Mirror: A History of Multicultural America* (Boston: Little, Brown, 1993), 191–192.

13. Ibid., 192.

14. Chan, *Asian Americans*, 8.

15. Treaty with China, January 26, 1860, 12 Stat. 1023, 1029.

16. Betty Lee Sung, *The Story of the Chinese in America*, (New York: Collier Books, 1967), 11.

17.   Fong, *The Contemporary Asian American Experience*, 11.
18.   Ibid., 14.
19.   *People v. Naglee*, 1 Cal. 232 (1850).
20.   *People v. Hall*, 4 Cal. 399, 404–406. (1854).
21.   Chan, *Asian Americans*, 54.
22.   As quoted in Charles J. McCain, *In Search of Equality: The Chinese Struggle Against Discrimina-tion in Nineteenth Century America* (Berkeley: Univ. of California Press, 1994), 10.
23.   Chan, *Asian Americans*, 91.
24.   Treaty with China, July 28, 1868, 16 Stat. 739 (1868).
25.   Ibid., 740 (1868).
26.   Ibid.
27.   Fong, *The Contemporary Asian American Experience*, 11.
28.   *Chinese Exclusion Case*, 130 US 581 (1888).
29.   Ibid., 595.
30.   Sung, *The Story of the Chinese in America*, 35.
31.   Ibid., 44.
32.   See McCain's *In Search of Equality* (1994) for a thorough treatment of the discrimination Chi-nese faced during the nineteenth century in California and the nation.
33.   *In re Tiburcio Parrott*, 1 Fed. 481, 494–95 (1880).
34.   Ibid. (emphasis theirs).
35.   McCain, *In Search of Equality*, 79–83.
36.   *Baker v. Portland*, 2 Fed. Cas. No. 473 (1877).
37.   Ibid., 475.
38.   *In re Tiburcio Parrott*, 1 Fed. 481 (1880).
39.   McCain, *In Search of Equality*, 88–89.
40.   Ibid., 491–92 (emphasis added).
41.   Ibid., 493.
42.   Ibid., 498.
43.   Ibid., 517–18.
44.   Ibid., 498.
45.   *Ho Ah Kow v. Nunan*, 12 Fed. Cas. 252 (C.C.C. D. Cal. 1879).
46.   Ibid., 255.
47.   Ibid., 256.
48.   Ibid.
49.   Ibid., 257.
50.   Treaty with China, November 17, 1880, 22 Stat. 826.
51.   Ibid., 827.
52.   Chinese Exclusion Act, May 6, 1882, 22 Stat. 58.
53.   Scott Act, October 1, 1888, 25 Stat. 504.
54.   Ibid.
55.   *Chinese Exclusion Case*, 130 US 581 (1889).
56.   *Chinese Exclusion Case*, 130 US 581, 595 (1889) (emphasis added).
57.   Ibid., 595–596.
58.   Ancheta, *Race, Rights, and the Asian American Experience*, 25.
59.   Sung, *The Story of the Chinese in America*, 52.
60.   *Chinese Exclusion Case*, 130 US 581, 606 (1889).
61.   Ibid., 609.
62.   Ibid.
63.   *In re Lee Sing*, 43 F. 359 (C.C. Cal. 1890).
64.   Ibid.
65.   Ibid., 360.
66.   Geary Act, May 5, 1892, 27 Stat. 25.
67.   McCain, *In Search of Equality*, 202.
68.   Geary Act, 27 Stat., 25, 26.
69.   McCain, *In Search of Equality*, 203–204.
70.   Ibid., 204–205.

71.   *Fong Yue Ting v. United States*, 149 US 698 (1892).

72.   Ibid., 724.

73.   Ibid., 741–42.

74.   Ibid., 744.

75.   Ibid., 746.

76.   Ibid., 754.

77.   Ibid., 759.

78.   Ibid., 763.

79.   Treaty with China, March 17, 1894, 28 Stat. 1210. See the treaty in Charles I. Bevans, ed., *Treaties and Other International Agreements of the United States: 1776–1949*, vol. 6 (Washington, DC: Department of State, 1968–1976), 691–694.

80.   Bevans, *Treaties and Other International Agreements*, 692.

81.   Ibid., 693.

82.   See Erika Lee, "Birthright Citizenship, Immigration, and the US Constitution: The Story of *Wong Kim Ark v. United States*," in *Race Law Stories*, eds. Rachel Moran and Devon W. Carbado (New York: Foundation Press, 2008).

83.   *United States v. Wong Kim Ark*, 169 US 649 (1898).

84.   Ibid., 693.

85.   Ibid., 709.

86.   Ibid.

87.   *Elk v. Wilkins*, 112 US 94 (1884).

88.   *United States v. Wong Kim Ark*, 169 US 649, 725.

89.   Ibid., 725–726.

90.   Ibid., 730.

91.   As Erika Lee showed in "Birthright Citizenship," despite this important case, the Chinese exclusion laws would not be repealed until 1943, and Chinese Americans continued to suffer profound discrimination.

92.   *United States v. Ju Toy*, 198 US 253 (1905).

93.   Ibid., 268.

94.   Ibid., 269.

95.   Ibid., 274.

96.   Sung, *The Story of the Chinese in America*, 56.

97.   Ibid.

98.   Immigration Act of 1924, May 26, 1924, 43 Stat. 153.

99.   Chan, *Asian Americans*, 121.

100. Sung, *The Story of the Chinese in America*, 77.

101. To Repeal the Chinese Exclusion Acts, December 17, 1943, 57 Stat. 600.

102. Ibid., 601.

103. Sung, *The Story of the Chinese in America*, 79.

104. Ibid., 95.

105. Chan, *Asian Americans*, 141.

106. To Amend the Immigration and Nationalization Act, October 3, 1965, 79 Stat. 911.

107. Roger Daniels, "Asian Americans," in Encyclopedia of American Social History, vol. 2, eds. Mary Kupiec Cayton, Elliott J. Gorn, and Peter Williams, 883 (New York: Charles Scribner's Sons, 1993).

108. Ibid., 886.

109. *Lau v. Nichols*, 414 US 563 (1973).

110. Ibid., 568.

111. As quoted in Ancheta, *Race, Rights, and the Asian American Experience*, 107.

112. Daniels, "Asian Americans," 884.

113. US Census Bureau, "The American Community–Asians: 2004" (Washington, DC: Department of Commerce, February 2007).

114. Fong, *The Contemporary Asian American Experience*, 65.

115. Ibid., 140–141.

116. Frank H. Wu, *Yellow: Race in America Beyond Black and White* (New York: Basic Books, 2002), 70.

117. Ancheta, *Race, Rights, and the Asian American Experience*, 72–73.

118. *Lee v. Department of Justice*, 413 F. 3d 53 (D.C. Circ. 2005), 55.
119. Spencer K. Turnbull, "Wen Ho Lee and the Consequences of Enduring Asian American Stereotypes," in *Asian American Politics*, eds. Don T. Nakanishi and James S. Lai, 308 (Lanham, MD: Rowman & Littlefield, 2003).
120. Ancheta, *Race, Rights, and the Asian American Experience*, 73.
121. Ibid., 73–74.
122. Turnbull, "Wen Ho Lee," 305.
123. Frank H. Wu, "Profiling Principle: The Prosecution of Wen Ho Lee and the Defense of Asian Americans," in *Asian American Politics*, eds. Don T. Nakanishi and James S. Lai, 298 (Lanham, MD: Rowman & Littlefield, 2003).
124. *Wen Ho Lee v. United States Department of Justice*, 287 F. Supp. 2d 15 (D.D.C. 2003).
125. *Lee v. Department of Justice*, 413 F. 3d 53 (D.C. Circ. 2005). One of the journalists, Jeff Garth, had his contempt verdict overturned because of insufficient evidence.
126. Sung, *The Story of the Chinese in America*, 281.
127. David J. O'Brien and Stephen Fugita, *The Japanese American Experience* (Bloomington: Indiana Univ. Press, 1991), 10.
128. Ibid.
129. Chan, *Asian Americans*, 9.
130. Takaki, *A Different Mirror*, 247.
131. O'Brien and Fugita, *The Japanese American Experience*, 18.
132. Takaki, *A Different Mirror*, 247.
133. Paula D. McClain and Joseph Stewart Jr., *"Can We All Get Along?" Racial and Ethnic Minorities in American Politics*, 4th ed. (Boulder, CO: Westview Press, 2006), 21.
134. Masakazu Iwata, "The Japanese Immigrants in California Agriculture," in *Promises to Keep: A Portrayal of Nonwhites in the United States,* eds. Bruce A. Glasrud and Alan M. Smith, 300 (Chicago: Rand McNally, 1972).
135. It was not until 1885 that the Japanese government modified its emigration policy to allow Japanese citizens to move to Hawaii and to California. (McClain and Stewart, *"Can We All Get Along?"* 21.)
136. Iwata, "The Japanese Immigrants," 300.
137. Ibid.
138. Ibid., 331–332.
139. O'Brien and Fugita, *The Japanese American Experience*, 15.
140. Ibid., 10.
141. Takaki, *A Different Mirror*, 247.
142. Amendment to Various Acts relative to Immigration and the Importation of Aliens, March 3, 1891, 26 Stat. 1084.
143. Ibid., 1085.
144. *Nishimura Ekiu v. United States*, 142 US 651, 652 (1891).
145. Ibid.
146. 29 Stat. 848.
147. Ibid., 853.
148. Sung, *The Story of the Chinese in America*, 69.
149. *United States v. Yamasaka*, 100 Fed. 404 (1900).
150. Ibid.
151. *Japanese Immigrant Case*, 189 US 86 (1903).
152. Ibid., 101 (emphasis added).
153. Ibid., 101–102.
154. Ibid., 102.
155. Thomas A. Bailey, *Theodore Roosevelt and the Japanese-American Crises* (Gloucester, MA: Peter Smith Publishers, 1964), 12.
156. Ibid., 10–11.
157. Iwata, "The Japanese Immigrants," 305.
158. Daniels, "Asian Americans," 876.
159. Bailey, *Theodore Roosevelt*, 33.
160. Ibid., 35.

161. Ibid., 142–143.
162. To Regulate the Immigration of Aliens into the US, February 20, 1907, 34 Stat. 898.
163. Chan, *Asian Americans*, 38.
164. Bailey, *Theodore Roosevelt*, 165.
165. Henry Steele Commager, *Documents of American History*, 9th ed. (Englewood Cliffs, NJ: Prentice-Hall, 1971), document no. 367.
166. As quoted in *Oyama v. California*, 332 US 633, 654, footnote 4 (1948).
167. Chan, *Asian Americans*, 68.
168. Ibid., 69.
169. O'Brien and Fugita, *The Japanese American Experience*, 20.
170. Treaty with Japan, February 21, 1911, 37 Stat. 1504.
171. *Oyama v. California*, 332 US 633, 654 (1948).
172. Ibid., 654–655.
173. Chan, *Asian Americans*, 47.
174. *Oyama v. California*, 332 US 633, 657 (1948).
175. Ibid.
176. Iwata, "The Japanese Immigrants," 306.
177. *Oyawa v. California*, 332 US 633, 661 (1948).
178. See Devon W. Carbado, "Yellow by Law: The Story of *Ozawa v. United States*," in *Race Law Stories,* eds. Rachel F. Moran and Devon W. Carbado (New York: Foundation Press, 2008) for a full account of this important case.
179. Ibid., 184.
180. *Ozawa v. United States*, 260 US 178 (1922).
181. To Establish a Uniform Rule of Naturalization, March 26, 1790, 1 Stat. 103.
182. *Ozawa v. United States*, 260 US 178, 195 (1922).
183. Ibid., 197.
184. Ibid., 198.
185. Ibid.
186. Ibid.
187. Ibid.
188. Roger Daniels, *The Politics of Prejudice: The Anti-Japanese Movement in California and the Struggle for Japanese Exclusion,* 2nd ed. (Berkeley: Univ. of California Press, 1977), 90.
189. *Oyama v. California*, 332 US 633, 659.
190. Chan, *Asian Americans*, 47.
191. *Oyama v. California*, 332 US 633, 667.
192. Ibid., 670.
193. *Asakura v. Seattle*, 265 US 332 (1924).
194. *In re Naka's License*, 9 Alaska 1 (1934).
195. *Tokaji v. State Board of Education*, 67 P2d. 1082 (1937).
196. Roger Daniels, "Incarceration of the Japanese Americans: A Sixty-Year Perspective," *The History Teacher* 35, no. 3 (2008), www.historycooperative.org/journals/ht/35.3/daniels.html.
197. O'Brien and Fugita, *The Japanese American Experience*, 46.
198. To Prohibit Certain Acivities, with Respect to Aliens, June 28, 1940, 54 Stat. 670.
199. *Annual Report of the Attorney General for Fiscal Year Ended June 30, 1942* (Washington, DC: Government Printing Office, 1943), 14.
200. Eugene V. Rostow, "The Japanese American Cases: A Disaster," *Yale Law Journal* 54, no. 3 (June 1945): 495.
201. Ibid., 520–521.
202. Ibid.
203. To Provide a Penalty for Violation of Restrictions in Military Areas, March 21, 1942, 56 Stat. 173.
204. Daniels, "Incarceration," 4.
205. Rostow, "The Japanese American Cases," 508.
206. O'Brien and Fugita, *The Japanese American Experience*, 74–79.
207. See Roger Daniels, *Concentration Camp USA: Japanese Americans and World War II* (New York: Holt, Rinehart & Winston, 1971) and Peter Irons, *Justice at War* (New York: Oxford Univ. Press, 1993) for good analyses of these cases.

208. *Hirabayashi v. United States*, 320 US 81 (1943).
209. *Minoru Yasui v. United States*, 320 US 115 (1943). This case dealt with the curfew issue, but the court relied on *Hirabayashi* to affirm Yasui's conviction.
210. Jerry Kong, "Dodging Responsibility: The Story of *Hirabayashi v. United States*" in *Race Law Stories,* eds. Rachel F. Moran and Devon W. Carbado (New York: Foundation Press, 2008).
211. *Hirabayashi v. United States*, 320 US 81, 96 (1943).
212. Ibid., 96–97.
213. Ibid., 99.
214. Ibid., 100.
215. Ibid., 106.
216. Ibid., 111.
217. *Korematsu v. United States*, 323 US 214 (1944).
218. *Ex Parte Mitsuye Endo*, 323 US 283 (1944).
219. Fred Korematsu's case was actually heard twice by the Supreme Court, once in 1943 and again the following year. See Chan, *Asian Americans*, 136–137 for details.
220. *Korematsu v. United States*, 323 US 214, 219 (1944).
221. Ibid., 223 (emphasis his).
222. Ibid., 232.
223. Ibid., 243.
224. Ibid., 233.
225. Ibid., 236–237.
226. Ibid., 239–240.
227. Ibid., 242.
228. Ibid., 246.
229. *Ex Parte Mitsuye Endo*, 323 US 283, 295.
230. Rostow, "The Japanese American Cases," 513.
231. *Ex Parte Mitsuye Endo*, 323 US 283, 291.
232. Ibid., 302.
233. Ibid., 309.
234. Ibid.
235. Chan, *Asian Americans*, 141.
236. Ronald O. Haak, "The Case of the Japanese-Americans," in *Promises to Keep: A Portrayal of Nonwhites in the United States,* eds. Bruce A. Glasrud and Alan M. Smith, 332 (Chicago: Rand McNally, 1972).
237. Japanese Evacuation Claims Act, July 2, 1948, 62 Stat. 1231.
238. O'Brien and Fugita, *The Japanese American Experience*, 74.
239. *Oyama v. California*, 332 US 633 (1948).
240. Ibid., 647.
241. Ibid., 644.
242. Ibid., 648.
243. Ibid., 663.
244. O'Brien and Fugita, *The Japanese American Experience*, 79.
245. Chan, *Asian Americans*, 174.
246. In 2009, the US Senate passed a unanimous resolution apologizing to African Americans for the practice of slavery. While welcomed by many as a long overdue measure, the resolution explicitly stated that the language of the resolution could not be used for reparation claims (www.washingtonpost.com/wp-dyn/content/article/2009/06/18/AR2009061803877.html). Also in 2009, the US formally issued a muted apology to Native peoples across the country. President Obama signed a resolution that apologized "on behalf of the people of the United States to all Native peoples for the many instances of violence, maltreatment, and neglect inflicted on Native peoples by citizens of the United States." Interestingly, this resolution was not a direct apology by the US to Native nations, and the Obama administration did not issue any statement accompanying the resolution, which was part of a defense appropriation spending bill. Thus, for many Native individuals, nations, and organizations there is a real question whether the US has, in fact, actually apologized for its historic treatment of indigenous peoples.
247. Ibid.

248. Daniels, "Incarceration," 7.

249. McClain and Stewart, *"Can We All Get Along?"* 74.

250. O'Brien and Fugita, *The Japanese American Experience*, 128.

CHAPTER 10: "IN THEIR 'BEST' INTERESTS": CHILDREN AND THE LAW

1. Samine Sengupta, "UN Session Begins to Tackle the Perils of Being Young," *The New York Times*, May 9, 2002.

2. The United States officially sanctioned the death penalty for juveniles until 2005, when the Supreme Court in *Roper v. Simmons* (543 US 551) held that the Eighth and Fourteenth Amendments forbade imposition of the death penalty on offenders who were under eighteen when their crimes were committed.

3. Barry Feld, *Bad Kids: Race and the Transformation of the Juvenile Court* (New York: Oxford Univ. Press, 1999), 333.

4. Jane Woldfogel, *The Future of Child Protection: How to Break the Cycle of Abuse and Neglect* (Cambridge: Harvard Univ. Press, 2001), 6.

5. Wendy Fitzgerald, "Maturity, Difference, and Mystery: Children's Perspectives and the Law," *Arizona Law Review* 36 (Spring 1994): 37.

6. Barbara Woodhouse, "'Who Owns the Child?'" *Meyer* and *Pierce* and the Child as Property," *William and Mary Law Review* 33 (Summer 1992): 1042.

7. Barbara Woodhouse, "'Out of Children's Needs, Children's Rights': The Child's Voice in Defining the Family," *Brigham Young University Journal of Public Policy* 8 (1994): 327.

8. Tom Campbell, "The Rights of the Minor as Person, as Child, as Juvenile, and Future Adult," in *Children, Rights, and the Law,* eds. Philip Aston, Stephen Parker, and John Seymour, 16 (New York: Oxford Univ. Press, 1992).

9. *Thompson v. Oklahoma*, 486 US 815, 825, n. 23 (1988).

10. Feld, *Bad Kids*.

11. Ibid., 17.

12. Michael Grossberg, "Children's Legal Rights: A Historical Look at a Legal Paradox," in *Children at Risk in America: History, Concepts, and Public Policy,* ed. Roberta Wollons, 116 (Albany: State Univ. of New York Press, 1993).

13. Michael Grossberg, "Balancing Acts: Crisis, Change, and Continuity in American Family Law, 1890–1990," *Indiana Law Review* (1995): 286.

14. Fitzgerald, "Maturity, Difference," 52.

15. Feld, *Bad Kids*, 52.

16. *Ex Parte Crouse*, 4 Whort. 9 [Pa. 1838].

17. Ibid., 3.

18. Lois A. Weithorn, "Protecting Children From Exposure to Domestic Violence: The Use and Abuse of Child Maltreatment," *Hastings Law Journal* 53 (2001): 42–43.

19. Grossberg, "Children's Legal Rights," 119.

20. Weithorn, "Protecting Children," 48.

21. Feld, *Bad Kids*, 37.

22. Ibid.

23. Weithorn, "Protecting Children," 52.

24. *Hammer v. Dagenhart*, 247 US 251.

25. Ibid., 280.

26. *Bailey v. Drexel Furniture Co.*, 259 US 20 (1923).

27. Woodhouse, "Who Owns the Child," 1067.

28. Ibid., 996.

29. *Meyer v. Nebraska*, 262 US 390, 400 (1923).

30. *Pierce v. Society of the Sisters*, 268 US 510, 535 (1925).

31. Ibid.

32. *Prince v. Massachusetts*, 321 US 158, 166 (1944).

33. Ibid., 170.

34. Ibid.

35. Grossberg, "Children's Legal Rights," 124.

36. *Brown v. Board of Education of Topeka*, 347 US 483, 493 (1954).

37. *In re Gault*, 387 US 1, 27–28 (1967).

38. Ibid., 13.

39. Janet L. Dolgin, "The Age of Autonomy: Legal Reconceptualizations of Childhood," *Quinnipiac Law Review* (1999): 447.

40. Feld, *Bad Kids*, 106–07.

41. Ibid., 107.

42. Grossberg, "Children's Legal Rights," 129–130.

43. Dolgin, "The Age of Autonomy," 422.

44. Fitzgerald, "Maturity, Difference," 22.

45. *McKeiver v. Pennsylvania*, 403 US 528, 547 (1971).

46. Albert R. Matheny, "*McKeiver v. Pennsylvania*," in *The Oxford Companion to the Supreme Court of the United States,* ed. Kermit L. Hall, 538–539 (New York: Oxford Univ. Press, 1992).

47. *Ingraham v. Wright*, 430 US 651, 681 (1977).

48. *Parham v. J.R.*, 442 US 584, 602 (1979).

49. *New Jersey v. T.L.O.*, 469 US 325, 341 (1985).

50. *Veronica School District v. Acton*, 515 US 646, 654, 662 (1995).

51. *Morse v. Frederick*, 551 US 393 (2007).

52. Ibid., 410.

53. Ibid., 435.

54. Fitzgerald, "Maturity, Difference," 19.

55. Woodhouse, "Out of Children's Needs," 327.

CHAPTER 11: "THE STATE OF NATURE": THE NATURAL WORLD AND THE LAW

1. Charles Reich, "The New Property," *Yale Law Journal* 73, no. 5 (April 1964): 739.

2. Raphael Minder, "Looking for Wedge From Spain, Catalonia Bans Bullfighting," *The New York Times*, July 29, 2010.

3. Martin Roberts, "Spanish Parliament to Extend Rights to Apes," Reuters, June 25, 2008, www .reuters.com/article/2008/06/25/us-spain-apes-idUSL256586320080625 (accessed 12/15/2008).

4. Donald G. McNeil Jr. "When Human Rights Extend to Nonhumans," *The New York Times*, July 13, 2008. In 1999, New Zealand's parliament enacted a bill that stopped short of conferring basic human rights on apes, but did extend them legal protection from scientific experimentation. Britain was the first state to prohibit experiments on chimpanzees, orangutans, and gorillas. See Lee Glendinning, "Spanish Parliament Approves 'Human Rights' for Apes," *Guardian*, June 26, 2008, www.guardian.co.uk/world/2008/jun/26/humanrights.animalwelfare (accessed 12/15/2008).

5. Deborah Ball, "Swiss Reject Law on Animal Rights," *The Wall Street Journal*, March 8, 2010, http://online.wsj.com/article/SB10001424052748703936804575107811656131100.html (accessed 7/12/2010).

6. See the *San Antonio Express-News*, May 21, 2008. Author has copy of the report by Ariane Willemson, ed. Published by the Federal Ethics Committee on Non-Human Biotechnology (Swiss Federation, April 2008).

7. Vine Deloria Jr., *C. J. Jung and the Sioux Traditions* (New Orleans: Spring Journal Press, 2009), 91.

8. Peter Singer, *Animal Liberation*, revised ed. (New York: Harper Collins, 2002), 6.

9. See Thomas G. Kelch, "Toward a Non-property Status for Animals," *New York University Environmental Law Journal* 6 (1998): 531; Jane Goodall and Stephen M. Wise, "Are Chimpanzees Entitled to Fundamental Legal Rights?" *Animal Law* 3 (1997): 61–73; and Derek W. St. Pierre, "The Transition from Property to People: The Road to the Recognition of Rights for Non-Human Animals," *Hastings Women's Law Journal* 9 (Summer 1998): 255–271.

10. St. Pierre, "The Transition from Property to People," 261.

11. Vine Deloria Jr., *The Metaphysics of Modern Existence* (New York: Harper & Row, 1979), 135.

12. Vine Deloria Jr., *C. J. Jung and the Sioux Traditions*, see chapter 9, "Jung and the Animals."

13. Peter Singer, *Animal Liberation*, 187.

14. Ibid., 206.

15. St. Pierre, "The Transition from Property to People," 261.

16. Steven M. Wise, *Rattling the Cage: Toward Legal Rights for Animals* (Cambridge, MA: Perseus, 2000), 43.

17. Ibid.

18. Roderick Frazier Nash, *The Rights of Nature: A History of Environmental Ethics* (Madison: Univ. of Wisconsin Press, 1989), 19.

19. Ibid., and see Singer, *Animal Liberation*, 7.

20. Wise, *Rattling the Cage*, 44.

21. Robert V. Percival, "Environmental Law," in *The Oxford Companion to American Law*, ed. Kermit L. Hall, 259 (New York: Oxford Univ. Press, 1992).

22. Ibid.

23. Nash, *The Rights of Nature*, 34.

24. Percival, "Environmental Law," 259.

25. Nash, *The Rights of Nature*, 63.

26. Deloria, *Metaphysics*, 135.

27. Leopold's book was written in 1948, but he died before it was edited and published by his son Luna in 1949.

28. Aldo Leopold, *A Sand County Almanac: With Essays on Conservation from Round River* (New York: Ballantine Books, 1966), xviii.

29. Ibid., xix.

30. Ibid., 238.

31. Rachel Carson, *Silent Spring* (Boston, MA: Houghton Mifflin, 1962).

32. Ibid., 8.

33. Ibid., 64.

34. Clean Air Act, 77 Stat. 401.

35. Wilderness Act, 78 Stat. 890.

36. Land and Water Conservation Fund, 78 Stat. 897.

37. Solid Waste Disposal Act, 79 Stat. 992.

38. Christopher Stone, "Should Trees Have Standing? Toward Legal Rights for Natural Objects," *Southern California Law Review* 45 (1972): 452.

39. Roger W. Findley and Daniel A. Farber, *Environmental Law*, 4th ed. (St. Paul, MN: West Publishing, 1996), 2.

40. Christopher Stone, *Should Trees Have Standing? And Other Essays on Law, Morals and the Environment* (Dobbs Ferry, NY : Oceana Publications, 1996), ix.

41. Ibid.

42. Stone, "Should Trees Have Standing," 455.

43. *Sierra Club v. Morton*, 405 US 727, 741–42.

44. Deloria, *Metaphysics*, 138.

45. Wise, *Rattling the Cage*, 44.

46. *Jennison v. Kirk*, 98 US 453.

47. Justice Field quoting from the *Congressional Globe*, 1st Session, 39th Congress, part IV, 3225–3228.

48. *Jennison v. Kirk*, 98 US 453, 457.

49. *Coffin v. The Left Hand Ditch Co.*, 6 Colo. 443.

50. This system of water law originated in California. It was specifically developed for the western states, which hold and receive far less water than the eastern part of the country. A central element in this doctrine is that the first appropriator of a water source has top priority over later arrivals. Rights depend on usage and not on who owns the land. And "once a person puts water to a beneficial use and complies with any statutory requirements, a water right is perfected and remains valid so long as it continues to be used." (David H. Getches, *Water Law*, 2nd ed. [St. Paul, MN: West Publishing, 1994], 5–6.)

51. This is the most common water law system. It is used in twenty-nine states, nearly all of which are located in the East and Midwest. Landowners who live adjacent a water source are denominated as riparians, as their adjacent location to water grants them certain rights to use the water next to their property. Two features of the riparian system are that (1) the riparian must make "reasonable" use of the water, and (2) if the water amount is reduced then all riparians must adjust their usage accordingly. (Getches, *Water Law*, 4).

52. *Coffin v. The Left Hand Ditch Co.*, 6 Colo., 443, 446.

53. Ibid.
54. *Commonwealth v. Turner*, 145 Mass. 296, 298 (1887).
55. Ibid., 299.
56. Ibid., 300 (emphasis added).
57. *Stephen v. State*, 65 Miss. 329 (1888).
58. Ibid.
59. Ibid.
60. Ibid.
61. Ibid.
62. Ibid.
63. Ibid.
64. *Hunt v. State*, 3 Ind. App. 383, 29 N.E. 933 (1892).
65. Ibid., 933.
66. Ibid.
67. Ibid.
68. Ibid., 934.
69. Wise, *Rattling the Cage*, 45.
70. *Geer v. Connecticut*, 161 US 519 (1896).
71. Ibid., 522.
72. Ibid.
73. *Hughes v. Oklahoma*, 441 US 322 (1979).
74. *State v. Karstendiek*, 39 L.R.A. 520, 49 La. Ann. 1621 (1897).
75. Ibid., 1624 (emphasis added).
76. Ibid.
77. See Laurence H. Tribe, "Ways Not to Think About Plastic Trees: New Foundations for Environmental Law," *Yale Law Journal* 38 (1974): 1315; and Elizabeth L. DeCoux, "In the Valley of the Dry Bones: Reuniting the Word 'Standing' With its Meaning in Animal Cases," *William and Mary Environmental Law & Policy Review* 29 (2005): 682.
78. Cited in *City of Shreveport v. Price*, 77 So. 883, 885 (1918). Mentioned in *State v. Martin*, 189 So. 109, 110 (1939); and *Warrenburger v. Folson*, 239 F.2d 846, 848 (3rd Circ. C. Pa) (1956).
79. *People ex. rel. Freel v. Downs*, 26 N.Y. Crim. R. 327; 136 N.Y.S. 440 (1911).
80. Ibid., 443.
81. Ibid.
82. Ibid., 444.
83. Ibid., 445.
84. Ibid.
85. *Scenic Hudson Preservation Conference v. Federal Power Commission*, 354 F.2d 608 (1965).
86. Stone, *Should Trees Have Standing?* (1996), 15.
87. Ibid.
88. *Scenic Hudson Preservation Conference v. Federal Power Commission*, 354 F.2nd 608 (1965).
89. Ibid., 608.
90. *Sierra Club v. Morton*, 405 US 727 (1972).
91. *Cappaert v. United States*, 426 US 128 (1970).
92. Ibid., 131.
93. Ibid., 138.
94. As quoted in Nash, *The Rights of Nature*, 132.
95. *Tennnessee Valley Authority v. Hull,* 437 US 153, 157 (1978).
96. Ibid., 172–173.
97. Ibid., 196.
98. Ibid., 210.
99. Nash, *The Rights of Nature*, 178.
100. *Palila v. Hawaii Department of Land and Natural Resources*, 471 F. Supp. 985 (1979).
101. See *Northern Spotted Owl v. Hodel*, 716 F. Supp. 479 (1988), *Northern Spotted Owl v. Lujan*, 758 F. Supp. 621 (1991), *Mt. Graham Red Squirrel v. Yeutter*, 930 F. 2d 703 (1991), *Hawaiian Crow v. Lujan*, 906 F. Supp. 549 (1991), *Florida Key Deer v. Stickney*, 864 F. Supp. 1222 (1994), and *Marble Murrelet v. Pacific Lumber Co.*, 880 F. Supp. 1343 (1995).

102.   Stone, *Should Trees Have Standing?* (1996),160.

103.   *Hawaiian Crow v. Lujan*, 506 F. Supp. 549 (1991).

104.   Ibid., 551–552.

105.   Ibid., 552.

106.   Ibid., 552–553.

107.   *Marbled Murrelet v. Pacific Lumber Co.*, 880 F. Supp. 1343 (1995).

108.   Ibid., 1346.

109.   *Whitman v. American Trucking Associations, Inc.*, 121 S. Ct. 903 (2001).

110.   Ibid., 904.

111.   Ibid., 908 (emphasis added).

112.   George W. Bush on Environment, www.ontheissues.org/Celeb/George_W__Bush_Environment.htm.

113.   *Massachusetts v. Environmental Protection Agency*, 127 S. Ct. 1438; 549 US 497 (2007).

114.   Linda Greenhouse, "Justices Say EPA Has Power to Act on Harmful Gasses," *The New York Times*, April 3, 2007. As a sign of the dramatically altered political landscape in Washington, DC, in the wake of Obama's election, the EPA on April 17, 2009, formally declared carbon dioxide and five other heat-trapping gases to be pollutants that threaten public health and welfare. This declaration sets in motion a process that will finally lead to the regulation of these dangerous gases for the first time in American history. (John M. Broder, "EPA Clears Path to Regulate Heat-Trapping Gases for First Time in US," *The New York Times*, April 18, 2009).

115.   *Massachusetts v. Environmental Protection Agency*, 127 S. Ct. 1438, 1446.

116.   Ibid., 1462.

117.   Ibid., 1463.

118.   Greenhouse, "Justices Say EPA Has Power."

119.   *Exxon Shipping v. Baker*, 128 S. Ct. 2605.

120.   *Winter v. Council of Natural Resources Defense Council*, 555 US 7 (2008).

121.   *Exxon Shipping v. Baker*, 128 S. Ct. 2605, 2608.

122.   Ibid., 2614.

123.   Ibid., 2615.

124.   *Maragne v. States Marine Lines, Inc.*, 398 US 375, 387 (1970).

125.   *Exxon Shipping v. Baker*, 128 S. Ct. 2605, 2638.

126.   Ibid., 2639.

127.   Adam Liptak, "Damages Cut Against Exxon in Valdez Case," *The New York Times*, June 26, 2008.

128.   Campbell Robertson and Clifford Krauss, "Gulf Spill Is the Largest of Its Kind, Scientists Say," *The New York Times,* August 3, 2010.

129.   *Winter v. Council of Natural Resources Defense Council*, 555 US 7 (2008).

130.   Ibid., 28.

131.   Ibid.

132.   Ibid., 25.

133.   Ibid., 13.

134.   *United States v. Stevens*, 130 S. Ct. 1577 (2010).

135.   Depiction of Animal Cruelty Act, December 9, 1999, 113 Stat. 1732.

136.   Percival, "Environmental Law," 264.

137.   US Congress, House, *Hearing Before the Subcommittee on Crime, Terrorism, and Homeland Security of the Committee on the Judiciary*, 109th Congress, 2nd Session on HR 4239, May 23, 2006, 1.

138.   Ibid., 2.

139.   Animal Enterprise Terrorism Act, November 27, 2006, 120 Stat. 2652 (2006).

140.   Caroline Paul, "Does the 'Terrorist' Label Fit the Crime?" *Los Angeles Times,* May 25, 2007.

CHAPTER 12: EXPANDING THE LEGAL UNIVERSE

1.   Charles Reich, "The New Property," *Yale Law Journal* 73, no. 1 (1964): 771.

2.   *Brown v. Board of Education of Topeka*, 347 US 483 (1954) (Statutory segregation of white and black schoolchildren denied the black children equal protection).

3.   *Cisneros v. Corpus Christi Independent School District*, 467 F.2d 142 (5th Cir. 1972) (Nonstatutory

segregation in public schools constituted state action for purposes of Fourteenth Amendment), *cert. denied,* 413 US 920, 922 (1973).

4.   *Lau v. Nichols,* 414 US 563 (1974) (Public school system must provide English language instruction to non-English-speaking students).

5.   *DeFunis v. Odegaard,* 416 US 312 (1974) (Concerning claim that state school's admission policies discriminated against a nonminority applicant).

6.   *Regents of the University of California v. Bakke,* 438 US 265 (1978) (Special minority admissions program at state medical school denied equal protection to nonminority applicant).

7.   *Pollock v. Farmers' Loan & Trust Co.,* 158 US 601 (1895).

8.   Ibid. at 534 (Argument of appellants' counsel).

BIBLIOGRAPHY

Alfange, Dean. *The Supreme Court and the National Will.* New York: Doubleday, Doran & Co., 1937.

Anaya, S. James. *Indigenous Peoples in International Law.* 2nd ed. New York: Oxford Univ. Press, 2004.

Ancheta, Angelo N. *Race, Rights, and the Asian American Experience.* 2nd ed. New Brunswick, NJ: Rutgers Univ. Press, 2006.

Annual Report of the Attorney General for Fiscal Year Ended June 30, 1942. Washington, DC: Government Printing Office, 1943.

Archibold, Randall C. "Arizona Blocked From Enforcing Immigration Law." *The New York Times*, July 29, 2010.

Arnold, Thurman. *The Symbols of Government.* New Haven, CT: Yale Univ. Press, 1935.

Baer, Judith. *Our Lives Before the Law: Constructing a Feminist Jurisprudence.* Princeton, NJ: Princeton Univ. Press, 1999.

———. *Women in American Law: The Struggle Toward Equality from the New Deal to the Present.* 2nd ed. New York: Holmes & Meier, 1996.

Ball, Deborah. "Swiss Reject Law on Animal Rights." *The Wall Street Journal*, March 8, 2010, http://online.wsj.com/article/SB10001424052748703936804575107811656131100.html (accessed 7/12/2010).

Bailey, Thomas A. *Theodore Roosevelt and the Japanese-American Crisis.* Gloucester, MA: Peter Smith Publishers, 1964.

Bardolph, Richard, ed. *The Civil Rights Record: Black Americans and the Law, 1849–1970.* New York: Thomas Y. Crowell, Co., 1970.

Barsh, Russel Lawrence, and James Youngblood Henderson. *The Road: Indian Tribes and Political Liberty.* Berkeley: Univ. of California Press, 1980.

Bauer, Jack L. *The Mexican War: 1846–1848.* Lincoln: Univ. of Nebraska Press, 1974.

Bedoya, Alvaro. "The Unforeseen Effects of *Georgia v. Ashcroft* on the Latino Community." *Yale Law Journal* 115 (2006): 2112–46.

Belz, Herman. "Affirmative Action." In *The Oxford Companion to the Supreme Court of the United States*, edited by Kermit L. Hall, 19. New York: Oxford Univ. Press, 1992.

Berger, Raoul. *Government by Judiciary.* Cambridge, MA: Harvard Univ. Press, 1977.

Bergman, Barbara R. *In Defense of Affirmative Action.* New York: Basic Books, 1996.

Berkhofer, Robert F. Jr. *The White Man's Indian.* New York: Vintage Books, 1978.

Bevans, Charles I., ed. *Treaties and Other International Agreements of the United States: 1776–1949.* Vol. 6. Washington, DC: Department of State, 1968–1976.

Black, Hugo L. "The Bill of Rights–James Madison Lecture." In *One Man's Stand for Freedom: Mr. Justice Black and the Bill of Rights*, 31–48. New York: Alfred A. Knopf, 1963.

Borrows, John. *Canada's Indigenous Constitution.* Toronto, ON: Univ. of Toronto Press, 2010.

Broder, John M. "EPA Clears Path to Regulate Heat-Trapping Gases for First Time in US." *The New York Times*, April 18, 2009.

Brown, Dorothy A. *Critical Race Theory: Cases, Materials, and Problems.* St. Paul, MN: Thompson/West, 2007.

Brown, Janelle. "The Taliban's Bravest Opponents." Salon.com, http://dir.salon.com/mwt/feature/2001/10/02/fatima/index.html. Accessed October 2, 2001.

Brown, Judith Olans, Lucy A. Williams, and Phyllis Tropper Baumann. "The Mythogenesis of Gender: Judicial Images of Women in Paid and Unpaid Labor." *UCLA Women's Law Journal* 6 (Spring 1996): 458–539.

Burnette, Robert. *The Road to Wounded Knee.* New York: Bantam Books, 1974.

Campbell, Tom. "The Rights of the Minor as Person, as Child, as Juvenile, and Future Adult." In *Children, Rights, and the Law*, edited by Philip Aston, Stephen Parker, and John Seymour. 1–23. New York: Oxford Univ. Press, 1992.

Carbado, Devon W. "Yellow by Law: The Story of *Ozawa v. United States*." In *Race Law Stories*, edited by Rachel F. Moran and Devon Carbado. 171–231. New York: Foundation Press, 2008.

Cardozo, Benjamin N. *The Nature of the Judicial Process.* New Haven, CT: Yale Univ. Press, 1949.

———. "The Paradoxes of Legal Science." In *Selected Writings of Benjamin Nathan Cardozo*, edited by Margaret E. Hall. 251–70. New York: Fallon Publications, 1947.

Carson, Rachel. *Silent Spring.* Boston: Houghton Mifflin, 1962.

Castile, George Pierre. *To Show Heart: Native American Self-Determination and Federal Indian Policy, 1960–1975.* Tucson: Univ. of Arizona Press, 1998.

Castillo, Richard Griswold del. "The Treaty of Guadalupe Hidalgo." In *US-Mexico Borderlands: Historical and Contemporary Perspectives,* edited by Oscar J. Martinez. 2–9. Wilmington, DE: Scholarly Resources, Inc., 1996.

Chan, Sucheng. *Asian Americans: An Interpretive History.* New York: Twayne Publishers, 1991.

Chan, Sucheng, and Spencer Olin, eds. *Major Problems in California History: Documents and Essays.* Boston: Houghton Mifflin, 1997.

Cohen, Adam. "Last Term's Winner at the Supreme Court: Judicial Activism." *The New York Times,* July 9, 2007.

Cohen, Felix S. *Handbook of Federal Indian Law.* Washington, DC: Government Printing Office, 1942. Reprint ed., Albuquerque: Univ. of New Mexico Press, 1972.

———. *On the Drafting of Tribal Constitutions.* Edited by David E. Wilkins. Norman: Univ. of Oklahoma Press, 2006.

Cohen, Morris Raphael. *Reason and Law: Studies in Juristic Philosophy.* Glencoe, IL: Free Press, 1950.

Commager, Henry Steele. *Documents of American History.* 9th ed. Englewood Cliffs, NJ: Prentice-Hall, 1971.

Cortner, Richard C. *A Mob Intent on Death: The NAACP and the Arkansas Riot Cases.* Middleton, CT: Wesleyan Univ. Press, 1988.

Cott, Nancy F. *No Small Courage: A History of Women in the United States.* New York: Oxford Univ. Press, 2000.

Coulter, Robert T. "The Denial of Legal Remedies to Indian Nations Under United States Law." *American Indian Journal* 3 (1977): 5–11.

Countryman, Edward. *The American Revolution.* New York: Hill and Wang, 1985.

Cramer, Renee Ann. *Cash, Color, and Colonialism: The Politics of Tribal Acknowledgment.* Norman: Univ. of Oklahoma Press, 2005.

Cushman, H. B. *History of the Choctaw, Chickasaw, and Natchez Indians.* Edited by Angie Debo, 1899. Reprint ed., Norman: Univ. of Oklahoma Press, 1999.

Daniels, Roger. "Asian American." In *Encyclopedia of American Social History,* Vol. 2., edited by Mary Kupiec Cayton, Elliott J. Gorn, and Peter W. Williams. 873–90. New York: Charles Scribner's Sons, 1993.

———. *Concentration Camps USA: Japanese Americans and World War II.* New York: Holt, Rinehart & Winston, 1971.

———. "Incarceration of the Japanese Americans: A Sixty-Year Perspective." *The History Teacher* 35, no. 3 (2008).

———. *The Politics of Prejudice: The Anti-Japanese Movement in California and the Struggle for Japanese Exclusion.* 2nd ed. Berkeley: Univ. of California Press, 1977.

Davis, Natalie Zoman, and Jill Ker Conway. "The Rest of the Story." *The New York Times Magazine,* May 16, 1999, 81–85.

Debo, Angie. *And Still the Waters Run: The Betrayal of the Five Civilized Tribes.* Norman: Univ. of Oklahoma Press, 1984.

———. *A History of the Indians of the United States.* Norman: Univ. of Oklahoma Press, 1973.

DeCoux, Elizabeth L. "In the Valley of the Dry Bones: Reuniting the Word 'Standing' With its Meaning in Animal Cases." *William and Mary Environmental Law & Policy Review* 29 (2005): 681–764.

Deloria, Vine Jr. *Behind the Trail of Broken Treaties: An Indian Declaration of Independence.* Austin: Univ. of Texas Press, 1985.

———. *C. G. Jung and the Sioux Traditions: Dreams, Visions, Nature, and the Primitive.* Edited by Philip J. Deloria and Jerome S. Bernstein. New Orleans: Spring Journal Books, 2009.

———. *The Metaphysics of Modern Existence.* New York: Harper & Row, 1979.

Deloria, Vine Jr., and Clifford M. Lytle. *The Nations Within: The Past and Future of American Indian Sovereignty.* Austin: Univ. of Texas Press, 1984.

Deloria, Vine Jr., and David E. Wilkins. *Tribes, Treaties, and Constitutional Tribulations.* Austin: Univ. of Texas Press, 1999.

Deloria, Vine Jr., and Raymond DeMallie. *Documents of American Indian Diplomacy: Treaties, Agreements, and Conventions, 1775–1979.* 2 vols. Norman: Univ. of Oklahoma Press, 1999.

DeSipio, Louis. "Latino Voters: Lessons Learned and Misunderstood." In *The Unfinished Agenda of the Selma-Montgomery Voting Rights March*, edited by Dara N. Byrne. 135–42. Hoboken, NJ: John Wiley & Sons, 2005.

Dolgin, Janet L. "The Age of Autonomy: Legal Reconceptualizations of Childhood." *Quinnipiac Law Review* (1999): 421–50.

Dowling, Colette. *The Frailty Myth: Redefining the Physical Potential of Women and Girls*. New York: Random House, 2001.

DuBois, W. E. B. *Black Reconstruction in America, 1860–1880*. New York: Atheneum, 1935.

Duthu, N. Bruce. *American Indians and the Law*. New York: Penguin Books, 2008.

Ely, James W. Jr. *Railroads and American Law*. Lawrence: Univ. Press of Kansas, 2001.

Faludi, Susan. *Backlash: The Undeclared War against American Women*. New York: Crown, 1991.

Fehrenbacher, Don E. *The Dred Scott Case: Its Significance in American Law and Politics*. New York: Oxford Univ. Press, 1978.

Feld, Barry. *Bad Kids: Race and the Transformation of the Juvenile Court*. New York: Oxford Univ. Press, 1999.

Fenton, William N. *The Great Law and the Longhouse: A Political History of the Iroquois Confederacy*. Norman: Univ. of Oklahoma Press, 1998.

Findley, Roger W., and Daniel A. Farber. *Environmental Law*. 4th ed. St. Paul, MN: West Publishing, 1996.

Fitzgerald, Wendy. "Maturity, Difference, and Mystery: Children's Perspectives and the Law." *Arizona Law Review* 36 (Spring 1994): 11–111.

Fong, Timothy P. *The Contemporary Asian American Experience: Beyond the Model Minority*. Upper Saddle River, NJ: Prentice Hall, 1994.

Fung, Richard. "'Seeing Yellow': Asian Identities in Film and Video." In *The State of Asian American Activism and Resistance in the 1990s*, edited by Karen Aguilar-San Juan. 161–171. Boston: South End Press, 1994.

Gale, Mary Ellen. "Unfinished Women: The Supreme Court and the Incomplete Transformation of Women's Rights in the United States." *Whittier Law Review* 9 (1987): 448.

Gann, L. H., and Peter J. Dugan. *The Hispanics in the US: A History*. Boulder, CO: Westview Press, 1986.

Garcia, John A. *Latino Politics in America: Community, Culture and Interests*. Lanham, MD: Rowman & Littlefield, 2003.

Garrison, Tim Alan. *The Legal Ideology of Removal: The Southern Judiciary and the Sovereignty of Native American Nations*. Athens: Univ. of Georgia Press, 2002.

Gates, Paul W. *History of Public Land Law Development*. Washington, DC: Government Printing Office, 1968.

Getches, David H. *Water Law*. 2nd ed. St. Paul, MN: West Publishing, 1994.

Glendinning, Lee. "Spanish Parliament Approves 'Human Rights' for Apes." *Guardian*, June 26, 2008.

Goldberg, Carole. "What's Race Got to Do With It? The Story of *Morton v. Mancari*." In *Race Law Stories*, edited by Rachel F. Moran and Devon Carbado. 233–69. New York: Foundation Press, 2008.

Goldstein, Leslie Friedman. *The Constitutional Rights of Women*. 2nd ed. Madison: Univ. of Wisconsin Press, 1988.

Goodal, Jane, and Stephen M. Wise. "Are Chimpanzees Entitled to Fundamental Legal Rights?" *Animal Law* 3 (1997): 61–73.

Greenhouse, Linda. "Justices Say EPA Has Power to Act on Harmful Gases." *The New York Times*, April 3, 2007.

Grossberg, Michael. "Balancing Acts: Crisis, Change, and Continuity in American Family Law, 1890–1990." *Indiana Law Review* 28 (1995): 273–308.

———. "Children's Legal Rights: A Historical Look at a Legal Paradox." In *Children at Risk in America: History, Concepts, and Public Policy,* edited by Roberta Wollons. 111–40. Albany: State Univ. of New York Press, 1993.

Guinier, Lani, and Gerald Torres. *The Miner's Canary: Enlisting Race, Resisting Power, Transforming Democracy*. Cambridge, MA: Harvard Univ. Press, 2002.

Gutierrez, David G. "Introduction." In *Between Two Worlds: Mexican Immigrants in the United States*, edited by David G. Gutierrez. xi–xxvii. Wilmington, DE: Scholarly Resources, 1996.

Haak, Ronald O. "The Case of the Japanese-Americans." In *Promises to Keep: A Portrayal of Nonwhites in the United States*, edited by Bruce A. Glasrud and Alan M. Smith. 322–33. Chicago: Rand McNally, 1972.

Hamilton, Alexander, James Madison, and John Jay. *The Federalist Papers*. New York: New American Library, 1961.

Harring, Sidney L. *Crow Dog's Case: American Indian Sovereignty, Tribal Law, and United States Law in the Twentieth Century*. New York: Cambridge Univ. Press, 1994.

Heidenreich, Conrad E. "Huron." In *Handbook of North American Indians: Northeast*, Vol. 15, edited by Bruce G. Trigger. 368–88. Washington, DC: Smithsonian Institution, 1978.

Hendrick, Irving G. *California Education: A Brief History*. San Francisco, CA: Boyd & Fraser Publishing, 1980.

Hertzberg, Hazel W. *The Search for an American Indian Identity: Modern Pan-Indian Movements*. Syracuse, NY: Syracuse Univ. Press, 1971.

Hindery, Leo Jr., and Donald W. Riegle Jr. "The Jobs Solution." *The Nation* 288, no. 15 (April 20, 2009): 13–16.

Hovenkamp, Herbert. "Due Process." In the *Oxford Companion to American Law*, edited by Kermit L. Hall. 235. New York: Oxford Univ. Press, 2002.

Hutchinson, Dennis J. "*Brown v. Board of Education*." In *The Oxford Companion to the Supreme Court of the United States*, edited by Kermit L. Hall. 93–96. New York: Oxford Univ. Press, 1992.

Indian Law Resource Center. "Native Land Law Project: Draft General Principles of Law Relating to Native Lands and Natural Resources," General Edition. Little Canada, MN: Indian Land Tenure Foundation, 2010.

Institute for the Development of Indian Law. *Proceedings of the Great Peace Commission of 1867–1868*. Washington, DC: Institute for the Development of Indian Law, 1975.

Irons, Peter H. *Justice at War*. New York: Oxford Univ. Press, 1993.

Iwata, Masakazu. "The Japanese Immigrants in California Agriculture." In *Promises to Keep: A Portrayal of Nonwhites in the United States*, edited by Bruce A. Glasrud and Alan M. Smith. 298–315. Chicago: Rand McNally, 1972.

Jones, Dorothy A. *Critical Race Theory: Cases, Materials, and Problems*. St. Paul, MN: Thompson/West Publishing, 2007.

Jordan, Winthrop D. *White Over Black: American Attitudes Toward the Negro, 1550–1812*. Baltimore, MD: Penguin Books, 1968.

Kairys, David. *With Liberty and Justice for Some: A Critique of the Conservative Supreme Court*. New York: The New Press, 1993.

Kang, Jerry. "Dodging Responsibility: The Story of *Hirabayashi v. United States*." In *Race Law Stories*, edited by Rachel F. Moran and Devon Carbado. 307–39. New York: Foundation Press, 2008.

Kappler, Charles J., comp. *Indian Affairs: Laws and Treaties*. 2 vols. Washington, DC: Government Printing Office, 1903.

Karst, Kenneth L. "Women's Constitution." *Duke Law Journal*, no. 3 (1984): 447–508.

Kelch, Thomas G. "Toward a Non-property Status for Animals." *New York University Environmental Law Journal* 6 (1998): 531–54.

Kelso, Louis O., and Patricia Hetter. *Two Factor Theory: The Economics of Reality*. New York: Vintage Books, 1967.

Kidwell, Clara Sue. *The Choctaws in Oklahoma: From Tribe to Nation, 1855–1970*. Norman: Univ. of Oklahoma Press, 2007.

Kitano, Harry H. L., and Roger Daniels. *Asian Americans: Emerging Minorities*. Englewood Cliffs, NJ: Prentice Hall, 1987.

Kluger, Richard. *Simple Justice: The History of Brown v. Board of Education and Black America's Struggle for Equality*. New York: Knopf, 1977.

Kolchin, Peter. *American Slavery: 1619–1877*. New York: Hill and Wang, 1993.

Kristof, Nicholas D., and Sheryl WuDunn. "Why Women's Rights Are the Cause of Our Time." *The New York Times Magazine*, August 23, 2009, 28–39.

Lacy, Dan. *The Meaning of the American Revolution*. New York: New American Library, 1964.

Lambardo, Paul A. "Three Generations, No Imbeciles: New Light on *Buck v. Bell*." *New York University Law Review* 60 (April 1985): 53.

Lee, Erika. "Birthright Citizenship, Immigration, and the US Constitution: The Story of *Wong Kim*

Ark v. United States." In *Race Law Stories*, edited by Rachel F. Moran and Devon Carbado. 85–105. New York: Foundation Press, 2008.

Leopold, Aldo. *A Sand County Almanac: With Essays on Conservation from Round River.* New York: Ballantine Books, 1966.

Liptak, Adam. "Damages Cut Against Exxon in Valdez Case." *The New York Times*, June 26, 2008.

———. "Dissenters Argue That Ruling Will Corrupt Democracy." *The New York Times*, January 22, 2010.

———. "The Most Conservative Court in Decades." *The New York Times*, July 25, 2010.

Locke, John. *Of Civil Government: Two Treatises.* London: J. M. Dent & Sons, 1924.

———. *Two Treatises of Government.* New York: New American Library, 1963.

Lofgren, Charles A. *The Plessy Case: A Legal-Historical Interpretation.* New York: Oxford Univ. Press, 1987.

Lopez, Ian Henry, and Michael A. Olivas. "Jim Crow, Mexican Americans, and the Anti-Subordination Constitution: The Story of *Hernandez v. Texas.*" In *Race Law Stories*, edited by Rachel F. Moran and Devon Carbado. 269–306. New York: Foundation Press, 2008.

Marable, Manning. "Staying on the Path to Racial Equality." In *The Affirmative Action Debate*, edited by George E. Curry. 3–15. Reading, MA: Addison-Wesley, 1996.

Martinez-Ebers, Valerie, and Manochehr Dorraj. *Perspectives on Race, Ethnicity, and Religion: Identity Politics in America.* New York: Oxford Univ. Press, 2010.

McCain, Charles J. *In Search of Equality: The Chinese Struggle Against Discrimination in Nineteenth Century America.* Berkeley: Univ. of California Press, 1994.

McCaslin, Wanda D., ed. *Justice as Healing: Indigenous Ways.* St. Paul, MN: Living Justice Press, 2005.

McClain, Paula D., and Joseph Stewart Jr. *"Can We All Get Along?" Racial and Ethnic Minorities in American Politics.* 4th ed. Boulder, CO: Westview Press, 2006.

McNeil, Donald G. Jr. "When Human Rights Extend to Nonhumans." *The New York Times*, July 13, 2008.

Meier, Matt S., and Feliciano Ribero. *Mexican Americans/American Mexicans: From Conquistadors to Chicanos.* Revised ed. New York: Hill and Wang, 1993.

Mitchell, Donald Craig. *Sold American: The Story of Alaska Natives and Their Land, 1867–1959.* Hanover, RI: Univ. Press of New England, 1997.

Mohawk, John. *Utopian Legacies: A History of Conquest and Oppression in the Western World.* Santa Fe, NM: Clear Light Press, 1999.

Montesquieu, Baron de. *The Spirit of Laws.* In *Great Books of the Western World*, Vol. 38, edited by Robert Maynard Hutchins. Chicago: Encyclopedia Britannica, 1952.

———. *The Spirit of Laws.* Edited by David Wallace Carrithers. Berkeley: Univ. of California Press, 1977.

Moran, Rachel F., and Devon W. Carbado, eds. *Race Law Stories.* New York: Foundation Press, 2008.

Nakanishi, Don T., and James S. Lai, eds. *Asian American Politics: Law, Participation, and Policy.* Lanham, MD: Rowman & Littlefield, 2003.

Nash, Roderick Frazier. *The Rights of Nature: A History of Environmental Ethics.* Madison: Univ. of Wisconsin Press, 1989.

Newcomb, Steven T. *Pagans in the Promised Land: Decoding the Doctrine of Christian Discovery.* Golden, CO: Fulcrum Publishing, 2008.

Newton, Nell Jessup. "Federal Power Over Indians: Its Sources, Scope and Limitations." *University of Pennsylvania Law Review* 132 (1984): 195–288.

Nieman, Donald G. *Promises to Keep: African Americans and the Constitutional Order, 1776 to the Present.* New York: Oxford Univ. Press, 1991.

Norgren, Jill. *The Cherokee Cases: Two Landmark Federal Decisions in the Fight for Sovereignty.* Norman: Univ. of Oklahoma Press, 2004.

Norgren, Jill, and Serena Nanda. *American Cultural Pluralism and Law.* 2nd ed. Westport, CT: Praeger, 1996.

Northrop, F. S. C. *The Taming of the Nations: A Study of the Cultural Bases of International Policy.* New York: MacMillan, 1952.

Norton, Mary Beth, and Ruth M. Alexander, eds. *Major Problems in American Women's History.* 2nd ed. Lexington, MA: D. C. Heath & Co., 1996.

Oakes, James. "Slavery." In *Encyclopedia of American Social History*, Vol. 2., edited by Mary Kupiec Cayton, Elliott J. Gorn, and Peter W. Williams. 1407–19. New York: Charles Scribner's Sons, 1993.

O'Brien, David J., and Stephen Fugita. *The Japanese American Experience*. Bloomington: Indiana Univ. Press, 1991.

O'Brien, David M. *Storm Center: The Supreme Court in American Politics*. 7th ed. New York: W. W. Norton & Co., 2005.

Otis, D. S. *The Dawes Act and the Allotment of Indian Lands*. Edited by Francis P. Prucha. Norman: Univ. of Oklahoma Press, 1973.

Otten, Laura A. *Women's Rights and the Law*. Westport, CT: Praeger, 1993.

Pasquaretta, Paul. *Gambling and Survival in Native North America*. Tucson: Univ. of Arizona Press, 2003.

Paul, Caroline. "Does the 'Terrorist' Label Fit the Crime?" *Los Angeles Times*, May 25, 2007.

Pearce, Roy Harvey. *Savagism and Civilization: A Study of the Indian and the American Mind*. Baltimore: Johns Hopkins Press, 1953.

Percival, Robert V. "Environmental Law." In *The Oxford Companion to American Law*, edited by Kermit L. Hall. 258–264. New York: Oxford Univ. Press, 1990.

Pitkin, Hannah. "Obligation and Consent." *American Political Science Review* 59, no. 4 (December 1965): 990–99.

Plucknett, Theodore F. T. *A Concise History of the Common Law*. 2nd ed. Rochester, NY: The Lawyers Cooperative Publishing, 1956.

Polin, Raymond. "The Rights of Man in Hobbes and Locke." In *Political Theory and the Rights of Man*, edited by D. D. Raphael. Bloomington: Indiana Univ. Press, 1967.

Porter, Robert Odawi. *Sovereignty, Colonialism and the Indigenous Nations: A Reader*. Durham, NC: Carolina Academic Press, 2005.

Power, Lucas A. Jr. *The Warren Court and American Politics*. Cambridge, MA: Belknap Press of Harvard Univ. Press, 2000.

Preston, Julia. "Fueled by Anger Over Law, Immigration Advocates Rally for Change." *The New York Times*, May 2, 2010.

Price, Don K. *The Scientific Estate*. Cambridge, MA: Belknap Press of Harvard Univ. Press, 1965.

———. *America's Unwritten Constitution: Science, Religion, and Political Responsibility*. Baton Rouge: Louisiana State Univ. Press, 1983.

Price, Melanye T., and Gloria T. Hampton. "Linked Fates, Disconnected Realities: The Post-Civil Rights African American Politics." In *Perspectives on Race, Ethnicity, and Religion: Identity Politics in America*, edited by Valerie Martinez-Ebers and Manochehr Dorraj. 121–37. New York: Oxford Univ. Press, 2010.

Pritchett, C. Herman. *The American Constitution*. New York: McGraw-Hill, 1959.

Rakove, Jack N. *Original Meanings: Politics and Ideas in the Making of the Constitution*. New York: Alfred A. Knopf, 1996.

Rawls, John. *Collected Papers*. Cambridge, MA: Harvard Univ. Press, 1999.

———. *Justice as Fairness: A Restatement*. Edited by Erin Kelly. Cambridge, MA: Harvard Univ. Press, 2001.

———. *The Law of Peoples*. Cambridge, MA: Harvard Univ. Press, 1999.

———. *Political Liberalism*. New York: Columbia Univ. Press, 1993.

———*A Theory of Justice*. Cambridge, MA: Harvard Univ. Press, 1971.

Reews, Terrance J., and Claudette E. Bennett. "We the People: Asians in the United States." Washington, DC: US Bureau of the Census, 2004.

Reich, Charles. "The New Property." *Yale Law Journal* 73, no. 5 (April 1964): 733–87.

Roberts, Martin. "Spanish Parliament to Extend Rights to Apes." Reuters, June 25, 2008. www.reuters.com/article/2008/06/25/us-spain-apes-idUSL256586320080625. Accessed December 15, 2008.

Robertson, Campbell, and Clifford Krauss. "Gulf Spill Is the Largest of Its Kind, Scientists Say." *The New York Times*, August 3, 2010.

Robertson, Lindsay G. *Conquest by Law: How the Discovery of America Dispossessed Indigenous Peoples of Their Lands*. New York: Oxford Univ. Press, 2005.

Rostow, Eugene V. "The Japanese American Cases: A Disaster." *Yale Law Journal* 54, no. 3 (June 1945): 489–533.

Rusco, Elmer R. *A Fateful Time: The Background and Legislative History of the Indian Reorganization Act*. Reno: Univ. of Nevada Press, 2000.

Schultz, Jeffrey D., and Laura Van Assendelft, eds. *Encyclopedia of Women in American Politics*. Phoenix, AZ: Oryx Press, 1999.

———. *Encyclopedia of Minorities in American Politics.* Vol. 1, *African Americans and Asian Americans.* Phoenix, AZ: Oryx Press, 2000.

Scott, Daryl Michael. *Contempt and Pity: Social Policy and the Image of the Damaged Black Psyche, 1880–1996.* Chapel Hill: Univ. of North Carolina Press, 1997.

Scott, James Brown. *James Madison's Notes of Debates in the Federal Convention of 1787 and Their Relation to a More Perfect Society of Nations.* New York: Oxford Univ. Press, 1918.

Seed, Patricia. *American Pentimento: The Invention of Indians and the Pursuit of Riches.* Minneapolis: Univ. of Minnesota Press, 2001.

Sengupta, Samine. "UN Session Begins to Tackle the Perils of Being Young." *The New York Times,* May 9, 2002.

Shavers, Anna Williams. "A Century of Developing Citizenship Law and the Nebraska Influence: A Centennial Essay." *Nebraska Law Review* 70 (1991): 462–518.

Sigerman, Harriet. "An Unfinished Battle: 1848–1865." In *No Small Courage: A History of Women in the United States,* edited by Nancy F. Cott. 237–88. New York: Oxford Univ. Press, 2000.

Sinclair, Andrew. *The Savage: A History of Misunderstanding.* London: Weidenfeld & Nicolson, 1977.

Singer, Peter. *Animal Liberation.* Revised ed. New York: Harper Collins, 2002.

Skeery, Peter. "The Ambivalent Minority: Mexican Americans and the Voting Rights Act." *Journal of Political History* 6, no. 1 (1994): 73–95.

———. *Mexican Americans: The Ambivalent Minority.* Cambridge, MA: Harvard Univ. Press, 1993.

Skogen, Larry C. *Indian Depredations Claims, 1796–1920.* Norman: Univ. of Oklahoma Press, 1996.

Skrentny, John D. *The Minority Rights Revolution.* Cambridge, MA: The Belknap Press of Harvard Univ. Press, 2002.

Slotkin, Richard. *Regeneration Through Violence: The Mythology of the American Frontier, 1600–1800.* Middletown, CT: Wesleyan Univ. Press, 1973.

Starna, William A. "Cooper's Indians: A Critique." In *James Fenimore Cooper: His Country and His Art,* edited by George A. Test. 63–76. Oneonta: State Univ. College of New York, 1991.

Stevenson, Richard W. "Capitalism After the Fall." *The New York Times,* April 19, 2009.

St. Pierre, Derek W. "The Transition from Property to People: The Road to the Recognition of Rights for Non-Human Animals." *Hastings Women's Law Journal* 9 (Summer 1998): 255–71.

Stewart, Paul H. "Financing Self-Determination: Federal Indian Expenditures, 1975–1988." *American Indian Culture and Research Journal* 14, no. 2 (1990): 1–18.

Stone, Christopher. "Should Trees Have Standing? Toward Legal Rights for Natural Objects." *Southern California Law Review* 45 (1972): 450–501.

———. "Should Trees Have Standing? Revisited: How Far Will Law and Morals Reach? A Pluralist Perspective." *Southern California Law Review* 59 (November 1985): 1–154.

———. *Should Trees Have Standing? And Other Essays on Law, Morals and the Environment.* Dobbs Ferry, NY : Oceana Publications, 1996.

Strossen, Nadine. "Women's Rights Under Seige." *North Dakota Law Review* 73 (1997): 207–30.

Strum, Philippa. *Mendez v. Westminster: School Desegregation and Mexican-American Rights.* Lawrence: Univ. Press of Kansas, 2010.

Sung, Betty Lee. *The Story of the Chinese in America.* New York: Collier Books, 1967.

Suzuki, Bob H. "Education and the Socialization of Asian Americans: A Revisionist Analysis of the 'Model Minority' Thesis." *Amerasia* 4, no. 2 (1977): 23–51.

Swindler, William F. *Court and Constitution in the Twentieth Century.* Indianapolis: Bobbs-Merrill, 1974.

Takaki, Ronald. *A Different Mirror: A History of Multicultural America.* Boston: Little, Brown, 1993.

Taub, Nadine, and Elizabeth M. Schneider. "Women's Subordination and the Rule of Law." In *The Politics of Law: A Progressive Critique,* 3rd ed., edited by David Kairys. 328–55. New York: Basic Books, 1998.

Tibbles, Thomas Henry. *The Ponca Chiefs: An Account of the Trial of Standing Bear.* Edited by Kay Graber. Lincoln: Univ. of Nebraska Press, 1972.

Tocqueville, Alexis de. *Democracy in America.* Edited by J. P. Mayer. New York: Doubleday, 1969.

Tribe, Laurence H. "Ways Not to Think About Plastic Trees: New Foundations for Environmental Law." *Yale Law Journal* 83 (1974): 1315–48.

Tsosie, Rebecca. "Sacred Obligations: Intercultural Justice and the Discourse of Treaty Rights." *UCLA Law Review* 47, no. 6 (August 2000): 1615–72.

Tsuk Mitchell, Dalia. *Architect of Justice: Felix S. Cohen and the Founding of American Legal Pluralism.* Ithaca, NY: Cornell Univ. Press, 2007.

Turnbull, Spencer K. "Wen Ho Lee and the Consequences of Enduring Asian American Stereotypes." In *Asian American Politics: Law, Participation, and Policy,* edited by Don Nakanishi and James S. Lai. 303–16. Lanham, MD: Rowman & Littlefield, 2003.

Tushnet, Mark. *The NAACP's Legal Strategy Against Segregated Education: 1925–1950.* Chapel Hill: Univ. of North Carolina Press, 2004.

US Congress. American Indian Policy Review Commission. *Final Report.* Washington, DC: Government Printing Office, 1977.

US Congress. House. *Hearing Before the Subcommittee on Crime, Terrorism, and Homeland Security of the Committee on the Judiciary.* 109th Congress, 2nd session on HR 4239, May 23, 2006.

US Congress. Senate. *The Effect of the Fourteenth Amendment on Indian Tribes.* Senate Report No. 268, 41st Congress, 3rd session, 1870.

Valencia, Reynaldo Anaya, Sonia R. Garcia, Henry Flores, and Jose Roberto Juarez Jr. *Mexican Americans and the Law.* Tucson: Univ. of Arizona Press, 2004.

Velez, Carlos G. "The Nonconsenting Sterilization of Mexican American Women in Los Angeles." In *Twice a Minority: Mexican American Women,* edited by M. B. Melville. St. Louis, MO: C.V. Mosby, 1980.

Warren, George A., ed. *Decisions of the Department of the Interior. Solicitor's Opinions.* Washington, DC: Government Printing Office, 1938.

Weithorn, Lois A. "Protecting Children From Exposure to Domestic Violence: The Use and Abuse of Child Maltreatment." *Hastings Law Journal* 53 (2001): 1–52.

Wells, Samuel T., and Rosanna Tubby, eds. *After Removal: The Choctaw in Mississippi.* Jackson: Univ. Press of Mississippi, 1986.

West, Robin. "Jurisprudence and Gender." In *Feminist Legal Theory: Readings in Law and Gender,* edited by Katharine T. Bartlett and Rosanne Kennedy. 201–234. Boulder, CO: Westview Press, 1991.

Whitaker, Robert. *On the Laps of Gods: The Red Summer of 1919 and the Struggle for Justice That Remade the Nation.* New York: Crown, 2008.

Whitehead, Alfred North. *Adventure of Ideas.* New York: MacMillan, 1933.

Wilkins, David E., and Tsianina Lomawaima. *Uneven Ground: American Indian Sovereignty and Federal Law.* Norman: Univ. of Oklahoma Press, 2001.

Williams, Robert A. Jr. *The American Indian in Western Legal Thought: The Discourses of Conquest.* New York: Oxford Univ. Press, 1990.

Williams, Wendy W. "The Equality Crisis: Some Reflections on Culture, Courts, and Feminism." In *Feminist Legal Theory: Readings in Law and Gender,* edited by Katharine Bartlett and Rosanne Kennedy. 15–34. Boulder, CO: Westview, 1991.

Wise, Steven M. *Rattling the Cage: Toward Legal Rights for Animals.* Cambridge, MA: Perseus, 2000.

Woldfogel, Jane. *The Future of Child Protection: How to Break the Cycle of Abuse and Neglect.* Cambridge, MA: Harvard Univ. Press, 2001.

Woodhouse, Barbara. "'Out of Children's Needs, Children's Rights': The Child's Voice in Defining the Family." *Brigham Young University Journal of Public Policy* 8 (1994): 321–40.

———. "'Who Owns the Child?' *Meyer* and *Pierce* and the Child as Property." *William and Mary Law Review* 33 (Summer 1992): 995–1122.

Wright, Benjamin F. *The Growth of American Constitutional Law.* Chicago: Univ. of Chicago Press, 1967.

Wu, Frank H. "Profiling Principle: The Prosecution of Wen Ho Lee and the Defense of Asian Americans." In *Asian American Politics: Law, Participation, and Policy,* edited by Don Nakanishi and James S. Lai. 297–301. Lanham, MD: Rowman & Littlefield, 2003.

———. *Yellow: Race in America Beyond Black and White.* New York: Basic Books, 2002.

CASE REFERENCES

Adkins v. Children's Hospital, 261 US 525 (1923)
Asakura v. Seattle, 265 US 332 (1924)
Austin v. Michigan Chamber of Commerce, 494 US 652 (1990)
Bailey v. Drexel Furniture Co., 259 US 20 (1923)
Baker v. Portland, 2 Fed. Cas. No. 473 (1877)
Bank of Augusta v. Earle, 38 US 519 (1839)
Berea College v. Kentucky, 211 US 45 (1908)
Board of Education of Independent School District of Pottawatomi County v. Earls, 536 US 822 (2002)
Bradwell v. Illinois, 83 US 130 (1873)
Brown v. Board of Education of Topeka, 347 US 483 (1954)
Brown v. Board of Education of Topeka, 349 US 294 (1955)
Buck v. Bell, 274 US 200 (1927)
Bush v. Vera, 517 US 952 (1996)
Cappaert v. United States, 426 US 128 (1970)
Cherokee Nation v. Georgia, 30 US (5 Pet.) 1 (1831)
Chicago, Burlington and Quincy Railroad Company v. Iowa, 94 US 155 (1877)
Chicago, Milwaukee and St. Paul Railroad Co. v. State of Minnesota,134 US 418 (1890)
Chinese Exclusion Case, 130 US 581 (1889)
Cisneros v. Corpus Christi Independent School District, 342 F. Supp. 599 (1970)
Citizens United v. Federal Election Commission, 130 S. Ct. 876 (2010)
City of Sherrill v. Oneida Indian Nation of New York, 544 US 197 (2005)
City of Shreveport v. Price, 77 So. 883 (1918)
Civil Rights Cases, 109 US 3 (1883)
Coffin v. The Left Hand Ditch Co., 6 Colo. 443
Colliflower v. Garland, 342 F.2d. 369 (1965)
Commonwealth v. Turner, 145 Mass. 296, 298 (1887)
Connecticut General Life Insurance Co. v. Johnson, 303 US 77 (1938)
Davis v. Sitka School Board, 3 Alaska 481 (1908)
DeFunis v. Odegaard, 416 US 312 (1974)
Dobbs v. the United States and the Apache Indians, 33 Ct. Cls. 308 (1898)
Dothard v. Rawlinson, 433 US 321 (1977)
Dred Scott v. Sandford, 60 US 393 (1857)
Elk v. Wilkins, 112 US 94 (1884)
ex Parte Crouse, 4 Whort. 9 (Pa. 1838)
ex Parte Crow Dog, 109 US 556 (1883)
ex Parte Mitsuye Endo, 323 US 283 (1944)
Exxon Shipping v. Baker, 128 S. Ct. 2605 (2008)
Federal Election Commisson v. Wisconsin Right to Life, 551 US 449 (2007)
Florida Key Deer v. Stickney, 864 F. Supp. 1222 (1994)
Fong Yue Ting v. United States, 149 US 698 (1892)
Geduldig v. Aiello, 417 US 484 (1974)
Geer v. Connecticut, 161 US 519 (1896)
Goesaert v. Cleary, 335 US 464 (1948)
Gong Lum v. Rice, 275 US 78 (1927)
Gratz v. Bollinger, 539 US 244 (2003)
Griswold v. Connecticut, 381 US 479 (1965)
Grutter v. Bollinger, 539 US 306 (2003)
Guadalupe v. Tempe Elementary School District, 587 F.2d 1022 (1978)
Hall v. De Cuir, 95 US 485 (1877)
Hammer v. Dagenhart, 247 US 251 (1918)
Hardy v. De Leon, 5 Tex. 211 (1849)
Hawaiian Crow v. Lujan, 906 F. Supp. 549 (1991)

Hernandez v. New York, 500 US 352 (1991)
Hernandez v. Texas, 347 US 475 (1954)
Hirabayashi v. United States, 320 US 81 (1943)
Ho Ah Kow v. Nunan, 12 Fed. Cas. 252 (C.C.C.D. Cal. 1879)
Hoyt v. Florida, 368 US 57 (1961)
Hughes v. Oklahoma, 441 US 322 (1979)
Hunt v. State, 3 Ind. App. 383 (1892)
Independent School District v. Salvatierra, 33 S.W.2d 790 (Sup. Ct. 1930)
Ingraham v. Wright, 430 US 651 (1977)
In re Gault, 387 US 1 (1967)
In re Lee Sing, 43 F. 359 (C.C.Cal. 1890)
In re Naka's License, 9 Alaska 1 (1934)
In re Rodriguez, 81 F. 337 (D.W.D. Tex. 1897)
In re Sing Too Quan, 43 F. 359 (C.C.Cal. 1890)
In re Tiburcio Parrott, 1 Fed. 481 (1880)
Japanese Immigrant Case, 189 US 86 (1903)
Jennison v. Kirk, 98 US 453 (1879)
Johnson v. McIntosh, 21 US 543 (1823)
The Kansas Indians, 72 US 737 (1867)
Kilpatrick v. Sisneros, 23 Tex. 113 (1859)
Korematsu v. United States, 323 US 214 (1944)
Late Corporation of the Church of Jesus Christ of Latter-Day Saints v. United States, 136 US 1 (1890)
Lau v. Nichols, 414 US 563 (1973)
Lee v. Department of Justice, 413 F. 3d 53 (D.C. Cir. 2005)
Leegin Creative Leather Products Inc. v. PSKS Inc., 551 US 877 (2007)
Lochner v. New York, 198 US 45 (1905)
Lone Wolf v. Hitchcock, 187 US 553 (1903)
Louisville, Cincinnati and Charleston Railroad Co. v. Letson, 2 How. (43 US) 497 (1844)
Madrigal v. Quilligan, 639 F.2d 789 (9th Cir., 1981)
Maragne v. States Marine Lines, Inc., 398 US 375 (1970)
Marbled Murrelet v. Pacific Lumber Co., 880 F. Supp. 1343 (1995)
Massachusetts v. Environmental Protection Agency, 549 US 497 (2007)
McClanahan v. State Tax Commission of Arizona, 411 US 174 (1973)
McConnell v. Federal Election Commission, 540 US 93 (2003)
McKeiver v. Pennsylvania, 403 US 528 (1971)
McKinney v. Saviego, 59 US 235 (1855)
Mendez v. Westminister School District, 64 F. Supp. 544 (1946)
Meyer v. Nebraska, 262 US 390 (1923)
Milwaukee and St. Paul Railroad Co. v. State of Minnesota, 134 US 418 (1890)
Minor v. Happersett, 88 US 162 (1875)
Minoru Yasui v. United States, 320 US 115 (1943)
Montoya v. United States, 180 US 261 (1901)
Moore v. Dempsey, 261 US 86 (1923)
Morgan v. Virginia, 328 US 373 (1946)
Morse v. Frederick, 551 US 393 (2007)
Morton v. Mancari, 417 US 535 (1974)
Mt. Graham Red Squirrel v. Yeutter, 930 F.2d 703 (1991)
Muller v. Oregon, 208 US 412 (1908)
Native American Church v. Navajo Tribal Council, 272 F.2d 131 (1959)
New Jersey v. T.L.O., 469 US 325 (1985)
Nishimura Ekiu v. United States, 142 US 651 (1891)
Northern Spotted Owl v. Hodel, 716 F. Supp. 479 (1988)
Northern Spotted Owl v. Lujan, 758 F. Supp. 621 (1991)
Orr v. Orr, 440 US 268 (1979)
Oyama v. California, 332 US 633 (1948)
Ozawa v. United States, 260 US 178 (1922)

Palila v. Hawaii Department of Land and Natural Resources, 471 F. Supp. 985 (1979)
Parham v. J.R., 442 US 584 (1979)
Passamaquoddy Tribe v. Morton, 528 F.2d 370 (1975)
Paul v. Commonwealth of Virginia, 75 US 168 (1869)
People ex. rel. Freel v. Downs, 26 N.Y. Crim. R. 327; 136 N.Y.S. 440 (1911)
People v. De La Guerra, 40 Cal. 311 (1870)
People v. Hall, 4 Cal. 399 (1854)
People v. Naglee, 1 Cal. 232 (1850)
Perez v. FBI, 707 F. Supp. 891 (1988)
Philip Morris USA, Inc. v. Williams, 128 S. Ct. 2904 (2008)
Pierce v. Society of the Sisters, 268 US 510 (1925)
Plessy v. Ferguson, 163 US 537 (1896)
Pollock v. Farmers' Loan and Trust Co., 158 US 601 (1895)
Prince v. Massachusetts, 321 US 158 (1944)
Radice v. New York, 264 US 292 (1924)
Reed v. Reed, 404 US 71 (1971)
Regents of the University of California v. Bakke, 438 US 265 (1978)
Roe v. Wade, 410 US 113 (1973)
Roper v. Simmons, 543 US 551 (2005)
Rostker v. Goldberg, 453 US 57 (1981)
San Antonio Independent School District v. Rodriguez, et al., 441 US 1 (1973)
Sanchez v. State, 156 Tex. Crim. 468 (1951)
San Mateo County v. Southern Pacific Railroad Company, 116 US 138 (1885)
Santa Clara County v. Southern Pacific Railroad Co., 118 US 394 (1886)
Scenic Hudson Preservation Conference v. Federal Power Commission, 354 F.2d 608 (1965)
Shaw v. Reno, 509 US 630 (1993)
Sierra Club v. Morton, 405 US 727 (1972)
Sinking Fund Cases, 99 US 700 (1879)
Slaughter-House Cases, 83 US 36 (1872)
Standing Bear v. Crook, 25 F. Cas. 695 (C.C.D. Neb. 1879) (No. 14,891)
Stanford v. Kentucky, 492 US 361 (1989)
State v. Karstendiek, 39 L.R.A. 520, 49 La. Ann. 1621 (1897)
State v. Martin, 189 So. 109 (1939)
Stephen v. State, 65 Miss. 329 (1888)
Stephens v. Cherokee Nation, 174 US 445 (1899)
Talton v. Mayes, 163 US 366 (1896)
Taylor v. Louisiana, 419 US 522 (1975)
Tennnessee Valley Authority v. Hull, 437 US 153 (1978)
Thompson v. Oklahoma, 486 US 815 (1988)
Tokaji v. State Board of Education, 67 P2d. 1082 (1937)
Toledo v. Pueblo de Jemez, 119 F. Supp. 429 (1954)
Trustees of Dartmouth College v. Woodward, 17 US 518 (1819)
United States v. Bitty, 208 US 393 (1908)
United States v. Cruikshank, 92 US 542 (1875)
United States v. Debell, 227 Fed. 775 (1915)
United States v. Dege, 364 US 51 (1960)
United States v. Ju Toy, 198 US 253 (1905)
United States v. Kagama, 118 US 375 (1886)
United States v. Lucero, 1 N.M. 422 (1869)
United States v. Mazurie, 419 US 544 (1975)
United States v. Morrison, 579 US 598 (2000)
United States v. Osborn, 2 F. 58 (1880)
United States v. Sandoval, 231 US 28 (1913)
United States ex rel. Standing Bear v. Crook, 25 F. Cas. 14,891 (1879)
United States v. Stevens, 132 S.Ct. 1577 (2010)
United States v. State Tax Commission of Mississippi, 505 US 633 (1974)

United States v. Thind, 261 US 204 (1923)

United States v. Virginia, 518 US 515 (1996)

United States v. Waller, 243 US 452 (1917)

United States v. Washington, 384 F. Supp. 343 (1974)

United States v. Wong Kim Ark, 169 US 649 (1898)

United States v. Yamasaka, 100 Fed. 404 (1900)

Veronica School District v. Acton, 515 US 646 (1995)

Wabash, St. Louis and Pacific Railway Co. v. Ilinois, 118 US 557 (1886)

Waldron v. United States, 143 Fed. 413 (1905)

Warrenburger v. Folson, 239 F.2d 846 (3rd Cir. C. Pa, 1956)

Wen Ho Lee v. United States Department of Justice, 287 F. Supp. 2d 15 (D.D.C. 2003)

West Coast Hotel Co. v. Parrish, 300 US 379 (1937)

Whitman v. American Trucking Associations, Inc., 531 US 457 (2001)

Winter v. Council of Natural Resources Defense Council, 555 US 7 (2008)

Worcester v. Georgia, 31 US 515 (1832)

INDEX

ABOUT THE AUTHORS

Vine Deloria Jr. was named by *Time* magazine as one of the greatest religious thinkers of the twentieth century and was a leading scholar who authored many acclaimed books.

Professor David E. Wilkins holds the McKnight Presidential Professorship in American Indian Studies at the University of Minnesota.